The Elizabethan conque

This book is about the impact of the Nine Years' War on central and local government and society in the English and Welsh shires in the 1590s. It contains fascinating new insights into the centrality of Ireland to England's problems in the crucial last decade of Elizabeth I's reign.

However, this is in no sense a conventional military history of the Irish war, 1594–1603, but rather a history of the social impact of the war and the strains it put upon the Elizabethan government. Based on painstaking primary research, it also covers the recruitment of levies for Ireland, their shipping, their service in Ireland and the limited extent of aftercare given to the sick and wounded. The book therefore helps towards an understanding of why the Elizabethan conquest took so long to complete and why it proved to be more severe than at first intended.

John McGurk, formerly Head of History at Liverpool Hope University College, is a Visiting Lecturer in Irish History and Fellow of the University of Liverpool and is a Fellow of the Royal Historical Society.

The Elizabethan conquest of Ireland

JOHN McGURK

MANCHESTER UNIVERSITY PRESS

Manchester and New York

Copyright © John McGurk 1997

The right of John McGurk to be identified as the author of this work has
been asserted by him in accordance with the Copyright, Designs and
Patents Act 1988.

Published by Manchester University Press
Oxford Road, Manchester M13 9NR, UK
and Room 400, 175 Fifth Avenue, New York, NY 10010, USA
www.manchesteruniversitypress.co.uk

Distributed exclusively in the USA by
Palgrave, 175 Fifth Avenue, New York NY 10010, USA

Distributed exclusively in Canada by
UBC Press, University of British Columbia, 2029 West Mall,
Vancouver, BC, Canada V6T 1Z2

British Library Cataloguing-in-Publication Data
A catalogue record for this book is available from the British Library

Library of Congress Cataloging-in-Publication Data
A catalog record for this book is available from the Library of Congress

ISBN 13: 978 0 7190 8051 7

First published in hardback 1997 by Manchester University Press
This paperback edition first published 2009

Printed by Lightning Source

To peace in Ireland

Contents

Tables

Preface

This is a study of how the prosecution of the Nine Years' War in the last decade of Elizabeth I's reign impinged on government and society at central and local levels in the shires of England and Wales. And although we need to ask and give some answer to why the war was fought out to a bitter end, the book offers no dramatically new interpretation of the causes; rather it might be said to make a contribution to our understanding of the crises of the 1590s in both islands. Not least among those crises arose when the long unsettled state of Ireland, by inviting Spanish intervention, called forth an unprecedented English war effort in men, arms, money, horses, impedimenta, as well as the ships necessary to get them all into field and garrison in Ireland.

An overview of the scale of those operations is attempted in Chapter 3 while subsequent chapters in Part I are detailed studies of the demands made on the shires there selected. In the sixteenth century it would be true to say that there had been general neglect of the government of Ireland in real terms but certainly not among the myriad writers on Ireland and the Irish in the period. By concentrating on the three main military ports of Chester, Bristol and Barnstaple, the billeting and transportation of the troops levied for Ireland are considered in the chapters of Part II, but for the sake of completion of the theme some less important ports used in the prosecution of the war are also studied. This section exposes the practical problems and looks at how local and central government overcame them successfully to assemble and ship recruits and reinforcements as well as the habiliments of war to supply the commanders in Ireland for nearly a decade. Without becoming embroiled in the long-established controversy of 'the military revolution', it is now clear that society was virtually on a continual war footing in both islands in the 1590s, while at the same time the distinction between the soldiery and the civilian populace was emerging but perhaps not at the same rate in Ireland, where the soldier/colonist/farmer became a familiar enough figure among the officer cadre at the end of the war, though research is steadily showing that the rewards of lands and offices of an Irish military career have likely been exaggerated. The chapters of Part III establish that the life of the Elizabethan soldier was hard and cheerless, fighting a campaign that he barely understood and from which he was not expected to return. However, in the final chapter I have taken on a largely neglected theme, which could bear more investigation, in considering what welfare measures were taken for the sick and wounded as well as the relief given to those who did return maimed from the war.

My interest in the subject goes back to the 1960s when studying lieutenancy in Kent and finding in the William Salt Library, Stafford, the then recent accession of the

Leveson lieutenancy records; many of the extensive bundles dealing with Kentish levies for the wars abroad included some papers on those sent to Ireland. My deeply rooted familial passion for Irish history was quickened not just by the find but by the historical revolution in the subject, partially and tragically triggered off by the 'Troubles' since the 1970s. And in any case, I have ever had the normal pacifist's obsession with soldiers and war. My debts to many of the pioneers of that revolution will be evident in the bibliography, many of whom, sadly, are no longer with us: Professors Joel Hurstfield and Sir John Neale of the Institute of Historical Research and in Ireland those two pillars of the historical revolution Professors R. Dudley Edwards and G. A. Hayes-McCoy, in particular. For encouragement to persevere and for references my thanks are due to Professor D. B. Quinn, Professor N. Canny, Dr B. Bradshaw, Professor S. Ellis and above all to Dr Michael Power, whose painstaking supervision and sound advice at every stage of the original thesis proved to be a constant inspiration. Apart from indicating how long this work has been in a state of fermentation, the footnotes and bibliography will also show my indebtedness to a younger generation of researchers who have increased our knowledge not only of English–Irish relations, Elizabethan military affairs, and the underlying ideologies but also of the logistics and practicalities of local and central Elizabethan government. Finally, I am grateful to Professor Simon Lee, Rector of Liverpool Hope University College, for sabbatical leave at the end of my teaching career to complete the work.

The dating used throughout the text is in accord with customary practice of New Style for the year and Old Style (when used) for the day and the month.

Acknowledgements

The author and publishers are indebted to the Controller of Her Majesty's Stationery Office for permission to reprint Crown copyright material from the Public Record Office and from the Public Record Office Calendars. Permission was kindly granted by the following to reproduce parts from my already published articles: the Honourable Society of Cymmrodorion, the Society for Nautical Research, the Society for Army Historical Research, and the Kent Archaeological Society.

It is a particular pleasure to acknowledge my thanks to Mrs Jean Johnson, without whose patience and skills in word-processing the whole enterprise may have been well nigh impossible. And this would clearly have been the case without the good-humoured promptings of many at Manchester University Press, especially from Carolyn Hand. The debts incurred in writing any book are many, varied and difficult to recall, so that a general acknowledgement to all who have helped me (too numerous to list) over a lifetime of lectures, classes, discussions and correspondence may seem inadequate. However, I should like to exonerate them all from any responsibility for the errors that undoubtedly remain.

Abbreviations

AFM	*Annals of the Four Masters*
APC	*Acts of the privy council*
BAO	Bristol Archives Office
BL	British Library
Cal. Carew MSS	*Calendar of the Carew papers*, Lambeth Palace Library, London
CCR	Chester City Record Office
CCRO	Cheshire County Record Office
CSPD	*Calendars of state papers, Domestic*
CSPI	*Calendars of state papers, Ireland*
DNB	*Dictionary of national biography*
HMC	Historical Manuscripts Commission
IHS	*Irish Historical Studies*
KAO	Kent Archives Office
LRO	Lancashire Record Office
PRO	Public Record Office
SP	State Papers
SRO	Staffordshire Record Office

PART I

Men and arms for the Nine Years' War

But if the plains of Crecy, like a book
Contain in characters their heavy doom
If Bologne, Tournai, Poitiers, pale do look
To think what hath, or may hereafter come;
If they be witnesses how ill we brook
Disembling lips, when truth the goal hath won
Treading on falsehood: Why not then Tyrone?

'England's hope against Irish hate, 1600', unpaginated booklet, Lambeth Palace Library,
endorsed 'Thomas Heyes, his coppy'

CHAPTER ONE

Background to the Nine Years' War

The condition of Ireland was one of the many difficulties facing Queen Elizabeth I at her accession; the mere mention of rebellion in Ireland is supposed to have made her 'sick and ill'.[1] The country was rarely free from political and social unrest throughout the forty-five years of Elizabeth's reign; as late as 1596 the queen reminded the Irish council in Dublin that she would reform the disordered state of Ireland with the sword to the obstinate and with justice to the oppressed. Ireland was perhaps the most complex and intractable problem for the Elizabethan government, a most 'unwelcome inheritance from Henry VIII'.[2]

One major feature of Irish life in the sixteenth century which affected the whole history of Anglo-Irish relations lay in the different cultural groups in the population. Four of these may be distinguished: the native Gaelic Irish, the Old English of the Pale and the towns, the Scots, and the New English, the last being the newer adventurers who planted the subdued parts of Munster, Leinster and Connaught, and who became the officials of church and state in the Dublin administration. The native Irish, the majority of the population, were represented by sixty or more Gaelic lords or chiefs and were different in their society, religion, language and laws from those of the newcomers, so that in effect two nations lived in Ireland.[3] In Ulster the Gaelic population predominated and was led by the chiefs of the O'Neills, O'Donnells, O'Reillys, O'Rourkes, Maguires and McMahons, to name but the more notable. In Connaught, Burkes, O'Malleys, O'Connors and O'Kellys represented the names of the Irish family networks of the westward seaboard, and to the south and west, in the province of Munster, O'Sullivans, McCarthys and O'Briens were the leading Gaelic lords, and though Leinster had been the most anglicised of the provinces of Ireland O'Connors, O'Mores, O'Byrnes, and O'Tooles headed notable family groupings outside the English Pale and the towns.[4] Many of the Old English had hibernicised, adopting the Gaelic way of life through intermarriage with native Gaelic stock and had long since thrown off their English allegiance. Such were the Fitzgeralds, the Roches, the Powers, Butlers, Dillons, Tyrells and Savages. The English referred to them as 'English rebels' and 'Irish enemies'; these are the more polite expressions used for these families who had become more Irish than the Irish themselves. Of the third group, the Gaelic Scots, strongest in the north-east of Ulster, the most representative were the MacDonalds and the MacSweeneys.[5] The New English had been going to Ireland throughout the Tudor period but in greater numbers from *circa*

1537, as would-be colonisers, leaders of expeditionary forces and officials in the Dublin administration in state, church and army; many of their names are celebrated in Elizabethan history – Sidney, Perrot, Ralegh, Gilbert, Frobisher, Spenser, Bagenal, Norris, Russell, Fitzwilliam, Essex and Mountjoy. Lesser-known names of captains and military men who went into the country with the levies we shall have cause to mention throughout the book. Many of them came from the squirearchy providing the volunteer officer cadre but their men were mainly conscripts from the other end of the social scale.

To understand the background to the Elizabethan reconquest, two important consequences of earlier attempts to subdue Ireland need to be emphasised: first, after the Anglo-Norman twelfth-century invasion, kings of England claimed to be lords of Ireland; second, the association of kingship with landownership emerged and stood in sharp contrast to Gaelic tradition, in which a king or chief was the elected leader of his people with no hereditary rights to land or offices. The effective owners of the land were the families who historically inhabited and tilled it. No kingdom of Ireland existed in legal fact until the Dublin parliament of 1541 recognised and made Henry VIII and his successors not lords of Ireland but kings thereof.[6] Henry's intention was to bring about a revolution in the government of Ireland; the 'sundry sorts' of people who made up the Irish population, certainly less than a million by mid-sixteenth century, were henceforth all to be anglicised and treated as the king's subjects. Gaelic lords were ordered to hold lands as fiefs of the crown of England and in this way the crown would technically recover its *de facto* hold over the island of Ireland. The policy is generally called 'surrender and re-grant', and the king's deputy, then Anthony St Leger, began to carry out the long process of negotiation with the Gaelic lords.[7] By Henry VIII's death in 1547 forty of the principal Gaelic and Old English lords had made their peace with the crown and undertaken to observe the various conditions consequent on surrender and re-grant, the most important being obedience to English laws. In return the king gave them English titles, earldoms for example to Conn O'Neill in Ulster, MacWilliam Burke in Connaught and Murrough O'Brien in Thomond, seats in parliament, English schooling for their sons, and permission to receive confiscated church lands within their own territories. Henry introduced the new reformed religion, although ultimately the Protestant reformation had little success in Ireland.[8]

In the schemes for reform there were weaknesses in theory and difficulties in practice despite the obvious overtures of conciliation with the Gaelic lords. The family communities were the traditional holders of the land in Gaelic Ireland and there had also been a renaissance of Gaeldom in the fifteenth century which has been underestimated by Tudor historians. By negotiating with the lords and overlords the crown ignored the majority of families whose traditional Brehon laws and customs recognised no association of landownership and tenures of public offices, but in practice by the sixteenth century political control meant the personal headship of the dominant kin or family group and the absorption of their territory in return for protection and representation. Succession under Irish law was by election of the chief and his *tanaiste* or second in command by the gentry of a lordship. The chief was inaugurated with a series of elaborate rituals at a hallowed place, Tullahogue in the case of the O'Neills of Tyrone and Kilmacrenan for the O'Donnell of Tyrconnell. In an English feudal sense the Henrician policy assumed the absolute ownership of all the land of Ireland and in surrender and re-grant confused the office of Gaelic chieftainship, an elective one, with landownership, held by primogeniture. The various agreements made with various chieftains who could not under Brehon law bind their successors to keep these covenants with the English crown became recipes for future troubles. Traditional feuds and endemic domestic intrigues between Irish families exacerbated the confusion. On their part many of the Irish chiefs were willing enough to covert unstable land interests into firm feudal tenures but they could not change overnight the staunchly held traditions of their peoples. These also varied in the regions and indeed on the aggrandisement or otherwise of individual Gaelic overlords in exacting rents, dues, military support and a whole series of exactions generally referred to as 'coign and livery'.[9]

The breakdown of the Henrician piecemeal reforms have been well commented upon by recent writers on sixteenth-century Ireland – their initial successes, later modifications and final failure in the outbreaks of rebellion against royal policy, anglicisation and religious reformation. Two to three generations of violent reaction culminating in a nine years' war would follow before the final downfall of the Gaelic system. By 1603 there had been an extension of royal power and a secular conquest accomplished but without a religious reformation; consequently the seventeenth century would see the last wars of religion fought out in Ireland.

In general, Elizabeth's policy towards Ireland proved to be a continuation of her father's, reforms not military conquest, persuasion and not the sword, and like the early Tudor system it was cheap and undemanding; few offices were created. It was not until 1560, for example, that Elizabeth created a royal privy seal for Ireland with a principal secretary to keep it. And while the royal courts of justice in Ireland were mirror images of those in England there were fewer established posts for the common lawyers to climb to high office. In the Dublin executive there was a constant struggle for power between the New English and the Old English and on the Irish bench concomitant battles between English and Irish judges, though their inaction and senility caused worse problems in the 1560s. And although Ireland had constitutionally been a kingdom since 1541, it infuriated the gentry and lawyers of the Pale that the courts in England remained superior, in that Irish cases could be reviewed on that side of the Irish Sea. From about 1547 Irish Tudor policy ignored the pleas and wishes of the Old English in the government of Ireland as the trends tended to military conquest, colonisation and therefore anglicisation by force; this was to be the revolution in government in Ireland, and it was to be Elizabethan, not Henrician or Cromwellian.[10]

The difficulties of governing Ireland were always exacerbated by the assimilation of the chief governor's office and indeed lesser offices, such as chancellor, treasurer-at-war, and presidencies in Munster and Connaught, into the orbit of the English court and politics. It is one of the chief arguments implicit in this book that the overall Elizabethan conquest had a major impact on the developments of the English state itself in the late sixteenth century; the very machinery of government was hardly adequate to carry out the tasks Tudor Irish policy demanded of it; one instance may suffice here. The overambitious plans for the plantation of Munster and their attempted execution in the years after the Desmond rebellions were quite beyond the administrations of London and Dublin. No wonder private enterprises became the government's cheap solution, but these too needed supervising as the uncontrolled activities of the adventurers both in Munster and in the more spectacular failures in Ulster between 1571 and 1573 forced the administration to fall back on coercion and martial law to carry out what it could not do in the civil manner.

Naturally, Irish and at times Old English reaction showed itself at first in resentment, then rebellion and finally outright armed conflict with foreign aid. In the late 1580s in Connaught the leading family of the Burkes rose in rebellion, saying that they would have a MacWilliam Burke, not an English earl, and if not they would go to Spain for one and that they would 'tolerate no sheriff nor any of them or their people answer to any court of assize or sessions of the peace'.[11] Outside the English Pale rebellious attitudes became commonplace. Still, the policy of voluntarily securing the individual loyalty of the dynastic lords was never completely abandoned, especially if this could be achieved by exploiting feuds between hibernicised families like the Butlers and the Geraldines.[12]

In the complex series of attempts to govern Ireland in the 1570s and '80s some general trends have been discerned: efforts at conciliation, the continuation of individual surrender and re-grant policies, gradual efforts to introduce English shire administration and English common law; these attempts were frequently followed by outbreaks of rebellion which in turn led to the confiscation of lands, and plans and efforts to plant and colonise the confiscated areas. Events in the province of Munster from the 1570s to 1598 provide an example of such trends in English policy.[13] The province was rich, fertile and accessible and therefore a magnet for the land-hungry adventurers from the English West Country. Munster was on the sea route to Spain, the Azores and, significantly for those with long-term colonising objectives such as Humphrey Gilbert and Walter Ralegh, Munster could be considered a trial run to the Americas. Within the province the feuds between the Butlers and the Fitzgeralds provided opportunities for government interference. From 1569 to 1573 Munster was in a state of rebellion led by James FitzMaurice Fitzgerald. Well established Anglo-Irish lords like MacCarthy, the Earl of Clancarty, joined the rebellion because of the harassments of the New English Sir Peter Carew, who pursued a form of legal imperialism, seeking out ancient claims of his twelfth-century ancestors to parts of the province. With the help of Gilbert, Hawkins, Frobisher and Ralegh, Carew was prominent with Sir John Perrot and the Earl of Ormond in crushing the insurrection. FitzMaurice escaped to the courts of Europe, collected an invading force of Spaniards and Italians and made a landing in Kerry in July 1579. This second Desmond rebellion was put down with severity; by November 1583 Munster was quiet, and the way cleared for the confiscation of the Desmond estates. Petitions for letters patent for these estates stressed the benefits which would accrue from a settled plantation. Between 1585 and 1598 native landowners were gradually dispossessed and replaced by loyal West Country men. But the Munster plantation was not destined to last. The last native Gaelic resurgence of the queen's reign, which began with the Ulster lords under Hugh O'Neill, gradually disaffected the entire country, bringing disaster to the

Munster colonists in 1598. Many, like the celebrated Edmund Spenser, hastily returned to England; some may have joined the Irish insurgents and others less fortunate were killed.

In Connaught, west of the River Shannon, the government aimed at destroying local Gaelic independence through a settlement negotiated with the lords; this is known to history as 'The Composition of Connaught'. It confirmed the lords in their estates and introduced money rents instead of services and contributions in kind and as a result it was hoped that, in time, all Gaelic captaincies, jurisdictions, elections and customary divisions of lands would disappear. Recent research has shown that the system did not settle land titles, nor did it prevent land speculation by outsiders. There were at least twenty-four members of the New English or Pale gentry purchasing estates in Connaught by 1585.[14] But, all told, the experiment was one of the more successful achievements of Sir John Perrot as lord deputy of Ireland 1584–1588. The experiment may well have been non-violent but the provincial governor or president of Connaught, Sir Richard Bingham, became a by-word in cruelty. His harsh rule drew the hostility of the Connaught peasantry and in their opposition they were aided by the O'Donnells of Tyrconnell, modern Donegal, who in any case had ancestral claims and interests in many areas of north Connaught. Red Hugh O'Donnell led this opposition and kept the province unsettled.

Of the four provinces Ulster proved the most intractable to conquest and anglicisation. It was mountainous and then much afforested; all its southern approaches were through wood, bog and lough, so it must have presented the appearance of an impenetrable fortress. The most inaccessible part lay around the Sperrins and the great forest of Glenconkeyne, the homelands of the O'Neills, ancestral lords of so much of the entire province of Ulster. The rivers Foyle, the Erne (with its series of loughs), the Blackwater, Lough Neagh and the Upper and Lower Banns formed an almost continuous and veritable water barrier to the province. The main passages into it were from the south-west where, at Ballyshannon, the waters of the Erne flow into the Atlantic and where a ford provided a passage into south Donegal. The difficulties of that passage are much commented upon by Sir Henry Docwra, who in 1600 had tried to establish a sub-garrison there. Amphibious operations were clearly necessary to make any inroads into Ulster, a fact much appreciated since the days of Shane O'Neill's rebellion in the 1560s. Further east on the isthmus between Upper and Lower Lough Erne, Enniskillen with Maguire's noted castle became a prized site to garrison and thereby control the passage into south-west Ulster. To the south-east there was the historic Gap of the North, the gorge in the hills between Dundalk and Newry, better known in the sixteenth century as the Moyry Pass, a traditional gateway into Ulster from the south. And at Armagh, near the Blackwater river and barely fifteen miles from O'Neill's principal seat at Dungannon, English commanders maintained a precarious foothold in the war years until 1598.[15] By the beginning of all-out hostilities under O'Neill in 1593/1594 the only government footholds around the province were small garrisons at Enniskillen (Maguire's castle having been taken and retaken a number of times), Carrickfergus, Olderfleet and Carlingford. Belfast then was unimportant though Captain Thomas Lee, a notorious double agent in the war, advocated fortifying Belfast rather than the traditional Norman keep at Carrickfergus to command the sea around Carlingford, especially to prevent Scots mercenaries joining the Irish.[16]

The difficult terrain of south-east Ulster is clearly illustrated in a map of a portion of south Armagh in the areas of the Blackwater. It is attributed to Richard Bartlett, a military engineer and map maker with Mountjoy's forces who was beheaded in 1603 before he had finished mapping in Donegal.[17] Sir John Davies, later the first Attorney General of Ireland in James's reign, considered Ulster to be 'a very wilderness the inhabitants having for the most part no certain habitation in any towns or village'.[18]

Apart from 'plotts' and 'plans' of the forts and garrisons made by military map makers such as Richard Bartlett, John Thomas and Robert Ashby on the fringes of Ulster, the interior of the province remained uncharted until the Jacobean plantations. The Irish are not known to have much used maps except those they captured or stole to send on to Spain.[19] There were general descriptions of the province in the many 'Discourses, Discoveries, Plots and Plans' that proliferate in the state papers, and one particularly fulsome description by Sir Henry Bagenal, who had the command of the Newry garrison, which in 1586 was the most northerly part of the Pale (at the queen's accession this included the counties of Dublin, Louth, Meath, Westmeath and Kildare). Professor Canny has reminded us that by then there was too much Gaelic influence in the Pale, manifest in the Irish language of the labourers and tenants who had moved in on either a permanent or seasonal basis. Stanihurst, notable writer and Palesman and friend of Edmund Campion, states that many in the Pale spoke 'neither good English nor good Irish,' but rather a gallimaufry of both. Gaelic lords bordering the Pale had little respect for the English customs or concepts of social order; traditionally therefore the gentry of the Pale looked to the crown of England to preserve them from Gaelic aggression and, much to the irritation of the queen and council, in their frequent pleas they thought of themselves more deserving of royal favour than the queen's subjects in England.[20] The political and above all the religious dilemmas of the Old English of the Pale, adherents, as they were generally were, to Catholicism, became more critical after the excommunication of Elizabeth I by the papal bull *Regnans in excelsis*, as loyalty to the old faith and to the crown appeared untenable. The theme is much discussed as religion and politics merged in the sixteenth and seventeenth centuries. The dilemma of the Old English Catholics in Ireland become a minority interest, not just for the ecclesiastical and intellectual historian, as they were driven to rebellion and eventually to join company with their erstwhile enemies, the native Gaelic Irish.[21]

According to Fynes Moryson, Mountjoy's secretary for a time, many English people regarded the frequent occurrence of rebellion in Ireland lightly, 'thinking them rather profitable to exercise the English in arms than dangerous to disturb the state'.[22] Sir William Fitzwilliam, lord deputy 1588–1594, had made the provinces of Munster and Connaught generally quiet in his vigorous efforts to establish the queen's sovereignty following the efforts of Perrot. Historically, Fitzwilliam has been regarded as the corrupt and cruel governor who did more than most to trigger off the Nine Years' War. A recent assessment by Dr Hiram Morgan proves the point.[23] Many contemporaries in the Dublin administration were of the opinion that the new outbreak of rebellion in Ulster in the early 1590s would soon be crushed and the example previously set in the Composition of Connaught would then follow naturally; that, in fact, the rebellion stirring under the second Earl of Tyrone, Hugh O'Neill, would hardly be more difficult to quell than Shane O'Neill's had been.

Such attitudes underestimated the strength of Gaelic Ulster, and above all the charismatic figure of Hugh O'Neill, a leader at home in both worlds, English and Gaelic, a subtle politician, organiser of genius and a soldier with the rare gift of patience and the ability to inspire loyalty among erstwhile feuding chieftains. From 1594 to 1599 O'Neill with O'Donnell and their confederate chiefs were largely successful in keeping the English out of Ulster. The battles of Clontibret in Monaghan (1595) and the Yellow Ford (1598), on the borders of Armagh and Tyrone, were their best-known victories. By then O'Neill appears to have been able to unite most elements of opposition to the crown in almost every part of Ireland by presenting his cause, not merely as an Ulster one of defence, but as an Irish one of freedom from English control. With the aid of Spain and with assurances from Rome he was able to adopt the Catholic cause and present his struggle as a religious crusade in the restoration of traditional Catholicism.[24]

Though the Irish fought an heroic and defensive war with traditional courage, and at times with uncharacteristic unity of purpose, they and their Spanish allies were defeated in 1601 by the greater resources of the Elizabethan state. The queen's ships had the command of the seas, which checked further foreign help to the Irish, and by the same means the English field army and garrisons were kept victualled and supplied as the last and unquestionably the most able of the Elizabethan lord deputies, Charles Blount, Lord Mountjoy, conquered Ireland for Queen Elizabeth. For the first time in Ireland's history all its inhabitants became the subjects of one authority. The military victory ensured that that authority would be English.

The *Pacata Hibernia* was won at a dreadful cost and while it can be said that by 1603 Ireland was managed and controlled, it was hardly pacified. This book, however, is not to be regarded as a history of the Nine Years' War *per se* – rather it seeks to explore the English effort which that war entailed. The recruitment, transportation and conditions of military service in those years in Ireland has not attracted a major study in all of those pragmatic aspects – yet, many historians have hastened to narrate the conquest of Ireland in the last years of Elizabeth's reign in terms of impatience to end what had become a dreary chapter in unfinished business. This first part of the book attempts to find out why the war was fought and demonstrates the demands made upon the shires of England and Wales for manpower to conduct the war, thereby putting into effect the policies of the late Elizabethan privy council – which were not always the actual wishes of the queen. Part I therefore makes some attempt to show the effects the Irish war had on the late Elizabethan state, especially in the way the war helped to bring about an eventual military organisation, though not necessarily an efficient one. The effects of the Nine Years' War are generally treated in English histories in the broader context of the Elizabethan struggle with Spain, Ireland being ambiguously regarded now as an item of domestic policy, then, with Spanish intervention there in the winter of 1601, as foreign policy, and naturally, because of Ireland's proximity, a decided danger to the very safety of the English realm. Furthermore, there is no secondary work on the embarkation and transportation of troops into Ireland in the 1590s. The second part of the book may be said to go some way to fill this particular gap. The third and final part, by focusing on the impact of the war on the common soldier, provides insights into the comparatively neglected world of service conditions of the foot soldier in Ireland and of his welfare or lack of it, in both field and garrison. Lastly, it is possible through petitions and similar evidence to see something of the relief measures and aftercare provided for the sick and wounded soldiery both in Ireland and, for those who were fortunate enough to make their return, in their native English or Welsh parishes, where they could benefit from the meagre measures of poor relief to which they were entitled by statute. The historiographical background to the war has a long pedigree and has recently been rehearsed in the works of such representative authors as Brendan Bradshaw, Wallace MacCaffrey, Ciaran Brady, Nicholas Canny, Steven Ellis and Hiram Morgan. And yet, before the present revolution in the writing of Anglo-Irish historical relations, it needs to be pointed out that James Anthony Froude began it all at the beginning of the century, when he wrote that:

> The Queen's meaning towards Ireland was nothing but good; she detested persecution, she was scrupulously anxious, like her father, to protect the Irish owners in the possession of their estates, yet she pursued a policy the most fertile in disaster that the most malignant ingenuity could have devised.[25]

Readers hardly need reminding that at present there is a deep divide among historians of Ireland and, not to trivialise the revisionist debate, that division may be said to focus on the discovery of the roots of Irish or Gaelic nationalism.[26] Before the present debate, those who wrote on sixteenth-century Anglo-Irish relations very often uncritically repeated contemporary and justificatory commentaries which in themselves have an historiographical pedigree stretching back to the strictures of Gerald of Wales in the twelfth century.[27] His account of the partial subjection of Ireland in the later twelfth century enjoyed popularity among English and Old English as well as among the politicians and literate military caste of Elizabethan England and Ireland. A world picture of Ireland and the Irish was virtually created in the Irish Pale by the Old English writers such as Stanihurst, Spenser and Campion, and in England by Camden. Modern historians with perhaps a clearer understanding of both sixteenth-century English and Irish societies present a more sophisticated picture while still showing how the peoples of an emergent renaissance state were in conflict with a much older civilisation which still retained in the late sixteenth century its own pattern of internal warfare, its own system of law and of land-holding and one of bewildering alliances and counter-alliances among its leading aristocratic families. The modern historiography of the subject is still a matter of debate, as many of the writers mentioned differ on their interpretations of government policies at various stages in the government of Ireland. It is still difficult to distinguish war propaganda from policy and, in the psychology of war aims and justifications, to sort out the genuinely held opinions from the specious and self-interested commentaries found throughout the state papers, Ireland, to name but one major collection. The bad-tempered comments of the less literate military captains in

10

Ireland against the Irish are amusing and conceited but they should not be taken as government policy!

It is of interest that those who are victorious generally have a vested interest in the bad state of the country and people they hope to rule and colonise. The themes or allegations of Gaelic barbarism and superstitious popery which proliferate the writings of the Elizabethans have often served as a distraction from the fact that the Old English ruling caste were also Catholic but were being ousted as the effective governors by the New English Protestant adventurers. Ancestral dispossession was not just the preserve of the Gaelic Irish.

The immediate responses of the Gaelic Irish lords to government policies in the post-Armada period have recently been teased out by Hiram Morgan in his *Tyrone's rebellion*. The reaction of the Old English to their ambiguous position in Ireland as Catholic and English is still a subject that could bear further investigation than Colm Lennon and Nicholas Canny have so far given it.[28] The devastation wrought by the military conquest under Lord Mountjoy and the severity of his mopping up of resistance after his victory over the Irish and Spanish at Kinsale hardened native Irish attitudes. Surely then the seeds of a later Irish Catholic nationalism were finding a fertile soil which would burgeon forth in the middle of the seventeenth century?[29] The Gaelic Irish emerged as a nation but without a state, in the sense that England became such by Elizabeth's reign and in Ireland itself the Old English had been a state in formation but in no sense were they ever a distinct nation. Ironically, the New English adventurers, colonists and political aggressors survived in Ireland simply because they had no indigenous identity and indeed from that very survival the celebrated 'Irish question' was born. In the present historiographical controversies Steven Ellis's position may be singled out, for he has cogently argued that the Old English of the Irish Pale presented similar problems faced by the Tudor state in its government of other frontier lands such as Wales, the northern shires bordering Scotland, and Cornwall. It must be stated that his argument, while having force for the early Tudor period in Ireland, takes on a different hue as the late Elizabethan state was confronted not with a localised rebellion in Ireland but with all-out war aided and abetted by the papacy and Spain.[30]

Foreign intervention in Ireland was the ever-present fear since the defeat of the 1588 Armada and before that Christopher Hatton, known to history as Elizabeth's dancing master, noted that Ireland even in 1561 could easily become a 'postern gate through which those bent on the destruction of the country might enter'.[31] The majority of sixteenth-century English people believed that the continental enemies of England were certain of a *céad mile fáilte* by the Irish lords. The moves made towards peace with France in the 1570s clearly had internal national English security in mind and the same motives governed what the Elizabethans called 'strong practical reasons' for pursuing a vigorous policy in Ireland. Sir William Fitzwilliam declared that the loss of Ireland would be far worse than the loss of Calais, 'for Ireland being a whole region, furnished with so many notable havens, so inhabited with stout people, and so near our mainland would no doubt shake this whole state and part thereof more dangerously'.[32] From about 1593 Spanish aid was daily expected for Hugh O'Neill's growing rebellion, which threatened to unite all elements of opposition to English rule; then reasons of strategy dictated to queen and council a policy of repression that hardly needed a justificatory ideology. The aim of the war then in Ireland became nothing less than the very defence of England itself. Such a pragmatic approach had little to do with the intellectual arguments of renaissance humanism;[33] that practical attitude can be seen in the commissions and communiqués of the state papers and indeed is enshrined in the terms of the lord deputy's oath of office:

> Ye shall defend her majesty's castles, garrisons, dominions, people ... and repress her rebels and enemies... and all other things for the preservation of this her majesty's peace among the people and execution of justice.[34]

And despite the recent arguments surrounding the interpretation of Spenser's *View of the present state of Ireland*, written in 1598 but not published until 1633, the plain and brutal solutions he prescribed for the ills of Ireland were pragmatic, if too expensive at the time.[35]

The sixteenth-century reconquest was probably the first time since the twelfth-century conquest that large numbers of English people came into direct contact with the Gaelic Irish in their native habitat. Ireland had never been fully united in a political sense either by the Irish or by Anglo-Irish lords and so it can be argued too that, with the attempt at the establishment of strong centralised government in England under Elizabeth, it was almost inevitable a similar attempt would be made to bring Ireland under more effective English control, perhaps even without the threats of continental invasion to justify a strong policy of intervention. In Ireland itself there were few political institutions surviving from the pre-Norman conquest; those that did or that were revived in the fifteenth century were in fact local, not nationwide, and could be said to promote division rather than unity; this trend in itself was sufficient to invite interference from England.[36]

Therefore, political institutions to govern Ireland were imported from England and run by the New English, whose steady influx brought about a divided population between old survivals and new arrivals, and between them and the Gaelic Irish. The whole superstructure of institutions – a central castle authority in Dublin, a system of English law administered by royal justices (many of the Old English judges were described as 'speechless and senseless on the bench') – and the entire local administration represented by shires and sheriffs were all, in Beckett's felicitous analogy, 'like a clock whose face was in Dublin while the works were in England'.[37] In overall charge were the lords deputy (a few, like the second Earl of Essex, were called lord lieutenant); there were no less than seventy-six of them throughout the sixteenth century and they had varying success in governing Ireland.[38] During the Elizabethan reign it was considered an overall aim to make the lord deputy's nominal authority under the crown more effective over the whole island; this was given greater or less emphasis depending on the urgency and seriousness of rebellion and on resources in England. Within that context a variety of English concerns can be discerned – the fear of Spanish intervention in Ireland, the queen's interest as nominal sovereign, and the religious colour of the struggle. The opinions and comments of contemporary writers on Ireland, many of them little more than propagandists for the conquest, give an insight into Elizabethan attitudes to the Irish. These were summarised in the work of D. B. Quinn in his *The Elizabethans and the Irish*.[39]

English aims

Most historians would now agree that the war in the late 1590s, once begun, gathered its own momentum and became more of an all-out conquest as the safety of England itself appeared to be at stake. In the parliament of 1597/1598 Francis Bacon underlined the dangers by pointing to four main events which had increased those dangers: the king of France had turned Catholic; Calais had fallen to the Spanish, thereby 'knocking at our doors'; furthermore, 'that ulcer of Ireland … hath run and raged more, and must attract the attentions of Spain'; and finally, 'the last two sea exploits, Cadiz and the Islands Voyage must surely spur the King of Spain on to take his revenge'.[40] By the 1601 November parliament Bacon's prophecy had come to pass; a Spanish force of twenty-three ships and some 4,500 men had landed at Kinsale on 23 September 1601. Cecil's opening speech dwelt on the Spanish presence in Munster, whose intention he averred was 'to tear her Majesty's subjects from her,' and he remarked, 'there we have an army and nothing but an army, fed, even, out of England … it is time to open our coffers'. The queen's need of about £300,000 before Easter was the main purpose of calling that parliament. And, as Cecil also pointed out, no one was so foolish as to believe an end to the danger even if the Spanish were expelled from Ireland: 'if we had been of that mind,' he concluded, 'when the king of Spain had that great overthrow of his Invincible Navy in *anno* 1588 we had been destined to perdition'.[41]

Lord Burghley reflected on the advantages of peace with Spain during the last years of his life,[42] and from Ireland Sir George Carew, president of Munster, counselled such a peace in a 'Discourse of Ireland' (1598), which he sent to Sir Robert Cecil. He appeared to have every confidence that the forces in Ireland would be able to expel the Spaniards and suppress the rebellion though he feared it would cost England a dearer price than Ireland was worth. Peace with Spain was not possible in 1598 or thereafter for the foreseeable future, hence Carew suggested that the surest way to effect the pacification of Ireland was by means of a 'sharp prosecution'; he was aware that those who had inheritances in Ireland and 'such as live by the wars' wanted a final solution 'by the sword' and would not heed the losses of men and money 'that must be consumed in finishing the work'.[43]

Charles Blount, Lord Mountjoy, sounded just as belligerent and determined when he heard the Spaniards had actually landed at Kinsale. He wrote to Sir Robert Cecil: 'I cannot dissemble how confident I am to beat these Spanish Dons, as well as ever I did our Irish Macs and Oes, and to make a perfect conclusion of the war of Ireland.'[44]

From the highest levels of policy making it was seen that unless Ireland was brought into submission and the Spaniards expelled, the island would ever prove a safe haven for England's enemies. The truth of the old saying 'He who would England win With Ireland must begin' must have been self-evident in October 1601.[45] The queen and council determined to oppose with all the military potential possible an Irish force which aimed at the elimination of English sovereignty in Ireland. In asking the clergy to provide horses that October the queen wrote to Archbishop Whitgift:

> the king of Spain and the Pope having long succoured by underhand means our Rebels in Ireland have now of late discovered their malice in more open manner by sending into that kingdom a navy and an army of men who are landed in our province of Munster pretending both to restore there the superstitions of Rome and to reduce that Realm under Spanish tyranny.[46]

Likewise, in her letters to the lords lieutenant she stressed the seriousness of the situation, pointing out that not only was the king of Spain aiding 'our rebels' but that he wished to make himself 'owner of that kingdom'.[47] The chauvinistic tone, beginning to be common in English government pronouncements against Spain since 1588, hardened with the actual intervention of their troops in Ireland. The government did not underestimate the military task ahead. When Mountjoy's men fought at Kinsale they did so as much to repel a Spanish invasion as to put down an Irish revolt. The war assumed an international dimension which it had lacked since the Desmond revolts of 1579–1583.

Whether the Elizabethan government was right to be worried by Spanish forces is perhaps doubtful. Modern historical opinion on Spanish strength in the late sixteenth century seems to indicate that England overestimated its military power; Geoffrey Parker calculated that plague wiped out 8 per cent of the Iberian population between 1598 and 1602 with the result that captains failed to fill their bands in the Spanish army.[48]

It is generally correct to identify English policy with the queen's in all foreign and military affairs; to her, Ireland was ever considered 'our realm of Ireland', or 'our kingdom of Ireland'; Munster was 'our province' and even 'our rebels of Ireland'.[49] Privy councillors and the lord treasurer and the principal secretary might well propose policies but it was the queen who gave the orders. Elizabeth often called her councillors together about Ireland and strengthened them with her wisdom in advising how to suppress rebellion. She disliked the human and financial costs of warfare and favoured moderate and indirect rule as long as possible, inefficient and unsatisfactory though it may have been in the hands of her officials in the Dublin administration. As long as the situation in Ireland was not especially urgent, the queen did not want to spend more than was strictly necessary there. Sir Robert Cecil, who likely knew the queen better than most, wrote of her to Sir George Carew in these terms: 'I speak it to you confidently, that (but myself) I know not one man in this kingdom that will bestow six words of argument to reply if she deny it'.[50]

In proclamations, through privy council orders and in the preambles to statutes she made it clear that it was her will and wish to keep Ireland 'in perfect obedience'.[51] Pronouncements about moderation in policy in Ireland seem to appear *after* bouts of severe repression; for example, when Sir John Perrot had hoped to heal the wounds inflicted by Lord Grey in quelling the Desmond rebellion, 1579–1583, we find hints that the repression may have gone too far.[52] Lord Mountjoy, too, after his definitive conquest, speaks of 'politic proceedings' of 'appeasement' and of *proemis* rather than *poena*.[53] Sir Arthur Chichester, the tough governor of Carrickfergus, and more significantly one of the main architects of the Jacobean plantations in Ulster, advocated educating the Irish to civility 'by gentle persuasion and force of example', but did so at the end of a forceful military career devastating north-east Ulster.[54]

One should hardly look for a consistent policy in the many letters of the queen to her servants in Ireland, nor is it realistic to expect one in the changing circumstances in the last years of her reign. Apparently it had been spread abroad that the queen of England 'intendeth the utter extirpation of the Irish' but the council wanted to assure Dublin that the queen had no such intention or had ever made such a declaration. Rather she wanted it broadcast in Ireland that:

> no subject of hers shall be oppressed by any, if they live in obedience, but if any think of tyrannizing over others to fashion themselves any greatness, no formal submission shall preserve them from the rod of her justice.[55]

From the royal point of view the Irish were to be regarded as the common subjects of the crown. Rebels, whether in England or in Ireland, were simply traitors. If there is a consistent note in the queen's letters to Ireland it is undoubtedly her reluctance to give approval to expensive schemes of military conquest.[56] Cecil wrote to Carew that the queen was 'apter to approve *facta* than *facienda*'.[57]

In spite of the frequent dispatches from Ireland the queen and her council had difficulty in knowing what or whom to believe as intriguers: 'trimmers', adventurers and crooked administrators pursued their own purposes, often to the impoverishment both of the crown and of Ireland. The jealousies, factions and divisions in the English court and council could also be replicated in the Dublin administration.[58] Such divisions appear to have been well known to the Irish enemy too: 'Trust not in the English, for they are not sound among themselves ... the Council is divided,' Donnell MacCarthy reported to the Bishop of Cork.[59] In the last major crisis that threatened the safety of the realm after Essex's failure the Elizabethan government made unprecedented efforts to support Mountjoy in the final subjugation – the time to end caution and compromise had then arrived. From 1599 until the queen's death, soldiers, money and arms were sent across the Irish Sea and though the military potential of late Elizabethan England was limited by resources and weakness in the administration of them, yet the final result, the eventual submission of Ulster, proved to be the nearest match of performance with intention achieved by the Elizabethan state.[60]

In terms of army costs, Sir Julius Caesar's accounts show the charge of Ireland to have been £1,845,696 between October 1595 and the end of the reign.[61] Lord treasurer Middlesex in 1620 considered that Ireland had cost Elizabeth more than £3 million and near the lives of 100,000 – a widely exaggerated mortality figure as may be seen in Chapters 3 and 10 (see especially Table 17).[62] As the number of sacrifices mounted, the government appeared to be determined not to lose sovereignty over Ireland at the end of the day. Among others, John Clapham articulated that opinion:

> Indeed, the wars in Ireland, gathering strength by continuance of time and being maintained with the loss of so many worthy men and the expense of such a mass of

_easure might seem a matter dishonourable. But if the quality of the place and the condition of the people be duly weighed, it will appear that it had been more easy to have conquered a kingdom elsewhere than to have reduced that land to obedience.[63]

The queen echoed those sentiments, dwelling on the anguish the war had brought to many, 'the alienation of Our people's mind from Us' and the burdens it all had placed on the exchequer.[64] Mountjoy's aim was to prosecute the war to the bitter end; and this dictated a ruthless campaign in burning crops, destroying cattle and starving out the rebellious. In a memorable sentence to Cecil he summed up his determination: 'And till it [Ulster] be so reduced and the name of O'Neill or Earl of Tyrone utterly suppressed never look for a sound peace in Ireland'.[65]

To argue that England's war aims were simply the pursuit of a pragmatic programme of total conquest to establish sovereignty and that indeed such a programme was justified by rebellion and England's safety from its continental enemies omits discussion of the religious dimension of the conflict. In the propaganda of the day rebellion in Ireland was often confounded with an adherence to Catholicism and popery. Mistakenly, as it proved, many Elizabethans thought that if submission to Rome was weakened or loyalty to the Pope removed then the cause of English law, order and reform must prevail. Many of the New English already in Ireland and perhaps with a vested interest in the cause of the reformed religion did not distinguish that cause from government policy.[66] Barbarity and paganism became the polemic of conquest to justify the killing of non-combatants. Among others, Nicholas Canny has explored the mental attitudes of the New English in the 1560s and 1570s towards the Irish and sees the lines hardening to justify a regime of inhumanity.[67] To have acknowledged the Irish as Christian would necessarily mean to have acknowledged them as civilised; many articulate Elizabethans were not prepared to do this. Historians find it strange that so many of the renaissance soldier-administrators, well read in the classics and well travelled, should have been apparently blind to an appreciation of early Christian Gaelic culture. It was, however, a commonplace in renaissance writing that a barbaric people must first be brought to civility before they could be taught the truths of Christianity.[68] Many Protestant clergy were at one with the majority of the officials and adventurers in Ireland in a policy of coercion once the rebellion was bravely on. The proselytising work of zealots like Adam Loftus and Thomas Jones is well know; their complaints of slackness in the Court of High Commission to Whitgift is telling evidence. Of the queen's attitude to the promotion of the reformation, they wrote that:

her majesty hath expressly directed them not to stir or meddle in matters of religion ... that the work of the Commission had been discontinued for six years ... priests had been given their liberty which many had used to encourage rebellion ... it would seem her Majesty was prepared to allow constant breaches of the law.[69]

William Lyon, bishop of Cork, preached against all 'cessations' and truces with the Gaelic Irish saying that they never did any good 'to this savage and barbarous nation, only service' – the usual euphemism for military service or oppression; he advocated 'justice without partiality', by which he meant English justice.[70]

The earlier Protestant proselytising programme seems to have weakened in the 1590s; perhaps in the shibboleths of the day many believed that the reform of religion was impossible before the conquest was complete; however, all feared that Irish Catholicism had already made the reconquest difficult to achieve. Hence the activities of friars, priests and Jesuits were not regarded as Christianising but rather as part and parcel of fuelling Gaelic resistance. To take but one example of support for this attitude, Myler McGrath, the ex-friar and convert Protestant archbishop of Cashel, in writing to Cecil on 19 January 1600, claimed that the priests were 'the very root and spring of whom all traitors do grow' and professed incredulity that the government did not have them caught and banished, otherwise, he said, 'Ireland will never be quiet'.[71] Did the belligerence of the New English in the 1590s help counter-reformation activities and entrench the trend of identifying Gaelic Ireland with Catholicism? It is of interest to see that, in the welter of 'Plans', 'Plans', 'Discoveries', and 'Projects' for the reformation of Ireland, 'reformation' is not in the context of religious reformation but of repression in those last years of the reign.[72] It would be all too easy to build up an unfavourable picture of the Protestant clergy in Ireland, who were supposed to have been the driving force in the promotion of the reformation of religion. Spenser clearly had a bad opinion of them; they were either 'unlearned' or 'men of some bad note, for which they had forsaken England'. Even if England sent good and honest ministers, Spenser remained pessimistic: 'what good shall any English minister do amongst them by preaching or teaching which either cannot understand him or will not hear him'.[73] Naturally, the failings, especially their lack of loyalty, of the Catholic clergy are better known in the state records of the decade. In this period too one finds the outbursts of the anti-clerical who castigates both English and Irish, Catholic and Protestant clergy as 'lewd and ignorant'; one such anti-clerical wrote:

> divers of the English have not one word of latin, divers of the Irish broken latin, meeter for the tavern than the temple ... tippling of ale and acqua vitae, getting of bastards and never giving themselves to study or preaching.[74]

Twenty years later William Lithgow, who travelled Ireland in 1619, was writing in the same vein of the clergy:

> Sermons and prayers they never have any ... the alehouse is their church ... their text, Spanish sack ... their singing of psalms the whiffing of tobacco.[75]

Comment on Ireland and the Irish in the sixteenth century flowed easily from the pens of statesmen, clerical and lay, and from commanders and captains with a barely disguised interest in colonisation. Some of the best-known English renaissance scholars wrote on Ireland: Spenser, the foremost poet, Campion, historian and poet, John Davies, philosopher, poet and lawyer, Fenton, classicist and noted translator of Guicciardini, John Hooker, lawyer and biographer of Sir Peter Carew, the mid-Tudor adventurer who typified the land-hungry West Country man.[76] Fynes Moryson was especially perceptive and prolific, though nonetheless prejudiced, as was Thomas Stafford, Sir George Carew's apologist in his celebrated *Pacata Hibernia*. Some of the titles betray a specious polemic, as we have seen. The not so well known 'Discoverie, recoverie and apologie' of the unfortunate Captain Thomas Lee is typical of the genre; he favoured medical analogies:

> I find it is good to deal with Ireland as a careful surgeon is accustomed to deal with a body full of dangerous and infested wounds, that is to apply medicines to those parts which are nearest unto the head and the heart before they do practice upon the rest of the members.

Lee went on to liken Munster to the head, and the Pale to the heart, while Connaught was 'the belly or somewhat lower' and Ulster 'a leg ... remote member full of foul canker and other gross diseases'.[77] Barnaby Rich, in his 'A looking glass for her Majesty wherein to view Ireland', writes similarly but he also made the interesting claim that, since the wars in Ireland began, 'the greatest cause has been wrong information delivered unto your Majesty and honourable council,' suggesting that the government was badly informed on the state of Ireland.[78] Rich was not of the persuader school in his proposed remedy to the queen: like Spenser, he chillingly recommended what had virtually become a formula for the 1590s – 'this reformation must be settled by force, yet famine must be an especial means whereby to accomplish it' and 'a barbarous country must first be broken by a war before it will be capable of good government'.

Racism reinforced the cant of conquest. The conquistadors are in such tracts made paladins of rectitude and their victims brutish monsters. John Baynard advised famine and force as the sole means to subdue Ireland. Thomas Stafford compared the people of Munster to the Italian 'bandetti ... who live between the power of the king of Spain and the Pope'.[79] 'Tartarian' was so frequently used as an adjective of Gaelic society that it became an Elizabethan cliché.

The reduction of Ireland to English renaissance civility clearly meant the obliteration of the Gaelic polity and way of life, and this was also to be achieved by fostering divisions among the Irish themselves on the classical principle of *divide et impera*.

Some writers, mainly from the Pale, contented themselves with statements of high indignation on how the law was flouted. Sixteenth-century English writers on Ireland tell us as much about themselves as they do of their subject; they are, as David Quinn has summarised, 'curious, surprised, hostile, censorious, nationalistic, reforming and paradoxically at times, sympathetic and brutal almost in the same breath'.[80] Motivated often by land hunger and personal ambition they were hardly impartial and objective witnesses of the sixteenth-century Irish scene. But in those ambitions many of the Elizabethan adventurers were frustrated, for, by the end of the century, many of their class lamented the misery, poverty and desolation the war had entailed, not to mention the disastrous consequences to their profits that the debasement of the Irish coinage and the tying of trade to England implied. John Chamberlain, commenting on the minting of base coin for Ireland, feared that such a practice was but a prelude 'to purge our own money of the best juice'.[81] Spenser saw the envy and greed of the governing class as the major hindrance to good order; 'the country suffered,' he wrote, and 'good government became impossible for conscientious men'.[82]

While good government may have suffered, some of the official class made Irish fortunes. It was said of Sir William Fitzwilliam, 'Never a man went from Ireland of his calling with more money and less love'.[83] Richard Boyle is perhaps the best-known example.[84] Roger Wilbraham feathered his nest as solicitor general of Ireland, as Lord Burghley's endorsements to charges brought against him in 1597 suggest.[85] Sir George Carey, treasurer-at-war, 1599–1606, amassed wealth out of his office. Years after his death the legal actions against his heirs and executors indicated fraudulent dealings and peculation in the order of £150,000.[86] Less dramatic instances of captains and muster masters who turned public money to their private gain will be noted later. Service in Ireland could equally break lesser men, for example those who had pinned their hopes on land gains at the end of the war.[87] If large debts can be construed as evidence of honesty it may be that Lord Mountjoy was above suspicion; he complained to Cecil that he was likely to return from Ireland a beggar.[88]

Many of the Elizabethan adventurers who occupied positions in the army and administration were aggressive and greedy in enriching themselves. Some, like Sir Richard Bingham and Sir Conyers Clifford in Connaught, posed as the champions of the common people against the exactions of the 'hellhounds' of lords whose only principle, according to Barnaby Rich, towards their tenants was 'defend me and spend me'.[89] Captains lost no opportunity to stress the 'tyranny' of O'Neill and O'Donnell when they wrote to the privy council or to Cecil.[90] They seemed anxious to stress their rôle as the deliverers of the common people to justify a harsh or 'forward' policy, which frequently ended in the seizure of property.

How far official English policy went along with these attitudes of the adventurers in Ireland is difficult to assess. It would be also difficult to sustain the contention that an overall empirical policy of total conquest, much talked of in the 1590s and 1570s, was ruthlessly and systematically followed. The queen's government could not afford a consistent policy of total conquest. At times official policy was at variance with what many captains and commanders in the field thought best. The military situation was never static; textbook strategy was often rendered useless by a quick-witted and quick-footed enemy. In such circumstances individual commanders often took severe courses of action formerly denounced by government. It is scarcely surprising that the subjugation took so long.

In the official mind there seems to have been only one name for troubles in Ireland – 'rebellion' – and the main cause of its occurrence was assumed to be the half measures taken by England.[91] Elizabethan statesmen who had anything to do with Ireland spoke with a superior confidence of the 'godly conquest' and the 'perfecting of Ireland to obedience'. Their schemes for the settlement of Ireland wrongly assumed that the English themselves would not be divided by dissensions such as the feuds between Sir William Russell and Sir John Norris,[92] between Sir Geoffrey Fenton and Sir Richard Bingham,[93] and that between Sir Ralph Lane and Maurice Kyffin, the latter sent to reform abuses in the muster office headed by Lane.[94] Personal antagonisms hindered smooth administration in both civil and military establishments, and at times advantaged the enemy. The queen and council in England bemoaned the enormous cost in lives, money and supplies the reconquest of Ireland entailed. The Earl of Sussex, hampered by difficulties as lord deputy, once wished the island of Ireland sunk in the sea.[95] The queen grew weary with reading the Irish dispatches, and Sir Robert Cecil confessed to Lord Thomas Howard in 1600, 'It cost me some labour before I went to bed and I protest it brake my sleep (no easy matter, I thank God) to contemplate how that land of Ire has exhausted this land of promise'.[96]

Irish aims

From the Irish point of view the war was clearly a defence against the spread of English administration and an alien religion, and in defence of the Gaelic order, which, as it proved, was in the last decade of its autonomous existence. Historical scholarship has begun to give detailed surveys of Gaelic society, sympathetic to its values, and arguing that over centuries the Gaelic way of life was sufficiently flexible and attractive to absorb many English settlers.[97] G. A. Hayes-McCoy's writings in particular have shown a resurgent Gaelic society in Ulster in the late sixteenth century sufficiently organised and equipped under Hugh O'Neill to withstand subjugation by English culture and customs or anglicisation.[98] Nicholas Canny traced the hibernicisation of the Pale in the 1560s and 1570s and demonstrated that Gaelic society was far from being in the arrested state of development claimed by contemporary English renaissance writers.[99] And, in a recent case study in Gaelic ideology, Brendan Bradshaw sees an emergent self-conscious nationalism articulated in bardic poetry, though not of the faith and fatherland variety beloved of Irish nationalistic historians since the seventeenth century.[100]

In one of the more perceptive and objective passages of Fynes Moryson's *Itinerary* he attempts an analysis of why the native Gaelic Irish resisted the English advance so stubbornly. His list of causes include the treasons practised by Hugh O'Neill as Earl of Tyrone, the severity of Sir Richard Bingham as governor of Connaught and, to quote:

> the hatred of the conquered against the Conquerors, the difference of religion, the love of the Irish to Spain … the extortions of the sheriffs and sub-sheriffs buying these places, the ill government of the Church among our selves, and the admitting Popish Priests among the Irish.[101]

He went on to claim that the 'fier of Rebellion now kindled' was allowed to become a 'devouring flame' because timely hands were not laid on the leaders 'to prevent their combination', and because 'Pardons and Protections' had been granted to many who had formerly abused this clemency. Finally, he blamed the employment of Irish in the English forces for the prolongation of the war.[102]

It is evident from the Irish state papers alone that the New English recognised that Irish hatred of them greatly increased from the late 1580s. The murders and mutilations that accompanied the rising in Munster to exterminate the English colony in October 1598 left them in no doubt. William Saxey, chief justice in Munster,

reported to Cecil the horrors that had taken place. The English had had then
cut, but had not been killed, and:

> Some with the tongues cut out of their heads others with their noses cut off ... infants
> taken from the breast and the brains dashed against the walls ... and the heart plucked out
> of the body of a husband in view of his wife.[103]

A summary of the state of Ireland in 1597 claimed universal hatred for the English
and that no part of Ulster was free from hostility to the queen.[104] A discourse sent to the
queen in 1598 stated that 'there could be no agreement possible between two equal
contraries, English and Irish' – yet another Spenserian barb.[105]

Hugh O'Neill saw Catholicism as a potent unifying force; it united the Anglo-Irish
and the native Gaelic, it crossed barriers between town and country and between lords
fighting for the restoration of their privileges and the people for their liberties.
Whether he liked it or not, the leaders of the Catholic Church saw in Hugh O'Neill
their deliverer from an imposed alien religion. O'Neill may have been brought up a
Protestant, but when in Ireland in the 1590s his allegiance to Catholicism is
undoubted. By then he had strengthened his position in the O'Neill lordship to have
himself inaugurated 'the O'Neill', the symbol of Irish independence, encouraged it
was said by the Catholic bishops.[106]

To O'Neill there were many advantages in projecting the war as a crusade in league
with the papacy and Spain against the new religion of the invader and coloniser. No
other factor would bring together those disparate elements more thoroughly than a
common Catholicism. One of the earliest occasions in which O'Neill stated the
restoration of Catholicism as a war aim can be seen in the joint letter with O'Donnell of
September 1595 to Philip II of Spain declaring the renewal of the war in the name of
religion. They asked for two or three thousand soldiers, money and arms 'to restore the
faith of the Church and secure you a kingdom'.[107] At the same time Francis Mountford,
a Catholic English priest, wrote in similar vain to Don Carolo.[108] Both letters were
intercepted by the English intelligence service,[109] and it was thought that the queen
generally made a point of reading such letters.[110] In his July 1596 call to the gentlemen
of Munster to join the rebellion, O'Neill stressed that 'the highest to the lowest shall
assist Christ's catholic religion and join in confederacy and make war with us'.[111] His
letter from Dungannon in November 1599 to rouse support in the towns stated this
war aim categorically: 'upon my salvation I fight chiefly and principally for the catholic
faith to be planted throughout all our poor country as well in cities as elsewhere,' and
ends by 'praying God to move your flinty hearts to prefer the commodity and profit of
our country before your own private ends'.[112] He urged Cormac McDermott 'to expel
the enemies of the Church'.[113] He upbraided Barry of Cork for 'serving against us and
the Church',[114] and told him a week later (25 February 1600) that by not joining his
forces he had 'separated himself from the unity of Christ, his mystical body, the
Catholic Church'.[115] And he told John FitzEdmonds and his sons to 'fight for your
conscience and the right'.[116]

The Anglo-Irish lords of Cork and Limerick, unmoved, were visited by O'Neill in a
ferocious incursion or 'journey of retribution'; he burned and pillaged the towns and

villages on Lord Barry's lands in particular; the state papers give 220 such towns and villages, a palpable exaggeration; towns here are confused with town lands, the subdivision of land-holdings, sept or clan lands, the approximate Gaelic equivalent to folk land in England.[117] Lord Barry of Cork was treated as a defector by O'Neill. Whereas in the Desmond rebellion, 1579–1583, his forces were the mainstay of the rebels, in the 1590s Barry was a firm supporter of the English.[118]

During the prolonged negotiations of 1596 with the council in Dublin, and through it with the queen and privy council, O'Neill and O'Donnell stressed liberty of conscience in their petitions.[119] The queen was annoyed that her representatives had given ear 'to such presumptious and disloyal petitions', and that her commissioners in Ireland had made a truce on terms she did not like. Her answer on the question of 'free liberty of conscience' was that O'Neill and O'Donnell did not mention this in their earlier submissions, and that the petition of March 1596 demonstrated 'a later disloyal compact made betwixt them and other rebels without any reasonable ground'.[120]

However much O'Neill tried to use the common Catholicism of rebel Gaelic and loyal Old English to bring about a common hostility, he did not greatly succeed. The harshness of the war effort alone achieved as much. There was little evidence in the Pale of any general movement to join O'Neill, or indeed in the towns. They did not equate their Catholicism with rebellion and saw no incompatibility between their loyalty to both crown and Catholicism. What did strain their loyalty was the new class of bureaucrats, soldiers and would-be land and office holders who moved into Dublin and the Pale, and as the allegiance of the Anglo-Irish to the English crown grew lukewarm, they came increasingly under suspicion. Nor did Protestantism unite all on the English side; not all of the new bureaucratic class were loyal Protestants. Some were English recusants seeking a haven in Ireland, where there was a greater degree of tolerance for Catholicism than could be found in the England of the 1590s.[121]

In his efforts to make the war a crusade, O'Neill wanted assurance that the Pope would excommunicate those who supported the English crown policy.[122] Although Pope Clement VIII did not give such an assurance, O'Neill used the threat of excommunication to bring him support which the English government believed would have been otherwise withheld. Dermot McGrath, bishop of Cork, and Owen Hogan, vicar apostolic, helped O'Neill by threatening Lord Barry of Cork with excommunication, claiming they had 'received an excommunication from the Pope against all that doth not join in this Catholic action.'[123] The most O'Neill gained from Clement VIII was an indulgence of the type usually given those setting out to fight for the recovery of the Holy Land; in its terms O'Neill was entitled 'Captain General of the Catholic Army in Ireland'. The indulgence was not the same thing as a papal command to Irish Catholics to take up arms, still less an excommunication of those who did not join O'Neill's forces.[124]

At the court of Rome, O'Neill had much support from Peter Lombard, the papal nominee to Armagh.[125] There, too, he had enemies who were not prepared to believe that his motive was primarily the defence of the Catholic faith. They may have cast doubts on the purity of O'Neill's motives to the Pope, who clearly was not going to give him unqualified support.[126]

At the Irish college in Brussels Catholic loyalist students assured the papal nuncio that Hugh O'Neill was chiefly concerned to establish his own ascendancy. As proof they put forward to the nuncio the rumoured allegations that O'Neill was in conspiracy with the Earl of Essex in 1599, and that O'Neill's declarations that he fought for the freedom of the Catholic religion ought to be distrusted.[127]

The terms of the truce he had won with Essex, and those he wished to have ratified with the English government in 1599–1600, show O'Neill to have had genuine religious concerns. Ireland was to be reconciled to the Holy See, prisoners of religion were to be released, Irish Catholics were to be promoted to church livings, the churches were to be restored, Catholicism was to be preached, a Catholic university was to be founded, and he and his followers were to 'peaceably enjoy all lands and privileges that did appertain to their predecessors two hundred years past'.[128]

The demand for the restoration of lands was inextricably mixed up with his war aims; but for O'Neill, land, religion and former rights all simply added up to the removal of English rule, a veritable declaration of all-out war. When Cecil read the terms O'Neill outlined, he wrote on the margin of the original copy from O'Neill 'Eutopia'.[129] Once again the queen advised that the reformation of religion should not be insisted on as it made the people more obdurate; she did not wish to make persecution in religion an excuse for rebellion. In advising Sir George Carew in September 1600 the privy council wrote:

> that it is as yet inconvenient to take any sudden or sharp course for reformation of their blind superstitions, being with strong head so generally carried away with opinion of conscience; so we must put a great difference betwixt the secret exercise of their religion and practice of treason under colour of religion.[130]

The privy council went on to command Carew to show great wisdom and discretion in the just execution of the law with 'the offenders in treason without any inconvenient disturbance for matter of religion'.[131] The penalties for recusancy were not vigorously pursued in Ireland, as the government did not have the machinery or personnel to carry them out. Some repressive measures against the Catholic clergy were, however, enforced; they were, for instance, specifically excluded from the general pardon issued in 1600 for all in the province of Munster for their part in the 1598 rebellion.[132]

As much as Elizabeth and her council wanted to keep religion out of the war in Ireland, O'Neill and his followers wished to have it brought to the forefront of their war aims. O'Neill intensified his appeals to Rome, to Spain and to the Cardinal Archduke Albert, Spanish ruler of the Low Countries, requesting the last, for example, to grant licence to all Irish soldiers in the Low Countries to return to Ireland to assist against the English.[133] In his negotiations with Rome O'Neill stressed that he never made terms which did not include liberty of conscience,[134] and in his many dealings with Spain he emphasised 'the extirpation of heresy' from Ireland.[135] The Spanish council reporting to Philip III in July 1600 on the state of Ireland noted, 'Most nations dislike Spain, the Irish love it. It is just that they be succoured.'[136]

Contemporaries leave much evidence of their war aims, yet it would be misleading to interpret their writings to present a Herculean conflict of civilisations, a struggle of

English renaissance civility against a primitive Gaelic barbarism. The private ambitions of Gaelic lords like O'Neill, O'Donnell and Maguire, of Anglo-Irish nobility such as the Earl of Ormond and Lord Barry, and of parvenu royal officials like Fenton, Cary and Chichester, cannot be divorced from the higher-flown statements of war policy. In this sense it is not easy to identify nationalist, patriotic or religious sentiments as the only motives in the war.

Notes

1 J. Morrin, ed., *Calendar of patent and close rolls of Chancery in Ireland, Henry VIII – Elizabeth* (hereafter *Calendar of patent rolls, Ireland*) (Dublin, 1862), vol. ii, p. lxiii.

2 Cited in N. P. Canny, *The Elizabethan conquest of Ireland: a pattern established, 1565–1576* (Hassocks, 1976), 11.

3 K. W. Nicholls, *Land, law and society in sixteenth century Ireland* (Dublin, 1976).

4 G. A. Hayes-McCoy, 'Gaelic society in the late sixteenth century', *Historical Studies*, 4 (1963), 45–61.

5 G. A. Hayes-McCoy, *Scots mercenary forces in Ireland 1565–1603* (Dublin, 1937), *passim*.

6 33 Henry VIII, c. 1, and see *Irish statutes* (1786 edn), I, 176.

7 W. F. T. Butler, 'The policy of surrender and re-grant', *Journal of the Royal Society of Antiquaries, Ireland*, 43 (1913).

8 See the bibliography under such authors as R. D. Edwards, A. Ford, P. Corish, B. Bradshaw, N. Canny, C. Brady, and C. Lennon.

9 K. W. Nicholls, *Gaelic and Gaelicised Ireland in the later middle ages* (Dublin, 1972).

10 C. Brady, 'Court, castle and country; the framework of government in Tudor Ireland', in *Natives and newcomers: essays on the making of Irish colonial society 1534–1641*, eds C. Brady and R. Gillespie (Dublin, 1986) and for a more descriptive account see S. Ellis, *Tudor Ireland: crown, colony and the conflict of cultures, 1470–1603* (London, 1985), ch. 6. For a detailed analysis of the government of Ireland up to the Henrician regime see the same author's *Reform and revival: English government in Ireland, 1470–1534* (Woodbridge, 1986).

11 *Calendar of state papers, Ireland* (hereafter *CSPI*) (1586–1588), 68, 98; *ibid.* (1588–1592), 173, 506.

12 G. A. Hayes-McCoy, 'Conciliation and coercion and the Protestant Reformation 1547–1571, 1571–1603', in *A new history of Ireland, vol. iii, Early modern Ireland, 1534–1691*, eds T. W. Moody, F. X. Martin and F. J. Byrne (Oxford, 1976), 88–92.

13 M. MacCarthy-Morrough, *The Munster plantation: migration to southern Ireland 1583–1641* (Oxford, 1986). For the causes of these rebellions see C. Brady, 'Factions and the origins of the Desmond rebellion of 1579', *Irish Historical Studies* (hereafter *IHS*), 22 (1981), 289–312, and for a narrative account of both rebellions see J. J. N. McGurk, 'The fall of the noble house of Desmond, 1579–83', *History Today*, 29 (1979), 578–585, 670–675.

14 B. Cunningham, 'The composition of Connaught in the lordships of Clanrickard and Thomond, 1577–1641', *IHS*, 24 (1984), 1–14.

15 G. A. Hayes-McCoy, *Ulster and other Irish maps c. 1600* (Irish Manuscripts Commission, Dublin, 1964).

16 British Library (hereafter BL) Additional MSS, 33, 743, f. 89, Lee's 'Discoverie, recoverie and apologie'.

17 Public Record Office (hereafter PRO) MP\F, 36 and for further details on the map see PRO NI, T2125\2\4.

18 Sir John Davies, *A discovery of the true causes why Ireland was never entirely subdued ... until ... his majesty's happy reign* (1612) (facsimile edn, Shannon, 1969).

19 *CSPI* (1601–1603), 529, the deposition of Jordan Roche before Sir George Carew in Cork, 19 November 1602.

20 N. P. Canny, *The formation of the Old English elite in Ireland* (Dublin, 1975); Rowland White, 'Book on the state of Ireland, 1571' in PRO state papers (hereafter SP) 63\31\32, ff. 75–114.

21 See the bibliography under B. Bradshaw, A. Ford, P. Corish, R. Dudley Edwards and N. Canny.

22 Cited in C. L. Falkiner, *Illustrations of Irish history and topography* (London, 1904), 287.

23 H. Morgan, *Tyrone's rebellion: the outbreak of the Nine Years War in Tudor Ireland* (Dublin, 1993).

24 Hiram Morgan, '"Faith and fatherland or Queen and country", an unpublished exchange between O'Neill and the state at the height of the Nine Years War', *Dúiche Néill (Journal of the O'Neill Country Historical Society)*, no. 9 (1984), 9–65.

25 J. A. Froude, *The English in Ireland* (1901), 52.

26 C. Brady, ed., *Interpreting Irish history* (Dublin, 1994).

27 Notably the *History and topography of Ireland*, trans. and ed. J. J. O'Meara (London, 1982) and Gerald's *Expugnatio Hibernica*, eds A. B. Scott and F. X. Martin (Dublin, 1978).

28 N. P. Canny, *The formation of the Old English elite in Ireland* (Dublin, 1975); C. Lennon, *Richard Stanihurst, the Dubliner, 1547–1618* (Dublin, 1979).

29 B. Fitzpatrick, *Seventeenth century Ireland; the war of religions* (Dublin, 1988).

30 S. Ellis, *Tudor Ireland: crown, community and the conflict of cultures 1470–1603* (London, 1985) and his 'Historiographical debate; representations of the past in Ireland: whose past and whose present?', *Irish Historical Studies*, 27 (1991), 108.

31 Sir Henry Nicholas, *Memoirs of the life and times of Sir Christopher Hatton* (London, 1847), 158.

32 Cited in J. E. Neale, *Elizabeth I and her parliaments, 1584–1603* (London, 1953–1957), 56.

33 N. Canny and C. Brady, 'Spenser's Irish crisis', *Past and Present*, 120 (1988), 201–215.

34 *Calendar of patent rolls, Ireland*, ii (1862), 29.

35 P. Coughlan, ed., *Spenser and Ireland* (Cork, 1989) and particularly the essay by C. Brady, 'The road to the view....' in that volume.

36 J. C. Beckett, 'The study of Irish history', *Confrontations: studies in Irish history* (London, 1972), 18.

37 J. C. Beckett, The making of modern Ireland (2nd edn, London, 1981); and quotation in S. Ellis, *Tudor Ireland: crown, community and the conflict of cultures, 1470–1603* (London, 1985), 159, from F. E. Ball, *The judges in Ireland, 1221–1921* (London, 1926), vol. i, 141–142.

38 *Calendar of patent rolls, Ireland*, i, preface, xvii, xviiii, lii. For the definitive secondary work on the governors of Ireland in the early modern period see C. Brady, *The chief governors: the rise and fall of reform government in Tudor Ireland 1536–1588* (Cambridge, 1994).

39 D. B. Quinn, *The Elizabethans and the Irish* (Ithaca, 1966).

40 J. E. Neale, *Elizabeth I and her parliaments*, vol. ii (London, 1957), 360.

41 *Ibid.*, 411, 413.

42 PRO SP12/266/3, 2 January 1598.

43 *Calendar of the Carew MSS preserved at Lambeth Palace Library* (1867–1873) (hereafter *Cal. Carew MSS*), iv, 168–171, discourse of Ireland to Cecil, 1601.

44 In Fynes Moryson, *An itinerary ... and a description of Ireland*, vol. ii, ed. J. Machlehose (Glasgow, 1907), 461 (hereafter Fynes Moryson, *Itinerary*).

45 Cited by Richard Hawkins to the privy council, 10 June 1602, in PRO SP12/284/28, 29.

46 Lambeth Palace Library MS 2009, f. 141.

47 PRO SP12/282/33.

48 G. Parker, *The army of Flanders* (Cambridge, 1972), 43.

49 Lambeth Palace Library MS 2009, f. 141, and PRO SP12/282/33.

50 J. Maclean, ed., *The letters of Sir Robert Cecil to Sir George Carew* (Camden Society, old series, lxxxviii, London, 1864), 139.

51 For examples see PRO SP12/282/33, 34, and throughout *Acts of the privy council of England 1542–1631* (London, 1890–1907) (hereafter *APC*), xxix–xxxii.

52 C. Brady, 'Court, castle and country; the framework of government in Tudor Ireland', in *Natives and newcomers: the making of Irish colonial society 1534–1641* (Dublin, 1986).

53 Historical Manuscripts Commission (hereafter HMC), *Salisbury*, xiv, 241.

54 For one assessment of his part in the conquest see *New History of Ireland*, iii, *s.v.* Chichester. However, as lord deputy (1605–1615) Chichester was forced to resign for opposing the severity of anti-Catholic laws in 1614.

55 *Cal. Carew MSS*, iii, 121. Russell was lord deputy from June 1594 to May 1597. His Irish journal is in the BL Additional MSS 4728 and summarised in *Cal. Carew MSS*, iii, 220–260.

56 *Cal. Carew MSS*, iv, 362.

57 *Ibid.*, 98 – there is a draft of the queen's letter giving the lord deputy authority to pardon dated 29 June 1601.

58 For some of the queen's censures on the Dublin councillors see *CSPI* (1599–1600), 114–117, 178, 212, 216.

59 *CSPI* (1600), 71.

60 See the tables in Chapter 3.

61 BL Lansdowne MSS, 156, ff. 253–258.

62 F. C. Dietz, *English public finances, 1558–1641*, vol. ii (1964), 435; for earlier government expenditure on Ireland see S. Ellis, *Tudor Ireland: crown, community and the conflict of cultures 1470–1603* (London, 1985).

63 John Clapham, *Certain observations concerning the life and reign of Queen Elizabeth*, eds E. Read and C. Read (Philadelphia, 1951), 58.

64 Cited in Fynes Moryson, *Itinerary*, vol. iii, 225.

65 *CSPI* (1601–1603), 8.

66 R. Dudley Edwards, *Church and state in Tudor Ireland* (Dublin, 1935), is a standard authority on the religious aspect of the war. But also see A. Ford, *The Protestant Reformation in Ireland 1590–1641* (Frankfurt am Main, 1985) and Hiram, *Duiche Neill (Journal of the O'Neill Country Historical Society)*, 9 (1984), 9–65.

67 N. P. Canny, *The Elizabethan conquest of Ireland; a pattern established, 1565–1576* (Hassocks, 1976) and for a critique of Canny see B. Bradshaw, 'The Elizabethans and the Irish', *Studies*, 66 (1977), 38–50.

68 E. Spenser, *A view of the present state of Ireland*, ed. W. L. Renwick (Oxford, 1970).

69 *CSPI* (1600), 76–80.

70 *CSPI* (1599–1600), 475–478, and for trenchant comments on what the extension of justice meant see Viscount Baltinglas's letter to the Earl of Ormond in *Cal. Carew MSS* (1575–1588), 289.

71 *CSPI* (1599–1600), 407–408.

72 *Cal. Carew MSS*, iii, 105, 180, 333; *ibid.*, iv, 478 and *CSPI* (1596–1597), 234–235, 250, 254, 266, 292, 403; *ibid* (1598–1599), 160, 162–165, 171–172, 328–329.

73 E. Spenser, *A view of the present state of Ireland*, ed. W. L. Renwick (Oxford, 1970), 88, 89.

74 *CSPI* (1595–1599), 430.

75 W. Lithgow, 'Adventurers in Ireland', *Ulster Journal of Archaeology*, 17 (1911), 90.

76 N. P. Canny, *The Elizabethan conquest of Ireland; a pattern established, 1565–1576* (Hassocks, 1976), Chapter 4, *passim*.

77 BL Additional MSS, 33, 743, ff. 1–188 give the full 'Discoverie, recoverie and apologie' – for the citations see ff. 53, 54, 146.

78 PRO SP63/205/no. 72, ff. 1–10, May 1599, and in Rich's *Description of Ireland* (1610), Chapter 4, his theme is largely unchanged.
79 Thomas Stafford, *Pacata Hibernia*, vol. ii, ed. S. O'Grady (London, 1896), 305.
80 D. B. Quinn, *The Elizabethans and the Irish* (Ithaca, 1966), 191.
81 S. Williams, ed., *Letters of John Chamberlain* (Camden Society, lxxix, London, 1861), 101, Chamberlain to Carleton, 3 February 1601.
82 H. Morley, ed., 'Spenser's view of the present state of Ireland', in *Ireland under Elizabeth and James* (London, 1890), 130–132.
83 BL Additional MSS, 4793, f. 78.
84 N. P. Canny, *The upstart earl: a study of the social and mental world of Richard Boyle, first earl of Cork* (Cambridge, 1982) but specifically on how Boyle accrued his fortune see T. O. Ranger, 'Richard Boyle and the making of an Irish fortune', *IHS*, 10 (1957), 257–297.
85 PRO SP63/201, 154.
86 H. Hall, *Society in the Elizabethan age*, 2nd edn (London, 1901), 123–129.
87 M. MacCarthy-Morrough, *The Munster plantation: migration to southern Ireland 1583–1641* (Oxford, 1986), and D. B. Quinn, 'The Munster plantation; problems and opportunities', *Journal of the Cork Historical and Archaeological Society*, 71 (1966), 19–41.
88 *CSPI* (1600–1601), 174; *CSPI* (1601–1603), 570.
89 *CSPI* (1592–1596), 407; *CSPI* (1598–1599), 130.
90 *CSPI* (1598–1599) 158, 447, 451; *CSPI* (1600) 66, 96, 126; *CSPI* (1600–1601), 166, 167.
91 H. Morley, ed., Sir John Davies' 'A Discovery of the True Causes why Ireland was never entirely subdued…', in *Ireland under Elizabeth and James* (1890), 218–221.
92 *CSPI* (1596–1597), 21, 49, 51, 54, 138–139, 158, 159, 207–209, 242, 304, 496.
93 *Ibid.*, 37, 68, 77, 112–113, 131–132 (Fenton and Bingham's quarrels).
94 *Ibid.*, 190, 214, 215, 252, 263, 292, 305, 314, 318, 337, 391, 464–465, Lane and Kyffin's differences.
95 *Cal. Carew MSS*, i, 302.
96 HMC, *Salisbury*, x, 345.
97 See the bibliography under K. Nicholls, S. O'Domhnaill, G. A. Hayes-McCoy, N. P. Canny, B. Bradshaw, R. D. Edwards, A. Clarke and D. B. Quinn.
98 Especially G. A. Hayes-McCoy, 'Gaelic society in the late sixteenth century', *Historical Studies*, 4 (1963), 45–61.
99 N. P. Canny, 'Hugh O'Neill and the changing face of Gaelic Ulster', *Studia Hibernica*, 10 (1970), 7–35; *The Elizabethan conquest of Ireland, a pattern established 1565–1576* (Hassocks, 1976), Chapters 1 and 7.
100 B. Bradshaw, 'Native reaction to the westward enterprise: a case study in Gaelic ideology', in *Westward enterprise*, eds K. R. Andrews, N. P. Canny and P. E. P. Hair (Liverpool, 1978), 65–85.
101 Fynes Moryson, *Itinerary*, vol. ii, 189–192.
102 See Chapter 2.
103 PRO SP63/202, part iii, no.127, William Saxey to Sir Robert Cecil, 26 October 1598.
104 *Cal. Carew MSS*, iii, 179, 216.
105 PRO SP63/202, part iv, no. 59 – endorsed 'A brief discourse of Ireland by Spencer'.
106 HMC, *Salisbury*, iv, 565. The date of his inauguration as 'the O'Neill' is variously given as 1593, 1595, 1597. The entire question of O'Neill's religious motives have been raised again by Hiram Morgan, *Duiche Neill (Journal of the O'Neill Country Historical Society)*, 9 (1984), 9–65; and they are more popularly exposed in Morgan's article 'Faith and fatherland in sixteenth century Ireland', *History Ireland*, 3 (1995), 13–20.
107 *Cal. Carew MSS*, iii, 122, translation of the Latin copy to Spain.
108 *Ibid.*, 123, signed *Amicus tuus ignotus* – O'Neyll and countersigned *Franciscus Monfortius*.

Don Carolo was likely Don Luis de Carillo, Governor of Corunna, cf. C. Maxwell, *Irish history from contemporary sources* (1923), 187, n. 2.

109 *Ibid.*, 122, 123 endorsed 'Intercepted'.
110 HMC, *Salisbury*, xii, 93.
111 *Cal. Carew MSS*, iii, 179, O'Neill from Strabane, 6 July 1596.
112 Cited in C. P. Meehan, *The fate and fortunes of Hugh O'Neill* (Dublin, 1886), 21, 23.
113 PRO SP63/207, part i, no. 85a, 3 February 1600.
114 *Ibid.*, no. 123(i), 13 February 1600.
115 *Ibid.*, no. 130, 25 February 1600.
116 *Ibid.*, no. 131, 23 February 1600.
117 PRO SP63/207, part i, no. 132, names of towns and villages destroyed between 13 February and the 27 February 1600.
118 J. O'Donovan (ed. and trans), *Annals of the kingdom of Ireland by the four masters* (Dublin, 1851) (hereafter *AFM*), vol. vi, 2150.
119 *Cal. Carew MSS*, iii, 133, 151, 152, 153–159, for these petitions and answers.
120 *Ibid.*, 167, 'Answers to the rebellious Earl of Tyrone'.
121 R. D. Edwards, 'Ireland, Elizabeth I and the Counter-Reformantion', in *Elizabethan government and society*, eds S. T. Bindoff, J. Hurstfield and C. H. Williams (London, 1960), 319, 331, and for the impact of the reformation on one English shire see, for example, K. E. Wark, *Elizabethan recusancy in Cheshire* (Chetham Society, 3rd series, xxix, Manchester, 1971).
122 J. Hagan, ed., 'Some papers relating to the Nine Years' War from the Borghese Collections of MSS Vat. Archives', *Archivium Hibernicum*, 3 (1914), 241–296.
123 *Cal. Carew MSS*, iii, 362–363.
124 For a printed Latin copy of the indulgence see PRO SP 63/207, part ii, no. 95.
125 J. J. Silke, 'The Irish Peter Lombard', *Studies*, 64, no. 254 (1975), 143.
126 J. J. Silke, 'Hugh O'Neill, the catholic question and the papacy', *Irish Ecclesiastical History*, 5th series, 104 (1965), 65–79.
127 J. Hagan, 'Some papers relating to the Nine Years War from the Borghese Collections of MSS Vat. Archives', *Archivium Hibernicum*, iii (1914), 274–285.
128 *CSPI* (1599–1600), 279–280.
129 *Ibid.*
130 *Cal. Carew MSS*, iii, 457–459.
131 *Ibid.*
132 *Ibid.*, 501–502.
133 J. Hagan, ed., 'Some papers relating to the Nine Years War from the Borghese Collections of MSS Vat. Archives', *Archivium Hibernicum*, iii (1914), 274–285.
134 *Cal. Carew MSS*, iii, preface, lvi, lvii.
135 *Ibid.*, 350.
136 *Calendar of state papers, Spanish* (1587–1603), 674

CHAPTER TWO

The machinery for the Irish war

'Levies of soldiers and arms for Ireland' is such a frequent entry in the state papers and the registers of the privy council that it is surprising the subject has not attracted scholarly attention in its own right. The works of C. G. Cruickshank, L. Boynton and G. Parker have provided insights into the theory and practice of military affairs in the period but there is little on the matter of sending troops to Ireland. C. Falls' pioneering work on Elizabeth's Irish wars deals primarily with the military actions against the Irish rebellions in the queen's reign. Wallace T. MacCaffrey's recent *Elizabeth I: war and politics 1588–1603*, by absorbing so much research work, including my own, in a synthesis, may now be said to have dated not only Falls' book but also that of A. L. Rowse on Ireland, and yet MacCaffrey, despite the concentration on Irish military affairs in the final volume of his trilogy, has not superseded the work of Ireland's premier military historian G. A. Hayes-McCoy in the *New history of Ireland* (edited by T. W. Moody *et al.*), or indeed the specialised work of the handful of historians working on Tudor Ireland such as Nicholas Canny, Ciaran Brady, Steven Ellis and Hiram Morgan. From the English side the Irish war loomed large in the government of Elizabethan England.[1]

Apart from the *State papers, domestic, State papers, Ireland*, the Carew collections and the privy council registers, the primary material must be sought among lieutenancy papers and other local records. Enough can be gleaned to show the theory and practice of sending troops to Ireland, and the composition of those forces in Ireland and the machinery of war. It is commonplace in sixteenth-century history to notice the gulf between government pronouncements about the Irish war and the practical implementation of policy. The difference between theory and practice is even clearer in the recruitment of forces for armed service. By statutes of 1557/1558, every able-bodied man between the ages of sixteen and sixty was subject to military service when needed, and was required to fit himself out with arms commensurate with his income and station in life according to a ten-point scale from £5–£10 a year up to £1,000 and over in land and goods. In times of emergency even citizens below the lowest income limit were assessed by the commissioners for musters and justices of the peace with regard to furnishing some 'warlike equipment or furniture'. The obligation of men to supply their own equipment was checked by means of inspection to see that it was in fact provided; a missing bow could carry a fine of 10s and a 'missing' horse as much as £10.[2]

Such detailed provision formed part of a militia act which brought about a radical change in the military organisation of the nation. It set the landed classes firmly within a national system, and marked an end to the quasi-feudal system of individual lords and gentlemen raising troops for the crown from their tenantry. Elizabeth inherited a unitary and efficient military organisation; in practice it was far from perfect. Shire authorities pleaded inability to meet the crown's demands, or put up opposition to the government's muster masters, often refusing to pay their salaries. Some towns, long after official attempts to subordinate municipal corporations to the authority of the lords lieutenant of the shires, continued to cite the privileges of their ancient charters to avoid mustering with the shires, at times refusing to send their quotas of men. The clerical estate sought to maintain ancient exemptions; so too did servants in the households of the nobility, and at times individuals evaded or refused to perform their military obligations.[3]

Orders to raise soldiers for the war came down in a chain of command from the queen and privy council to the lord lieutenant, the figurehead in late-Elizabethan local government; then to the justices of the peace who were not deputies, and eventually to the constables of the hundreds and the churchwardens in the parishes.[4] Wherever and whenever there was no lord lieutenant, the council addressed its instructions to the justices of the peace acting as commissioners for musters, or exceptionally in this period to the high sheriff.[5]

Such then was the formal procedure for the communication of orders from central to local government. At the local level we can gain as much insight into the process of raising levies from contemporary and popular literature as we do from militia and muster records. Captain Barnaby Rich, who had seen long army service in Ireland, wrote prolifically on military matters. This passage from his tract 'The manner of choosing soldiers in England' illuminates the simplicity of the theory and the complexity of the actual practice:

> The Prince, or Council sends down their warrant to certain commissioners of every such shire where they mind to have such a number of soldiers to be levied and appointed. The commissioner he sends his precept to the High Constable of every Hundred; he gives knowledge to every Petty Constable of every Parish within his circuit that upon such a day he must bring two or three able and sufficient men to serve the Prince before such Commissioners to such and such a place.... The Petty Constable when he perceives the wars are in hand foreseeing the toils, the infinite perils ... that is incident to soldiers, is loath that any honest man, through his procurement should hazard himself among so many dangers; wherefore, if within his office there hap to remain any idle fellow, some drunkard or seditious quarreller, or a privy picker ... these shall be presented to the service of the Prince; and what service is to be looked for among such fellows I think may easily be deemed.[6]

Later evidence will corroborate the accuracy of Shakespeare's representation in so many of the characters portraying local administration and military life. Dogberry, Elbow and Dull are likely drawn directly from life, as John Aubrey assures us.

As soon as the number of recruits required from each village and hundred was complete, the company was transferred to the charge of a conductor to the port of embarkation. The recruits were paid 'coat and conduct money' to provide for the expenses of the march. This was the only institutional arrangement for the movement of troops in the sixteenth century – the coat money being the soldier's uniform allowance, and conduct money the daily rate of 8*d* to cover food and lodgings. They were expected to cover a dozen or so miles a day. The conductor of the men out of the shires to the ports was not invariably the same conductor that took them on the second stage of their journey to Ireland. In the ports the mayor, commissioners for musters and the government muster master took the responsibility for keeping the men under control. Sometimes the government muster master in the port was given full authority over the troops, relieving the local authority of some of its responsibility. Maurice Kyffin, for instance, at Chester in 1595, helped the port to requisition ships for the levies, was their paymaster while in Chester and took responsibility for food supplies, and yet his proper task and office was simply to muster the levies as they came in from the shires to Chester. Once aboard the men became the responsibility of their captains and the shipmaster, and once in Ireland they awaited orders from the commanders. Then they were destined for either the garrisons or the field army, if they had not already deserted or made their way to the Irish enemy. Their service in Ireland in the last decades of the queen's reign was a mixture of police action, skirmishes and guerrilla warfare.

The levies were mustered, armed, clothed and billeted at the expense of the local shires with some financial help from the crown in the time-honoured institution of coat and conduct money. At least this administrative machinery did mean that an army could be assembled when needed and disbanded when its task was done, especially in the case of an overseas amphibious expedition. It was also much cheaper than a standing army or the more time-honoured hiring of mercenaries.

The use of lieutenancy gave the government much greater, and more systematic, control over the whole problem of raising troops than had the earlier system of commissions of array – a quasi-feudal procedure whereby an individual was authorised by the monarch to recruit a given number of men. There are isolated instances of the use of lieutenancy earlier in the reign, for example when the queen ordered Sir Matthew Morgan to levy 200 'shot' for the siege of Rouen.[7] Contracts with individual noblemen to provide soldiers was not favoured by Elizabeth.

Incidentally, the indentures or contracts mentioned in Elizabethan records about soldiers are not such contracts but simply receipts to record that the privy council's orders had been executed. Once the lord lieutenant received the council's orders he passed them on to his deputies and to those justices of the peace who were not on the martial commission and they in turn communicated the orders to the constables of the hundreds of the shire, and then to the responsible parish officers such as the petty constables and even the churchwardens. Each shire had a quota, normally in multiples of fifty or a hundred, and the number had to be made up by impressment from the whole county, in practice not more than two or three from one parish. The frequency of demands in the 1590s made the entire exercise burdensome and expensive on the localities. Everything to be done to prepare the conscripted man for active service in Ireland became the responsibility of the local authorities; this ended only when the troops were aboard ship and out of port. The system was a centralising one, intended to make queen and council strong enough to disregard exemptions and privileges and, above all in time of national emergency, to ignore the age-old custom whereby the trained bands of the shires could not be sent abroad on military service. In theory all fit men were liable to service with the home militia but by the end of the sixteenth century the historic notion of an entire male population trained and fully armed for defence of the realm was fast becoming a romantic ideal. The national militia was only an occasional force, but for foreign expeditions a distinction was still made between trained and untrained soldiers. The queen did not have the resources to keep a permanent, state-financed army, but the development of a system of trained hands was the next best thing and gave some recognition to specialisation for war. The influences of the continental military revolution were beginning to make some impact in England but military historians see it happening in small ways and rather slowly; the organisation, training and arming of the bands with firearms and the developments of fortifications of garrisons are but a few of the indications of this.

Training, especially in firearms, was costly; trained soldiers were clearly the best material for an army, but it was considered imprudent to send them out of the country. They were the mainstay of national defence and hence exempt from foreign service. This exemption, however, had the undesired effect that on occasion of impressments for Ireland and elsewhere the trained bands became a refuge for those trying to escape going abroad with the army. As the demands for men for Ireland increased, it little profited the reluctant recruit when the trained bands themselves were raided for the Irish service.

The army proved ever more costly as the Nine Years' War enveloped the nation; the number of garrisons multiplied and the numbers in the field army increased so that under the commands of the second Earl of Essex and later of Mountjoy, Elizabethan drafts to Ireland amounted to a permanent army. Indeed, at the end of Mountjoy's conquest of Ulster in 1602 there was a proposal, which came to nothing, for the establishment of a permanently paid militia to be trained and employed in Ireland.[8]

Ideally the government wanted the yeomen farmers and better-class labourers and tradesmen in both the army in Ireland and in the trained bands at home, because they were thought better able to pay for their own training and weapons.[9] On one occasion a number of good labouring men were drafted for Ireland, but as it became generally known that their employers were unwilling to take them back into work once their military service was finished, the privy council decided to rescind the order and have the labourers replaced by the sons of freeholders who would make good soldiers without exacerbating the unemployment problem on their return.[10] Official fears were expressed about the possible foolhardiness of arming the lower orders of Elizabethan society. In Kent, William Lambarde pointed out to his lord lieutenant, William Lord Cobham, the dangers in first arming men and 'then insulting them'.[11]

Throughout the 1590s the privy council's advice, and occasionally that of the queen, was to choose freeholders' sons, husbandmen and farmers' sons for the war. And they would have liked the drafts of unwilling recruits or conscripts to be very much leavened by a goodly number of ordinary and gentlemen volunteers, as they made the better soldiers. There were indeed many gentlemen volunteers for the war, usually enthusiastic sons of the gentry and yeomanry, who may have had many reasons for joining the forces but mostly the hope of a captaincy. Yet their ambition when fulfilled was often less than glorious, for command of a company could provide a lucrative income at the soldier's and queen's expense.

Near the end of the queen's reign lord chief justice Popham indicated the ideal type needed for military reinforcements when he wrote to Sir Robert Cecil:

> New supplies might be of gentlemen of the best sort, to be accompanied with their friends, neighbours and tenants, who would keep their companies full for their own safety, and expedite the service for their speedier return.[12]

As the demands for the Irish war grew, there was little likelihood that the government could gain the numbers or the types they wanted without the county authorities resorting to arbitrary conscription.

The privy council, commanders in Ireland, and literate external observers could paint the picture of the ideal recruit needed in the wars but in practice the rogues, vagabonds and idlers, 'the masterless men', were drafted for service in Ireland in a policy of social cleansing, which was often achieved at the expense of the army. That the Elizabethan government regarded vagabondage as a major social problem can be seen in the numerous proclamations in the 1590s dealing with ruined smallholders and the unemployed farm workers who roamed the countryside living on nothing a year at the expense of the respectable.[13]

The evidence for this from the records and returns sent in by commissioners for musters, muster masters, mayors of the ports of embarkation, such as Chester, Bristol and Barnstaple, as well as the receiving military commanders in Ireland, is overwhelming in indicating that most troops for Ireland were unsatisfactory. After viewing and mustering a levy brought to Bristol for embarkation the commissioners there wrote to the privy council by way of report:

> There was never beheld such strange creatures brought to any muster ... they are most of them either lame, diseased, boys, or common rogues. Few of them have any clothes; small weak starved bodies taken up in fairs, markets and highways to supply the places of better men kept at home.[14]

Sir Edward Wingfield, one of the commissioners at Bristol, wished he could paint so that 'he might have sent a picture of those creatures who have been brought to him to receive for soldiers'. Sir Robert Cecil, he mused, might have wondered how it was possible to find in England and Wales 'so many strange decrepid people ... except they had been kept in hospitals'.[15] Matthew Sutcliffe, a noted contemporary writer on military matters, deplored the fact that local captains deliberately used the impressment 'to disburthen the parish of rogues, loyters, drunkards, and such as no other way can live'. And, if better men were selected, he went on, 'It is for some private grudge and of those that are chosen if they have either friends, favor or money, most of them are dismissed'.[16]

In August 1600 the privy council complained that troops recently sent from the City of London to Ireland were not raised by a properly conducted levy but by a search for rogues and vagabonds, who then deserted; the City's authority was promptly ordered to implement the original instructions, as out of the original 350 men ordered only 140 had arrived at Chester for embarkation.[17] The privy council concurred with the generally accepted view that it was those who were the least worthy in a community who could be best spared for the wars, but once, at least, the council positively commanded such a course of action: 'Idle persons to be pressed in Kent ... and those who do live by shiftings and bad meanes in places neere the city' was the order given the lord lieutenant in 1601.[18]

It was the proper business of the muster masters viewing levies at the ports to see that the men sent to Ireland were 'serviceable' and their arms adequate; it is not surprising that at various times their reports give a bad reputation to certain shires on account of the 'insufficient' or 'lewd' persons whom they had recruited. The lord lieutenant of Huntingdonshire, Lord St John Bletso, had fifty of his recruits sent back from Chester by the mayor as they were 'of low stature and having other defects'.[19] Henry Hardware, the mayor of Chester, wrote to Cecil to say he had refused the whole batch from Huntingdon.[20] 'Northampton has sent very ill men, not forty good ones (out of a hundred). Never a county send such hither as they,' reported John Baxter to Cecil.[21] Various contingents from the Welsh shires were also refused; the Earl of Pembroke was reprimanded for the poor quality of fifty recruits from Radnor in 1598.[22] But if the Welsh levies come in for more criticism than most it is simply because the Principality was heavily drawn upon for the Irish war.

Often the fault for under-strength companies and for the bad quality of the soldiers lay with the conductors from the shires and with the captains taking the men to Ireland. Once a contingent had reached port it was too late to improve its quality if the wind served; John Baxter had to go ahead with his unsatisfactory company from Northampton.[23] Abuses began with the first muster in the shire, then multiplied *en route* to the port, where a second muster by the mayor, and by specially appointed commissioners, revealed discrepancies from the numbers originally ordered and inadequacy in the quality of the recruits.

It was the captain's responsibility to fill his company by replacing those who were refused or who deserted, and often they did this by pressing in the criminal. At Rochester in October 1601, captains Hugh Kenrick and Henry Fortescue, for example, found their companies thirty-seven short of the levy sent out of Suffolk, so they made up their numbers by taking up idle men in Kent and from those 'that pass to and fro in the Gravesend barge'. They also wanted a warrant from the Earl of Nottingham, the lord admiral, then at Rochester, to take up 'tapsters, ostlers, chamberlains,' with whom, they said, 'the country now abounded'.[24]

Captains and conductors found a profitable sideline in defrauding the crown by pocketing bribes to have men discharged, occasionally by encouraging desertion, therefore gaining on coat and conduct money, and by drafting 'stand-ins' at the review and muster in the ports. It was, for example, reported from Barnstaple that the conductor of a levy from Hampshire allowed seven men to run away.[25] A conductor of a Derbyshire levy to Chester in 1600 stood accused of releasing seven soldiers on his way to the port and of replacing them with others.[26] And, in the same county, there is a confession of William Ward about bribes taken by Captain John Tolkerne and two other officers for discharging soldiers in March 1598.[27] Thomas Allen, a yeomen of Staffordshire, gave five pounds to Captain Norton in 1596 'for not serving her Majesty on her last voyage in her wars'.[28] When twenty-two escaped from the Lancashire and Lincolnshire levies sent to Chester, the council sent their names to the shire commissioners, instructing them to find out from those arrested how much they paid for their liberty.[29]

Under martial law desertion was a capital offence, and yet in Ireland during these war years it appears to have been rife. Evidence of desertion to the enemy is also found. Soldiers, often unpaid, were tempted by offers of higher pay and better victuals from the Irish.[30] Indeed, by the end of the century the council in Dublin reported that desertion was common and that they could do nothing about the problem, and they set the blame firmly on the roguery of the captains.[31] It was said that entire companies melted away as soon as they reached Ireland.[32]

Complaints of abuses in the system of raising troops tend to attract more notice in the sources than messages of congratulation for services well performed. Not all comments were bad. Improvements in the type of men recruited and of the good quality of their equipment are occasionally noted. The mayor of Chester specifically commended to the privy council a particular levy of fifty men from Anglesey in 1601:

> They came to this city very well apparelled with caps, cassocks, doublets, breeches, nethersocks, shoes and shirts, which gave great discontentment to the residue of the soldiers which had no apparell and to us some trouble for their pacification.[33]

The privy council congratulated a levy from Oxfordshire and Berkshire in December 1598 on the speed with which the men were assembled and on the good quality of men and equipment. Lord John Norris, the lord lieutenant, whose sons and brothers served in high commands in Ireland, was commended for the excellence of that particular piece of service.[34] The Earl of Bath, when viewing a draft of soldiers from the West Country in October 1601, reported to Sir Robert Cecil that many of the thousand men mustered and viewed 'are very tall men and well armed and willing to serve'.[35] Therefore not all the drafts to Ireland in these years were the unsatisfactory rogues, vagabonds and gaol-birds of Elizabethan England. Companies of untrained raw recruits were often given some training by the muster masters and captains while waiting in the ports for favourable winds for Ireland; such companies were leavened with some of the militia from the trained bands and also with a handful of gentlemen volunteers.

The majority of the levies sent into Ireland consisted of pressed men, who had little stomach for the task of subduing an enemy fighting a guerrilla war in a terrain of bog, bush and mountains, and with the prospect of death from disease or hostilities. There was a great reluctance to serve in Ireland; 'Better be hanged at home than die like dogs in Ireland' became a common saying in Chester. It was ever difficult for commanders in Ireland to keep full ranks.[36] Sir George Carew, the commander and president in Munster, commiserated with Lord Mountjoy, the lord deputy, on how difficult it was to 'keep unwilling minds together that are not inclined to be soldiers, and how fearful the name of Ireland is to pressed men in England'.[37]

There is little in the privy council's letters to the shire authorities to make the service sound attractive; any note of encouragement that they might well profit is noticeable by its absence and in this respect these letters are very different from the prospectus-type publicity given to would-be adventurers and planters when the government encouraged younger sons to colonise parts of Ireland in the wake of rebellions and land confiscation. In the Staffordshire local records of Edward Sulyard one mention is found which hints that service in Ireland need not be disastrous: 'If there be any tall and gallant minded fellows that will go this journey and be able in good sort to furnish himself he may see great service'.[38]

Companies arrived in Dublin, Waterford and Cork, major troop ports in the years 1595–1602, but also at Lough Foyle, Carrickfergus and Olderfleet from 1600 to 1603, which had been depleted by desertions.[39] Delays at sea meant that the soldiers' supplies of victuals had been spoiled on the journey or had run out on arrival so that some men were ready to sell their arms and equipment for food. If appointed to remote garrisons on the borders of O'Neill's and of O'Donnell's lands, the long marches wearied them or else gave them a further chance to slip their captains. 'Troops, arms, money, victuals and munition,' it was said, 'disappeared as though in some Serbonian bog,' so that a company was often reduced to a skeleton band within a month of its arrival in Ireland. 'It is strange to see how suddenly our new English soldiers doth decay,' wrote Sir Richard Bingham, governor of Connaught, to the queen, 'For of the last thousand, one fourth part are run away.'[40]

While the reports of captains and the complaints of commanders are convincing evidence of the unsuitable type of soldiers sent to Ireland, it is but one reason for the weakness of the English army, as can be seen from reports to Sir Robert Cecil. Lack of regular pay and of victuals compounded the general weakness. Deprivation caused a mutiny among Sir Thomas Norris's troops in Dublin on 28 May 1590.[41] On another occasion the council in Dublin was so fearful of a mutiny that it borrowed £4,000 to pay soldiers by putting its plate in pawn.[42] And at about the same time an anonymous captain reported:

> It is well known and of a truth to be avouched that there have been divers garrisons in many places of Ireland which have lived without taste of bread or drink, but of relief only of beef-water, some the space of six months, some eight, some more. [43]

Sir John Dowdall, of some twenty years' experience of warfare in Ireland, wrote to Cecil about why the English forces were 'so weak and poor'; he mentioned delays in sending reinforcements, their insufficiency when they arrived in Ireland and the habit the newly arrived soldiers had of getting rid of their armour, following the fashion of the disarmed companies that came out of Picardy and Brittany 'desiring a scald rapier before a good sword, a pike without carettes or burgennett and a hagbutter without a morion'[44] – in other words, a disregard for what Dowdall considered proper armour for an infantryman. There were plenty of Irish merchants ready to buy up such armour and weapons and munitions from the disaffected English. These were some of the reasons why he found the enemy 'so strong, so well armed, apparelled, victualled and moneyed,' and for the English forces for the most part seeming 'poor beggarly ghosts more apt for their graves than to fight a prince's battles'.[45]

The common soldier's lack of regular wages, food and sometimes clothing was frequently laid at the door of the captains. Sir John Dowdall reported to Cecil that one of the primary causes for all the troubles with the queen's forces in Ireland lay in the choice made of captains, many of whom were elected to office from favour, not merit. Many of them were unsuited for the leadership of soldiers and were 'more inclined to dicing, wenching, and the like ... and rather than spare a penny will suffer their soldiers to starve, as is daily seen in this kingdom'.[46]

The privy council reserved the right to appoint captains, but their appointment was frequently left to the commander-in-chief in Ireland, who was expected to know the relative merits of candidates.[47] Mountjoy was accused of favouritism in his appointments, but he claimed in his own defence that those appointed were men of ability.[48] Mountjoy had a free hand in appointments but petitions from his 'divisional' commanders and from minor and ambitious lieutenants may have limited his personal choice of leaders. Mountjoy gave authority to Sir Henry Docwra at Lough Foyle to appoint his own captains when vacancies occurred; to the chagrin of Sir George Carew in Munster this type of authority had not been given to him.[49]

The basic unit for administrative purposes was the company, and its captain was the linchpin between the higher command and his men – in theory their representative and defender, responsible for arming, clothing and feeding them, in practice the exploiter of their labour and their pay. The system whereby expenses were charged against the company and settled between the treasurer-at-war, or his deputies, and the captains played into the hands of those who were intent on fraud: 'only the common soldier shared the honour of being a mere victim with the Queen'.[50] Even after reforms in the muster office in Ireland in the 1590s, when muster masters were appointed to large garrisons such as that at Lough Foyle to check the abuses, the captains continued to profit from the fraudulent distribution of food, clothing and arms because the subordinate company officers were chosen by them; a lieutenant, ensign, sergeant, drummer, preacher, cannoneer, surgeon and about six corporals became the establishment in a normal company of 130 infantrymen. Preachers and cannoneers, positions normally filled by the gentlemen volunteers, were paid in Ireland out of the captain's allowances of 'dead pays'; six in every hundred became the customary quota in Ireland.[51] One muster master reported that there was not a single preacher in the entire province of Munster,[52] and as for cannoneers another report said that there was no need for them.[53] This was not strictly true as the use of heavy ordnance at some sieges is mentioned.

The main opportunity for peculation on the part of the fraudulent captains lay in the fact that lump sums were paid to them for their companies according to the numbers on their muster roll. Hence the captains practised every possible deception to present full companies on muster days by filling gaps with 'stand-ins' commandeered from companies not being mustered at the same time; this was one of the more common deceits. The company clerk, who kept and made the rolls, was in a good position to expose deceptions, but he had little authority and was in any case generally in league with his captain in outwitting muster masters and clerks of the check. Indeed, checks on some companies in Ireland saved no more than a few shillings over six months.[54] The crown was still paying for men who existed merely on the pages of the muster roll. In the opinion of one observer the queen would have been far better off to pay such captains a thousand pounds to keep them out of the army.

Absenteeism of captains became a serious problem. Many took unofficial leave, and in 1592 the queen ordered all captains absent from their charges in Ireland to make immediate return, as their absence encouraged the soldiers to plunder the countryside, much to the discomfort of native non-combatants.[55] Some of these recalcitrant captains when before the privy council swore they had no company in Ireland, others admitted their responsibility and were ordered back, and some were content to let their Irish companies to subordinates as long as there was no need for their physical presence to make the position profitable.[56]

Frauds and absenteeism hampered the efficiency of the military service in Ireland. Wholesale cheating of the crown was rampant. By means of disloyal trade the enemy became supplied with arms, munitions and lead, and from the selfsame merchants who supplied the English forces from Manchester, Liverpool and Birmingham.[57] O'Neill was occasionally supplied from Spain but more regularly from Scotland.[58] Throughout the war there is a proven link between the Irish forces and the English merchants in clandestine sales of war materials. The abuse must have been difficult to detect since captains and soldiers sometimes sold their weapons, which eventually found their way into the hands of the enemy. 'Divers of the captains,' wrote the privy council, 'under colour of fetching powder and victual for her Majesty's store continually furnish the rebels'.[59] Both councils, in Dublin and in London, blamed the corrupt practices of the captaincy for the near state of starvation and beggary of the rank and file.[60]

The captain, between the queen's officials and his men, was mainly responsible for the distribution of the soldiers' food, clothing and arms. By acting as an entrepreneur and keeping his company impoverished he helped the enemy indirectly by impairing the fighting efficiency of his men. It is not then to be greatly wondered at if some companies mutinied for their pay, or took out their anger on the local peasantry and townsfolk, inflicting on them the harassment they were, in theory, paid to do to the enemy.[61] Spoliation in any case was an established procedure in sixteenth-century warfare. Captains in the Pale had a notorious reputation for allowing their men for want of pay 'to spoil the subjects as if they were rebels'.[62]

But if the captains were in the army to make money, so too some of the civil servants of the crown fraudulently used their positions to supplement the low official fees. The most lucrative in this respect was the treasurer-at-war's office. To single out but one example, Sir George Carey, treasurer-at-war in Ireland 1599–1606, is thought to have defrauded the crown of £150,000 in keeping back soldiers' pay, in speculating on the debased Irish currency, and in conniving at frauds with the clothing merchants who supplied the army.[63] Administration, however, is only a means to the maintenance of a fighting force, and though malpractices such as these weakened or impaired the efficiency of the fighting arm, a military system must be judged in the final analysis by its results.

It is not reasonable to suppose that all military recruits were rogues, that all the captains were such as Sir John Dowdall had described, or that, like Sir George Carey, all paymasters were corrupt, otherwise the reconquest of Ireland could hardly have been possible. Many of the officer class sent to Ireland were of England's best military stock: Norrises, Binghams, Bagenals, Chichesters and the two Earls of Essex, to name the more prominent. Of those exercising the highest military command in Ireland, Charles Blount, Lord Mountjoy, proved to be the most outstanding, but the reconquest of Ireland, which in great measure is attributable to him, may not have been possible without seasoned leaders like Sir George Carew in Munster and Sir Henry Docwra and Sir Arthur Chichester in Ulster. Chichester, like many who had served in Ireland, also saw service with Essex at Rouen in 1591 and at Cadiz in 1596; it was Essex who appointed him to the vacant governorship of Carrickfergus Castle in April 1599.[64]

In Part III we shall see military services in Ireland in much greater detail. Meanwhile, in considering the composition and build-up of the armies in Ireland, two further elements must now be delineated: the redeployment of veteran troops from the continent and the use of Irish and Scots soldiers in the English fighting arm in Ireland.

The first major contingent of hardened English troops to arrive in Ireland from the continent came on the successful conclusion of Sir John and Sir Henry Norris's campaign in Brittany, when 1,500 seasoned infantrymen were brought to Waterford in March 1595, when 'the entire Province of Ulster rose up in one alliance, and one union against the English'.[65] Weak from their sea journey and accustomed to short marches in France, some of their captains were hesitant to march their men on to Wicklow. When they were eventually mustered and viewed in the presence of the new lord deputy, William Russell, 'at the greene in Dubline,' he professed disgust at their defective arms and clothing, 'both worn out with long use and not lately supplied'. 'What, quoth he, are these the old soldiers we hear of? They look as if they come out of the gaols in London'.[66] Russell had them dispatched to the then newly appointed general of the forces in Ulster, Sir John Norris.

Jealousies and difficulties had grown up between Russell (no mean military leader, as can be seen from his journal[67]) and Sir John Norris, then appointed 'Lord General of her Majesty's forces in Ulster'; Norris had formerly been lord president of Munster.[68] His new command was a difficult one, for the Ulster garrisons at Armagh, Newry, Dundalk and Monaghan were beleaguered by the increasing numbers and efficiency of the enemy. Norris's veterans saw action by May 1595 in repeated attempts to re-establish and strengthen these garrisons.[69] He told Burghley, the queen's chief minister, that the northern rebels were stronger in arms and munitions than formerly, and that he dare not, even with 1,700 of the best foot and 300 horse, make the journey between Dundalk and Newry, a distance of barely twelve miles.[70]

Not all the veteran captains from Brittany served directly under Sir John Norris; Captain Baker, for instance, who accompanied his men from Brittany, served under lord deputy Russell when he essayed a 'journey' to the Blackwater to aid the Armagh garrison.[71] Ever since the defeat of marshal Sir Henry Bagenal at Clontibert earlier in May 1595 – O'Neill's first major victory against the queen's forces – garrisons at Armagh and Newry became liabilities every time they ran out of supplies.[72] Sir Henry Power had been instructed to take his Brittany force to help the Earl of Ormond in Leinster, though Power's chief sphere of military action was in Munster under Sir George Carew. Power was promised promotion to a colonelcy but failed to get it. He complained bitterly to the privy council about his twenty years' service to her majesty which had been lightly regarded by their lordships.[73] Sir John Norris's first contacts with the northern enemy convinced him that he could not do much against them without more men. Later that year, in August, 1,000 infantrymen and 100 horse arrived from England, but in the commander's opinion they were nearly 'all poor old ploughmen and rogues'.[74]

In the build-up of the Earl of Essex's celebrated 'army of Ireland', a force of some 16,000 foot and 1,300 horse, in 1598/1599, a large redeployment exercise took place when 2,000 experienced troops from the Low Countries were ordered to Ireland in exchange for the same number of raw recruits to be levied in England.[75] This was a measure of the determination of the Elizabethan government to subdue Ireland.[76] A royal proclamation declared reasons for sending Essex with plenipotentiary powers to Ireland:

> This is therefore the cause that after so long patience we have been compelled to take resolution to reduce that kingdom to obedience, which by the laws of God and nature is due unto us by using an extraordinary power and force against them.[77]

The gathering of Essex's army illustrates every facet of the recruitment process: all classes of men in every shire of England and Wales were drawn from parish, town and village, hastily trained and shipped to Ireland. Apart from the unwilling recruits, Essex's army attracted gentlemen volunteers; he was especially inundated with petitions for posts of conductors and captains, both for the leadership of men leaving the Low Countries and for those leaving England to replace those of the Low Countries. The states general took the raw recruits in replacement for veterans but refused to employ the officers sent over from England with the recruits; those left without positions hastily volunteered for service in Ireland under Essex.[78]

At the earliest sign that Essex was to take Ireland in hand, Sir Henry Docwra offered his services, which were accepted 'to his unspeakable contentment'.[79] He then became the chief conductor of the Low Countries' veterans to Ireland for the Earl of Essex. From England, Sir William Knollys was responsible for dispatching the recruits to replace them in the Low Countries. The privy council ordered 1,400 to be taken out of Sir Francis de Vere's companies in the field and 600 from Sir Edward Norris and the garrison at Ostend; missing numbers or defects were to be made up from Sir Robert Sidney's garrison at Flushing.[80]

In this triangular redeployment exercise, affairs did not move smoothly. Both Docwra's and Knollys' letters to the Earl of Essex tell a tale of bad management and lack of cooperation on the part of Sir Francis de Vere in the Low Countries. Sir Thomas Knollys wrote that when he arrived in Flushing nothing was ready for the reception and disposal of the raw recruits; only 400 of the old troops had arrived in Zealand and were 'without a captain or any other officer to conduct them to Ireland'. There were no arrangements made for billeting and victualling his men and he did not know what was to become of the captains he had with him.[81] Essex wanted the best and the most experienced of the Low Country troops. What he obtained were men from Sir Francis de Vere's broken companies, that is to say, discharged companies, described by Knollys as 'the worst men and the worst armed',[82] and by Docwra as 'far inferior in their experience and readiness to your lordship's expectation'.[83] The contingent for Ireland was in any case 500 short of the total, and those brought together for embarkation to Ireland do not appear to have been paid.[84] Tempers frayed and a feud grew up between Docwra and de Vere which must have deepened when the privy council sent severe reproaches to de Vere.[85] Five of the companies were supposed to have been sent from the Brill garrison, but Dudley Carleton in his letter to John Chamberlain marvelled that such a number could be ordered from a garrison that had but 'two companies left and those for the most part Dutch and married men'.[86]

The general opinion persisted that veterans from the continental wars made better fighting material for the forces in Ireland than hastily trained raw recruits. The Earl of Nottingham, the lord admiral, thought 2,000 of them worth 8,000 of the so-called trained men from England. 'There were never a Prince so deceived as Her Majesty had been with this word of trained men,' he wrote to Cecil on the occasion of new demands for reinforcements for Essex's fast-dwindling army.[87]

Many of the delays and difficulties in the recruitment and build-up of his 'Irish army' were caused by the lack of shipping. Essex wrote from Ireland in April 1599 requesting ships for 4,000 foot and 100 horse to be landed in June. The government insisted that he should first exhaust all shipping possibilities in Ireland; consequently nothing was done in England while the Earl scoured the Irish ports for ships, and in vain.[88] By the 1590s the Netherlands, on the other hand, had become known as a practical training ground for troops for Ireland. Ever since the formal alliance of 1585 the queen kept a force of some 5,000 foot and 1,000 horse in return for the possession of Flushing and Brill. The garrisons there needed constant reinforcements and each time, according to Francis de Vere, their commander, they were sent 'the very scum of the world', swept from the gaols and taverns, and as soon as they had been trained into competent soldiers they were ordered elsewhere.[89]

Less well known than the mere replacement of seasoned troops by recruits from England is the tendency on the part of military authorities to use Irish and Scots men for the wars in the Low Countries to replace veterans. Robert Dudley, Earl of Leicester, for instance, wanted to have '600 or a 1,000 of your idle Irish men ... very meet to be out of the country, for they be hard and abide more pains than our men ... till they have been as well trained with hardiness as they have.'[90]

Sir John Perrot, lord deputy in Ireland 1584–1588, advised the council in Dublin to send Irishmen into Flanders.[91] Such a trend or policy could misfire, as it did when Sir William Stanley defected with his Irish companies to the Spaniards at Deventer.[92] If there were risks involved in employing the Irish in the wars abroad, to employ them in the queen's forces in Ireland was considered doubly dangerous.

The recruitment of Irishmen into the English forces became a vexed problem during the last years of the reconquest, although there was hardly a time when Irish soldiers did not fight for England on the continent or in Ireland, for instance with Henry V at Agincourt or in the service of Henry VIII.[93] Early in the queen's reign it was decided not to permit more than five or six Irish soldiers to serve in the royal companies, for it was thought to be dangerous for Irish troops to outnumber English in any company. There could be no certainty of their loyalty, particularly when their countrymen proved to have the upper hand in an engagement.[94]

There were, however, good strategic arguments for their employment. To recruit some Irishmen into the companies prevented them from serving with the enemy and saved England supplies. Was it not, too, the classical policy of an occupying army to divide the enemy? Lord Mountjoy, like many military commanders, had read Caesar's *Gallic wars* and tried to apply classical precedents in typical renaissance vein.[95] He requested the privy council's permission on one occasion 'to wage some of these Irish by agreement and for a certain time whereby by them I should consume many of the rebels and by the rebels consume many of them and both for the good of the service'.[96] In seeking the granting of such a request it is presumed that the motives of the chief commander were more honourable than those of some of his captains who were keen to fill their companies with the Irish on the assumption that they would accept lower pay; the Irish thereby became a means 'to cover their frauds and make gains'.[97] The hope that there would be but five or six Irishmen in each English company was a pious one. In 1602 the council was very concerned in a letter to Mountjoy that there were 'six whole companies of mere Irish in Connaught, and those Connaughtmen ... especially whilst they are employed in their own countries and at their own doors'. Mountjoy was advised to reform that situation as soon as possible, and oddly told that Irish companies may expect no money for apparel which they 'are known never to use' and that their pay should not necessarily be equal to that the English soldiers.[98]

In Munster Sir George Carew denied that the Irish would 'serve under the colours at less pay than the queen allows'; he had a deep distrust of the Irish in his companies.[99] The blustering Captain Nicholas Dawtrey, the original for Shakespeare's Falstaff, pointed out the advantages to the queen of employing the Irish if they were taken abroad to fight. He offered to lead a company of them to fight with him in Brittany. His reasoning may be cited:

> The queen shall leave at home many of her people of England ... disarm her ill-disposed subjects of Ireland whose rebellions are supported by those trained soldiers ... she shall save the spending of more treasure in Ireland and fourthly they [the Irish soldiers] will do more spoil upon the enemy than three as many soldiers of any other nation ... for there can be no better soldiers upon the earth than they be, either for the use of their weapons or the strength of their bodies and minds ... they will keep health when others with a little extremity will lie by the wall.[100]

It was not so much regard for the fighting qualities of the Irish which led to the recruitment of Irishmen but the urgent need to replace the dead, the deserted and the wounded. Many captains could not wait on the vagaries of the wind to bring fresh levies out of England and the temptation to fill their places with Irish was very great. Many, like Dawtrey, preferred the Irish fighting man to the inferior pressed man from England or Wales, and made a virtue out of necessity; Irish courage and hardihood became proverbial.[101]

Most Englishmen remained cautious about the use of Irishmen. Fynes Moryson complained about filling up companies with Irish soldiers and estimated, perhaps for effect, that at least one-third of the queen's forces in Ireland was Irish.[102] Philip O'Sullivan Beare, writing later than Fynes Moryson, reckoned that the Irish comprised about half the armed forces in Ireland in the latter part of the queen's reign, remarking that the Irish were conquered not so much by the foreigner as by one another.[103] Many of these Irish troops were supplied by Anglo-Irish lords like Ormond, Barry of Cork and the Kildare FitzGeralds, whose role in the war is likely underestimated.

Sir Robert Cecil may have been remote from Ireland but few had a better grasp of the overall difficulties than he did, for he was constantly in receipt of captains' reports either by their writings or by word of mouth when they came to the council and to the court. He warned Mountjoy to observe 'what hath been the fruit of entertainment of the Irish in companies either with Sir Henry Docwra or Sir Arthur Chichester,' advising that it would be a better policy to give the chiefs of the Irish good pensions and 'leave them to maintain the rascals as well as they can' rather than that the queen should entertain their followers as well.[104]

In the final years of the reconquest of Ireland the government suggested that Irishmen who wanted to serve should be sent to the continental wars and their places taken by levies out of England, and that the number already serving in English companies should be allowed to decline through natural wastage.[105]

Official policy clearly disapproved of the practice of using Irish soldiers in the queen's army but in practice no lord deputy in Ireland could do without them. Sir John Perrot, when lord president of Munster in the 1570s, said the Irish were indispensable to the forces. Sir George Carew in Munster, Sir Henry Docwra and Sir Arthur Chichester as commanders in Ulster, and Lord Mountjoy as lord deputy and overall commander in the field, continued to have Irish soldiers in their companies. Mountjoy expressed the hope that when the army was strengthened with Englishmen he could 'begin to chase the Irish out of our companies'. In a lengthy memorandum to the privy council of June 1601 Mountjoy said that the Irish in the army must be necessarily maintained, for we take so many men from the rebels and give unto ourselves ... facility to plant the foundation of their own ruin, and both with us and against us waste them by themselves.' Here was the practical counter-argument to official policy. Mountjoy went on to give the council instances of how such was the case in the course of the war.[106]

The Irish element in the English fighting force, that is, those on the queen's payroll, and in effect mercenaries, must be distinguished from the hosting of 'risings out', which loyal Irish chiefs and Anglo-Irish lords did to raise soldiers temporarily for service with English commanders. Although they often proved less dependable than those on the payroll, their value as allies outweighed the dangers of their return to the rebels. At their most cooperative they could police their own districts, provide guides and scouts in difficult terrain, help in the transportation of supplies to garrisons, provide intelligence of enemy movements and in skirmishes aid the regular troops. If it was a risk to employ native Irishmen in the armies, it was equally a risk to let them go.

The lord deputy often urged that whenever the armed forces were reduced no great haste should be used in disbanding the Irish in the companies because discharged men provided ready-trained soldiers for the Irish side.[107] When O'Neill won at Clontibret in

Monaghan in 1595, and uncharacteristically in a set battle, Sir Henry Bagenal's men were astounded to see a contingent of musketeers 'in red coats like English soldiers' coming over against them.[108] During the period of his loyalty to the crown, O'Neill had the services of six English captains to train soldiers to fight the Irish rebels. He managed to change the men being so trained under these captains so that many more than the intended 600 received training in firearms at the hands of these captains, thereby ensuring O'Neill a trained force when he threw in his lot on the Gaelic Irish side. These English captains in O'Neill's service included Hugh Mostyn, a Flanders veteran, Alexander Walshe, a Brittany veteran, Richard Tyrell and the brothers Richard and Henry Hovenden; the last became O'Neill's secretary.[109] Hayes-McCoy proved that O'Neill had an army trained in firearms, divided into companies, and the system of 'dead pays' had also been adopted, all of which followed English convention and custom.[110]

In a report of 'divers Welshmen concerning the Earl of Tyrone' of January 1599, it was said that O'Neill had in his service 500 Welshmen, whom he had made officers and 'rewardeth with double pay above the Irish nation,' and that therefore on no account should Welshmen be used in service against Irishmen 'because they were not to be trusted'.[111] It was a vain wish, as will be seen from the recruitment in the Welsh shires (Chapter 3).

One further way to counteract the serious loss of soldiers advised by the privy council was the employment of Scottish mercenaries, especially for the period of the O'Neill suppression. They argued that the Scots were 'inured to the manner of the Irish war ... especially to tread the bog and the bush'.[112] Like the Irish, it was said, the Scots were accustomed to suffer cold, hunger and long marches, and were 'a great deal more desperate' so that they would be glad to serve the queen for little pay and 'will meet the Irish in their own form of fighting'.[113] Their employment would deprive O'Neill and O'Donnell in Ulster of some of the aid they traditionally received in men, munitions and supplies, especially out of Argyllshire.[114]

In every plan put forward for the settlement of Ireland, the English always considered the expulsion of the Scots from Ulster a preliminary step for peace. It is then interesting that there was serious discussion of employing Scots as mercenaries against the Irish. In Queen Mary's reign an act of parliament forbade the sending in of any Scots to Ireland, 'retaining them or intermarrying with them,' to prevent any alliance between the Irish and the Scots.[115] Throughout all the rebellions in Ulster the terms of this act were more honoured in the breach, as can be seen from the numerous orders to the Ulster chiefs, O'Neills' and O'Donnells', to expel any Scottish mercenaries they had employed.[116]

By 1594 O'Neill had firmly come out on the side of the Gaelic Irish. The council in Dublin took up the question of raising Scots mercenaries by sending an experienced sea captain and negotiator, Captain George Thornton, to bargain with the Earl of Argyll and the clan of the McLeans for a body of 'redshank' soldiers as they were called. But nothing was effected by October 1595.[117] Sir William Russell, lord deputy in 1596, then recommended to the English privy council the policy of employing Scots. By 1596 all Ulster and Connaught lay under the sway of the northern rebels. Russell wrote:

> If a force of 3000 Scots, well chosen and governed by some honourable commander ...
> might be drawn into Ulster to serve upon the back of the Earl [of Tyrone], and the same
> 3000 Scots to be joined with the garrison of Lough Foyle ... it would be to good purpose
> for the speedy achieving of this war.[118]

The recommendation fell on deaf ears, probably because too much was hoped for from
the truce that year. In any case, a garrison at Lough Foyle was still a matter of
discussion, not of reality. The time for negotiating with King James VI of Scotland was
ill chosen, for it is thought that he was then probably helping O'Neill; however, no
proof of this can now be brought forward.[119]

After a disastrous defeat at the Yellow Ford in August 1598 the proposal to employ
Scots was again considered by the council in Dublin. It wanted King James to raise an
army of Lowland Scots but, clearly timorous of such a measure, the Dublin council
wanted the Scots' king to promise a full withdrawal when they had completed their
service.[120]

During 1600 the council in Dublin continued to importune Sir Robert Cecil to have
the scheme for Scottish mercenaries put into effect. They seemed to be unable to make
up their minds on the desirability or otherwise of Highlanders or Lowlanders. Adam
Loftus would have liked a force of Highlanders to move against O'Byrne's men, who
held sway in the Wicklow mountains, south of Dublin and the Pale. The Highlanders
were, he thought, especially suited to mountain warfare and, he added, they could be
'hired good cheap'.[121]

By November 1600 nothing had been done about employing Scots but the English
privy council informed Sir Henry Docwra, the commander of the Lough Foyle
garrisons, that they had had overtures from a Scottish chieftain, then at feud with
Hugh O'Neill, to recruit a force of his men for Docwra.[122] A force of mercenaries was
apparently enlisted, but they never served with Docwra; indeed, shortly after this
information was received, a small body of Scots were found serving under O'Neill
instead.[123] Throughout this period King James and the estates in Scotland seemed
lukewarm about Anglo-Scottish collaboration in Ireland. Highlanders were never
actually sent against the Irish. Given the nature of the war in the north of Ireland it was
a more pertinent English policy simply to keep the Scots from aiding their kinsmen,
particularly in Antrim.[124]

The English commander Sir Arthur Chichester was firmly set against the
involvement of the Scots. His hostility to them is well attested;[125] he distrusted the
comings and goings of Sir Randall MacDonnell's kinsmen; they normally resulted in
conspiracies, such as happened when his brother, Sir John Chichester, was slain in
1597. At Carrickfergus he always had the Scots on his doorstep, not just from the
proximity of the Mull of Kintyre and the isles, but from their presence in Olderfleet
Castle on the haven above Carrickfergus, for that fortress had been sold to them in
December 1597.[126] Sir Arthur's commission, dated 8 April 1600, gave him authority
'to pursue with fire and sword such Scots as are there landed or shall land'.[127] He could
not put this into effect until the English privy council and Sir Robert Cecil had made
up their minds whether or not, in difficult negotiations with King James, the Scots
should be treated as friends rather than as allies of the northern rebels.[128] Sir Arthur

Chichester's relations with the Scots, the McSorleys and the MacDonalds, in times both of truce and of hostility, were little different from his experience against the Irish enemy.

In the discussion on the employment of Scottish mercenaries, 'gallowglasses' and 'redshanks', the common-sense and cautious view prevailed: there was the risk of their changing sides and the difficulty of controlling or eventually expelling them once they were in Ireland. Sir Geoffrey Fenton, secretary to the Dublin council, stated these views and won the day; he wrote that it had ever been 'the rule of policy in this government to keep the Scots out of Ireland, as a people that have wild pretences to Ulster and have long time footed in some parts thereof'.[129]

The evidence on the late-sixteenth-century Irish war indicates the majority of recruits were unwilling conscripts with little or no training, especially when their presence was urgently wanted. Military service in Ireland had a notorious reputation. The conscripted man faced serious handicaps; his pay was usually in arrears, he was frequently defrauded by his captain and often left short of life's necessities. The common rumour was that few soldiers returned from Ireland, for if the enemy did not end their lives, want and sickness did.

It is not to be greatly wondered if such men were mutinous, or deserted when they had the opportunity, either when unfavourable winds detained them at the ports of embarkation or whenever a chance came in Ireland, and once there some went over to the Irish enemy. Muster masters and mayors of ports were quick to blame losses on the criminal and quasi-criminal types recruited. The government put the blame on the captains' and conductors' inefficiency and fraud; even after attempts to reform the recruiting system through the appointment of muster masters and commissaries for food and clothing, abuses continued.

Under the competent military leaders sent over to end the war after Essex's debacle, English soldiers in Ireland and their Irish allies eventually proved successful against an elusive enemy fighting a type of war of which the English had little experience. Those who were in agreement with the queen and council's wishes that there should be as many English as possible in the ranks of the army insisted that the English soldier was just as brave and enduring as his Irish or Scots counterpart. The author of a 'Discourse of Ireland', written during the war, opined:

> The Irish churl will never bear arms nor fight in his own defence; but the English farmer or clown, after he hath been once or twice upon service, will serve as sufficiently and as valiantly as most soldiers in garrison and therefore the more English the better for the State.[130]

But the problem of carrying out this policy was highlighted by Thomas Platter, who travelled widely in the English shires at the time of Essex's recruiting campaign for his army of Ireland:

> The country has good soldiers, but they do not care to go abroad; when soldiers are required, and idlers are found loitering in the towns, they are given money, and whether

they will or no, are forced to leave forthwith, and if they are caught deserting their case has been dealt with and justice done forthwith.[131]

The mixed nature of the queen's forces in Ireland, made up as they were of English, Welsh and Irish, and of impressed men, volunteers and veterans from the Low Countries, would strongly suggest that it is too simplistic to polarise the protagonists in the war into English and Irish. When many Irish in the English forces fought their own countrymen, and English soldiers deserted to the Irish enemy, national identities became blurred after long service in Ireland. Christopher St Lawrence, a well known captain, when brought before the privy council to answer his alleged implication in the Essex plot, and there told he was an Irishman, replied 'I am sorry that when I am in England I should be esteemed an Irishman, and in Ireland an Englishman'.[132] May not this captain's identity crisis have been shared by many of the less articulate common soldiers? Between 1594 and 1602 large levies of them were recruited in the cause of conquering Ireland; the demands for these men and the money to equip them put heavy burdens on the shires of England and Wales, which the following chapter surveys.

Notes

1   Cited in A. V. Judges, ed., *The Elizabethan underworld* (London, 1965). See the bibliography under the authors mentioned.
2   4 & 5 Philip and Mary, c. 3, in *Statutes of the realm*, iv, 316–320.
3   PRO SP11/12, 18r, where the lords lieutenant are not to spare 'any lyte [leet] or town, borough, though the same be a county of itself'. J. J. N. McGurk, 'The clergy and the militia, 1580–1610', *History*, 60 (1975), 198–210.
4   For the evolution of lieutenancy in one shire see J. J. N. McGurk, 'Lieutenancy in Kent c. 1580 – c. 1620', MPhil thesis (University of London, 1971), Chapter 2.
5   *APC*, xxvii, 109–110; for an example of this in Kent, and for one in Cheshire see Cheshire County Record Office (hereafter CCRO), Cholmondeley's letter book, DDX. 358/1, f. 33v, August 1596.
6   Cited in J. Harland, ed., *The Lancashire lieutenancy under the Tudors and Stuarts*, part i (Chetham Society, xlix, Manchester, 1859), xxii.
7   HMC, *Salisbury*, iv, 183.
8   HMC, *Salisbury*, xii, 590, Edward Hayes to Sir Robert Cecil, 7 January 1603.
9   *APC*, xiv, 55–56.
10 *APC*, xv, 99–100.
11 Staffordshire Record Office (hereafter SRO), D 593/S/4/11/1 (i–iv), 13 December 1587.
12 HMC, *Salisbury*, xii, 315, 22 August 1602.
13 M. St Clare Byrne, *Elizabethan life in town and country* (London, 1957), 154; P. Hughes and J. F. Larkin, *Tudor royal proclamation* (New Haven, 1969), vol. iii, 762, 779; P. A. Slack, 'Vagrants and vagrancy in England 1598', *Economic History Review*, 27 (1974), 2nd series no. 3.
14 HMC, *Salisbury*, xii, 169, 29 May 1602.
15 *Ibid.*
16 M. Campbell, *The English yeoman under Elizabeth and the early Stuarts* (New Haven, 1942), 352.
17 *APC*, xxx, 620–621.

18 *APC*, xxxii, 74.
19 PRO SP12/274/69, the commissioners of musters to the lord lieutenant, 4 March 1600.
20 PRO SP12/274/92, Henry Hardware, mayor of Chester, to Cecil, 2 April 1601.
21 HMC, *Salisbury*, xii, 164, Baxter to Cecil, 22 May 1602.
22 *APC*, xxix, 43–44.
23 HMC, *Salisbury*, xii, 164.
24 HMC, *Salisbury*, xi, 441, 22 October 1601.
25 *Ibid.*, 431.
26 HMC, *Rutland*, i, 358–359, 1600.
27 College of Arms, Talbot MSS, N, f. 340.
28 S. A. H. Burne, ed., *Staffordshire sessions records* (Stafford, 1933), vol. iii, 170.
29 *APC*, xxxii, 359.
30 *CSPI* (1598–1599), 31.
31 *Ibid.*, 274.
32 *CSPI* (1596–1597), 179.
33 HMC, *Salisbury*, xi, 474.
34 *APC*, xxix, 398·
35 HMC, *Salisbury*, xi, 443.
36 *APC*, xxxii, 360, desertions from Lincolnshire; *ibid.*, 392, from Flintshire; and from the mayor of Chester's military papers, M/MP/8/45–52 for a batch of examples on desertions at Chester.
37 *Cal. Carew MSS*, iv, 338.
38 SRO, D172/3, 290, letter no. 21.
39 *CSPI* (1596–1597), 179, 358; *CSPI* (1598–1599), 31, 274.
40 *CSPI* (1598–1599), 340; and 1xviii of the preface.
41 *Cal. Carew MSS*, iii, 31–40.
42 *CSPI* (1598–1599), 357.
43 *Ibid.*, 149.
44 *Cal. Carew MSS*, iii, 353–355, Sir John Dowdall to Sir W. Cecil, 2 January 1600, from Youghal, Cork, 'sent by Mr. Henry Palmer'.
45 *Ibid.*
46 *Ibid.*
47 *CSPI* (1596–1597), 59.
48 *CSPI* (1600), 503.
49 *Cal. Carew MSS*, iv, 137, Carew to Mountjoy, 1 September 1601.
50 J. E. Neale, 'Elizabeth and the Netherlands, 1586–89', *English Historical Review*, 45 (1930), 373–396.
51 *APC*, xxvi, 277.
52 *CSPI* (1599–1600), 383.
53 *Ibid.*, 275, and see also the descriptive map of the siege of Glin Castle, Limerick, in the *Pacata Hibernia* (1810 facsimile edn), facing p. 112.
54 *APC*, xxxi, 130.
55 *APC*, xxii, 480.
56 *CSPI* (1599–1600), 192, 255, 424; *CSPI* (1600), 442, 505.
57 *CSPI* (1596 – December 1597), 323.
58 *Ibid.*, 383, 390, 393; *CSPI* (1598–1599), 332–333.
59 *APC*, xxx, 807, and for further instances of the same complaint, *ibid.*, 87, 98, 111.
60 *CSPI* (1598–1599), 429–430.
61 *Ibid.*
62 *Cal. Carew MSS*, iii, 260–265, 'Declaration of the present state of the English Pale of Ireland ...', June 1597.

63 For a review of the evidence against Sir George Carey see H. Hall, *Society in the Elizabethan age* (London, 1888), 125–132.
64 W. Pinkerton, 'The "overthrow" of Sir John Chichester at Carrickfergus in 1557', *Ulster Journal of Archaeology*, 5 (1857), 188–190.
65 *AFM*, vi, 1951.
66 Sir James Perrot, *Chronicle of Ireland, 1584–1608*, ed. H. Wood (Irish Manuscripts Commission, Dublin, 1933), 103.
67 BL Additional MSS, 4728, calendared in Carew MSS, Lambeth Palace Library, iii, 220–260.
68 *Cal. Carew MSS*, iii, 118–119, Sir John Norris's commission.
69 *Ibid.*, 113–119.
70 PRO SP63/180/8, 9.
71 *Cal. Carew MSS*, iii, 114.
72 G. A. Hayes-McCoy, 'Tudor conquest and counter-reformation, 1571–1603', in *A new history of Ireland, vol. iii, Early modern Ireland, 1534–1691*, eds T. W. Moody, F. X. Martin and F. J. Byrne (Oxford, 1976), 121.
73 PRO SP63/207, part i, no. 117.
74 PRO SP63/183, 21.
75 PRO SP63/202, part iv, no. 17. For the particular numbers ordered from the shires PRO SP63/194/114–116b; the entire volume SP12/270, is chiefly concerned with Essex's army.
76 PRO SP12/268, 123, the queen to the lords lieutenant, November 1598.
77 P. Hughes and J. F. Larkin, *Tudor royal proclamation* (New Haven, 1969), vol. iii, no. 798.
78 HMC, *Salisbury*, viii, 499, 507, 508, for examples.
79 HMC, *Salisbury*, ix, 22, 41, 42, Docwra to Essex, 25 January 1599, from Flushing.
80 PRO SP12/269, 12, 15, Sir Edward Norris, governor of Ostend to Sir R. Sidney.
81 HMC, *Salisbury*, ix, 36, 37, Knollys to Essex, two letters, 22 January 1599. Knollys also wrote despairingly to Sir Robert Cecil, 'There is a great fault somewhere in making new orders contrary to those of Council', PRO SP12/270, 27.
82 HMC, *Salisbury*, ix, 36.
83 *Ibid.*, 42.
84 *Ibid.*
85 *APC*, xxix, 621.
86 PRO SP12/270, 10.
87 HMC, *Salisbury*, ix, 338.
88 *CSPI* (1599–1600), 7, 19, 28, 92.
89 J. Fortescue, *History of the British army* (London, 1899), vol. i, 156.
90 J. Bruce, ed., *Correspondence of Robert Dudley, Earl of the years 1585 and 1586* (Camden Society, xxxvii, London, 1844), 26.
91 C. McNeill, ed., 'The Perrott papers', *Analecta Hibernica*, 12 (1943).
92 B. Jennings, ed., *The wild geese in Spanish Flanders 1582–1700* (Irish Manuscripts Commission, Dublin, 1964).
93 W. G. Strickland, 'Irish soldiers in the service of Henry VIII', *Royal Society of Antiquaries of Ireland*, 6th series, 13 (1923), 94–97.
94 *Cal. Carew MSS*, i, 355 with reference to the year 1563.
95 F. M. Jones, *Mountjoy: the last Elizabethan lord deputy* (Dublin, 1958).
96 *Cal. Carew MSS*, iv, 50, Mountjoy to the privy council, 1 May 1601.
97 *CSPI* (1598–1599), 258.
98 *Cal. Carew MSS*, iv, 219.
99 *CSPI* (November 1600–July 1601), 162.
100 HMC, *Salisbury*, iv, 567, Captain Dawtrey to Sir R. Cecil, 21 July 1584.

101 J. A. Froude, *The English in Ireland* (London, 1901), 11.
102 Cited in C. Hughes, *Shakespeare's Europe* (London, 1903), 185–260, from the fourth part of Fynes Moryson's *Itinerary*, although it is not in the McLehose Glasgow edition of the *Itinerary* (1907).
103 P. O'Sullivan Beare, *Historiae Catholicae Iberniae Compendium* (Lisbon, 1621), trans. and ed. M. J. Byrne in *Ireland under Elizabeth* (Dublin, 1903), 40, 41, 57, 69, 160.
104 *Cal. Carew MSS*, iv, 156, Cecil to Mountjoy, October 1601.
105 *CSPI* (1598–1599), 156.
106 *Cal. Carew MSS*, iv, 90, 91.
107 C. Hughes, *Shakespeare's Europe* (London, 1903), vol. iii under 1602/1603, citing Moryson's *Itinerary*.
108 *CSPI* (1592–1596), 322.
109 *Cal. Carew MSS*, iii, 87, 88, 89; *Cal. Carew MSS*, iv, 53, 54, 200.
110 G. A. Hayes-McCoy, 'The Army of Ulster, 1593–1601', *Irish Sword*, 1 (1950), 105–117.
111 *CSPI* (1598–1599), 462, see tables.
112 *Ibid.*, 330.
113 *Ibid.*, 437, 447.
114 G. A. Hayes-McCoy, *Scots mercenary forces in Ireland, 1565–1603* (Dublin, 1937).
115 *The statutes at large of England and Great Britain (1509–1708)* (London, 1811), vol. i, 329 for the Act 3 & 4 Philip and Mary. The act remained a dead letter until 1612 when a Dublin parliament repealed it.
116 *Cal. Carew MSS*, iii, 96, 162, 278, 522.
117 PRO SP63/183, 77, October 1595.
118 *Cal. Carew MSS*, iii, 197, 'A Declaration' by the lord deputy and council.
119 *CSPI* (July 1596–December 1597), 431, yet see G. A. Hayes-McCoy, *Scots mercenary forces in Ireland, 1565–1603* (Dublin, 1937), who also shows how equivocal James VI was in helping O'Neill – turning a blind eye to men and munitions going from Scotland to O'Neill.
120 *CSPI* (1598–1599), 329. For contemporary accounts of the battle of the Yellow Ford see *Cal. Carew MSS*, iii, 280–281; *CSPI* (1598–99), 227–228; P. O'Sullivan Beare, *Historiae Catholicae Iberniae Compendium* (Lisbon, 1621), trans. and ed. M. J. Byrne in *Ireland under Elizabeth* (Dublin, 1903). Though he wrote in 1621 O'Sullivan Beare had oral reports from many who had taken part; c.f. R. D. Edwards, *Ireland in the age of the Tudors: the destruction of the Hiberno–Norse civilization* (London, 1977), 191.
121 *CSPI* (April 1599–February 1600), 389, 409, 450.
122 PRO SP63/207, part vi, 16.
123 *Calendar of state papers, Scotland* (1589–1603), 789, 796.
124 G. A. Hayes-McCoy, *Scots mercenary forces in Ireland, 1565–1603* (Dublin, 1937), Chapter 2.
125 *CSPI* (November 1600–July 1601), xlv–xlvii.
126 *CSPI* (July 1596–December 1597), 492; *CSPI* (1598–March 1599), 6, 9.
127 G. A. Hayes-McCoy, *Scots mercenary forces in Ireland, 1565–1603* (Dublin, 1937), 318; *APC*, xxxi, 307–308.
128 Fynes Moryson, *Itinerary*, vol. ii, 326.
129 PRO SP63/194, 67, Fenton to Cecil, 6 February 1597.
130 *CSPI* (1601–1603), 252, footnote transcribing this marginal comment.
131 Thomas Platter, *Travels in England in 1599*, trans. and ed. C. Williams (London, 1937), 184.
132 A. Collins, ed., *Letters and memorials of state from the De L'isle and Dudley papers* (London, 1746), vol. ii, 137.

CHAPTER THREE

The demands of the war on the shires of England and Wales

All classes of Elizabethan society were affected by war. A few wrote of the bearing of arms in the service of queen and country as a noble profession, but by the 1590s their sentiments were shared neither by the conscripts sent into Ireland nor by those called upon to pay for the war.[1] Support for an unpopular war in terms of men, arms and money was grudgingly given; the complaints of rich and poor alike and their reluctance to give practical assistance to foreign campaigns are well attested. The rich withheld horses or sent their poorer specimens; and they generally passed on the military taxes imposed on them to those less able or less unwilling to pay. The well known antiquarian and justice of the peace William Lambarde said as much to William, Lord Cobham in 1587, remarking that dutiful men would find themselves more and more charged and 'theire chearfull rediness the cause that they are more urged on'.[2] Elsewhere, Lambarde pointed out how the impressed man 'comes as willingly to serve as does the beggar to the stocks or the dog to hanging.'[3]

The 1590s was a period of stress for the English people: outbreaks of plague, particularly severe in London in 1593, and a bad run of harvests from 1594 to 1597 coincided with heavy demands for war. Alongside increased taxation, price inflation continued, and a rise in population exacerbated the scarcity of goods and employment. Hardship was aggravated by soldiers returning from the war. The efforts of the 'political nation' to ameliorate these stresses are reflected in the statutes, proclamations and privy council orders. Parliament became critical of crown policies; at court there was factionalism, and in the nation at large sporadic outbreaks of disorder.[4] The Irish war was happening at a time when England was developing as a state with a corpus of officials without tenure of office and without any service tradition or fixed procedures. The troops should not be called an army; their leaders, commanders and captains were still individualistic but without the medieval war lord's responsibility to his men. Dublin officials were near enough to their London counterparts for rapid consultation and, in an age of sail with the prevailing westerly winds, for constant impingement on the agenda of the London privy council. The vagaries of the queen's temper – royal rages at inefficiency, waste and stupidities and constant demands from Ireland – frayed the nerves and tempers of her servants in their turn.

Before turning to the demands for soldiers for Ireland it would be helpful to know the size of the population drawn upon, but gaps and uncertainties in the evidence have reduced demographic estimates to calculated guesses; not until the census of 1801 do we have comprehensive information on the population of England and Wales. The data used by economic historians and those of the Cambridge Group for the History of Population and Social Structure from parish registers, subsidy and diocesan returns have all to be hedged about by qualifications, not least that these sources were not compiled for demographic purposes but for the fiscal, military and ecclesiastical needs of the Tudors.[5]

There is general acceptance among demographers that the population of England and Wales was increasing in the Elizabethan period.[6] The muster returns made in 1570 of the 'Whole numbers of the shires and towns fit to bear arms' gives a figure of 589,981, which when multiplied by the figure of six recommended by W. G. Hoskins gives a total population of 5,539,886.[7] W. G. Hoskins also estimated a total population of 3.80 million from the 1603 ecclesiastical census.[8] Although attempts to use such sources as a reasonable guide to population are not thought to have been successful by the Cambridge Group, E. A. Wrigley's and R. S. Schofield's estimates from parish register evidence, using back projection, are not dissimilar. Their figure for 1571 is 3,270,903; in 1591 they give a figure of 3,899,190, and in 1601 a figure of 4,109,981.[9] Whatever source is used, the upward trend in the population is clear. William Lambarde in Kent remarked that the decades of peace before the 1590s were 'the mother of riches ... the father of many children.'[10] And in one of his celebrated charges to the Maidstone juries Lambarde said that:

> The number of our people is much multiplied nowadays not only young folk of all sorts but churchmen of each degree do marry and multiply at liberty, which was not wont to be, and on the other hand we have not, God be thanked, been touched with any extreme mortality either by sword or sickness that might abate the overgrown number of us.[11]

Historical demographers suggest reasons for the increased Elizabethan population to have been more complex than Lambarde indicated; new methods of farming, the division of large estates, and the rise of local industries are more cogent reasons for relative overpopulation in the sixteenth century. The agrarian revolution and industrial reorganisation of late Elizabethan England created unemployment which the Elizabethan poor law and efforts to regulate trade tried to control.

About three-quarters of this population lived in the countryside in small village communities or, in some shires, on isolated farms; of those in the small market towns, provincial cities and in London the majority had been born and bred in rural conditions.[12] The more populous area lay south of a line running from the Wash to the Bristol Channel. Within this southern area some 20 per cent of the nation lived in the Thames Valley, the most populous shires being Kent, Surrey, Somerset, Devon, Gloucester, Norfolk, Suffolk and Essex.[13]

Out of the total population Sir Thomas Wilson reported that only 300,000 able-bodied men were said to be fit to bear arms in 1588. 'But to say that the half or 3rd part of them were fit to be *hommes d'armes* ... I can neither affirm nor believe'.[14] This pessimistic estimate of 100,000 eligible and fit men for military service who could be called upon for defence or for foreign wars does help to put into perspective the demands made upon the shires for soldiers for the Irish war in the 1590s. Only about

30,000 men were sent from England to Ireland, representing about 0.76 per cent of the English population. A suggestion was made in 1598 to the Earl of Essex by one Thomas Saltern that if each parish of England and Wales provided one or two able and serviceable men a large army could have been recruited to revenge the reverses then taking place in Ireland.[15] And yet at the period of greatest military pressure, 1598–1601, the 21,000 soldiers in field and garrison in Ireland proved a considerable burden on the late Elizabethan state. By conflating both Cruickshank's figures and my tables (see below), Professor Wallace T. MacCaffrey reckons that the land forces conscripted by the crown between 1585 and 1602 would result in a figure of 75,000, of whom 37,000 served in Ireland. This does not include mariners serving abroad. It is difficult to agree with MacCaffrey's later contention that the geographical spread was evenly handled by the privy council; this may be roughly true of the English shires but certainly not of Wales, which suffered a disproportionate set of demands on its manpower in comparison with England.[16]

Some contemporaries believed the realm was overpopulated and that men could be well spared for overseas adventure. Richard Hakluyt the Younger saw the nation 'swarminge at this day with valiant youthes' and he held out the hope that the large vagrant population might be shipped to the New World to better their ways.[17] D. B. Quinn, in investigating such writers, showed that those who had read their Machiavelli turned their thoughts to colonisation as an outlet for an unemployed surplus population. In this respect Ireland, as well as the New World, was viewed as a land to be colonised. Walter Ralegh, Thomas Smith, Edmund Spenser, the elder Essex and Francis Bacon were all concerned and involved in the first English colonial experiments in Ireland. But colonies in Ireland were mainly thought of as a way to solve the military problem of governing Ireland rather than a way of exporting surplus English population. This is evident in the way some Elizabethan writers recommend that Ireland be colonised by the Dutch or, as Sir Parr Lane advised, by a mixture of Dutch and Scots.[18] It was said of the sixteenth-century Dutch that they made very good colonists since they were steadfast and 'had lead in their boots'.

To interpret sixteenth-century Anglo-Irish relations, bad though they were in the 1590s, as a long drawn out and consistent conflict of Gael and Gall is to ignore much modern historical research, to simplify the aims of the protagonists in the wars, and consequently to misunderstand the nature of both English and Irish societies at the time. The stark contrasting of the emergent renaissance English state in conflict with an ancient Gaelic civilisation on the periphery of Europe has also been superseded by recent scholarship. The full modern historiography of the 1590s is still far from settled, as writers differ in their interpretations of government policy as well as on how that policy, if any, was made. What part Elizabeth played in the drama remains ambiguous as she strove to heal faction at court and in the privy council. Naturally, the personal motivation of the protagonists in the Nine Years' War is fraught with subjectivism as contemporary views of Ireland and the Irish ranged from the highest religious, patriotic, and altruistic ideals to the basest materialistic, power-seeking and greedy ambitions.

To the majority in both the Dublin and London councils, and certainly to the queen, it was axiomatic that the peoples of Ireland were the subjects of the crown but in reality those outside the Pale and the garrisoned towns gave their allegiance either to the feudalised Anglo-Irish lords or native Gaelic chieftains, whoever gave them protection in their localities on the ancient principle of 'defend me and spend me'. In Dublin overall authority under the crown lay with lord deputies; each had varying degrees of success in governing Ireland. Indubitably, it was an overall aim to make the lord deputy's authority more effective over the entire island of Ireland. Such was explicit in the articles of his commission but it was given more or less emphasis depending on the urgency or seriousness of rebellion in the country and on the resources of England to implement it. One must recall that effective English presence in sixteenth-century Ireland was very much dependent on sea power to supply it; every lord deputy recognised 'the commodity of the sea', as Lord Mountjoy put it.[19]

Within this over-riding and accepted war aim, a variety of English concerns about Ireland are hidden: the fear of Spanish intervention, the queen's own interests in the sister island, particularly its costs to her government and, the most difficult one to discern, the religious concerns of promoting the reformation there. To the minds of many young bloods on the move and on the make in Elizabethan England in an age of self-conscious expansion, private aggrandisement in colonial ventures was foremost.

In a pragmatic and strategic sense, Ireland could easily have become what the Netherlands were to Spain, 'a postern gate' for the enemies of England; here lay strong practical reasons for pursuing a vigorous policy in Ireland. When Spanish men, arms and money were daily expected from 1594 to aid Hugh O'Neill's growing rebellion then threatening to swamp not only Ulster but the whole of Ireland, the strategic reasons dictated to queen and council a policy of repression, more severe than first intended, and which hardly needed a justifying ideology – for nothing less than the defence of the realm was then seen to be at stake; after all, the nightmare of 1588 was of recent memory. See, for instance, how such war aims are enshrined in the proclamations, privy council letters and the lord deputy's oath of office.[20]

In periods later than the Elizabethan, the army provided a time-honoured career for penniless younger sons. A standing army, as such, did not exist in Elizabeth's reign, and her forces in the 1590s were chiefly drafts of conscripts. The totals of men sent to Ireland cover the period of the Nine Years' War. The figures to Ireland and to the continent are not directly comparable but they do give a rough indication of the relative demands for men.[21] The figures in parentheses in Table 1 indicate the rank of each county: London, for instance, stands first, sending most soldiers to the continent and Ireland, while Kent stands second in numbers sent abroad but only twenty-seventh in the numbers sent to Ireland. The figure for each county in column one in Table 1 is the 1577 muster. These muster returns also give a relative notion of the individual manpower of the shires.[22]

The English shires can be broadly grouped into five geographical categories: western maritime shires, inland shires, south-eastern, eastern, and south coastal shires. After London and Yorkshire, the western maritime counties, especially Devonshire, Gloucestershire, Lancashire and Somersetshire, are most heavily drawn upon for the Irish war. Gloucestershire can be considered maritime because the Severn estuary goes deep into the shire and because of its proximity to Bristol, the second most important port for the embarkation of troops to Ireland. Cheshire stands tenth in contribution of

Table 1   Overall prospectus of demands for troops sent to Ireland and to continental Europe

County	Muster figure (1577)	Population	Ireland (1594–1602)		Abroad (1585–1602)	
Bedfordshire	1,000	7,000	592	(28)	850	(16)
Berkshire	5,615	39,305	579	(29)	1,155	(8)
Buckinghamshire	4,302	30,114	669	(25)	1,055	(10)
Cambridge	1,000	7,000	479	(31)	600	(20)
Cheshire	1,640	11,480	869	(10)	150	(24)
Cornwall	7,043	49,301	815	(13)	350	(21)
Derbyshire	5,901	41,307	668	(24)	75	(26)
Devonshire	10,000	70,000	1,730	(3)	900	(14)
Dorsetshire	5,056	35,392	690	(22)	860	(15)
Essex	9,253	64,771	794	(16)	1,900	(5)
Gloucester	9,821	68,747	1,664	(4)	900	(14)
Hampshire	8,109	56,763	860	(11)	1,925	(4)
Herefordshire	6,102	42,714	956	(9)	300	(22)
Hertfordshire	2,600	18,200	439	(32)	1,275	(7)
Huntingdonshire	1,000	7,000	482	(30)	200	(23)
Kent	11,203	78,421	600	(27)	3,850	(2)
Lancashire	6,000	42,000	1,403	(5)	300	(22)
Leicester	1,040	7,280	725	(17)	150	(24)
Lincolnshire	5,348	37,436	1,045	(8)	600	(20)
London	–	250,000	2,269	(1)	7,915	(1)
Middlesex	6,293	44,051	295	(34)	850	(16)
Norfolk	9,148	64,036	700	(20)	1,050	(12)
Northampton	2,300	16,100	1,275	(6)	1,050	(12)
Nottingham	1,040	7,280	705	(19)	150	(24)
Oxfordshire	4,500	31,500	629	(26)	1,090	(11)
Rutlandshire	600	4,200	220	(36)	50	(27)
Shropshire	2,500	17,500	711	(18)	138	(25)
Somersetshire	12,000	84,000	1,234	(7)	1,660	(6)
Staffordshire	1,601	11,207	683	(23)	75	(26)
Suffolk	10,552	73,864	800	(14)	1,150	(9)
Surrey	6,865	48,055	225	(35)	750	(18)
Sussex	6,436	45,052	300	(33)	2,610	(3)
Warwickshire	3,170	22,190	841	(12)	625	(19)
Wiltshire	5,353	37,471	795	(15)	910	(13)
Worcestershire	1,500	10,500	691	(21)	–	
Yorkshire	40,187	281,309	2,160	(2)	800	(17)

The figure in parentheses after the Ireland total is a rank listing (from Table 2). A similar list is given in parentheses after the totals sent to the continental wars, for comparison.
– indicates unknown figure.

Irish levies, largely because it was the main hinterland to Chester, the most important of the ports for Ireland. Cornwall ranked thirteenth, a relatively high rating in view of the shire's small extent and 'traditional' poverty. This group of six shires contributed 25 per cent of the overall total of 30,592 infantry levies sent to Ireland between 1594 and 1602, which indicates that it was government practice to recruit heavily from the shires nearest to Ireland.

The inland shires were not so heavily drawn upon. Northamptonshire's 1,275 infantry indicates that it was the sixth most heavily drawn upon. Herefordshire's figure of 956, high for an inland county, putting it ninth in the overall ranking, may be explained by the heavy recruitment by the Earl of Essex, for it was a county in which he held much land and influence. Herbert Croft, a deputy lieutenant in Herefordshire, pointed out Essex's heavy demands on the shire in a complaint to Sir Robert Cecil:

> The continuance of the Irish wars makes us in these parts to fear that our countries are like to feel the burden ere long of levying more soldiers with which we have been for these many years exceedingly afflicted by reason that my Lord of Essex has ever drawn a charge upon us such as we groan under but know not how to remedy.[23]

The other fifteen inland shires contributed 35 per cent of the overall total.

In the six shires of the third group, the south-east, London's contribution of 2,269 greatly exceeds that of any shire, representing 7.4 per cent of all the infantry levies sent into Ireland. This demand made upon the ever-expanding metropolitan area reflected its population of about 250,000 by the year 1600.[24] One way London met its military obligations was by levying vagrants, but when the government was hard pressed for soldiers on the occasion of the Spanish landing in Ireland in 1601 London was ordered to use 500 men from its trained bands.[25] Both measures, the drafting of vagrants and the raiding of trained bands, were also resorted to in the shires. Essex's figure of 794 is the second largest of the group but in terms of the national effort its contribution ranked sixteenth. As a group, London and the south-east contributed only 15 per cent of the overall total of men sent to Ireland.

Of the six eastern English shires, Yorkshire contributed the second highest figure of soldiers to the war, which reflects its size and the fact that its lord lieutenant, as president of the council of the north, could draw on the four most northerly counties of Northumberland, Durham, Cumberland and Westmoreland. These four counties do not appear in the tables, and the large Yorkshire number of 2,160 probably included small levies from them. Though geographically remote from Ireland, Lincolnshire's figure of 1,045 men sent there stands comparison with the four western maritime shires, which also sent out over 1,000 men. Clearly, the government thought Lincolnshire wealthy and populous enough to sustain its demands. These six eastern shires raised a total of 5,666 men, representing 19 per cent of the overall total of soldiers sent to Ireland.

The three shires of Hampshire, Dorsetshire and Sussex, the coastlines of which directly face the continent of Europe, contributed but 6 per cent of the overall total of Irish levies. The much greater demands made on these three counties for levies for the wars in France and the Low Countries than for that in Ireland is clear; Sussex, for example, while ranking thirty-third in Irish levies, ranks third for continental levies, though the longer period, 1585–1602, over which levies were raised for the continent must be taken into account.

The significance of geographical proximity to war is underlined by the number of troops sent abroad to the continental wars of France and the Low Countries. Table 1 shows that London and the south-east sent 43 per cent of all troops destined there, the large group of inland shires 20 per cent, the south-coast shires 14 per cent, the east 12 per cent and the western maritime shires only 11 per cent. London's contribution alone was enormous, representing 20 per cent of all troops sent to the continent, and in the case of its contribution to Ireland it stood pre-eminent.[26] Kent, Sussex, Hampshire and Essex, all close to the European mainland, were the next four shires most heavily drawn upon for continental levies. Rutlandshire, Staffordshire, Derbyshire and Shropshire were least drawn upon for these levies. In the instances of the shires to be studied in more detail in Chapters 4 and 5, Kent ranks second for foreign levies but twenty-seventh for Irish levies, Lancashire twenty-second abroad and fifth in Irish, and Cheshire twenty-fourth in foreign levies and tenth in Irish. The government drew heavily upon the populous London and Home Counties area for the wars abroad, but most heavily on the western maritime shires for the Irish war.

The muster returns of 1577 in Table 1, while not a fully reliable guide to population, as we have seen, show nevertheless a relative correlation between those counties with a high muster figure and those drawn upon heavily for either Ireland or the wars on the continent. Yorkshire, for example, with the highest muster figure was also second in the number of men sent to Ireland, but then Yorkshire is the largest county in England; Kent stands third in muster figures and second in troops sent abroad; and Devon, fifth in musters, is third in the number of its men sent to Ireland. On the other hand, Lancashire, but fifteenth in the 1577 muster, was nevertheless fifth in the number of its troops sent into Ireland, and Northamptonshire's low muster rank of twenty-sixth is at odds with its high figure of troops to Ireland, making the shire sixth in that respect.

If we turn to consider the counties' contribution of infantry levies (Table 2), a number of major points emerge.[27] During the Nine Years' War the government made demands for levies on sixteen separate occasions, but not from every county each time. Gloucestershire, Leicestershire and Northamptonshire were each levied fourteen times; Cheshire, Herefordshire, Lancashire, Nottinghamshire and Warwickshire were asked thirteen times; and Bedfordshire, Buckinghamshire, Derbyshire, Shropshire, Staffordshire and Worcestershire were levied on twelve occasions. These fourteen counties were most often called upon for Irish levies but this did not necessarily mean they sent the most men. Yorkshire, levied on only nine occasions, provided the second highest number of recruits, simply because each demand was so large. London, too, was levied infrequently but heavily.

Small but frequent demands could produce a high total figure from a comparatively small shire. Herefordshire, levied on thirteen occasions, provided an overall total of 956 troops for Ireland, which appears to give substance to the complaints of Herbert Croft to Sir Robert Cecil in 1599.[28] The shires on which small but infrequent demands fell are noticeable in Table 2: Sussex, Surrey, Middlesex and Rutlandshire. Sussex, for instance, was asked for Irish levies on only four occasions. Surrey and Middlesex also sent out troops to Ireland infrequently, though some of the large London levies drew upon their manpower resources of Surrey and Middlesex.[29]

Table 3 sets out how the Irish war impinged on Wales. Proximity to Ireland as well as the convenience of the ports of Chester, Bristol, Haverfordwest and other havens dictated that Wales would suffer much in the 1590s from the demands of war. Owen

Table 2   Infantry levies for Ireland from English shires, 1594–1602

Shire	1594	1595	March 1596	Oct. 1596	1597	1598	1599	Jan. 1600	June 1600	Dec. 1600	April 1601	Aug. 1601	Oct. 1601	Dec. 1601	Jan. 1602	July 1602	Shire total	Rank
Bedfordshire	–	40	54	50	33	200	50	50	–	15	20	–	30	–	20	30	592	28
Berkshire	–	50	44	50	–	100	–	100	50	20	25	–	60	–	30	50	579	29
Buckinghamshire	–	50	44	50	–	100	150	50	50	20	25	–	50	–	30	50	669	25
Cambridge	–	40	54	50	–	200	–	50	50	20	–	–	60	–	25	–	479	31
Cheshire	100	–	–	47	47	150	200	100	50	20	25	(25)	100	–	20	50	869	10
Cornwall	–	–	–	–	100	300	–	50	–	20	20	25	60	100	–	100	815	13
Derbyshire	100	–	–	50	23	100	50	100	50	15	–	50	60	20	–	50	668	24
Devonshire	–	–	–	–	300	400	–	100	–	40	40	100	300	350	–	100	1,730	3
Dorsetshire	–	–	–	–	–	200	–	50	50	20	20	50	100	200	–	–	690	22
Essex	100	60	34	–	–	–	150	100	50	30	–	–	300	–	100	–	794	16
Gloucestershire	100	60	34	–	200	200	200	150	50	30	40	100	200	200	–	100	1,664	4
Hampshire	–	–	–	–	–	300	100	50	50	–	–	100	100	–	60	100	860	11
Herefordshire	100	–	–	50	56	100	100	100	50	25	25	50	75	200	–	25	956	9
Hertfordshire	–	50	44	–	–	100	50	50	–	15	20	–	60	–	25	25	439	32
Huntingdonshire	–	25	64	50	23	50	50	50	–	–	–	50	50	–	20	50	482	30
Kent	–	–	–	–	–	100	–	100	50	–	–	–	200	–	100	50	600	27
Lancashire	100	–	–	47	56	200	200	200	150	30	40	(100)	150	–	180	50	1,403	5
Leicestershire	–	40	34	50	56	100	50	100	50	15	20	50	60	–	50	50	725	17
Lincolnshire	–	–	–	100	–	150	100	200	100	45	–	–	200	–	100	50	1,045	8
London	–	–	–	94	–	300	150	300	200	150	175	–	400	–	500	–	2,269	1
Middlesex	–	–	–	–	–	–	100	50	–	20	25	–	50	–	50	–	295	34
Norfolk	–	–	–	–	–	200	–	100	100	–	–	–	200	–	100	–	700	20
Northamptonshire	–	205	39	100	56	100	50	150	100	25	40	100	150	60	–	100	1,275	6

Table 2 *continued*

Shire	1594	1595	March 1596	Oct. 1596	1597	1598	1599	Jan. 1600	June 1600	Dec. 1600	April 1601	Aug. 1601	Oct. 1601	Dec. 1601	Jan. 1602	July 1602	Shire total	Rank
Nottinghamshire	–	40	54	50	56	100	50	100	50	15	–	50	60	–	30	50	705	19
Oxfordshire	–	40	54	50	–	200	–	50	50	20	25	–	60	–	30	50	629	26
Rutland	–	–	–	–	–	100	–	50	–	–	–	25	30	–	15	–	220	36
Shropshire	100	–	–	50	56	150	50	–	50	30	35	50	60	–	30	50	711	18
Somerset	–	60	34	–	–	150	50	–	100	40	50	100	250	300	–	100	1,234	7
Staffordshire	100	–	–50	33	100	–	100	50	30	30	50	60	–	30	50	50	683	23
Suffolk	100	–	–	–	–	200	–	100	100	–	–	–	200	–	100	–	800	14
Surrey	–	–	–	–	–	–	–	150	–	15	15	–	30	–	15	–	225	35
Sussex	–	–	–	–	–	–	–	100	50	–	–	–	100	–	50	–	300	33
Warwickshire	100	–	–	50	56	150	50	100	50	20	25	50	60	–	30	100	841	12
Wiltshire	–	–	–	–	–	100	–	–	100	30	40	100	125	200	–	100	795	15
Worcestershire	100	–	–	50	56	150	50	–	50	20	25	50	60	–	30	50	691	21
Yorkshire	–	–	–	–	400	400	–	200	200	60	–	300	300	–	150	150	2,160	2
Totals	1,000	760	587	1,088	1,607	5,450	2,000	3,300	2,050	805	805	1,450	4,410	1,630	1,920	1,730	30,592	

calculated the mid-sixteenth-century Welsh population at about a quarter of a million.[30] Over eight years Wales was asked on fourteen occasions to provide levies amounting to a total of 6,611 men. This represents 2.9 per cent of the Welsh population, compared with English levies amounting to only 0.76 per cent of the English population. Therefore in relation to its size and population Wales was the more heavily drawn upon for the Irish war. An official comparison made in 1595 supports that conclusion, showing that of 11,996 soldiers sent from both England and Wales between 1594 and 1598, Wales sent 2,996, a quarter of the total.[31]

There is an approximate relationship between the Welsh shires' population figures and the numbers of soldiers demanded from them for the Irish war. Anglesey, twelfth in population, is also ranked twelfth in the number of soldiers; Glamorganshire, with the second highest population figure, is also second in the number of soldiers; Merionethshire was eleventh in both respects; Montgomeryshire sixth in both; and Radnorshire, while ninth in population, was equal tenth in the number of soldiers for Ireland. In contrast, Carmarthenshire, with the highest population figure, was only third in the list of soldiers, while Denbighshire, doubtless because of its proximity to Chester and its long border on the Deeside estuary, sent the highest number of soldiers though but third in population. None of the Welsh shires are far from the coast but the greatest numbers were clearly recruited from Denbigh, Glamorgan, Carmarthen, and Caernarvon. The last seems to have been the most heavily drawn upon for Irish levies in relation to its population, a fact not lost on its deputy lieutenant, William Maurice, who registered a number of complaints about government demands from such a poor county.[32]

In Anglesey, likewise, the authorities objected to the constant demands for men, but it was in fact the least recruited part of Wales. The real objection from the justices in Anglesey stemmed from their claims for total exemption from Irish military levies on the grounds that their island was dangerously exposed to invasion, being 'very open with six places fit for enemies to arrive, well known to the French and Spanish nations'.[33] But the Elizabethan government gave no exemptions to privileged places; it did not take seriously the possibility of an invasion through Anglesey at this time. Anglesey and Pembrokeshire were anciently exempt from foreign service on account of their vulnerable locations, but past privileges of exemptions were more often than not ignored by the privy council in the 1590s.[34]

Every abuse in the conscription arrangements found in the late-sixteenth-century English shires can be paralleled in the Welsh; the justices and deputies in Wales were no better in financial probity at a time when justices were the unpaid officials of the state. In the English shires it was unusual to find a captain and conductor of conscripts rejecting recruits because they were mustered by the adherents of an opposing faction in the county. In Wales it was commonplace. Sir Richard Trevor, for example, raised a company in Denbigh and Flint, but his own quota from Denbigh arrived in Chester well under strength because he refused to have those recruits sent by Salisbury of Llewenni, his rival in West Denbigh.[35]

Apart from such idiosyncrasies in the Welsh service, the administrative orders and routine methods of raising a military levy followed the same pattern as in England. In Wales, however, the deputy lieutenants in the 1590s exercised a more pronounced authority over the justices and constables, and at times the sheriff, in having government orders for levies put into effect. In general, privy council demands came to them from the lord president of the council of Wales and the Marches, William Herbert, Earl of Pembroke, from his seat at Ludlow Castle. At other times they acted directly on the authority of the queen's letters.[36]

The problem of desertion was a particularly prevalent one in the coastal shires of Wales and in Chester in the late 1590s, so that the privy council had to send out special orders to the Earl of Pembroke to have his deputy lieutenants and the sheriffs and constables arrest and punish Welsh soldiers who had deserted from Ireland.[37] John Wynn, as deputy in Caernarvonshire, was zealous in carrying out these orders.[38] In June 1597, he issued warrants to all the constables in Caernarvon to have deserters brought before him for examination and he seems to have conducted thirty such examinations that month. Those he committed to prison appealed to his rival deputy, William Maurice.[39]

While distinctive colours of army coats for individual shires were not a feature of sixteenth-century levies, the recruits from Glamorgan prided themselves on their well-turned-out uniforms of blue coats lined with yellow cotton and some in red coats lined with green.[40] As for arms, the Welsh muster rolls, even in the late 1590s, show a preponderance of the pike as the distinctive arm of the infantryman.[41] In 1598 the deputies of Caernarvonshire were warned that since a particular levy was 'to go against the Spaniards [in Ireland] who use great store of muskets, their bows must be changed for muskets or other shot, and their brown bills for halberds'. And (a rare mention of red coats in the sixteenth century) 'the soldiers must wear a red livery of kersey or Bridgewater cloth, indented with black'.[42] It is also of interest to find some regard for humanity in what was the essentially brutal exercise of impressment: in Carmarthen married men were exempt; so, too, were those afflicted with venereal disease. If a would-be recruit could prove 'a grief of his legges' he could also gain a release from the duty.[43] It was in protest against the inhumanity of the constables in Llandybie in Carmarthen that the villagers rescued the fifty-five-year-old Morgan Harry from the draft.[44]

It is probably naive to interpret such exemptions on totally humanitarian grounds; it is more likely that they were all part of the context of a reluctance to serve in the Irish wars. Overt reluctance is not far to seek, though the objections to service may all have appeared reasonable. William Maurice and John Wynn would not agree that Caernarvonshire was particularly warlike. They explained to the Earl of Pembroke how the men of Caernarvon, having been 'bred in peace', did not easily become accustomed to a military way of life, so that this was one reason why many of them chose prison rather than service in Ireland.[45]

Welsh names are to be found in almost every garrison and theatre of warfare in the 1590s; it was chiefly to those garrisons established along Lough Foyle by the Yorkshire commander Sir Henry Docwra and to those around Carrickfergus established by Sir Arthur Chichester that the Welsh levies were especially directed. In the council's words when ordering reinforcements for those 'desperate assignments', their garrisons 'are planted in the very heart of the north of Ireland where the enemy most usurpeth.'[46] Many of the names in Sir Henry Docwra's muster lists, particularly

Table 3   Infantry levies for Ireland from Welsh shires, 1594–1602

Shire	Population estimate	Oct. 1594	June 1595	Mar. 1596	Oct. 1596*	Aug. 1598	Jan. 1599	Jan. 1600	June 1600	Dec. 1600	April 1601	Aug. 1601	Oct. 1601	Jan. 1602	July 1602	Total	Rank
Anglesey	9,770	–	46	30	–	–	–	50	50	–	–	–	50	10	–	236	12
Brecon	21,190	–	35	50	100	100	50	–	100	15	15	25	50	–	50	590	5
Caernarvon	14,920	–	46	30	50	100	50	50	100	15	15	40	60	20	30	606	4
Cardigan	17,320	–	46	30	100	50	50	–	50	15	15	25	30	–	–	411	10
Carmarthen	34,375	–	–	100	100	100	50	–	100	25	25	50	60	–	–	610	3
Denbigh	22,482	50	–	50	100	100	50	50	100	15	15	30	60	20	30	670	1
Flint	12,570	50	–	50	100	50	50	50	50	10	10	20	30	10	20	500	8
Glamorgan	29,493	–	35	50	100	100	50	50	50	20	20	50	50	–	–	625	2
Merioneth	10,520	–	46	30	50	50	50	–	50	10	10	25	30	20	50	371	11
Monmouth	–	–	35	50	100	100	50	50	50	20	20	30	40	–	–	545	7
Montgomery	18,972	–	46	30	50	100	50	–	100	20	20	40	60	20	30	566	6
Pembroke	20,079	–	35	50	100	–	–	–	100	15	15	40	40	–	75	470	9
Radnor	14,185	–	46	30	50	50	50	–	100	15	15	25	30	–	–	411	10
Totals	225,826	100	416	580	1,000	900	550	300	1,000	195	195	400	590	100	285	6,611	

*The October 1596 levy was discharged but then recalled in April 1597.

Sources:

1. PRO SP12/248/87; 261/51; 267/51; 268/55; 270/15,30; 274/27. PRO SP63/208, part iii; f. 261; 194/27, 165.

2. Chester City Record Office, mayor's military papers, M/MP/11–13; mayor's great letter book, M/L/1 (1595–1602); muster rolls – M/MP/7/ff. 24–38 – roll for the 1596 levies, M/MP/11, Flintshire roll of December 1600; M/MP/12/1–20, 22–25 (1601).

3. For population estimates see L. Owen, 'The population of Wales in the sixteenth and seventeenth centuries', Transactions of the Honorable Society of Cymmrodorion (1959), 99–113.

4. G. Owen, The taylor's cussion (sixteenth-century commonplace book of G. Owen (1552–1613) on Pembrokeshire), part I, facsimile edn (1906), ff. 52–83.

those of his captains, indicate their Welsh origin: Lloyd, Trevor, Vaughan, Mostyn, Morgan and Morris, for examples.[47] Many Welsh families lost relatives when, for instance, Sir Henry Bagenal's field army was annihilated at the battle of the Yellow Ford, near Blackwater, on Monday 14 August 1598, as the names in the casualty reports show. One instance may serve to illustrate the bravery of the Welsh in that conflict. Evan Owen, Sir Richard Percy's ensign, 'being a resolute man' and seeing that all was lost, broke the flag pole which he carried and wrapped himself in the colours, which were 'heavy and new, full of half moons' (the silver crescent of the badge of the Percys). Owen was cut to pieces, 'for he would not part with his colours until he was slain'.[48] In the extensive contemporary evidence relating to the battle of the Yellow Ford, the bravery of the Welsh captains who lost their lives there is clear. Many of the Welsh captains who survived the war became 'servitors' or hoped to be colonists, rewarded for their services with forfeited lands, and this long before the influx of Scottish planters in King James' reign. Sir Richard Trevor, for instance, was rewarded with the governorship of Newry; Captain John Lloyd was given land in the same area of South Armagh; Captain Edward Morris settled at Mountjoy in County Tyrone, Captain Sidney in Cavan, Sir William Windsor at Drogheda; and the Vaughans received estates in Kilmacrenan and Buncrana in the O'Dogherty lands of Innishowen.[49]

To conclude, Wales became a natural recruiting ground for military levies to be sent to Ireland. Chester and its 'member' ports were geographically the focal point for the north Welsh levies and Bristol the port of those raised from south Wales. Geographical convenience may have saved the Elizabethan government much expense but so heavily were the Welsh shires drawn upon that impressments for the Irish war of the 1590s seem to have given rise to more quarrels than usual among the Welsh gentry. 'How can your minds be united in public defence,' wrote the Earl of Pembroke in 1591, 'when they are dyvided by privatt quarrells? And what hope of succour in the field may anie man have from him who is his professed enemie at home?'[50] The pressures of privy council demands for men, money and arms led to a continual flow of complaints from shire authorities, a reluctance to serve on the part of the recruits and to a greater flood of complaints about the quality of the Welsh recruits. Desertions from their levies seem to have been more frequent than those from the English shires, yet the higher incidence of Welsh drafts for Ireland simply highlights all the ills of late Elizabethan local administration in raising and transporting troops. The difficulties in local administration reflect both the war-weariness of the shires in the last decades of the queen's reign, as well as the bureaucratic problems and financial straits of her government in bringing an unpopular war to a successful conclusion.[51]

There is no doubt about the impatience of the late Elizabethan government with the 'pretended privileges' of chartered towns and other 'exempt' areas wishing to ease themselves of the burdens of raising levies, but it is also clear from the increasingly sharp tone of the privy council's letters in the 1590s that it had a struggle to ignore the clamour for exemptions.[52] Gloucester City protested against an impressment of men in 1596 as a violation of municipal privileges; Macclesfield likewise in 1599, Coventry in 1601 and Exeter in 1602,[53] while the Cinque Ports in Kent and Sussex and the Stannaries in Devon looked to the patronage of their lords warden to protect their ancient privileges against the encroachments of the lieutenancy. Many corporation records, however, show no distinct impressments of soldiers, which may well indicate that lieutenancy officers and commissioners for musters were able by agreement and understanding with the mayors of many towns to take up vagrant and masterless men by drafting them into the shire levies for the Irish war;[54] this was certainly the case in London, Oxford, Chester and Bristol.[55]

Tables 1–3 show that the total infantry levies from the shires of England and Wales to the last Elizabethan war in Ireland was 37,203, an annual average of 4,640 troops. If we accept C. G. Cruickshank's estimate that the total number of able-bodied adult males eligible for military service was probably between 200,000 and 250,000,[56] the total number of men levied for Ireland represents between 14.9 and 18.6 per cent of the total number of men available.[57] While it would be foolhardy to conclude that the Irish war of the 1590s was an unprecedented drain on the manpower resources of the communities of the realm, this proportion was nevertheless considerable. It must, however, be recalled that there was an increase in the English population and that towns used the Irish draft to rid themselves of undesirables; such considerations place the demands for men for Ireland in a more balanced way than has sometimes been presented. However, the demands to meet the various crises were relentless. No shire escaped. It may be noted from Tables 2 and 3 that when the Spanish landed at Kinsale in September 1601 almost every English and Welsh shire raised levies to fight them in October 1601. Thereafter the three further levies of the reign show some government attempt to spread the burdens of raising troops; all ten of the English shires and seven Welsh shires were exempt from the demands in January 1602. And for the final levy, in July 1602, nine English shires from those not exempted in January 1602 were passed over and five more exempt in Wales.

Table 4 sets out the numbers of the much smaller levies of horse bands sent to Ireland in the four crisis years of the war, 1598–1601. These levies represented the responses of the justices, the clergy and the recusants, the traditional providers of horse. In the normal procedure for raising horse levies, the privy council sent letters under the sign manual signifying the queen's orders to individually named country gentlemen each to provide a light horse and rider, fully accoutred. These letters make clear that the horses were to be raised 'without a common chardge of the meaner sorte'. In other words, the gentry were to bear the financial burden and not pass it on to their tenants.[58] To equip horse and rider and have them sent into Ireland was more expensive than, for instance, sending out a small levy of twenty pikemen; a fully equipped cavalryman cost about £30, a fully armoured pikeman only about 30s.[59]

It would be unwise to claim that a county which provided many horse must have been wealthy. Nevertheless, there does seem to be a correlation between wealth (as measured by the 1522 loan) and the provision of horse. Several of the wealthier shires sent relatively large numbers of horse: Kent, Essex, Norfolk, Suffolk, Hampshire, Lincolnshire and Hampshire were noted as traditional shires for the breeding of horses.[60] The link between the wealth of counties and the recruitment of horse levies cannot, however, be made in every case: Wiltshire, Devonshire and Somersetshire, among the very wealthiest counties, rank only twelfth, fourteenth and tenth, respectively, in providing horse. And Lancashire, considered among the poorest

Table 4   Horse levies and wealth of English shires

County	1522 loan yield £	rank	1598–1601: horse provided	Ranking in horse provision
Bedfordshire	2,413	23	10	20
Berkshire	5,035	13	13	17
Buckinghamshire	2,661	22	20	10
Cambridgeshire	3,332	17	17	13
Cheshire	–		17	13
Cornwall	2,106	19	4	24
Derbyshire	953	31	15	15
Devon	10,576	5	16	14
Dorset	4,630	14	14	16
Essex	11,207	3	47	2
Gloucestershire	5,850	11	14	16
Hampshire	6,293	10	37	6
Herefordshire	1,088	29	7	22
Hertfordshire	3,070	20	18	12
Huntingdonshire	2,342	24	11	19
Kent	13,164	1	51	1
Lancashire	–		20	10
Leicestershire	2,803	21	10	20
Lincolnshire	7,417	8	35	7
London	20,000		10	20
Middlesex	1,707	26	17	13
Norfolk	11,771	2	46	3
Northamptonshire	6,995	9	23	8
Nottinghamshire	1,065	30	12	18
Oxfordshire	3,363	16	19	11
Rutlandshire	712	32	8	21
Shropshire	1,249	28	18	12
Somerset	9,097	7	20	10
Staffordshire	1,500	27	13	17
Suffolk	10,444	6	44	4
Surrey	3,631	15	6	23
Sussex	5,810	12	22	9
Warwickshire	3,221	18	10	20
Wiltshire	11,190	4	18	12
Worcestershire	2,055	25	15	15
Yorkshire	–		43	5
Total			720	

Annual totals of horse: 117 (1598), 110 (1599), 183 (1600), 310 (1601).
Sources:
1. Column 1 from W. G. Hoskins, *The age of plunder, 1500–1547* (London, 1976), 22, 23.
2. Column 2 correlated from *APC*, xxviii, 588, 589, 590; *APC*, xxix, 116–118; *APC*, xxx, 435, 440; *APC*, xxxi, 313; *APC*, xxxii, 278–286.
3. According to these schedules in the privy council's registers the two years of heaviest horse demands were 1600 and 1601.
4. The privy council was not always well informed before making demands of individual gentry; in Lincolnshire, for example, one gentleman charged with providing a light horse in 1601 had been dead for many years – HMC, *Salisbury*, xii, 439.
5. The provision of light horse had become the special responsibility of the justices of the peace; compare the list of those asked for horse in 1601 in *APC*, xxxii, 275–277, with the rosters of the commissions of the peace for the same year in the appendices to J. H. Gleason, *The justices of the peace in England, 1558–1640* (Oxford, 1969).

counties of the realm, provided a good number of horse, perhaps because of the convenience of its ports. London, despite its undoubted wealth, was exempt from the provision of horse; the fact that ten were levied in 1599 simply shows that some of the gentry with London residences and business ventures had not been able to play off their London interests against their county responsibilities to the war effort. The privy council wrote to the lord mayor of London in July 1601 on the problem of 'men of good substance' whose 'estates lyeth in divers parts of the realm ... harbouring in London' so that they lived 'unprofitable to the State'. The problem was of long standing and the lord mayor was ordered to cooperate with the privy council in finding out the names of those 'shifting themselves from the burden of such taxes,' especially those who were justices of the peace in shires bordering London.[61]

The role of the cavalry in the Irish war was limited. The highest demand for horse coincided with the Spanish landing in September 1601 and then only 310 horses were asked from the gentry. There is plenty of evidence that both cavalry and infantry levies were widely unpopular throughout England and Wales, but to what extent the demands for soldiers turned public opinion against the war in Ireland is an imponderable question. Before considering the year-by-year demand for soldiers in more detail, it must be emphasised that the numbers of men ordered by the privy council and the numbers of men in action in Ireland were more often than not very different.

At the outset of his rebellion, in February 1595, Hugh O'Neill, second Earl of Tyrone, was believed to have an armed strength of 4,000 musketeers, 1,000 pikemen and 1,000 cavalrymen.[62] O'Neill had taken the isolated fort on the Blackwater in Armagh, which was a veritable gateway into his own lands; he was then in open defiance and in effect waging formal war. A draft proclamation against O'Neill as a traitor was prepared but its promulgation was now left to the new leader of the forces, Sir John Norris – the queen thought that even at the last hour it might have been possible by secret diplomacy to divide O'Donnell from O'Neill. But at last Dublin persuaded London of the gravity of the situation so that they decided to withdraw 2,000 veterans from Brittany to aid Sir John Norris, the absentee president of Munster, in a projected campaign directly against the Ulster Gaelic confederacy.[63]

Under the year 1595 the celebrated *Annals of the Four Masters* record that 'the entire province of Ulster rose up in one alliance and one union against the English.'[64] At the same time the English force in the field army under Sir Henry Bagenal, marshal of the army, was reported at 1,500 foot and 250 horse.[65]

The strength of the redeployment exercise can be followed in the report of Sir Henry Norris, who led them out of Brittany; 1,616 veterans embarked at Paimpol. Of these, 1,553 were fit when they put in at Plymouth for revictualling, and when the force eventually mustered in Dublin in April 1595 its strength was down to 1,400, the shortfall being accounted for by sickness, desertion and 'dead pays'.[66] Earlier, in October 1594, privy council orders had been issued to ten English shires and two Welsh shires to raise 1,100 new recruits for Ireland (see Tables 2 and 3). The levy both of veterans and of the new recruits proved inadequate as the reversal of English arms at the battle of Clontibret in Monaghan demonstrated in May 1595. In the following month, further orders went out to thirteen English shires and ten Welsh to raise another 1,176 men for Ireland (see Tables 2 and 3).

By August 1595 the certificate of the army musters in Ireland gave the following totals: 4,040 infantrymen, 657 horsemen, and 158 Irish kerne, a grand total of 4,855.[67] In October 1595, Hugh O'Neill, by then the undisputed leader of the Irish, made a truce with the government's forces which was to last until the new year, and despite minor outbreaks of hostilities the truce was prolonged by further negotiation until May 1596.[68] Matters were not helped by the constant bickerings between the lord deputy, Sir William Russell, and the commander in chief, Sir John Norris. Then the reinforcements were held up at Chester by contrary winds, so that no further action could be hoped for before the spring of 1596.[69]

The year 1596 in Ireland was one of uneasy truce, of warlike declarations and preparations for further fighting. Russell was of the opinion that 'this kingdom is not otherwise to be kept than by force'.[70] In consultation with the Irish council in Dublin he outlined what was necessary to suppress the northern rebellion 'in the prosecution of a sharp war'. Their recommendations to the English privy council may be summarised:

(1) in Ulster – 3,920 foot, 400 horse, 200 pioneers, 400 kerne, and in addition to launch an expedition to Lough Foyle of 1,000 foot, 100 horse and 200 pioneers;
(2) in Connaught – 3,000 foot, 300 horse, 100 pioneers, 200 kerne;
(3) in Munster – 200 foot;
(4) in Leinster and the Pale – 1,000 foot.

Finally, a force of 3,000 'well chosen and governed Scots' would be required.[71] The total establishment of over 14,000 men recommended proved to be far too ambitious for the English government to accept. Anticipating this reaction, perhaps, Dublin prepared more modest estimates. Reckoning from the muster masters' books that there were but 4,510 foot and 555 horse fit for service, not counting those in garrisons or in broken companies, that is, under-strength companies, Dublin reported that the minimum reinforcements needed were 4,600 foot, 245 horse and 200 pioneers.[72] But the total effect of the year's levying in England and Wales of 3,255 (Tables 2 and 3) was to raise the number of troops in Ireland only to 5,732 foot and 617 horse;[73] another report gave the army's strength then as 5,432 foot and 492 horse.[74] The total was far short of what the Dublin council would have liked.

The lack of spectacular success against O'Neill was laid at the door of scant supplies. The treasurer-at-war, Sir Henry Wallop, ever the prophet of doom in his letters to the privy council, reminded them that present troubles would prove to be 'the longest, most chargeable and most dangerous war' in memory in Ireland.[75] By a series of delicate negotiations the truce was extended to May 1596, mainly because preparations were under way for the celebrated Cadiz expedition, hence demands for soldiers for Ireland were discouraged. The Dublin council and particularly Wallop spelled out how the Irish situation had changed for the worse: the ominous unity of the Gaelic chiefs of both Ulster and Connaught under O'Neill and O'Donnell, the increasing professionalism of their fighting forces, which they proved at Clontibret by meeting English arms in the open and winning, and finally their determination to recover their lands and status. Wallop was certainly not a persuader, but was one of the more vocal advocates of the sword. Once again he called for a grand strategy and for a full army under some noble personage. He pointed out that an assault on three fronts would be the ideal: directly against O'Neill from Dublin and the Pale; an attack on O'Donnell from the province of Connaught; and lastly, by landing an amphibious force to establish garrisons along the Lough Foyle, to divide O'Neill and O'Donnell and thereby establish forces for an assault on their rear as well.[76]

During the summer of 1596 O'Neill's position was strengthened by the constant rumours of Spanish aid in arms, men and money; and on many occasions there had been expectations of an actual landing. While O'Neill was negotiating truces in the spring a Spanish delegation under Alonzo Cobos had landed in the north and promised that if they should continue the war they would lack for nothing from Philip of Spain. O'Neill passed on Philip of Spain's letter to the Dublin council, with his own and O'Donnell's reply saying they were now in the queen's favour and could not possibly satisfy his conditions.[77] Not many were taken in by his candour; negotiations became clogged but O'Neill had taken pains to make the English government aware that Spanish arms and money were coming in and that a Spanish army was a possibility; this situation raised his bargaining powers and enhanced his ambitions. Meanwhile, on the English side, morale was low in the forces; there was disorder in Munster and Connaught; desertion was rife; and the mortality rate was high. There were divisions both in the council and in the army command; Bingham in Connaught was in disgrace and so he set out for London to defend himself, but without permission and soon found himself in prison. Sir Conyers Clifford took his place in Connaught; he was a protégé of Essex and a veteran of the Rouen and Cadiz campaigns, but without extra resources his position was constantly under threat from O'Donnell. On the eve of 1597 in the Dublin council there was a rift between the secretary, Geoffrey Fenton, and the lord deputy, Russell – both wanted to leave Ireland. At a special meeting in London the queen decided to recall Russell and replace him by Thomas, Lord Burgh. Sir Henry Wallop's three-pronged assault on the north and west was rejected on the grounds of the difficulties of victualling the project.[78] But still the war party in the council in Ireland kept saying that the 'most honourable and assurdest course' would be 'a royal war', an all-out military conquest without heed to expense. The state of Ireland in the winter of 1596 made this extremely difficult, for it is worth recalling that both islands were then suffering from the worst dearth of the century; so short was food that victuals had to be procured from the Baltic and the continent before 2,000 men waiting to sail for Ireland could be sent. A defensive policy was advised instead of an aggressive one.

From that winter there was much marking of time until May 1597 and the arrival in Ireland of the new deputy Thomas, Lord Burgh, who is accredited with being the most obscure of all the Elizabethan lord deputies of Ireland; the destiny of English fortunes in Ireland was once more entrusted to a second-string figure.[79] Despite the reinforcement of 2,500 troops, Burgh accomplished little other than re-establishing what Ormond called the scurvy fort at the Blackwater. Grain and cattle were in short supply. Requests for more funds from England got frosty answers. The queen was much 'distasted' by the charge of Ireland, of £12,000 a month. Once again the idea of a three-pronged assault on the north had to be abandoned. By August Burgh was in retreat into Newry and then to Dublin; his hasty march in October back to Newry brought him to his death after a brief illness. A few days later Sir John Norris also died.[80]

Although something like 10,300 men appeared in the muster lists, Burgh had difficulty in fielding 1,700, of whom only some 400 or 500 were English. Clifford in Connaught had some 1,500 and two-thirds of those were Irish. By December 1597 Ormond could only find 500 men out of eighteen companies (nominally 1,800) and of those 100 were unable to bear arms. As general of the forces after Burgh's death, Thomas Butler, Earl of Ormond, had to maintain the Pale and hold on to existing garrisoned positions. By December 1597 the policy was once again to negotiate with O'Neill; Ormond as general of the army had full military responsibility and acted under privy council orders. But within a few months of cessation of hostilities, a build-up of forces was going on and to this we now turn.

During 1588–1589 the Irish administration constantly pressed for more soldiers and particularly horses even though fighting had virtually ceased in Ulster.[81] Russell, as we have seen, was glad to prolong the truce with O'Neill for, as he admitted, the army was in a sorry state, 'very unable to make head against O'Neill.'[82] Both Burgh and Sir John Norris died in October 1597 so that civil and military authority in Ireland was put into the hands of a committee of justices under Ormond. No lord deputy was appointed to succeed Burgh until the Earl of Essex was appointed with the title of lord lieutenant general in 1599.[83]

Prior to Russell's recall in May 1597, the English privy council sent out warrants to the lords lieutenant of twelve English shires to raise 600 foot to be sent to Ireland under Francis Croft as conductor,[84] and on the insistence of Lord Burgh a further 1,000 were ordered to be raised from Yorkshire, Gloucestershire, Devonshire and Cornwall (see Table 2). Burgh's insistence was strengthened by rumours of Spanish aid to be sent into Munster and acted as a spur to the English administration.[85] The privy council ordered the Welsh levies and others which had been discharged the previous October 1596 to reassemble at the ports in April 1597 (see Table 3). Six dead pays were allowed in each 100 but the number of deserters, especially in the Welsh, Derbyshire and Staffordshire levies, was high.[86]

After the year's programme of reinforcements to Ireland the government expressed its annoyance to Lord Burgh that by June 1597 little had been accomplished, and that the muster books came over 'alwaies very generallie and uncertainlie' and, considering they were the muster master's, the books were most disorderly.[87] Sir Ralph Lane was then muster master general in Ireland and his books purported to show 8,000 men on the payroll.[88] On his return Sir William Russell, who had generally been a failure in Ireland, told the government plainly that in his view there were hardly 5,000.[89] By July 1597 the government issued a set of orders to reform the musters and pay of the queen's army in Ireland.[90] Maurice Kyffin, appointed to check the muster office in Ireland, reported by the end of the year that there were twenty-one bands of horse, and seventy-eight companies of foot. The horse band in Ireland was normally fifty strong, and the foot band 100. Therefore Kyffin's total of 7,800 foot and 1,050 horse was higher than the official figure given by Sir Ralph Lane.[91]

'A summary report' of the state of Ireland from the Irish council at the end of 1597 made it clear to the English government that 'all the late rebellions in Ireland have had their beginning in Ulster,' and that the latest rebellion amounted to 'a universal Irish war, intended to shake off all English government'.[92] In response to the grave situation in that year the government called for an unparalleled effort from the shires. The overall total for 1598 was 5,450, the highest annual total for the war years (see Table 2).[93]

Early in February 1598 1,100 veterans were mustered in Picardy for Ireland. The Earl of Ormond was told to expect 900 of them in Munster, but only 612 arrived in the port of Waterford.[94] The privy council ordered 1,500 to be levied from England and in July 1598 a force of 1,472 landed in Dublin from England, 28 short. Early in August Sir Samuel Bagenal, brother of the marshal, Sir Henry Bagenal, had orders to conduct 600 men from Chester to Olderfleet, near Carrickfergus, and at the same time Colonel Egerton was to conduct 1,350 from the port of Plymouth; both contingents and 100 horse were intended to form a garrison to be 'planted' at Lough Foyle.[95] Nineteen shires were asked to contribute numbers varying between 50 and 200; London was first asked for 400 but this was later abated to 300 (see Table 2). This force did not sail until 28 October 1598, too late to prevent the greatest disaster ever to happen to an English army in Ireland, the Battle of the Yellow Ford on 14 August.[96] As a result of the disaster it was considered too dangerous to go ahead with the plans for Lough Foyle, and Bagenal's and Egerton's recruits were landed instead at Cork, Kinsale and Waterford; their arrival was reported by Edmund Spenser on his return to England, who said that though the soldiers were untrained raw recruits they were well equipped and that Sir Thomas Norris, president of Munster, was taking their training in hand.[97]

In November of the same year, a further 1,050 men were called from Bedfordshire, Berkshire, Worcestershire, Oxfordshire, Dorsetshire, Wiltshire, Leicestershire and Warwickshire.[98] This force was destined for Connaught to reinforce Sir Conyers Clifford, governor of that province. They arrived in Dublin under the conduct of Sir Arthur Savage, whence they marched to Athlone, the assembly place for entry into Connaught, and arrived by the end of January 1599.[99] In December 1598 redeployment of troops was again tried as we have seen in some detail in the last chapter; 2,000 veterans from the Low Countries were sent to Ireland. In this way the Netherlands became a training ground for English soldiers fighting in Ireland. Both the November and December levies became part of the large army build-up for the Earl of Essex's takeover in Ireland the following year. Perhaps because of the fluidity of numbers in the Irish service at this time there is no satisfactory estimate of the strength of the forces from the Irish administration until the following year. On the other hand, we know from Captain Francis Stafford's report of December 1598 that Hugh O'Neill's armed strength had increased to 1,043 horse and 3,540 foot, and that his military successes had done much to spread the rebellion throughout Ireland, encouraging the most southerly province of Munster to rise against the English colonists there.[100] By the winter of 1598 the Dublin council again warned the privy council in London: 'this rebellion is now thoroughly sorted to an Irish war, whose drifts and pretences are, to shake off all English government, and subtract the kingdom from Her Majesty, as much as in them listeth'.[101]

Recruitment for the Earl of Essex's forces continued through the winter of 1598/ 1599. To aid the build-up of his army in Ireland a great levy of 3,000 was demanded from the English shires in January 1599, speedily followed by a further demand in February and, except from Anglesey and Pembrokeshire, all the Welsh shires to make up an additional levy of 1,000 men.[102] In Tables 2 and 3 the totals for 1598 and 1599 necessarily overlap to indicate this winter levying for Essex. No previous commander in Ireland had had such an army, an official establishment of 1,300 horse and 16,000 foot. Before Essex's fatal truce with O'Neill and return to England, it is thought that his effective forces had decreased to about 925 horse and 11,250 foot.[103] At long last the queen and council began to face up in a realistic way to the demands of Ireland. In all, Essex's army at full muster was 16,000 infantry backed by 1,300 horse and fully supplied with food, munitions, clothing and ships. The queen remarked that it was 'a royal army paid, furnished in other sort than any king of this land hath done before'; in fact it was three times the size of the expeditionary force in the Netherlands and its projected annual cost was the immense sum of £290,000, or twice the annual charge of the Dutch service.[104] To the authors of the *Annals of the Four Masters* it was the strongest force sent into Ireland since the twelfth-century invasion under Strongbow in the reign of Henry II.[105] If the general aspect of this army was spectacular so too were the failures: the failure to meet O'Neill in the field, its retreat from the Lough Foyle project, its allowing O'Neill to take the initiatives in making a truce and above all in his treasonable return to England.[106]

When Mountjoy was appointed lord deputy on 21 January 1600[107] he inherited the forces left by Essex, under 12,000 foot and under 1,000 horse. In the government's instructions to him it was stated 'We have resolved to maintain an army of 12,000 foot and 1,200 horse ... you are not to exceed these numbers except for some notorious peril to the kingdom'.[108]

Fynes Moryson, later in 1600 to be Mountjoy's secretary, states that the lord deputy Mountjoy signed 'The lyst of the Army to bee a direction to the Treasurer at warres, for the payment thereof, from the first of Aprill in the yeere 1600,' which gives a total of 14,000 foot and 1,200 horse.[109] The discrepancy of 2,000 foot between what the government intended and the list signed in Ireland highlights the perennial difficulty in these years of knowing the exact strength of the army in Ireland. However, in January 1600 levies of 3,300 in the English shires and 300 in the Welsh shires were raised for Ireland for the designated force to be sent to Lough Foyle under Sir Henry Docwra, but under the supreme command of Mountjoy.

In the first months of the year 1600 all the military advantages appeared to lie with O'Neill and his confederates. The uncertainties aroused by Essex made it possible for O'Neill to make a veritable 'royal progress' throughout Munster in the winter of 1599/1600. None opposed him. However, the arrival in Ireland of Mountjoy, Carew and Docwra began to turn the tide of Irish successes by May 1600. Carew was to break O'Neill's grip on Munster, Docwra would lodge garrisons in his rear along the Foyle, driving a wedge between O'Neill and O'Donnell, and Mountjoy, consummate soldier-administrator, would harass and spoil the enemy at large on his many 'journeys', especially to the borderlands of Ulster, where lay the centre of the rebellion.[110] To supply this programme of reconquest the government sent frequent reinforcements to strengthen and set up garrisons, to aid the field forces and to resist the Spanish who landed at Kinsale in September 1601.

Meanwhile, in June 1600, a total of 2,050 recruits were ordered from England and 1,000 from the Welsh shires, the third and last time during the war that Wales was asked to provide such a high number. From Tables 2 and 3 it will be seen that shires heavily recruited in June 1600 were given a lighter order for the admittedly smaller demand of 1,000 recruits for the December 1600 levy from both England (805) and Wales (195). Nine English shires were exempt from the December levy, and though only Anglesey was exempt in Wales its overall total of 195 may represent the government's awareness of its large contribution in June.

From 1598 to 1600 there had been a growing demand for cavalry contributions from the traditional providers of horse, the justices, the clergy and the recusants. The greater expense of sending out fully equipped horsemen, the unpopularity of its use in armed combat in Ireland at this time, and the reluctance of the gentry to provide horses all dictated that the numbers sent to Ireland would be small: 117 in 1598, 110 in 1599 and 183 in the year 1600 (see Table 4).[111] In these years, and indeed to the end of the war, small groups of gentry sometimes went part share in satisfying privy council demands for horses; in Lancashire, for example, seven gentlemen joined in partnership to send out a single light horse.[112] And in 1598 and 1600 the clergy provided horse for Ireland through the diocese. 'Recusant horse' came under the jurisdiction of the lieutenancy in most cases.[113] In 1600 the gentry of Kent, Yorkshire, Lincolnshire, Norfolk, Suffolk and Essex supplied the greatest numbers; Surrey, Herefordshire, Leicestershire and Rutland provided two each, Cornwall and Devonshire none.[114] Ireland's foremost military historian, G. A. Hayes-McCoy, has long since shown how horse were used in the Irish wars to a greater extent than hitherto appreciated.[115]

In Ulster Sir Henry Docwra's garrisons at Lough Foyle needed reinforcement by April 1601; sickness and desertions had thinned down his original 4,000 foot to half that number. In April the government decided to levy 1,000 foot and 40 horse from England and Wales to supply these losses.

In Munster Sir George Carew's forces were in the most vulnerable part of Ireland in view of the rumours circulated by June 1601 of a Spanish invasion to land probably on the Munster coasts. Carew wrote to the privy council:

> six thousand men might be levied for this service; whereof two thousand to be sent presently for Waterford, and the rest to be in a readiness at an hour's warning to make speedy repair to the sea-coast upon the first notice of this invasion.[116]

The privy council responded by ordering a levy of 2,000 from thirty-three shires in England and Wales; 275 to be embarked at Barnstable by 6 August, 830 at Chester, and 895 at Bristol by 9 August.[117] When the privy council's original and general order of 23 July 1601 for 2,000 came to be shared out among the shires it can be seen from Tables 2 and 3 that the total was in fact 1,850. The discrepancy can only be accounted for by the vagaries of the Elizabethan council's arithmetic. All were so seriously delayed by contrary winds that they did not begin to arrive until the first week of September, a few weeks before the Spanish landfall in Munster.[118] Don Juan del Aguila and 4,000 Spanish soldiers put in at Kinsale on 23 September 1601, an event that changed the direction of the war in Ireland from Ulster to Munster, and one which evoked the largest programme of reinforcement since 1598/1599. News of the landing appeared to take a long time to reach London, but in the first week of October orders fell thick and fast on the shires of England and Wales to call up 5,000 men for Ireland (see Tables 2 and 3). Some 2,000 were to sail from Rochester, 2,000 from Bristol and Barnstaple, and 1,000 from Chester.[119] At the same time clothing contracts were made with merchants to supply winter suits. The clergy and gentry were asked to contribute nearly 300 horse, and the lawyers were to pay graduated contributions of £10, £20 or £30 towards the expense of sending them. John Wood, a victualling merchant, won the contract to provide food to feed 8,000 soldiers in Munster at an estimated cost of £13,300.[120]

The greatest demand for horse came at this crisis. The queen's orders under the sign manual were sent out to 275 individually named country gentlemen in the English shires and to sixteen in the Welsh counties each to furnish a fully accoutred light horse and rider for Munster. The shires sending most horses were Lincolnshire, Devonshire, Northamptonshire, Yorkshire and Hampshire, in that order; those sending least were Surrey and Cornwall, and five Welsh shires contributed a total of sixteen. From the named list of gentry eighty-seven asked to contribute were knights. Hampshire had the most of these, at twelve. And by a comparison with the rosters in the commissions of the peace, the majority asked for horses were justices of the peace.[121] The clergy of both provinces were to supply sixty – Canterbury forty-five and York fifteen.

The privy council analysed the results of this levy. Of the total 351 ordered from both the gentry and the clergy, forty-six horses were missing and thirty-one were sent back from the ports as 'insufficient', and 'therefore there were wanting in all the number of 77'. This should have left 274 to be transported; but the privy council's analysis under the heading of 'Sent and transported' gives 291.[122]

Contrary winds, especially at Bristol and Barnstaple, delayed the reinforcements; they began to arrive in Ireland from about 10 November.[123] Mountjoy reminded Sir Robert Cecil that the Spaniards had begun 'the war of the Lowe Countries and hath bin maintained with few more natural Spaniards than are arrived here already'.[124] By 14 November the queen's ships and the forces from Rochester under admiral Sir Richard Leveson had arrived at Cork.[125] The Irish council in Dublin remarked that this news was:

> a matter of great comfort to us, as we perceive it is most joyful to his lordship [Mountjoy] ... God has sent us these great succours, prepared by her sacred Majesty and expedited by her most honourable and careful mynestery.[126]

Mountjoy, writing to Sir George Carew, was less sanguine about the newly arrived levies. Many of them were raw recruits much upset by a bad voyage, so that numbers died on their first night in Ireland. Of others Mountjoy said, 'I think there be not ten of them that can shoot in a gun'. He sent 1,000 of them to Cork to rest until cabins were made for the sick.[127] The Irish council reported the safe arrival of 1,000 foot and 100 horse from Bristol, and 1,000 foot and 140 horse from Barnstaple and Ilfracombe, where some of the Bristol contingent had been blown off course. They disembarked at Cork, Youghal and Waterford by 12 November 1601.[128] Fynes Moryson reckoned

10,100 foot and 1,000 horse as the army's strength at the beginning of 1601 and in his 'Lyst of the Army at Kinsale' for November/December 1601 he gives 11,800 foot and 857 horse. The difference made by the arrival of recruits is apparent in the infantry's case but not in the instance of horse.[129]

Following the demands of October 1601 the privy council was almost apologetic in asking for a further levy of 2,000; but, as may be seen in Table 2 under December 1601, when the individual shires, mainly in the West Country, were given their quotas the total demands of this occasion came to 1,630. These were also delayed, and though the siege and battle of Kinsale had been fought and won on Christmas Eve 1601 the government did not cancel the levy in the new year, but on insistence from Ireland for more men decided instead to increase the original order of 2,000 to 4,000, 'notwithstanding the often and great levies of late in this kingdomme'. The first batch of 2,000 was ordered to sail on 10 January 1602, and the second on 20 January.[130]

The reasons for the increased demand for men even after the victory at Kinsale are not far to seek: sickness, desertion and mortality took a severe toll during the winter's siege.[131] It was also generally assumed that the Spanish defeat would 'sharpen and stir the King of Spain to a further stomach and fresh invasion'.[132] The lord deputy, and particularly Sir George Carew in Munster, were for a long time in great fear of their return.[133] To the privy council the lord deputy wrote: 'it will not then any longer be the war of Ireland, but the war of England in Ireland to the infinite danger and cumber of them both'.[134] Their fears were well founded for King Philip III of Spain had ordered a second fleet and an even stronger land force than the one which had fought at Kinsale, but it was not clear to English intelligence whether these forces were intended for Ireland, for the Netherlands, for England, or simply for the defence of Spain itself.[135]

The ability also of the Irish enemy to continue the struggle in Munster, and in Ulster on O'Neill's return there, was far from broken. Apart from fears of a Spanish return Carew in Munster needed new forces to mop up pockets of resistance, and in particular to take the strong fortification of Dunboy.[136] In Ulster, Docwra was not in a position to plant further garrisons, least of all the long-awaited one at Ballyshannon, and needed about another 1,000 troops.[137] Mountjoy confessed to the weakness of the army in the field, which badly needed men and victuals for what proved to be his final 'journeys' to aid Docwra and Chichester in Ulster.[138]

It was to supply these needs that 4,000 soldiers first ordered in December 1601 were asked to be sent in January 1602. The severity of this and previous demands seems to have induced the privy council, contrary to previous orders and practice, to allow the shires in certain cases to take the men out of the trained bands of the home militia, which happened in Kent, Lancashire and Northamptonshire. On this occasion London sent out the unprecedented figure of 500 of its trained men.[139] In general, the response from the shires was reluctant and there were exceptionally long delays in the arrival of men in Ireland; some reports of their arrival in Ireland from the military commanders are dated in May, June, and, in one instance, July 1602.[140]

A final levy, of 2,015, from England and Wales was ordered in July to sail in August. On 9 August 1602 the privy council informed Carew that '2,000 men levied in sundry shires of this realm are appointed to be embarked at Chester, Bristol and Barnstaple and transported to Cork' to sail on 15 August.[141] Mountjoy told Carew that they needed 'that number at least to fill our weak companies'.[142]

By the first week of September 1602 these levies were still in port. While 1,000 were supposed to have gone to Chester, only 850 embarked there on 4 September. This contingent was then blown on to the Wirral, and at another attempt only got as far as Beaumaris.[143] From Bristol it was reported that of the 800 ordered to the port their number was greatly diminished by desertion; this levy, too, suffered on account of the perversity of the winds. It is not clear how many in fact embarked at Bristol.[144] Of the 200 ordered to embark at Barnstaple, the mayor reported that 165 sailed on 24 August before the winds became contrary.[145] Reports from Ireland mention troop landings not at Cork, their original destination, but at Waterford on 22 September and 11 October.[146]

No further military levies were needed. As the winter of 1602 approached, Mountjoy began to reduce the army in Ireland. A full army list from Carew's papers for January 1603 shows totals of 12,100 foot and 1,000 horse.[147] In January and February Mountjoy and his commanders completed the reconquest in a campaign of attrition in Ulster which amounted to a harrying of the north. Those fifteen months mopping up the last pockets of resistance have been underestimated by historians, as Kinsale is too often taken to mark the final end of the war. In the last months of her life Elizabeth still had to make a major decision about the status of O'Neill; she did not live to make it. O'Neill, on the other hand, unaware of the accession of James in England, made his submission to the dead queen Elizabeth in the person of her last deputy at Mellifont Abbey on 30 March 1603. Mountjoy knew of the queen's death on 24 March. Had O'Neill known also, it is probable that he would have negotiated more favourable terms with James.[148]

Historians of the last years of the queen's reign now recognise that Ireland was her great problem; she was as much deluded about the realities there as those of her ministers who believed that the royal writ should have run as easily in Mayo as in Middlesex. English vacillations in policy between the use of the sword and of persuasion, royal delays, unwillingness to commit resources, muddled compromises, rag- and bob-tailed expeditionary forces, ramshackle armies until after 1598 all led eventually to a war which entailed much suffering and loss on both sides. Indeed, this unwelcome legacy was bequeathed to the Stuarts and it cast long shadows on future generations. In the judgement of a foremost scholar of the Elizabethan regime, Wallace T. MacCaffrey, 'the conquest was one of the great success of Elizabethan arms and the most disastrous failure of Elizabethan policy making'.[149]

To correct the view that Ireland absorbed the total military resources of England and Wales it must be recalled that during the same period that Elizabethan England was fighting the war in Ireland large forces were sent to France and the Netherlands; in addition there were the notable expeditions to Cadiz (1596) and Puerto Rico (1598). Also, home defences had to be prepared on account of the renewed attempts by Spain at invasion of England itself in 1596 and in 1599. These defence measures and the continuing state of war in Ireland, by increasing the number of combatants, put military organisation on a firmer basis, but the system of musters and levies did not develop into a standing army. And yet, the force maintained in Ireland was the nearest approach to a paid army of 'professionals' that Elizabethan England and Wales made. The government constantly harped upon the need for an efficient military organisation in the interests of economy, but it also wanted a policy of social cleansing at home which, in the end, did not lead to efficiency among the forces; in that conflict of aims lay some of the troubles in raising, organising and transporting these military levies into Ireland in the 1590s.

A perusal of the council's registers in any one of these crisis years will clearly indicate the demands made on the government; Ireland was high on the agenda of the 1590s and through to the very last months of the queen's reign. Appointments to all manner of offices, answering petitions, recommending courses of action, sending out orders to the shires, receiving reports and recriminations from commanders in the field, from the Dublin council and from irate and recalcitrant mayors of ports – the day-to-day evidence of all these activities and more fill the registers. The privy council would appear to have been an omnicompetent body – at one time acting as a war cabinet, at other times as a foreign office, indeed a colonial office managing England's oldest colony – and as the war in Ireland gathered momentum the privy council became involved in coat and conduct money, military taxation, shipping, and even strategies and tactics, not to speak of the factional politics and complexities of the Dublin council.

The last decade of the queen's reign was one of disenchantment, of war weariness exacerbated by harvest failures and plague, and although there were localised outbreaks of riot and disorder in opposition to royal demands there was no large-scale revolt against them while the queen lived. A 'precarious balance' between order and disorder, between the demands of the crown and the ability of the nation to pay, was maintained. The response to these demands for an unpopular war in Ireland is some measure of governmental success in the interests of centralisation, unity and order. The queen and privy council may have established a unitary military organisation by the 1590s but this did not mean that it was an efficient military machine; privileged persons and places were able to escape, evade or minimise military exactions, counties were able to change, ignore and contest demands, and captains and conductors of troops appear to have been able to practise fraud at will.

Notes

1 See the bibliography under B. Rich, T. Digges, T. Churchyard, W. Harrison and J. Derricke.
2 SRO, D 593/S/4/11/1, Lambarde to Cobham, 13 December 1597. This letter is not in the Folger edition of Lambarde's works.
3 Cited in P. Clark, *English provincial society from the Reformation to the Revolution: religion, politics and society in Kent, 1500–1640* (Hassocks, 1977), 222.
4 P. Clark and P. Slack (eds), *Crisis and order in English towns 1500–1700* (London, 1972); B. Sharp, *In contempt of all authority: rural artizans and riot in the west of England, 1558–1660* (London, 1980).
5 See for example the caution used by W. G. Hoskins, *The age of plunder, 1500–1547* (London, 1976), 219–220, when discussing such sources for population, and E. A. Wrigley

and R. C. Schofield, *The population history of England 1541–1871: a reconstruction* (Cambridge, Mass., 1981), Appendix 5, 563–569.

6   E. A. Wrigley, ed., *An introduction to English historical demography* (London, 1966), 266.

7   E. E. Rich, 'The population of Elizabethan England', *Economic History Review*, 2nd series, 2 (1950), 248, 251, 255.

8   W. G. Hoskins, *The age of plunder, 1500–1547* (London, 1976), 219.

9   E. A. Wrigley and R. S. Schofield, *The population history of England 1541–1871: a reconstruction* (Cambridge, Mass., 1981), 569.

10   SRO D 593/S/4/11/1, Lambarde to Cobham, 13 December 1587.

11   Cited in C. Read, ed., *William Lambarde and local government* (Ithaca, 1962), 182.

12   J. Thirsk, ed., 'The farming regions of England', in *The agrarian history of England and Wales, 1500–1640* (Cambridge, 1967), vol. iv, 1–20.

13   H. C. Darby, ed., *Historical geography of England* (Cambridge, 1963), 304–309.

14   F. J. Fisher, ed., *The state of England anno domini 1600 by Sir Thomas Wilson* (Camden Miscellany, 3rd series, xvi, London, 1936), 16–23.

15   HMC, *Salisbury*, viii, 426.

16   Wallace T. MacCaffrey, *Elizabeth I: war and politics, 1588–1603* (Princeton, 1992), 13.

17   W. Notestein, *The English people on the eve of colonization* (New York, 1954), 256.

18   D. B. Quinn, ed., 'A discourse on Ireland, c. 1599', *Proceedings of the Royal Irish Academy*, 47 (1942), 151–166; and for Sir Parr Lane's comments see the little-known treatise on Ireland in the Bodleian Library, Tanner MSS, 458, ff. 65–71, not dated.

19   Fynes Moryson, *Itinerary*, vol. ii, 392.

20   *Calendar of patent rolls in Ireland*, ii (1862), 29.

21   C. G. Cruickshank, *Elizabeth's army* (2nd edn, Oxford, 1970), Appendix 3. I have not used this author's totals of men to Ireland.

22   The 1577 muster returns are the most reliable one before the 1590s demands: see E. E. Rich, 'The population of Elizabethan England', *Economic History Review*, 2nd series, 2 (1950), 251–254.

23   HMC, *Salisbury*, ix, 420, Croft to Cecil, 29 December 1599.

24   F. Freeman Foster, *The politics of stability* (Royal Historical Society, London, 1977), 7.

25   *APC*, xxx, 620, 621; *APC*, xxxii, 27, 145; W. H. Overall and H. C. Overall, eds, *An analytical index to the series of records known as Remembrancia, AD 1579–1664* (London, 1878) (hereafter *Remembrancia*), 245, January 1601.

26   V. Pearl, *London and the outbreak of the Puritan revolution: city government and national politics* (London, 1964), Chapter 1.

27   Table 2 is based on correlated figures from PRO SP12/260, 40; SP12/268, 124; SP12/274, 15; SP12/275, 12; SP12/271, 37; SP12/285, 20; and PRO SP63/208, part iii, nos 194/27, 261; and PRO E101/65, 5–28; E101/66, 19; E101/67, 4.

28   HMC, *Salisbury*, ix, 420.

29   *Remembrancia*, 236, 237, 245; *APC*, xxxii, 27, 145.

30   L. Owen, 'The population of Wales in the sixteenth and seventeenth centuries', *Transactions of the Honorable Society of Cymmrodorion* (1959), tables pp. 107–113; and for a population density map based on this article see J. Thirsk, *The agrarian history of England and Wales, 1500–1640* (Cambridge, 1967), vol. iv, 144.

31   PRO SP12/268, 124, 125, schedule of soldiers sent to the wars (1598).

32   J. Ballinger, ed., *Calendar of Wynn papers* (Aberystwyth, 1926), nos 159, 173, 183.

33   E. G. Jones, 'Anglesey and invasion, 1539–1603', *Transactions of the Anglesey Antiquarian Society* (1946), 26–37.

34   J. J. N. McGurk, 'A survey of the demands made on the Welsh shires to supply soldiers for the Irish War 1594–1602', *Transactions of the Honorable Society of Cymmrodorion* (1983), 56–68.

35   E. S. Jones, *The Trevors of Trevalyn and their descendants* (privately printed, 1955).

36 *Dictionary of national biography* (Oxford) (hereafter *DNB*), *s.v.*, Herbert, William, third Earl of Pembroke.

37 *APC*, xxvii, 68, and a copy in J. Ballinger, ed., *Calendar of Wynn papers* (Aberystwyth, 1926), no. 181.

38 J. Ballinger, ed., *Calendar of Wynn papers* (Aberystwyth, 1926), nos 181, 182, 183, 184.

39 J. Ballinger, ed., *Calendar of Wynn papers* (Aberystwyth, 1926), no. 183, Maurice to Wynn with the petition from John William Pritchard later referred to as John Williams.

40 J. M. Traherne, ed., *Stradling correspondence* (London, 1840), 203.

41 CCRO M/MP/7, ff. 24–38, muster roll of Welsh levies in 1596; CCRO M/MP/11, 11, an individual indenture from Flint, December 1600; CCRO MP/12, 1–20, 22–25, Welsh muster rolls in May 1601.

42 J. Ballinger, ed., *Calendar of Wynn papers* (Aberystwyth, 1926), no. 201, 1 November 1598; and for a reference to English red-coats at the battle of Clontibret (Monaghan, Ireland) 1595 see *CSPI* (1592–1596), 322, and P. O'Sullivan Beare,'s *Historia Catholicae Hibernia Compendium* (Lisbon, 1621), trans. (in part) by M. Byrne as *Ireland under Elizabeth* (Dublin, 1903), 153–156.

43 Cited in G. D. Owen, *Elizabethan Wales: the social scene* (Cardiff, 1962), 72, 73.

44 I. O. Edwards, *A catalogue of Star Chamber proceedings relating to Wales* (Cardiff, 1929), no.1, 45.

45 Cited in A. H. Dodd, *History of Caernarvonshire, 1284–1900* (Caernarvon, 1968), 28.

46 *APC*, xxxi, 315.

47 A great number of these muster lists from Docwra's garrisons can be more readily consulted in the four volumes of the *CSPI* between 1599 and 1602.

48 Cited in G. A. Hayes-McCoy, *Irish battles* (London, 1969), 124.

49 J. C. Erck, ed., *Repertory of the inrollments on the patent rolls of Chancery in Ireland*, James I, i (1846), ii (1852) under the names mentioned above.

50 T. Jones Pierce, ed., *Calendar of Clenennau letters and papers* (*National Library of Wales Journal*, supplement, 4th series, part i, 1947), 31.

51 J. J. N. McGurk, 'Lieutenancy in Kent c. 1580 – c. 1620', MPhil thesis (University of London, 1971), 535 ff.

52 J. J. Goring, 'Military obligations of the English people, 1511–1558', PhD thesis (University of London, 1955), 197–199.

53 *APC*, xxvi, 277–278; *APC*, xxx, 788, 789; *APC*, xxxii, 191.

54 The published corporation records of Nottingham, Ipswich, St Albans, Norwich, Southampton, Exeter and Plymouth show no distinct impressments for Ireland.

55 *Remembrancia*, 245; *Oxford Council Acts*, ed. H. E. Salter for the Oxford Historical Society (Oxford, 1928).

56 C. G. Cruickshank, *Elizabeth's army* (2nd edn, Oxford, 1970), 24.

57 These figures have been accepted by both Wallace T. MacCaffrey and Ian F. W. Beckett for his contribution to *The Manchester history of the British army* (Manchester, 1991), vol. vii.

58 *APC*, xxxii, 275–277.

59 For examples of these costs see the following chapters.

60 J. Thirsk, ed., 'The farming regions of England', in *The agrarian history of England and Wales, 1500–1640* (Cambridge, 1967), vol. iv.

61 *APC*, xxix, 639; *APC*, xxxii, 47–49.

62 *Cal. Carew MSS*, iii, 107, 'An anonymous discourse for Ireland, 1595'.

63 *CSPI* (1592–1596), 298–300, 309–314, 317.

64 *AFM*, vi, col. 1959.

65 *Ibid.*, 190, report of Lieutenant Tucher, 1 June 1595.

66 PRO SP12/178/90, Sir Henry Norris to Lord Burghley, 13 March 1595.

67 *Cal. Carew MSS*, iii, 127, 'Certificate of the horse, foot and kearne in her Majesty's pay in Ireland, 1595'.

68 *CSPI* (1592–1596), 441–450.
69 *Ibid.*, 363, 396, 402–406.
70 HMC, *Salisbury*, vi, 351–352, Sir William Russell to the queen, 28 August 1596.
71 *Cal. Carew MSS*, iii, 196–199, 'a declaration by the lord deputy'.
72 *Ibid.*, iii, 198.
73 PRO SP63/196, 38.
74 HMS, *Salisbury*, vi, 543–544, 'A list of her Majesties forces in Ireland', September 1596.
75 *Ibid.*, 402.
76 *CSPI* (1592–1596), 467, 468, 469; and for Wallop's projects, see BL Cotton MSS, Titus, C, vii, ff. 156–161.
77 *CSPI* (1592–1596), 325, 330, 371, 383, 390; for the invasion cares of 1596 and for the Spanish mission to O'Neill, *ibid.*, 406, 409, 518, 519, 526, 527, and *CSPI* (1596–1597), 50.
78 *CSPI* (1596–1597), 160s, 170s, 180s.
79 Lord Burgh lacks an entry in the *DNB*. He was a governor of the cautionary town of Brill, owed his appointment to Essex, was not in favour at court, and he had no previous experience of Ireland.
80 *APC* (1597), 24, 26, 27, 240–245, 388; *CSPI* (1596–1597), 371–373, 398, 399–401.
81 HMC, *Salisbury*, vi, 543–544, 'A list of her Majesties forces in Ireland', December 1596.
82 T. Birch, *Memoirs of the reign of Queen Elizabeth from the year 1581 till her death ...* (London, 1754), vol. i, 277.
83 G. A. Hayes-McCoy, 'Tudor conquest and counter-reformation, 1571–1603', in *A new history of Ireland, vol. iii, Early modern Ireland, 1534–1691*, eds T. W. Moody, F. X. Martin and F. J. Byrne (Oxford, 1976), 124.
84 *Calendar of state papers, domestic* (hereafter *CSPD*) (1595–1597), 383, 404.
85 *APC*, xxvii, 90.
86 *Ibid.*, 68, 69, 76.
87 *Ibid.*, 243, the privy council to Lord Burgh, 22 July 1597.
88 *Ibid.*
89 *Ibid.*
90 *Cal. Carew MSS*, iii, 266–268.
91 PRO SP63/97, 89, 91, 99, 39; *APC*, xxvii, 243.
92 *Cal. Carew MSS*, iii, 271–273.
93 The November and December levies 1598 from the Low Countries were for the Earl of Essex's forces in 1599.
94 PRO SP63/202, part i, 88.
95 *APC*, xxviii, 524, 527.
96 *Cal. Carew MSS*, iii, 280–281.
97 PRO SP63/202, part iv, 15.
98 *APC*, xxix, 312.
99 HMC, *Salisbury*, vii, 487, 488.
100 *Cal. Carew MSS*, iii, 287.
101 *CSPI* (1598–1599), vii, 305.
102 *APC*, xxix, 237, 312, 358, 388, 491, 547, 572.
103 Fynes Moryson, *Itinerary*, vol. ii, 222–229; *Cal. Carew MSS*, iii, 292–295, Essex's army.
104 *Cal. Carew MSS*, iii, 292–295, Essex's army.
105 *AFM*, iii, 2111.
106 Wallace T. MacCaffrey, *Elizabeth I: war and politics, 1588–1603* (Princeton, 1992), Chapter 21.
107 *Calendar of patent rolls, Ireland* (1862), ii, 564.
108 *Cal. Carew MSS*, iii, 356.
109 Fynes Moryson, *Itinerary*, vol. ii, 290–293.

110 G. A. Hayes-McCoy, in *A new history of Ireland, vol. iii, Early modern Ireland, 1534–1691*, eds T. W. Moody, F. X. Martin and F. J. Byrne (Oxford, 1976), 130.

111 Numbers of horse from the schedules in *APC*, xxviii, 588, 590; *APC*, xxix, 116–118; *APC*, xxx, 435, 440.

112 L. Boynton, *The Elizabethan militia* (London, 1967), 182.

113 J. J. N. McGurk, 'The clergy and the militia, 1580–1610', *History*, 60 (1975), 198–210.

114 *APC*, xxxi, 323.

115 G. A. Hayes-McCoy, *Irish battles* (London, 1969), *passim*.

116 Thomas Stafford, *Pacata Hibernia*, ed. S. O'Grady (Dublin, 1896), vol. i, 318.

117 *APC*, xxxii, 82, 83.

118 See Part II.

119 *APC*, xxxii, 241–242.

120 *Ibid.*, 222, 234, 249, 251, 266, 278–286.

121 *Ibid.*, 275–277, 278–286, gentry lists; J. H. Gleason, *The justices of the peace* (Oxford, 1969).

122 *APC*, xxxii, 405.

123 HMC, *Salisbury*, xi, 443, 454, 461, 468, 484.

124 Fynes Moryson, *Itinerary*, vol. iii, 10.

125 *CSPI* (1601–1603), 181, 182.

126 *Ibid.*

127 *Cal. Carew MSS*, iv, 164.

128 *CSPI* (1601–1603), 182.

129 Fynes Moryson, *Itinerary*, vol. ii, 385–389; and in vol. iii, 40–43.

130 *APC*, xxxii, 475–477.

131 *Cal. Carew MSS*, iv, 179–204, for a collection of English and Spanish eyewitness accounts.

132 *CSPI* (1601–1603), 261.

133 *Cal. Carew MSS*, iv, 223, 225, 235, 236, 265, 277, Sir G. Carew's fears of Spain.

134 *Ibid.*, 284.

135 *Calendar of state papers, Spanish* (1587–1603), 711–716.

136 P. O'Sullivan Beare, *Historia Catholicae Hibernia Compendium* (Lisbon, 1621), trans. (in part) by M. Byrne as *Ireland under Elizabeth* (Dublin, 1903), 153–156.

137 *CSPI* (1601–1603), 263, 360, 391, 488, 534.

138 *Ibid.*, 377–381.

139 *Remembrancia*, 845, the government promised to pay for the apparel and arms.

140 HMC, *Salisbury*, xii, 154, 196.

141 *Cal. Carew MSS*, iv, 293.

142 *Ibid.*, 306.

143 HMC, *Salisbury*, xii, 346.

144 *Ibid.*, 369.

145 *Ibid.*, 320.

146 *Cal. Carew MSS*, iv, 338.

147 *Ibid.*, 396–398.

148 N. Canny, 'The treaty of Mellifont and the re-organization of Ulster, 1603', *Irish Sword*, 9 (1969/1970), 249–262.

149 Wallace T. MacCaffrey, *Elizabeth I: war and politics, 1588–1603* (Princeton, 1992), 57.

CHAPTER FOUR

Military levies raised from Kent, 1594–1602

The shires of Kent and Lancashire and Cheshire (in the next chapter) have been studied in detail to find out how Kent, a shire remote from Ireland, was affected by the government's demands for the Irish war, in comparison with the maritime shires of Lancashire and Cheshire, proximate to Ireland. The differences and similarities of their abilities to meet the demands and their responses to them will illustrate how little the government was able to insist on demands for men, money, horses and supplies at a time when the state was beginning to make distinctions between soldiers and civilians, as the latter were no longer needed to train in the old militia systems except for local defence in emergency. The evidence from these three shires shows how military taxation impinged on all classes of society in the 1590s, when the state was becoming the greatest purchaser of food, arms, clothing and all manner of other martial equipment for men and horses, as well as the ships to supply them. The opportunities for entrepreneurial activity on the part of captains, conductors of troops and owners of ships multiplied and so too did the chances of corrupt dealings. The captains could enrich themselves at the expense of the state and of the troops as the government could exercise only a rudimentary supervision, especially of captains in Ireland. The centralising of men in garrisons meant that the government's muster master had more control over the captains, when he was allowed to carry out his duties. Corruption and chicanery were not confined to Ireland – it is found at every stage of raising troops and in the necessary taxation to have them sent to Ireland from the shires. The bad health of the levies sent, the trying nature of the Irish climate, the misconduct of the leaders, the corruptions in the musters, the lack of money to pay the men, the difficulties in the distribution of food and clothes when they arrived, the outrages committed by both English and Irish soldiers on the civilian populations as well as the general dearth in the 1590s exacerbated the nature of the war.

Unlike the men of Devon, prominent in Irish martial activity and colonisation, the men of Kent (and Kentish men) are but scantily noticed in this context. Kent as a maritime county was heavily recruited for the wars of the Low Countries and France in the post-Armada period. From 1595 until the queen's death Ireland was high on the government's agenda and considerably taxed the resources of the realm. Whereas in the early 1590s it was the northern shires and Wales that were drawn upon to provide men, horses, arms and armour for the Irish war, in the final phase of the reconquest levies were raised from all over the country as the government exercised extraordinary zeal to prevent a Spanish foothold, if not sovereignty, in Ireland.[1] Kent was a rich and populous shire. Although population figures are calculated guesses, Edward Hasted thought that 200,000, of whom 60,000 were able bodied men, roughly represented the Elizabethan Kentish population. W. K. Jordan reckoned a Kentish population in 1570 of about 140,000 and Peter Clark, the latest historian of the shire, calculated a population rise from about 85,000 in the year 1500 to about 130,000 a century later.[2]

On the basis of muster returns, not very reliable in themselves, we gain an impression of the martial strength of the shire: the 1577 muster returned 11,203 able-bodied men; the 1580 one, 12,131; and the year prior to the Armada that figure had hardly increased, at 12,694. These muster lists are the only indication we have of the manpower base of the county and suggest that between 12,000 and 15,000 men were nominally fit for the demands of war.

In the official correspondence of Sir John Leveson, principal deputy lieutenant to the Lords Cobham, is found a tabulation of all the men ordered to be levied in Kent from March 1591 until the coronation of King James in July 1603 for both the continental and Irish wars.[3] The aim seems to have been a complete survey of the demands for soldiers on Kent within and without the realm, for it mentions troops sent up to London 'to guard her Majesty at the execution of Essex' and a similar contingent raised to guard King James at his coronation. Among lieutenancy records it is an unusual checklist. Over the twelve-year period Kent's contribution was 1,353; 53 were light horse, 600 infantrymen directly for Ireland and 700 were raw recruits for the Low Countries so that an equivalent number of seasoned veterans could be sent to Ireland. Overall the war in Ireland made lesser demands on the shire of Kent than did the continental wars. This total of 1,353 Irish levies from a possible mustered manpower of about 15,000 represented a 9 per cent drain on the county's labour force. We must also recall that the years 1594–1597 were ones of high mortality rates from outbreaks of plague and of near famine following bad harvests, which affected the loss of manpower not only to military service but the labour force in general. Sir Thomas Scott of east Kent remarked that 'there be not now in the parts about here such store of men as heretofore'.[4]

To administer the raising and sending out of levies, Kent had a complex mixture of institutions, medieval survivals and new arrivals, such as the centralising institution of lieutenancy, but the actual business was still based on the ancient Kentish hundreds, grouped into the time-honoured six lathes of east and west Kent. By the final years of Elizabeth's reign the lathe was becoming a residual administrative base, having been overtaken by the new petty sessional districts for judicial and administrative purposes.[5] Likewise, the rise to importance of lieutenancy saw the virtual demise of the sheriff's traditional role but his traditional unit of jurisdiction, the lathe, continued to be used for military organisation under deputy lieutenants. In their latter capacity they made their assessments for military taxation on the subsidy books, which valued a man within his parish of residence. There were 413 parishes in the county. Gentry families often had the bulk of their incomes from outside their parishes of residence and many, like the Scotts, Levesons, Culpeppers, Sidneys and Cobhams, from outside the county of Kent.[6] We are not here concerned with the many corporate liberties with their complex exemptions and the relationship of the lieutenancy and military taxation to the Cinque Ports on the Kent coasts, since their contribution was traditionally that of providing ships to transport armies to the continent and to defend the realm.[7]

Throughout the period of heavy recruitment the lieutenancy of Kent was held by the Brooke family, William and Henry Brooke, tenth and eleventh Lords Cobham; it was their deputies who had military expertise and the more prominent in the period included Sir John Leveson, Sir Thomas Fane (the younger), Sir Thomas Walsingham, Sir Peter Manwood, Sir Thomas Scott of Scotts Hall and Sir Thomas Wilsford. The outstanding leader of this group was Sir John Leveson of Halling. The son of a metropolitan newcomer into Kent, he had married into the Manwoods and was neighbour and friend to the Cobhams as well as colleague on the bench with William Lambarde, the premier topographer and historian of the shire. He took a prominent part in the defence arrangements of the shire during the Armada crisis, served with Lord Willoughby in France, and throughout the 1590s served as the chief deputy lieutenant for the Lords Cobham. He was also responsible for averting the Essex rebellion in the City of London in 1601. It is remarkable that he did not earn an entry in the *Dictionary of national biography* whereas his cousin Sir Richard Leveson did.[8]

The Leveson papers are particularly detailed with regard to the raising, equipping and the sending out of military levies to Ireland and more comprehensive than like records in most other English shires; therefore a closer analysis is justified for Kent's arrangements than for the other shires to be hereafter considered.[9] The abundance of the evidence dictates a severely chronological approach for the sake of clarity. This apparent simplicity will put the spotlight on the military organisation of one shire and thereby substantiate the general picture given in the previous chapters of the national levies. There is also sufficient variation in the detail of each levy, as well as in the performance and results achieved, to make a recital of routine administration meaningful.

1595–1599

The government may have been mindful of the burden of former Kentish contributions to the wars in France and the Netherlands[10] when in the summer of 1595 the county was asked to send only six light horse when O'Neill's rebellion was under way.[11] That summer the county mustered its trained bands in the five lathal divisions of Sutton-at-Hone, Aylesford, St Augustine's, Scray and Shepway.[12] The government's request for six horsemen became administratively eccentric, a fact not lost on the county authorities – the lord lieutenant William, Lord Cobham, managed to have an abatement of one of the light horse.[13] One horse, one rider, one set of accoutrements and arms suitable for light cavalry were to be levied on each of the five ancient divisions of the shire. Doubts were cast by the justices of the peace as to whether the cost should be a common charge on the county or should be borne by those who traditionally kept horses, in other words, themselves.[14] The justices should have been well aware that provision of light horse for overseas warfare had come to be regarded by the government as the special provenance of the justices of the peace, the clergy and recusants of substance.[15]

The justices did not want the burden to fall on their own shoulders; they resolved their doubts at a meeting in the Star Inn, Maidstone, on 18 June 1595, where they agreed that for the setting forth of the five horsemen they would make a collection on the basis of the last subsidy from those rated at £10 in land and those at £15 in goods.[16] Did they not bear burdens as landowners over and above the services they rendered as justices? Did they not supply horses, equip, train and maintain them? And were they not further taxed to finance the infantry musters of the shire?[17] They agreed that £27 8s was sufficient to buy the horse, equip both horse and rider, and leave enough money to supply an allowance for the rider's purse to feed himself and his horse on the way to the port of Chester.[18] In the event Sir John Leveson, the principal deputy lieutenant and justice, found that it cost £31 8s to send his man, Hugh Southern, fully equipped to Chester. Inflation would not have come as a surprise to the Kentish justices, though war as a cause of inflation in the late sixteenth century does not appear to have been intensively studied by historians.[19]

From their experience in sending out troops to the continental wars, such local officials as Sir John Leveson, Sir Thomas Scott and Robert Bing were well versed in the routine ordinances 'for the raising, arminge, conductinge and transportinge of men' and of choosing 'a mete and sufficient person to take chardge of leadinge them to the porte',[20] and in those tasks, as Sir Peter Manwood complained of being subjected 'to the displeasures of our friends and enemies'.[21] In 1595 the council thought the levy of horse well performed and the lord lieutenant was congratulated on his county's efforts.[22] There were disputes about the liability to pay for the horses and great difficulties arose in finding suitable men to ride them. William Place, for instance, who had been invited to be one of the horsemen, excused himself: 'because of the late dangerous sickness I am fallen into an infirmity called the piles whereof I am scarce able to go much less sit upon a horse'.[23]

When the five horsemen reached Chester they were delayed, waiting for an easterly wind, so they had to petition Sir John Leveson for further means of sustenance, claiming they were becoming destitute at Chester.[24] They were but a small part of the 100 horse and 1,000 foot hourly expected by general Sir John Norris, who, with the lord deputy, William Russell, was preparing an expedition to Ulster.[25] But these reinforcements did not arrive in Ireland until late August 1595.

During the uneasy truce in Ireland with O'Neill in November 1595 both sides built up military strength, but Kent was not asked for forces in the recruitment for Ireland which went forward between February and September 1596. The one exception to this was that the clergy of the province of Canterbury were asked to furnish 300 horses and 285 foot;[26] the privy council's letter to Lord Cobham stated that the soldiers supplied by the clergy of Kent were not to be mixed with the forces of the county because they were to be 'used for her Majesty's special service' – a phrase which at this time meant the Irish service; but 'if any of the clergy cannot find sufficient men to their armour and furniture the lord lieutenant may choose some able men for the purpose'.[27]

The county was exempted from the national levy of over 1,000 men called to Ireland in October 1596, when nineteen shires contributed.[28] Kent's commitment to the sieges of Boulogne (May and September 1596) may well have been the cause of its exemption. There was mounting resentment in any case over the deployment of 2,000 of its trained bands for Calais in April 1596.

This deployment may explain why the privy council did not make any demand for the crises in Ireland from Kent in 1597.[29] In this year continental demands fell heavily on Kent: 300 soldiers had been armed and apparelled, and trained at the county's cost for the Earl of Essex at Calais in May at a charge of £1,200; 50 men had been sent into Picardy in July; and 400 had been levied, armed and sent to Dover for Ostend. Their impressment and conduct cost the county £100.

The lack of military demands for Ireland on Kent in these two years was the lull before the storm. O'Neill had been consolidating his position in Ireland and without speedy reinforcement the English military position in Ireland was on the verge of collapse. The Dublin council reported on 5 November 1597 that there was no part of Ulster 'that standeth for her Majesty'.[30] Lord Semple wrote that many English were fleeing to Galloway in Scotland, so strong was O'Neill in Ireland.[31] John Chamberlain wrote on 17 May 1598 to Dudley Carleton: 'Matters in Ireland grow daily worse and worse so that unless they have round and speedy succours all is like to go to wreck'.[32] And Lord Burghley reflected on 2 January 1598, shortly before his death, how profitable and convenient it would have been for the queen to make peace with Spain so that Ireland then could 'be reduced to quietness'.[33]

Lord Burghley did not live to see the nadir of English military fortunes in Ireland, O'Neill's victory at the Yellow Ford on 14 August 1598, which had encouraged every rebellious element in Ireland. That event spurred the government to order new levies of 1,500 men from nineteen shires, and of this total the shire of Kent was asked to contribute 100 men and four horse.[34]

The county's deputy lieutenants decided on a proportion of nineteen soldiers to be recruited from each of the five lathes, thereby allowing for the customary dead pays. The company was armed at the county's cost in the proportions of twenty-five pikes, fifty calivers and twenty muskets, but of the calivers only twenty were 'fully furnished with sword, dagger, touch-box, bullet-bagg, flask, match and mould'. Sir John Leveson reckoned the cost to each lathe at £25 15s 4d but considered that Scray (being the smallest) should contribute half that amount, at £12 17s 8d.[35]

In the directives of 26 August from the privy council on behalf of the queen, the reasons for the levy are stated: 'forasmuch as the necessities of our service in our Realm of Ireland doth require a further reinforcement of men to be sent thither by reason of a late accident fallen out there'.[36] The order to have the soldiers levied, mustered, furnished with coats, armour and weapons with all expedition is followed by what was becoming a customary complaint in the 1590s: 'And for that in former like levies there hath been so little regard had both to the personablenesse and abilities of bodies in the men, and to their furniture also that a very great part of them hath been found utterly insufficient to be used in the service of the wars'.[37]

Two days later, on 28 August 1598, the privy council wrote to Henry, Lord Cobham, elaborating on the former strictures, telling him that his deputies had taken up 'loose and idle people' to disburden the county of the unprofitable classes without any consideration for 'the advancement of her Majesty's service or regard of her direction'. Had not the queen told him that such levies were a hindrance to the service, a trouble to her subjects, and the men so levied a danger to their own lives? Did they not know that the result of such recruitment was desertion? These complaints were made by way of warning, for at that time the deputies and constables had not put the machinery of recruitment into action.[38]

In response Leveson sent out instructions to the constables who took up the men in the villages and parishes. He underlined that they had to be 'of able bodies and of convenient years' and warned his constables that before the men were brought to the general muster the justices themselves would see them. In former levies the making of a muster roll had been neglected. His instruction was that precautions 'be taken to write the names, surnames, out of what parish and division every soldier was taken'. This precaution also helped to trace the place of origin of 'such men as do run away'.[39]

The levy was ordered to be ready by 15 September 1598, which gave the country authorities two weeks to have the men rounded up and equipped. Further instructions, when their conductor to Chester had been appointed, were sent to Lord Cobham, who ordered that the justices themselves 'repair to the villages to see that good choice is made of sufficient men in the required numbers' and that *they* were to make up the muster roll, that 'this service is to be performed by them *not* by the constables'.[40]

An apparently innocent postscript to the council's letter, asking the county to 'forbear to be at the chardge to provide the coates', caused a furore of protest. The government had contracted two London merchants, Babington and Bromley (see Chapter 8), to supply coats for the entire national levy, and have the coats delivered to the captains at the ports of embarkation.[41] At this point the county would be charged for the coats: 'the county shall then not presently be charged until the apparel is made ready at the port and then only at the rate as you have previously done'.[42]

The protest to lord lieutenant Cobham against these arrangements and against the London merchants came from influential landowners: Sir Thomas Fludd of Milgate, surveyor general of the Kent fortifications, erstwhile paymaster of the forces sent to France with Lord Willoughby in 1589; Sir Nicholas Gilborne of Charing, scout master general at the time of the Armada; and Sir Thomas Walsingham of Scadbury, deputy lieutenant and member of parliament for Rochester in 1597 and 1601, and later for the county in 1614. Their protest was written a few days after they had received Lord Cobham's summary of the privy council's orders, and they used the controversy over the coats to launch a list of grievances, exposing not only jealous feeling against the London monopolist merchants, but also against their opposition to the burden of government demands. They wrote: 'we and others the gentlemen of these parts do greatly mislike that the coats for the hundred men set forth out of this country for Ireland are appointed to be provided by some of the merchants of London'. They rounded on the council that 'they had scarcely had two days respite to furnish and set forth our men and sometimes lesse,' that of late they had 'great charges to have arms and armour and furniture ready upon any sudden occasion,' and that they had provided good strong and well lined coats for the winter use of soldiers 'for which we have long since disbursed ready money,' in which no one had made gains, 'which happly will not so fall out in the merchants provision'; they wanted their own arrangements to stand.[43] The government's intention was to centralise the supply of army coats by contracts with merchants and aimed at cutting out the frauds of captains and others who wanted to get their hands on the troops' clothing allowance.[44] The justices in Kent regarded the arrangement as novel, and may have wished to protect local tailors.

The levy of the 100 foot and four horsemen was ready by 15 September.[45] They went as part of the national levies to Munster, disembarking at Waterford, Cork and Kinsale in early October.[46]

1599–1602

It was governmental practice to recruit armies from those shires nearest the theatres of warfare, and when possible to release veterans from the continent for the Irish war. Kent, nearer to the Low Countries and France than to Ireland, was heavily drawn upon in January 1599. When the order went out in January 1599 to draft 2,000 men from the Home Counties and London for the Low Countries, so that a like number of Low Country veterans could go towards building up the Earl of Essex's expedition to Ireland, the shire of Kent was asked to contribute 400 to that total, whereas the country's total to Ireland was but 600.[47]

Perhaps the queen was conscious of the strain on the manpower resources of counties surrounding London when she wrote to their lords lieutenant, 'wee would not burden our subjects with these greater forces wheneverof our princely love to them we have every been sparing'.[48] The privy council's letter to Cobham in Kent, with detailed instructions for levying, arming and clothing the 400, was almost apologetic in tone, but the councillors went on to liken the state of Ireland to a disease for which speedy and effectual remedy was immediately required.[49] This mild tone to the authorities in Kent was a direct contrast to a letter the previous year when the county was directly accused of evading public burdens when 'the chardges of these levies ought to be borne chearfullie and willinglie … and leavied ratable and in due proportion uppon all … of habilitye, as hold in that countie any landes or any dwelling places.'[50]

The recruitment of the 400 in Kent went ahead. From the indentures made between the captains and the deputy lieutenants on behalf of the crown we can see that the men were taken up from all over Kent to make four companies of 100. The recruits were brought to Margate and allowed 8*d* a day for four days as conduct money. Each company was divided into equal divisions of 'shot' and pike, but the 'shot' was by now traditionally subdivided into those armed with calivers and muskets.[51] Two captains were appointed for their conduct into the Low Countries: Edward Scott of the family of Scott's Hall, prominent in military and public affairs in the eastern half of the county,[52] and Peregrine Wingfield, who had previously accompanied his father, Sir John Wingfield, on Essex's Cadiz venture in 1596. Peregrine Wingfield was specially recommended by the Earl of Essex for this task.[53]

These men who went out from Kent to the Low Countries that winter of 1599 replaced 2,000 supposedly experienced troops from the garrisons of Sir Francis de

Vere in the Netherlands. Sir Henry Docwra was given the charge of leading these veterans to Ireland to reinforce the great army of the Earl of Essex.[54]

At the same time the shire of Kent was indirectly assisting 'the service of Ireland' by releasing veterans, the officers of the lieutenancy were engaged in implementing the privy council's order that they should also furnish twenty-five horse to be sent to Essex in Ireland under the leadership of Captain John Brooke.[55] Sir John Leveson acted as coordinating deputy for this service and took the responsibility of seeing that the horses, riders, their arms and armour were well provided.[56] Squabbles broke out over his assessments of the five lathes to fund the undertaking. Those of Sutton-at-Hone argued that the charges 'were more than our arranged proportions in former times', and that they had 'not gathered that whole some of 83 li, iiis. because many do refuse to pay their taxes'. Sampson Lennard and Thomas Scott wanted direction: 'what course we shall take with them that thus refuse?'[57] This was one indication that the country was war weary from the demands for men, money and arms.[58]

Leveson and his fellow justices of the peace, who were familiar with the subsidy books of the county, decided upon a tax of 2s 2d in the pound on the value of lands held by a landowner in his parish of residence. They calculated that each lathe should contribute £150 to the total of £750 – twenty-five horses and riders, each costing £30.[59] However, the extant receipts of monies collected from the five lathes tell a different story. St Augustine's and Scray contributed £76 2s 9d; Aylesford, £80 2s 8d; Shepway, £72 0s 0d; and Sir John Leveson's own lathe of Sutton-at-Hone, £83 3s 0d. These totals, here summarised from the receipts, came to half the sum required to finance the service.[60]

But no slackness was imputed to Sir John Leveson; his zeal, on the contrary, caused complaints from his fellow justices and landowners.[61] If we look, for instance, at the total assessment of £1,425 in lands for Aylesford, then at the suggested rate of 2s 2d in the pound, about £158 should have been collected rather than the sum of £80 2s 8d. The under-achievement to meet the military expenses may have been caused by many landowners dwelling elsewhere as absentees and by others under-assessing themselves in the subsidy; both tendencies helped the landowners avoid the full burdens of military taxation.

The details of how the deficit was made good are not clear; perhaps, as happened on other occasions, the arms store in the county was drawn upon as a supplement, though this course of action was as much officially discouraged as was the practice of taking out men from the trained bands for overseas service.

In January and February 1600 the county of Kent was called upon to levy and arm 100 infantry and to have them sent to Chester.[62] The normal channels in a line of communication from privy council to the constables in the shire went into action under the direction of Sir John Leveson. His notes, lists, accounts, receipts and miscellaneous correspondence for this particular levy bespeak efficient organisation.[63]

The indenture drawn up by Henry Hart, the conducting captain, shows that ninety men were drafted, thereby allowing for 10 per cent dead pays. The geographical spread of the places from which they were recruited shows that rarely were two or more taken from the same village, town or parish. The highest incidence of soldiers then recruited from any one place shown on Hart's indenture is three from each of the following: Gravesend, Canterbury, Dartford, Edenbridge and Benenden.[64]

Under Sir John Leveson's direction the deputy lieutenants drew up a schedule indicating how the levy was to be armed: forty of them were to carry calivers, twelve to have 'bastard muskets', twelve to carry muskets of the heavier variety, requiring rests, twenty to have the full equipment of the pikeman, and six were to be halberdiers. To provide arms and the customary armour associated with each soldier's characteristic weapon – pikemen were always 'furnished with corslets' for example – the shire had to collect sums of money amounting to £379 8s 4d.[65] This sum was to be collected across the lathal divisions of the shire in the following proportions. Each lathe was to provide £75 17s 9d with the exception of Sutton-at-Hone, which was Sir John Leveson's division and which was to provide £76 1s 0d – the extra 3s 3d was for his clerk's fees; the surplus of 3s 8d in the sums to be collected is an arithmetical error on the part of Sir John Leveson's clerk.

The items of clothing provided for each soldier are given in Sir John Leveson's clothing accounts, but the list was drawn up by the privy council, which had given much thought to the winter clothing of the troops in Ireland.[66] The lord lieutenant, Lord Cobham, forwarded the list to Leveson; the list is of interest in that the privy council had clearly been persuaded by commanders in Ireland to make use of Irish mantles and brogues, the issue of which the council had formerly forbidden.[67] The details of the winter apparel of a levied soldier, which follow, have also been found for other Irish levies, for example from Derbyshire and Lancashire, which in turn suggests a standardisation by the year 1600 for each soldier, namely: a canvas doublet, a pair of broadcloth trousers, two shirts and two bands; a pair of shoes and two pairs of brogues, a pair of kersey stockings or two pairs of Irish frieze stockings; and a very long cassock of broadcloth or an Irish mantle.

Henry Hart took the men to Chester. His receipts came to £53 6s 8d. He left Dartford with his company on 11 February 1600 but did not arrive at Chester until 1 March. For his own entertainment Hart was allowed £4 16s.[68] The Kentish levy brought with it six targets, purchased in Kent at the rate of 30s 0d each,[69] and delivered by Hart to Sir Henry Docwra in Chester.[70]

The queen was troubled with the burden laid on the nation at large because of the Irish war, and wrote that this bothered her more than 'our infinite expenses there'; nevertheless, because Lord Mountjoy had made a good beginning that summer, 'the issue must be good, if the army there be reinforced for a few months' for O'Neill (called a monster of traitorous ingratitude) 'threatens the very safety and peace of England'.[71]

After the preamble of the queen's letter to the shires aiming to set out the reasons for the demands that inevitably followed from the privy council, the call went out to twenty-seven shires to draft the first levy of 2,000; of that number the county of Kent was asked to recruit fifty infantrymen.[72] Chester again was the port for the whole levy; they were to be there by 25 July 1600, that is to say, within a month of the original order. The urgency of this levy is reflected in the expeditious way in which the county authorities in Kent recruited and had the men sent under the conduct of Captain Edward Trevor to Chester. The entire exercise proved efficient owing largely to the work of the conducting captain. The Leveson papers once again are particularly informative on the levy.[73]

There was no delay in having the orders sent to the deputy lieutenants, Sir John Leveson, Sir Thomas Walsingham and Sir Peter Manwood.[74] The queen had informed the privy council on 25 June 1600,[75] the privy council wrote to Henry, Lord Cobham, on 26 June, and he had copies made and sent with his covering letter at five o'clock in the morning of 27 June.[76] Sir Richard Trevor and Sir John Trevor had already sent their letters strongly recommending Captain Edward Trevor to conduct the fifty from Kent together with the fifty from Sussex to Chester.[77] The manner in which he carried out his duties justified his relatives' recommendations. He arrived with his contingent four days earlier than required and, what is more remarkable, with all fifty from Kent. Although one, Gascome from Maidstone,[78] ran away, Trevor got another man in his stead and 'furnished' him at his own expense.[79] Lord Cobham received a letter of special commendation on behalf of the queen for 'The extraordinary regard and forward endeavours' of the officers of lieutenancy – captains, justices and constables.[80] Such is the barest outline of the welter of evidence for this particular levy from Kent; it is now necessary to take a closer look at its organisation.

From the government's angle the two most important aspects of any such piece of military service lay in the choice of reliable and fit fighting men, and the selection of an honest and competent captain to lead them. In this instance, since only one ran away and since Edward Trevor's work was lauded from all sides, the levy was carried out in an orderly and satisfactory manner.

The fifty soldiers were taken from every part of the shire and, as in Henry Hart's previous indenture, it may be seen that not more than three came from any town, village or parish. Two parts of the indenture survive: one with Trevor's signature, the other signed by Sir John Leveson and Sir Thomas Walsingham.[81] The proportion of firearms to pikes was the same as in Henry Hart's company, and because Trevor's numbers were half those of Hart, he had twenty with calivers, six with heavy muskets, six with light muskets, twelve pikemen and six billmen armed like the pikemen. Apart from the calivers all carried 'close hilted swordes and daggers'.[82] In earlier levies there had been in Kent 'verie ill choice' of swords and daggers, so apart from his specific weapon of pike, musket, bill or caliver, each infantryman was given a sword of 'good Turkey blade and of good close hilt', hence the emphasis here on this item. To the chagrin of those in Kent who had formerly supplied the army coats, the order went to the London merchants Babington and Bromley; but on this occasion the queen's allowance to the county for coat money was 8*s* per coat, so that in fact the county had to find less than half the cost, since in the 1590s the army coat cost about fifteen shillings. All the financial papers, even petty accounts from the hundreds, make the point that they did not include any allowance for conduct money 'because this county is not charged with any'.[83]

Sir John Leveson drew up the rates for buying the arms; at first his schedule was intended for west Kent but he persuaded Sir Peter Manwood to adopt the same rates for east Kent.[84] The schedule indicated that each pikeman's arm: and armour would cost 30*s* and the same for each billman and musketeer but 20*s* for the caliverman.[85]

These charges for buying arms were higher than the county had formerly experienced and Sir John Leveson thought fit to explain to the privy council the increases by noting that halberds or bills cost 6s 8d each and that the 'close hilted swordes and daggers cost iiijd the peece above the rate they have been accustomed'. Trevor also calculated that to hire carts to carry the arms to Chester would cost 6s 8d a day for thirty days 'to goe and com' but he hoped that the hire of carts would not be charged to the county.[86] This was so much hot air, because Captain Edward Trevor may not have been totally altruistic about saving the energies of his men or the county of Kent additional charges, for he was aware that his influential uncle, Sir Richard Trevor, was then one of the commissioners of musters appointed to view the men and arms when they arrived in Chester.[87]

The financial accounts for this levy were hastily compiled. They are complicated in that east and west Kent accounted separately, Leveson for the west and Manwood for the east. They show the total cost of the levy was £191 4s 0d, arrived at from the expenditure of £63 4s 0d on arms, £100 on coats, conduct money at 8d a day for fifteen days (£25) and an allowance of 4s 0d a day to Edward Trevor for his own conduct and entertainment. But in the accounts cast up for Trevor a total of £156 4s 0d is shown, arrived at in the following manner: £131 0s 0d for coat and conduct money, less £38 0s 0d on account of the government's allowance, leaving him £93 0s 0d, to which was added £63 4s 0d for arms. This last item is not specifically stated but assumed from the total of £156 4s 0d. There appears to be no record that Trevor disbursed £63 4s 0d at Chester for arms or that he did not.[88]

It would appear that there was some knavery and it should most likely be laid at Sir John Leveson's door. Two indications support this. The fact that the soldiers' clothing allowance was subsidised by the government's 8s 0d each for the coats is not made abundantly clear in his accounts, and in Sir Peter Manwood's accounts the 8s 0d is written as 4s 0d.[89] Furthermore, conduct money at 8d a day for fifteen days also appears in Leveson's accounts whereas the county was let off this expense in the privy council's directives.[90] It cannot, however, be proved that both deputies collected taxes from the county to raise money towards which the government had already provided an allowance.

In sharing the cost between east and west Kent there was a difference of opinion between Leveson and Manwood over the latter's claim that he had extra expense in hiring a barge 'to carry the soldiers from Gravesend to Blackwall'.[91] However, in his final set of accounts Sir John Leveson spread the 15s 0d in question across the five lathes so that each paid an extra 3s 0d to cover the hire of the barge. Sir Peter Manwood remained dissatisfied for he did not agree that Sir John Leveson paid one-half for the west part of Kent.[92] Rightly, he showed that he paid for arms £35 9s 5d, which was more than half the total. Perhaps this difference of opinion was another manifestation of the traditional rivalry between the 'two Kents' – east and west; Sir John Leveson frequently used the expression 'us of the west'; and when Kentish men spoke of 'the west' they were understood to mean west Kent.[93]

The usual beneficiaries of fraud in coat money were either the suppliers who sold short, or the captains, who were outbidding the clothiers in defrauding the crown and thereby depriving their own men.[94] A case was brought forward in Kent in 1618 which throws unfavourable light on the actions of the deputy lieutenants. An enquiry then was opened up by Sir Robert Brett, Sir James Semple and Thomas Hetley into charges that the deputies in Kent had fraudulently converted to their own use coat and conduct money paid out by the crown amounting to nearly £1,000 between the years 1592 and 1602.[95] Those named were Sir John Leveson, Sir Thomas Scott, Sir Thomas Sondes and Sir Thomas Wilford, by then all deceased. Their heirs and executors fought the case. The instigators of the enquiry were granted letters patent by King James to benefit from all such sums that had been wrongfully converted. The heirs petitioned the privy council showing that the patentees were ignorant of the past services of the deceased and since they expected to profit from the enquiry they were 'partial judges and unfit to censure the proofs and accounts'. Had they not also damaged the good reputation of these men and their heirs?[96] The privy council stopped the suit. The case was unusual as such frauds, common among captains, conductors of troops and merchants, were rare among deputy lieutenants, who often had more than a local importance.[97] If Sir John Leveson was guilty at this time then the remark of Captain Edward Trevor that he desired to conduct these men 'not out of any gain to be made by the exchange of men or by abusing the allowances' must have rang ironically in Leveson's ears.[98]

The private ambitions and differences of opinion between the deputies in Kent, and their possible frauds, may all have been momentarily forgotten in the glow of a private letter of thanks and commendation from the privy councillors on behalf of the queen addressed on 21 August 1600 to Lord Cobham and his deputies. Cobham's clerk, probably at his direction, underlined the more unctuous phrases and had the letter circulated.[99]

Captain Edward Trevor crossed with the levies to Ireland in August 1600 and saw action with Lord Mountjoy at the Moyry Pass – hills and woods between Dundalk and Newry – in the campaign of 25 September to 10 October.[100] One dispatch mentions 'Captain Trevor shot',[101] clearly not mortally, for he was again mentioned in the army lists of January 1603 as captain of a company of 100 foot in an unnamed garrison in Ulster.[102]

During the summer months of 1600 the government was determined to give as much help as possible to Lord Mountjoy in Ireland. Apart from the infantry levies there was a call on the gentry – individually named – of every English shire, and selected from those worth £20 a year in land, leases or fees, or at £100 value in goods, each to furnish a light horse.[103] The privy council's minute of 29 June to the named knights and gentlemen is specific:

> We do therefore hereby let you understand that her Majesty's pleasure is to require of you one light horse well furnished with a cuirass, a light horseman's staff of a good and sufficient length, one pistol, and especially a good sword, and withall a fit and able man to serve on the same.[104]

The cavalry levy was to be at Chester by 25 July. The privy council added, somewhat hopefully, that the gentry were in effect *lending* both man and horse for the queen's service, 'because it is intended at the ende of this action … both the one and the other

(God willing) shalbe returned unto you'.[105] The government's intentions are made clear in Sir Robert Cecil's notes:

> this is not meant to be an imposition but a tryall of men's affections; make a declaraccion of the cause, the use, and the good that is lyke to follow by applying a thorough remedy ... to recover a kingdome so neere loosing.

He even gave thought to which kinds of men should be approached, noting: 'the Cornmen are of the best ability,' and in the margin, 'Mawlt men, Sheep men, and grasiers'. The clerk refers to the war in Ireland as 'the breaking out of *civil* war in Ireland in Queen Elizabeth's reign'.[106]

The order was addressed countrywide to 183 named gentry of whom nineteen, the highest number, were Kentish gentry. These nineteen were selected from those who could have met the government's assessment of wealth.[107] Four knights head the list – Sir Moyle Finch, Sir Henry Cutts, Sir Michael Sondes and Sir John Roper; all nineteen names appear on a similar list of gentry providing light horse in 1595, or contributing to a levy of cavalry in that year.[108] But when a further 'tryall of men's affections' was made of the English gentry at the time of the Spanish landing in Ireland in October 1601, the Kentish gentry appear to have been exempt.

From a litany of the county's military expenditure we can see that this levy cost each one £30, a total of £570.[109] At Chester the commissioners found defects, and because of their delay in sailing and troubles made by their conductor, Captain Lisle, 'stirring the Kentish men to stand upon terms not much different from mutiny,' embarkation for Ulster did not take place until 19 August 1600.[110]

After the summer of 1600 no more were called for until April 1601, but only for three light horse, or petronels, so called from their characteristically dominant weapon, the long pistol. This was Kent's contribution to a national levy of 1,000 foot and 40 horse, intended for Sir Henry Docwra's garrison at Lough Foyle.[111] The queen's letter to Henry, Lord Cobham, pointed out there had been of late 'so many successes in all our prosecutions of those rebells ... [that] there must needes follow a speedie conclusion of that unnatural rebellion'. Reluctant to put the people to charges, the queen asked for a levy of three horse, advised the lord lieutenant 'to lay the charges upon the better sorte', and 'to make choice of good men', because defective levies only caused a renewal of the charges to both crown and country.[112]

Precise instructions followed from the privy council;[113] Lord Cobham had copies of both letters made and added his own letter to stress pertinent phrases of the queen's and council's letters for the benefit of his deputies. He asked for a list of names of suitable persons to meet the charge, which may indicate that he was not as conversant with 'the men of substance' in his lieutenancy as his father, William, Lord Cobham, had been.[114]

Service conditions in Ireland had a bad reputation. Perhaps to counter this reputation these official letters took pains to point out that the garrisons planted 'where the Archetraytor most usurpeth' were thoroughly accommodated with good lodgings and victuals, and had everything necessary for the subsistence of the army.[115] The privy council echoed the queen's comforting but hollow phrases to the lord lieutenants of the shires: 'in regard of her Majesty's dear affection to all that are exposed to peril for her and their country, she hath not spared for any charge how great soever the same hath been to her coffers'.[116]

Stress was placed on the quality of riders; they were to be well exercised horsemen, and therefore special choice should be made of *northern* men, 'because they are best skilled both to serve on horseback and do also know best how to use their horses well'.[117] The remark must have caused some ill feeling in Kent, Essex, Hampshire, Suffolk and Lincolnshire, which were also contributing to the cavalry.

The horsemen were to be armed 'with curattes, murryons, horsemen's staves and long pistols, Turkey swords with basket hilts and horsemen's coats'.[118] All were to be ready for embarkation at Chester by 20 May 1601, where ships had already been provided by the mayor for their transport to Lough Foyle.[119]

From Leveson's papers we can see how these directives were carried out, but whether or not he procured northern men to ride the horses is not mentioned. At the inspection of the three horses, one of them was returned as 'insufficient' but was speedily replaced 'for the bringinge of hym at the bolt', costing an extra 2s 0d.[120] The justices of the peace shared the cost of the operation at a total of £66 13s 4d, which was cheap when it is recalled that Sir John Leveson had sent out a horse to Ireland in 1595 at a cost of £31 8s 0d.[121] In this levy of three light horse, the accounts on the other hand show a low figure for the three horses themselves, 'for three trottinge geldinges, £30'. Other items of expenditure included:

> three saddles of buff with bit and stirrups – £3. 0s. 11d.; three longe french pistols – £3. 4s. 0d.; three coats of Kentish broadcloth lined through with white stayls and tricord with white lace and with white buttons – £6. 7s. 0d.; three suits of apparel, three hats, three pair of boots, three swords, and three hangers – £10. 0s. 0d.[122]

The carriage of their arms to Chester cost £102 0s 3d. Each rider was given 4s 0d a day for ten days' conduct money to feed himself and his horse. The records are silent on the names of the riders, their transport from Chester, or their arrival at Lough Foyle in Ulster, their intended destination.[123]

Before the year 1601 was out, the Spanish landing at Kinsale on 21 September drove the government to demand more men, horses, money and arms for Ireland; Kent did not escape. At first, on 6 October, 100 infantry were demanded, but this was almost immediately increased to 200 on 7 October.[124] They were to be assembled at Rochester and there join the national levy of 2,000 for shipping to Munster. Both exercises impinged on the resources of the county; Leveson became responsible for the levy within the county and for the arrangements at Rochester.[125]

From Leveson's correspondence it is plain that the levy of 200 was to be equally recruited from east and west Kent. In west Kent Aylesford was to recruit forty men; Sutton-at-Hone likewise was to provide forty; and the four hundreds of the lathe of Scray in west Kent, Milton, Tenham, Boughton and Faversham, were to provide five men each. From east Kent the lathes of St Augustine and Shepway were ordered to recruit forty men each, while the seven hundreds of Scray that lay within east Kent were to provide twenty men. In other words, the overall distribution of recruitment was simply that of forty men from each of the five lathes of Kent.[126]

Nevertheless, the proportion of pikes or 'corselets' to firearms or 'shot' differed between the recruits of east and west Kent: the west Kent recruits consisted of twenty-two corselets, eighteen calivers, forty muskets and twenty bills, while those from the eastern half of the shire comprised twenty-four corselets, forty calivers, twenty-four muskets and twelve bills. As firearms, such as muskets and calivers, were more expensive to supply, the total cost for east Kent came to £109 12s 0d, while the cost for the western part of the shire was £98 0s 0d, a total for the shire as a whole of £207 12s 0d, an average of a little over £1 for each soldier's arms.[127] Edmund Nicholson, a London arms supplier, had won the government's contract to fit out the entire levy of 2,000 men.[128] Leveson bought 180 swords of Turkish blades with basket-type hilts at 9s 8d each from Nicholson, and for other items of arms and armour he paid out a total of £103 12s 10d.[129] Other items included musket rests at 6d each, bandoliers and scabbards. The 200 suits of apparel cost £400, towards which the crown paid a 4s 0d allowance for the coats. Conduct money of 8d a day was provided for each soldier's march to Rochester, the overall cost coming to £53 6s 8d. The port was local and recruits from Shepway and St Augustine's were given a day to get to Rochester.[130] The conductors were Captains Blundell and Dodington and the Kentish levy of 200 (with 100 from Sussex) boarded the *Warspite* and set sail for Munster on 27 October 1601.[131]

Accounts for the levy to Rochester balance despite eccentric arithmetic, lack of doubly-entry bookkeeping, and the inconsistent use of Arabic and roman numerals. Such features serve to remind us of the essential amateurism in the execution of the many tasks of the Elizabethan justice and deputy lieutenant. A total of £620 had to be raised in the county to equip and send the levy.[132] In the normal method of financing a local levy, the justices worked out a rate of tax depending on abilities to pay and the severity of the demand for troops. The justices used the subsidy books, usually in their possession in the county, to decide who should pay and what amounts. In July 1594 the Kentish justices agreed on a rate of 3d in the pound on lands and 2d in the pound on goods on all in the subsidy books to raise money to have 250 soldiers sent to Brittany; the exact sum raised is unknown.[133] Likewise, in May 1596 the subsidy books were used to raise £89 3s 1d in taxes by charging all in the books 8d in the pound on their lands and 5d in the pound on their goods.[134] In the instance of the 1601 levy of 200 men to Rochester, the crown's financial contribution of £53 6s 8d represented about 9 per cent of the total of £620. Leveson's accounts do not say how the balance was raised in the county, but it is clear from two separate lists of identical names from the hundred of Eyhorne in the east division of Aylesford, one a list of subsidy assessments, the other a list of payments, that the information provided by the subsidy books was used to calculate a military tax.[135]

One indication that the tax was not considered equitable came from Scray, where the inhabitants resented bearing an equal share of the expenses because, they claimed, many of their lands lay in the less productive hundreds of the Weald of Kent, and they considered themselves poorer than the men of St Augustine's or of Sutton-at-Hone. Thomas Roberts of Glassenbury, one of their spokesmen, doubted if he could arm his recruits except out of the equipment of the trained bands, which, he asserted, 'will breed double mischief'.[136] Michael Sondes, a justice of the peace, also complained about the inequitable distribution of the recruits to be raised, and therefore of the unequal costs the quota would put on his area, the lathe of Scray.[137]

The last Elizabethan levies to leave Kent for Ireland were part of the national effort to wipe out pockets of resistance after the victory at Kinsale. Some in Kent, and elsewhere, may have wondered why there was need for a further call-up of 100 infantrymen in Kent in January 1602, and an additional fifty by July of the same year. The preambles to signet letters and privy council directives spelt out the necessity for these forces, even after so much had been achieved in Ireland. Leveson's records show how the chain of command went into action. The queen's signet letter, the privy council's directives and the more detailed instructions of the lord lieutenant, Henry, Lord Cobham, were all copied out by Leveson's clerk for the benefit of the deputy lieutenants.[138] This was normal procedure, but there are features which were not typical of earlier levies.

In the first place the queen's letter to Cobham is at great pains to let him know, and through him the entire local administration of the county, that the government was conscious of all the recent demands and was therefore making a generous gesture by freeing the shire 'from the charge of the arms and apparel as heretofore were directed to be paid for in the former levies shalbe now paid at our own charge'.[139] The county had to raise able-bodied men under a conductor to march them to Greenwich by 17 January, thence to sail to Southampton to join the rest of the troops by 26 January. The conductor's wages and the company's conduct money would be reimbursed to the county of Kent from the exchequer when the certificate was presented.[140]

The concession in the costs was doubtless pleasing to the county's authorities, but not the way the government proposed to give them – they asked that the whole levy be taken from the trained bands of the shire, a course of action the government had always forbidden. Hostility became great and was led by the lord lieutenant.[141] Was not such a procedure formerly condemned as unacceptable and reprehensible? Would it not lead directly to the 'decay' of the trained bands? Would it not deplete the county's store of arms, armour and all kinds of 'war-like furnitures'? Formerly an occasional few trained men were sent with drafts of raw recruits; now the government wanted to send out a completely equipped trained band. The county authorities had never liked the expedient of sending out even a handful of their trained men because the gaps so created in the bands had to be filled with 'men of like sufficiencie for the service'.[142] But no matter how strongly their arguments were put, the government unequivocally stated its demand:

> And because we have ben informed of late that the trained bands are both more sufficiently provided and abler of bodies than these untrained men ... we do hereby command you to levy this said number out of those trained bands.[143]

What may have given the government the idea was a full mobilisation of the trained bands the previous May. The government's muster master, Thomas Wyatt, had reported the military potential of the county and showed that it could well afford to have 100 trained men taken out for Ireland.[144]

Of nearly 4,000 men in the Kentish militia, over half were armed – 678 muskets, 628 calivers and 897 pikes.[145] But the demand to have 100 of them taken out of the shire for Ireland went against every local loyalty. Lord Cobham instructed his deputies on 8 January 1602 to use every possible means to avoid raiding the trained bands. He did not say why he was countermanding the government's order, other than that the trained bands 'be spared for divers greater considerations' and he trusted that his deputies would 'finde just as able-bodied and as serviceable men throughout the shire' because the total required was not that great.[146]

The outcome of this resistance is uncertain but it seems likely that the privy council's original order to have trained militiamen was disobeyed by the county's military administrators. Captain Thomas Stock, chosen as the conductor of the levy, listed seventy-five men on his muster roll, none of whose names appear on the county's muster roll of trained men in May 1601.[147] Stock's indenture, drawn up at Greenwich on 19 January, contains twenty names from each of the lathes of Aylesford, St Augustine's and Sutton-at-Hone, ten from Shepway and five from Scray. He was paid £10 conduct money to march his men to Greenwich and from there he put in a request for a further £28 5s 4d to conduct his levy to Southampton to join the rest of the forces going to Ireland.[148] But the weight of evidence suggests that his levy was discharged at Greenwich;[149] one item in the Leveson papers suggests that only twenty were 'staid' at Greenwich, which could mean that twenty men were rejected at the muster as unsuitable.[150]

By early summer 1602, Lord Mountjoy and other commanders in Ireland needed fresh men; the Spanish had landed munitions in May, while in Ulster Sir Henry Docwra wanted additional forces for Ballyshannon.[151] To meet these needs 2,000 were demanded of the English and Welsh shires, in what proved to be the last major levy of the reign. John Chamberlain gave a vivid description of how the levy was raised. Writing to Dudley Carleton on 8 May 1602, he said:

> we are sending 3000 men [*sic*] thither [to Ireland] which are levenying in the west and north country. Sir Francis Vere's voluntaries come not in so fast but that we are faine to come to a press of 1,000 men out of the neighbour shires and 2000 out of this town which is so disorderly performed by taking, and as it were, sweeping and carrying them violently to the ships that it is a general grievance and scandal at home and a great dishonour to be heard of abroad.[152]

Half were intended for the northern Irish garrisons of Carrickfergus and Ballyshannon, and the rest for other Ulster garrisons or for the lord deputy in the field. Kent was asked to supply fifty infantrymen. Unlike the January orders there was no mention in the queen's signet letter of 28 July 1602 that the government would pay for their arms and apparel, or that the men be taken from the trained bands.[153] Cobham ordered taxes to be collected to cover each soldier's expenses, estimated at £3 10s, a total cost of £175. The county was to pay all the expenses because 'the queen had of late a large financial burden in sending out the fleet to the coast of Spain'.[154] The men were to have 'able and serviceable bodyes'; 'only the ill-disposed could imagine that any cause could have moved Us to hazard our people's lives ... if we coulde prevent the peril of that State and Crown of Ireland by any other means'.[155]

Cobham's letters went out to the deputies at midnight 30 July and the men were to be equipped and marched to Bristol by 15 August.[156] Captain Thomas Stock was again chosen to conduct the hurriedly raised levy. His correspondence indicates that the men assembled at Dartford Heath on 8 August, which left only seven days to get to Bristol where 800 other soldiers were to sail for Dublin.[157]

The levies and the manpower resources of Kent

By treating in detail each levy sent out of Kent to Ireland between the years 1595 and 1602 we may see how government demands regularly impinged on the manpower resources of one shire to meet the main crises in Ireland: namely, the outbreak of the rebellion in 1595, the English losses sustained at the Yellow Ford in 1598, Essex's army of 1599, the Spanish landing at Kinsale of 1601 and the final campaigns to defeat O'Neill and O'Donnell in their homelands of Ulster in 1602. For in each crisis Kent made a contribution; its largest provision for the Irish war was in October 1601 of 200 for the army of 2,000 which was organised for shipping at Rochester.

By chronicling the military pressures in detail we get an impression of the relentless regularity of these demands, which by the late 1590s began to give rise to a host of grievances and to raise a number of questions, not least that of what had been gained by the wars – to many in Kent very little but hardships and a dire increase of taxation. It is often said that these taxes were passed down to those who could least afford to pay them but this oft-repeated allegation is difficult to prove. Disorder was averted after 1600 by the crown assuming part of the payments for equipping troops for overseas service. Economic historians have been keen to point to the credit and debit sides of warfare and to show that the financial strains were less significant than the general context of harvest failures, outbreaks of plague, and decline in domestic consumption, which were responsible for a severe economic slump in the last decade of the century. The total charge of military preparations borne by Kent between 1585 and 1603 was likely in excess of £10,000; while some of that revolved within the county's economy, it is difficult to believe that the government funds coming into Kent offset the outflow invested in the military expeditions. Most of the Home Counties had a similar experience. Rising military costs were partly a result of the major revolution taking place in arms, armour and fortifications which occurred in the period.[158]

The war was a considerable drain on Kentish manpower; many of those drafted into the expeditionary forces were vagrants and masterless men whose return to the county was not expected. Some died abroad but the majority returned maimed or diseased, or as deserters and poverty stricken. There is plenty of evidence to support the picture of the town suburbs and villages being infested with such soldiery raiding houses and terrifying the populace.[159] The deserting or returning soldier was common among the travelling poor of the shire and the frequent appearance of the recruiting officer often sent him into flight. Parish relief could not cope with the landslide into poverty of the 1590s and many worthies feared that any kind of large-scale relief in their parishes would attract the vagrant poor in their droves, who might prove difficult to send back to their own villages, parishes or towns. Despite the 1598 legislation which ordered neighbouring parishes to assist poorer communities, the practice was far from usual. The normal official agencies to help the statutory poor were inadequate to meet the scale of the problem in the 1590s but there was much private almsgiving, many charities and some public food provisioning at work alongside statutory poor relief.[160]

Apart from the poor, the vulnerable sectors of society were the small gentlemen farmers, the husbandmen and substantial craftsmen. None of the landowning class appear to have suffered any hunger pangs in the 1590s crises but neither were they totally immune – Henry, Lord Cobham, for example, had major financial difficulties in the 1590s though the economic crisis and royal demands were not the sole causes of his troubles.[161] And his leading political opponents, the Sidneys, were also heavily in debt by the time of the queen's death. But in the special pleadings which ever accompanied tax returns we also find that the middling gentry alleged considerable debts, such as the Scotts, the Willoughbys, the Wallers and the Lovelaces. According to P. Clark, many lesser gentry and the yeomanry were ruined by the crises of the 1590s.[162]

The local evidence also serves to illustrate the uniform system of raising troops for foreign war by means of the officers of the lieutenancy. Sir John Leveson proved to be the most energetic and efficient of the Kentish deputies. The chief conductors of the troops out of Kent, Henry Hart, Edward Trevor and Thomas Stock, seem to have been above reproach in their work, but the other military administrators, including deputy lieutenants, do not always appear to have been entirely honest in their financial management. Both halves of the shire shared the burden of recruiting the levies in equal proportions, but not without resentment and complaint from the inhabitants of Scray. Resistance to the use of trained bands for the Irish service was normal but the quality of troops raised appears to have been good. There were few deserters from Kent, for example, in comparison with recruits from north Wales. Captain Lisle, who accompanied troops from Chester to Ireland, thought well of the Kentish recruits, saying that 'except he might have Kentish men he would not conduct the supplies'.[163]

War weariness in Kent

Government demands for men, money and arms for the Irish war in Kent, as elsewhere, helped to bring about disillusionment with the Elizabethan regime. 'England,' one historian commented, 'generally grew weary of an old woman's government'.[164] By the beginning of the new century it was becoming increasingly difficult to raise levies as the government sensed and feared a hostile attitude. And though the government had reiterated that the rich bore the brunt of military taxes, it seems clear that many of the rich gentry escaped some of these burdens.[165] For instance, in 1597 defaulters 'included many of the principal men in the county of Kent'[166] – some alleging financial embarrassment, others claiming incorrect assessments, and some that the letters for loans had been addressed to the wrong people. Leveson wrote in 1601 of the discontent in the minds of some heavily charged that 'it has given us more experience of dislike than since our first acquaintance with the service of the county'.[167] In 1602 fifty-five persons in Kent were noted for their failure to pay ship-money tax, and a similar number for refusals to pay gunpowder tax.[168]

The grumbles of the Kentish gentry about the burden of official duties in levying men and money, billeting soldiers, in supervising the collections of the subsidies and purveyances, and in the frequent meetings of quarter and special sessions of the peace are much in evidence in Leveson's correspondence. Sir Peter Manwood, justice of the peace and deputy lieutenant, spoke for others in his position when he said, 'we stand upon slippery ground, subject to all men's censures and open to the displeasure of our friends and enemies'.[169] Military administration was only one burden. All who served as deputies in Kent during the years of war with Ireland were also justices of the peace, and as such their tasks multiplied in the 1590s.[170] By relying on men such as Leveson, Scott, Walsingham, Manwood, Lambarde and Fludd to carry out the duties of implementing government orders the Elizabethan regime enjoyed a cheap and reasonably efficient local government.

There were many in Kent, well provided with lands and houses, who managed to avoid all charge for the queen's service, so that an unjust burden was placed on those least able to bear it.[171] The chief offenders in this respect were 'citizens' of London, in other words, those Kentish landowners who had London residences and who managed to escape assessments on all or some of their property by means of this dual residence. The Lords Cobham maintained a London house at Blackfriars and Leveson one at Aldersgate.[172] Servants of great noblemen, by reason of their traditional exemption from taxes, also came under government censure: 'who by pretence of their service free themselves from the burden'. The lord lieutenant was instructed to exempt none, to rate all lands and houses in due proportion, to take bonds of those refusing, and to have them 'answer the same before the council board'.[173]

On their part, the county's gentry complained of the high price they had to pay for the queen's service. Thomas Scott the Younger blamed his debts in 1597 on his father's zeal for the royal service;[174] Michael Sondes protested to Leveson that if his services 'deserve not ordinary favour then I must hereafter more carefully look that my employments in her Majesty's service ... breed me less expenses',[175] and Sir Thomas Wilsford complained that because of his duties in the county he had lost £500 by not pursuing his legal practice in the Westminster courts.[176] Leveson, the recipient of so many complaints, did not complain about heavy financial exactions in the royal service, but he did cavil at times on account of the 'continual writing, postings of necessaries and toil'.[177]

Refusals to pay local and county taxes were among the more common offences at the Kent quarter sessions in the last years of the reign.[178] The Leveson papers suggest that rural opposition to royal demands was widespread in the county in 1599.[179] The county had difficulty in financing the gaols, the relieving of maimed soldiers and maintaining poor relief. The ordinary citizen in the late 1590s had a multitude of worries: fear of foreign invasion, hatred of spies, tax collectors and government purveyors, the fear that dwellings would be taken over by a captain to billet his men, or of disorderly conduct from disbanded and frequently unpaid troops or mariners. However, the cause of the eleven riots which occurred in Kent between 1585 and 1603 was shortage of food, not government or local taxation to finance military preparations.[180]

It is not easy to isolate the military costs of the Irish war on Kent from its commitment to defence or from its continental levies. Nor is it clear from accounts to

Table 5   Money raised in Kent to send levies to Ireland

Year	Levies	Cost (£.s.d)
1595	5 horses and riders	£137.0.0
1598	100 foot	£350.0.0
	4 horses and riders	£120.0.0
1599	25 horses	£750.0.0
1600	100 foot at £3 10s the man	£350.0.0
	50 foot at £3 10s the man	£175.0.0
	19 horses at £30 each	£570.0.0
1601	3 horses	£66.13.4
	200 foot	£620.0.0
1602	100 foot (stayed, yet assembly cost)	£10.0.0
	50 foot at £3 10s the man	£175.0.0
Total sum		£3,323.13. 4

what extent the crown shouldered part of the costs of the levies. The reluctance and refusals to pay military taxes suggest that the injection of government funds, especially its partial payment of coat money and full payment of conduct money, did little to alleviate the burden of fitting out armed expeditions to Ireland.

The actual sums of money raised within the county for the Irish war shows the price Kent had to pay for this war as well as the relentless regularity of the government's demands (Table 5).[181]

The crown had to raise loans during the 1590s to meet the extraordinary expenses of the war; many of these were raised on privy seals through the administration of the lieutenancy. The Kentish gentry, in a long litany of the county's financial burdens, claimed that they had given the crown nearly £7,000 under this system, and that ' no part as yet repaid, the forbearance whereof is grievous to divers who expected that they took up the same upon interest'.[182] They exaggerated, for on only one occasion, in 1596/1597, in the reign were such loans on privy seals not repaid.[183] The justices of the peace reckoned that Kent paid out a total of £10,911 13s 4d to meet the expenses of sending out men and arms to the Low Countries, France and Ireland from 1596 to July 1602.[184] Ireland, we have seen, accounted for £3,323 13s 4d, of this – a little over one-third of the total, or an annual average of £474 over a seven-year period of the Irish hostilities. Therefore, as with the numbers of levied men, Kent does not seem to have been unduly burdened with the cost of the war in Ireland. In the year 1601–1602, for example, one of particularly heavy military demands, Kent contributed £578 17s 0d to the costs of arming and clothing soldiers.[185] During the same year Lancashire paid £1,125 to the exchequer for the same costs, Dorset £650, Glamorganshire £782 10s 0d, Montgomeryshire £140, and Merionethshire £147 10s 0d.[186] Overall, the Irish war cost the Elizabethan government £1,845,696 during its last four years.[187] Sir Robert Cecil estimated that the war cost £300,000 a year when writing to Sir George Carew in

November 1602.[188] Beside such figures the war effort of the shire of Kent shrinks into perspective.

By the turn of the century refusals to pay local and county taxes were the common offences, apart from felonies at the county's quarter sessions. Defaulters in gaol money, poor rates and, as we have seen, royal exactions – the latter particularly crippling in 1599 – were all indicative that well before the end of the reign opposition to government levies and all kinds of demands was universal throughout the shire and growing all the time.[189]

Notes

1 J. J. N. McGurk, 'Levies from Kent to the Elizabethan wars, 1589–1603', *Archaeologia Cantiana*, 88 (1973), 52–72.

2 E. Hasted, *History and topographical survey of the county of Kent* (Canterbury, 1797), vol. i, 302; W. K. Jordan, 'Social institutions in Kent', *Archaeologia Cantiana*, 75 (1961); P. Clark, *English provincial society from the Reformation to the Revolution: religion, politics and society in Kent 1500–1640* (Hassocks, 1977), 6.

3 The Leveson lieutenancy collection is in the Staffordshire Record Office – SRO D593/S/ 4. This particular table is SRO D593/S/4/10/9, not dated but in a bundle of 1603. Dr Felix Hull brought that collection to my notice in the mid-1960s when it first went into the William Salt Library in Stafford then uncatalogued; I had the pleasure of being one of the first historians to work on it. Many of the bundles had been tied up in the 1590s by Leveson's clerk but someone had been busy in the eighteenth century removing seals from official letters!

4 Kent Archives Office (hereafter KAO), U1115/6/12 – Scott's official correspondence.

5 J. J. N. McGurk, 'Lieutenancy in Kent, c. 1580 – c. 1620', MPhil thesis (University of London, 1971).

6 T. E. Hartley, 'The sheriffs of the county of Kent, c. 1580–1625', PhD thesis (University of London, 1970) and for the lists of hundreds, lathes and so on, see BL Lansdowne MSS 276, ff. 185–186, and E. Hasted, *History and topographical survey of the county of Kent* (Canterbury, 1797), vol. i.

7 See J. J. N. McGurk, 'Lieutenancy in Kent, c. 1580 – c. 1620', MPhil thesis (University of London, 1971).

8 *Ibid.*, 241–246. The biographical information on Leveson now appears in P. W. Hasler, *The House of Commons, 1558–1603*, 3 vols (London, 1981), *s.v.* Leveson.

9 SRO D593/S/4/69, 1–11 contains the main section on the levies to Ireland from Kent.

10 SRO D593/S/4/22, 41.

11 Lambeth MSS, 1393, 5, 'Levies of arms and men in Kent'.

12 *Ibid.*, ff. 27–29d.

13 *Ibid.*, f. 28.

14 *Ibid.*, 8, 9, 22, 23.

15 J. J. N. McGurk, 'The clergy and the militia, 1580–1610', *History*, 60 (1975), 198–210, and 'Lieutenancy and Catholic recusants in Elizabethan Kent', *Recusant History*, 4 (1974), 157–170.

16 Lambeth MSS, 1393, f. 23.

17 *Ibid.*, 23d, but the discussion is elaborated in SRO D593/S/4, 37.

18 SRO D593/4/37, 3.

19 For the effects of war on early Tudor England see G. Elton, 'Taxation for war and peace in

early Tudor England', in *War and economic development*, ed. J. M. Winter (Cambridge, 1975).

20 BL, Harleian MSS, 168, 118.

21 G. Scott Thomson, 'The Twysden lieutenancy papers, 1583–1668', *Kent Records*, 10 (1926), 93.

22 Lambeth Palace Library, Twysden lieutenancy papers, MS 1393, 5, 'Levies of arms and men in Kent'.

23 SRO D593/S/4/33/3 – William Place to Sir John Leveson, June 1595.

24 *Ibid.*, 37, 3 (ii).

25 *Cal. Carew MSS*, 2009, 64.

26 Lambeth Palace Library, Archbishop's clerical muster book, MS 2009, f. 64.

27 G. Scott Thomson, ed., 'The Twysden lieutenancy papers, 1583–1668', *Kent Records*, 10 (1926), 103.

28 *CSPD* (1595–1597), 292–293.

29 BL Additional MSS, 34, 128, 87r.

30 *Cal. Carew MSS*, iii, 271–272, Irish council's report of 5 November 1597.

31 PRO SP12/252/15.

32 S. Williams, ed., *Letters written by John Chamberlain during the reign of Queen Elizabeth* (Camden Society, lxxix, London, 1861), 9, 17 May 1598.

33 PRO SP12/266, 3, 2 January 1598. Burghley's words echo those of his son when negotiating peace with Henry IV the previous year: HMC, *Salisbury*, xxiii (addenda), 45 – 23 March 1597.

34 *APC*, xxix, 156; SRO D593/S/4/66/3 (iii) the general order to the shires and the specific demand from Kent.

35 SRO D593/S/4/66/3 (iii), Leveson to the other deputies August 1598.

36 *Ibid.* (i), 'By the queene' to Lord Cobham, 26 August 1598.

37 *Ibid.*

38 *Ibid.* (ii), the privy council to Cobham, 28 August 1598.

39 *Ibid.* (iii), Sir John Leveson to the constables, September 1598.

40 SRO D593/S/4/67, 3 (ii), privy council to Lord Cobham.

41 *CSPD* (1598–1601), 151, for the sums they were paid later for this contract.

42 SRO D593/S/4/67/3 (ii), council to Lord Cobham.

43 SRO D593/S/4/66/3 (iv), sent by five justices from Bearsted, 2 September 1598.

44 Frauds against the crown were exposed in 1616 involving the treasurers-at-war in Ireland and the London merchants Babington and Bromley. H. Hall, *Society in the Elizabethan age* (London, 1888), 125.

45 BL Additional MSS, 34, 128, f. 87v.

46 *APC*, xxix, 94, 156.

47 PRO SP12/268, 121, draft copy, and 122, fair copy.

48 SRO D493/2/4/66/5 (i), Lord Cobham's copy of the queen's letter and sent out to his deputies.

49 SRO D593/S/4/65/5 (ii), the privy council's letter to Lord Cobham.

50 *APC*, xxix, 601, the privy council to Lord Cobham, 25 February 1598.

51 PRO E101/65/27, the two indentures made 8 and 9 January 1598.

52 KAO, U/1115/06, the official correspondence of Sir Thomas Scott as deputy lieutenant in east Kent.

53 SRO D593/S/4/66/5 (iv), the Earl of Essex commending Peregrine Wingfield as captain. Sir Edward and Sir Richard Wingfield were cousins and both were captains in Ireland. Sir Richard was created Lord Viscount Powerscourt (o.s.p., 1634), and Sir Edward succeeded to his Irish estates. *Cal. Carew MSS*, iv, 200, 233, 244, 400, 437.

54 HMC, *Salisbury*, ix, 41, 42, Docwra to Essex, 25 January 1599.

55 SRO D593/S/4/48/3 and S/4/66/2, two bundles which deal with this Kentish levy of horse; the latter, found later at Dubrobin Castle, were so clearly part of the Leveson collection that they were then catalogued with the full collection, SRO D593/S/4.
56 SRO D593/S/4/66/2, Sir John Leveson's arrangements for the levy.
57 *Ibid.*, 5, the justices of Sutton-at-Hone to Sir John Leveson, 4 January 1599.
58 BL Additional MSS, 34,128, f. 87v. During August 1599 the county's trained bands assembled at Sandwich to meet a Spanish invasion that did not materialise, but preparations cost the shire £1,000.
59 SRO D593/S/4/66/2.
60 *Ibid.*
61 Lambeth Palace Library, Twysden book of musters, MS 1392, 75–79.
62 SRO D593/S/4/68/1 (i), the privy council to Lord Cobham.
63 *Ibid.*, 1–4.
64 *Ibid.*, 2, Henry Hart's indenture, 15 February 1600.
65 *Ibid.*, 3 (i) – Leveson's accounts, February 1600.
66 *Ibid.*, 5.
67 *Cal. Carew MSS*, iii, 334; *CSPI* (1596–1599), 381, 383, 413.
68 SRO D593/S/4/68/2, the covering letter to Hart's indenture.
69 *Ibid.*, 3 (i, ii, iv).
70 *Ibid.*, vii, Sir Henry Docwra's acquittance for the targets.
71 PRO SP12/275, 10, 20 June 1600.
72 SRO D593/S/4/69/1 (i), the privy council to Lord Cobham.
73 *Ibid.* (i–ix); 69/2, the indenture and 69/3 (i–vi), accounts.
74 Sir Thomas Walsingham of Scadbury, near Chislehurst, d. 1630, Manwood of Hackington, near Canterbury, d. 1625.
75 SRO D593/S/4/66/4, from the queen to Lord Cobham, 25 June 1600; SRO D593/S/4/69/1 (i) is a copy of this letter.
76 *Ibid.* (ii); Leveson received his on 28 June at Dartford.
77 Sir Richard Trevor, knighted by Russell, the lord deputy in Ireland 1597 – *Cal. Carew MSS*, iii, 259; deputy lieutenant in Denbighshire and unsuccessful rival to John Salusbury in the parliamentary election of 1601.
78 SRO D593/S/4/69/1 (iii), Sir John Trevor to Sir John Leveson on behalf of Captain Edward Trevor, 4 July 1600.
79 *Ibid.* (vii) – privy council to Lord Cobham, 21 August 1600.
80 *Ibid.* (viii), Sir John Trevor to Sir John Leveson, 24 August 1600.
81 SRO D593/S/4/69/2, the indenture of Edward Trevor.
82 SRO D593/S/4/69/3 (i), the distribution of arms.
83 *Ibid.* (iii–vi) accounts of money received by J. Leveson.
84 SRO D593/S/4/69/4 (i), 'The charge of the arms *bought* in west Kent'; SRO D593/S/4/69/3 (vii), Sir Peter Manwood – his account.
85 *Ibid.* (i).
86 Note to Sir Peter Manwood: 'at these rates he [Trevor] will free us of hiring a carte' and hoped he would make speedy agreement on the rates so that he can 'continue with him [Trevor] for us all'. Attached to SRO D593/S/4/69/4.
87 *APC*, xxxi, 418; SRO D593/S/4/69/1 (i).
88 SRO D593/S/4/69/3 (iii, iv).
89 *Ibid.* (v), Sir Peter Manwood's accounts.
90 *Ibid.* (ii).
91 *Ibid.* (vi), Manwood to Leveson. Manwood was MP for Sandwich in 1589, 1592, 1597, 1601, for Kent in 1614, and for New Romney in 1620, *DNB*, s.v. Manwood, Peter.
92 SRO D593/S/4/69/3 (ii), as noted by Sir John Leveson.

93   A. Everitt, 'Kent and its gentry, 1640–1660', PhD thesis (University of London, 1957), 5.

94   C. G. Cruickshank, *Elizabeth's army* (2nd edn, Oxford, 1970) 91–101.

95   SRO D593/S/4/63/1 – a group of twelve documents dealing with the charges and countercharges made in 1618/1619. Further evidence of allegations of fraud in coat and conduct money in the Scott lieutenancy papers – KAO, 06/42.

96   SRO D593/S/4/63/1.

97   Sir John Leveson, d. 1615, Sir Thomas Scott, d. 1594, Sir Thomas Sondes, d. 1593 and Sir Thomas Wilford, d. 1610. There are brief biographies of these in J. J. N. McGurk, 'Lieutenancy in Kent, c. 1580 – c. 1620', MPhil thesis (University of London, 1971), Appendix III, 242–246.

98   SRO D593/S/4/69/1 (iii), reported by Sir John Trevor to Sir John Leveson on Edward Trevor's behalf.

99   *Ibid.* (vii), the privy council to Lord Cobham, 21 August 1600.

100 Fynes Moryson, *Itinerary*, vol. ii, 336, 342.

101 *Cal. Carew MSS*, iv, 498, 'The lord deputy's proceedings', November 1600.

102 *Ibid.*, iv, 397, 'The list of the army as it stands the 1st January 1602'.

103 Hatfield House, Cecil papers, 24/67 r.

104 *APC*, xxx, 434–440.

105 *Ibid.*, 434–435.

106 Hatfield House, Cecil papers, 24/26 r to 67 v, 'A consideration of divers things that do belong to the present execution of that contribution which the necessity of this present tyme doth require'.

107 Such as Sir John Leveson, Sir John Scott, Sir Thomas Walsingham of Scadbury, Sir Alexander Culpepper and Sir Thomas Waller. The nineteen named were: the four knights and Peter Manwood, Thomas Kempe, Samson Leonard, William Sidley, Martin Bareham, John Smith, James Cromer, Thomas Scott, Thomas Potter, John Hales, Norton Knatchbull, George Bing, Anthony Sucher, John Tufton and Richard Smith.

108 SRO D593/S/4/38/2, 'Names of those appointed to find launces, 1595'.

109 BL Additional MSS, 34,128, 87, under 'Anno 1600. A levy of 19 horse taken owte of the Countie by letters from their Honours to severall gents. at 30 li. each horse with his Rider and Furniture'.

110 HMC, *Salisbury*, xiv, 136.

111 *APC*, xxxi, 311–313, the total list given adds up to thirty-eight, not forty horse.

112 SRO D593/S/4/54/3 (i), the original of the queen's letter to Cobham; there is a copy of this in S/4/69/4 made by Cobham's clerk, 28 April 1601.

113 *Ibid.* (ii).

114 *Ibid.* (iv), Cobham's letter to his deputies, 30 April 1601.

115 SRO D593/S/4/69/4 (i), Cobham's copy of the queen's letter.

116 *APC*, xxxi, 312.

117 SRO D593/S/4/54/3 (i), the same remark in the queen's letter.

118 *Ibid.* (ii), the privy council's letter, Cobham's *vera copia*.

119 *APC*, xxxi, 312.

120 SRO D593/S/4/54/3 (iv).

121 SRO D593/S/4/37/3.

122 SRO D593/S/4/54/3 (vi), Leveson's accounts, which tally with the amount given in BL Additional MSS, 34,128, f. 87, of £66 13s 4d for the levy to Lough Foyle.

123 Like the other thirty-six horse at Chester, these were intended to fill up 'decayed' horsebands. The normal cavalry band was fifty strong at this time.

124 SRO D593/S/4/69/6 (i) and (ii), 6 and 7 October 1601.

125 See Part II.

126 SRO D593/S/4/69/7 and 8, S/4/54/2.

127 SRO D593/S/4/69/7, the account for west Kent; SRO D593/S/4/54/2, the account for east Kent, October 1601.
128 *APC*, xxxii, 472–473.
129 SRO D593/S/4/54/2; copies of draft accounts also in SRO D593/S/4/69/7 and 8.
130 SRO D593/S/4/69/8 (i–iv).
131 HMC, *Salisbury*, xi, 449.
132 BL Additional MSS, 34, 128, 88 r.
133 SRO D593/S/4/36/3–5.
134 *Ibid.*, S/4/46/6.
135 SRO D593/S/4/69/7 (i, ii).
136 SRO D593/S/4/54/2 (iii), Roberts to Leveson, 9 October 1601.
137 SRO D593/S/4/69/8 (v), Sondes to Leveson.
138 SRO D593/S/4/69/9 (i), the queen's letter, 6 January 1602, bearing the royal signature; (ii), a copy in which key phrases have been underlined, and repeated in other copies.
139 SRO D593/S/4/54/2, a further copy from Leveson's clerk.
140 SRO D593/S/4/69/9 (iii), privy council to Cobham, 7 January 1602.
141 *Ibid.* (iv), Cobham to the deputy lieutenants, Leveson, Scott and Walsingham, 8 January 1602.
142 *Ibid.*, and cf. *APC*, xxxi, 318–321.
143 SRO D593/S/4/69/9 (i), copy of the queen's letter, 6 January 1602, and another copy in SRO D593/S/4/54/2.
144 SRO D593/S/4/54/5, 'Lyst of Trained Bands in Kent, May 1601'.
145 *Ibid.*, the number of trained had increased in Kent since the 1591 certificate which shows a total of 3,223 under twenty-six captains – cf. SRO D593/S/4/58/13.
146 SRO D593/S/4/69/9 (iv), Cobham to his deputies, 8 January 1602.
147 *Ibid.* (v), 'Indenture of Thomas Stock made with the deputies Sir John Leveson, Sir John Scott and Sir Thomas Walsingham 19 January 1602'.
148 *Idid.* (v), Stock's request enclosed with the indenture.
149 BL Additional MSS, 34, 128, 88, 'a hundrede men at Greenwich ... agayne discharged'.
150 SRO D593/S/4/10/9.
151 *CSPI* (1601–1603), 274, 302, 380.
152 S. Williams, ed., *Letters of John Chamberlain* (Camden Society, lxxix, London, 1861), 130–131.
153 SRO D593/S/4/69/10 (i), the queen to Cobham, 28 July 1602.
154 *Ibid.* (iii), Cobham to Leveson for west Kent; the copy for Sir John Scott of east Kent in Scott family papers, KAO U1115/06/31.
155 SRO D593/S/4/69/10 (i), signet letter to Cobham, 28 July 1602.
156 PRO SP12/284/73, instructions to the vice-admiral on shipping this levy, 9 July 1602.
157 J. MacLean, ed., *Letters from Sir Robert Cecil to Sir George Carew* (Camden Society, lxxxviii, London, 1864), 126, 9 August 1602, where he tells him 'how her Majesty hath directed the other 800 men to Dublin'.
158 SRO D593/S/4/11/1; *CSPD* (1591–1594), 365.
159 M. Duffy, ed., *The military revolution and the state* (Exeter Studies, Exeter, 1980); KAO, QM/SB/145, for raids by vagrant troops.
160 W. K. Jordan, 'Social institutions in Kent 1480–1660', *Archaeologia Cantiana*, 75 (1961); E. Melling, ed., *Kentish sources: the poor* (Maidstone, 1964).
161 J. J. N. McGurk, 'Lieutenancy in Kent, c. 1580 – c. 1620', MPhil thesis (University of London, 1971).
162 P. Clark, *English provincial society from the Reformation to the Revolution: religion, politics and society in Kent 1500–1640* (Hassocks, 1977), Chapter 7.
163 HMC, *Salisbury*, xiv, 136, Captain Nicholas Dawtrey's report to Sir Robert Cecil from Chester, 19 August 1600.

164 G. Goodman, *The court of King James I* (ed. J. S. Brewer, 1839), vol. i, 97.

165 *APC*, xxiii, 39; *APC*, xxiv, 130 for examples.

166 SRO D593/S/4/42/4 – a bundle of fifty-three letters to Leveson seeking abatements.

167 SRO D593/S/4/42/3: S/4/54/1 – (1597).

168 SRO D593/S/4/55/12, not dated, but in bundles of 1602.

169 G. Scott Thomson, ed., 'The Twysden lieutenancy papers, 1583–1668', *Kent Records*, 10 (1926), 93.

170 W. Holdsworth, *A history of English law* (London, 1903), vol. i, 124.

171 *APC*, xxix, 601, the privy council to Lord Cobham.

172 A. M. Everitt, *Change in the provinces: the seventeenth century* (Leicester, 1969), 9, 17.

173 *APC*, xxix, 601.

174 SRO D593/S/4/42/4, letters and petitions to Leveson to be released from paying loans; some were addressed to William, Lord Burghley.

175 *Ibid.*, Sondes to Leveson.

176 *Ibid.*, Wilsford to Leveson; these three complaints are but samples.

177 G. Scott Thomson, ed., 'The Twysden lieutenancy papers, 1583–1668', *Kent Records*, 10 (1926), 91.

178 KAO, quarter sessions records, A/SR/1–5 and Q/SM/15, 8; and also letters from the justices of east Kent to Leveson on the 'manie that doe refuse to paie their taxes', SRO D593/S/4/66/5 (v), 4 January 1599.

179 SRO D593/S/4/11/9, 42/4.

180 P. Clark, 'Popular protest and disturbance in Kent, 1558–1640', *Economic History Review*, 2nd series, 29 (1976), 368 *et. seq.*

181 Total sums taken from BL Additional MSS, 34, 128, 87v–88, and from SRO D593/S/4/10/9, S/4/69, 4/66. Overall, Kent may have paid about £107,000 in direct and indirect taxation in the period 1589–1604.

182 BL Additional MSS, 34,128, 88.

183 J. J. N. McGurk, 'Lieutenancy in Kent, c. 1580 – c. 1620', MPhil thesis (University of London, 1971), Chapter 10.

184 BL Additional MSS, 34, 128, 87v.

185 PRO SP12/285, 65, 'Receipts of sums paid out of the shires from Michaelmas 43 Elizabeth to Michaelmas 44 Elizabeth'.

186 *Ibid.*, 61, 64, 67, 68, 71.

187 BL Lansdowne MSS, 156, ff. 253–258, from Sir Julius Caesar's accounts, and for a summary of 'The cost of Queen Elizabeth's Wars' see HMC, *Salisbury*, xv, 2. Other accounts show that *military* expenditure formed a major part of the *national* expenditure – PRO SP12/285, 21, 55–80 and 287/59; SP/63/212, 37.

188 J. Maclean, ed., *Letters of Sir Robert Cecil to Sir George Carew* (Camden Society, lxxxviii, London, 1864), 147–148.

189 SRO D593/S/4/66/5 and KAO, quarter sessions records, QM/SM/15, 8.

CHAPTER FIVE

Levies to Ireland from the maritime shires of Lancashire and Cheshire, 1594–1602

Background

In this period of Anglo-Irish hostility geographical convenience dictated that the Elizabethan government would draw large numbers of recruits from the maritime shires of Lancashire, Cheshire and Wales.[1] Soldiers from these areas could be assembled earlier and at less cost to the government than from inland and more distant shires. Convenience and economy may have dictated that the entire area of the north-west be treated as a whole for the purpose of levies, but Lancashire, Cheshire and above all Wales were disparate in character and tradition. Though the lieutenancy of the Stanleys, Earls of Derby, covered both Lancashire and Cheshire, two deputy lieutenants were appointed to act within each county.[2]

The government treated both shires and north Wales as a unit in 1575 when it was thought that the north-west could raise £20,000 a year to support the lord deputyship of Sir Henry Sidney in Ireland, but the scheme foundered because of Sidney's political ambitions.[3] The strategic importance of the north-west to the defence of the realm made the government view the area as a whole in the measures taken against invasion scares. The presence at the Spanish court of Sir William Stanley of Hooton, the notable betrayer of Deventer to the Spanish in 1587, increased the probability of an invasion directed at England through the north-west. In May 1590 the privy council warned the Earl of Derby that Stanley was to lead a Spanish attack by way of Anglesey as a base for an invading force into Lancashire and Cheshire. Derby was ordered to put both counties into a state of military readiness and to reinforce defences at Anglesey, but nothing came of the invasion scare.[4]

Commissions of lieutenancy to the Earls of Derby enabled the crown to centralise administration in an area comparatively remote from the centre of government. The Derbys held regular commissions of lieutenancy from 1551 to 1640, except for one notable break in continuity from 1594 to 1607. Henry, fourth Earl, died in September 1594, and Ferdinando, eldest son and successor, died in April 1595; thereafter financial disputes with Ferdinando's widow are thought to have weakened Derby influence in local and national affairs. William, sixth Earl (1594–1642), is not mentioned in county affairs until 1607, when he received his first commission of lieutenancy.[5] The period of the break in lieutenancy impinged on administration, hence government policies and orders for the raising of men and money fell to the sheriffs and commissioners of musters in both Lancashire and Cheshire.

Whether they held commissions of lieutenancy or not, the Earls of Derby regarded themselves as the chief magnates in Lancashire. Henry, fourth Earl, was sensitive about his position when he took his deputy, Sir Richard Molyneux, to task in 1591 for keeping privy council letters in his house, thereby ignoring 'the place and calling of his social superior'. The Earl wondered why privy council 'directions for matters in this county of Lancashire' should not have first been sent to him.[6] Derby power in Lancashire can be seen in the maintenance of large numbers of armed household servants and tenants well into the sixteen century, long after the nobility at large had discontinued the practice of retaining.[7]

Apart from the Earls of Derby, a coterie of about nine or more wealthy and powerful families in Lancashire acted as high sheriffs, knights of the shire, justices of the peace and commissioners for musters, and also sat on the many other commissions whereby Elizabethan government sought to centralise its control: the Heskeths of Rufford, Gerards of Bryn, Hollands of Denton, Houghtons of Houghton Tower, Molyneux of Sefton, Trafford of Trafford, Byrom of Newgate, Shireburnes of Stonyhurst and Leghs of Lyme. Likewise in Cheshire a group of about twelve families became the ruling elite of the shire: the Cholmondeleys of Cholmondeley, Fittons of Gawesworth, Venables of Kinderton, Breretons of Handforth and Brereton, Savages of Rock Savage, Warburtons of Arley, Smiths of Hough Hatherton, Stanleys of Hooton, Davenports of Davenport, Booths of Dunham Massey, Wilbrahams of Woodhey and Duttons of Hatton and Dutton. Such families formed the backbone of local administration at county level, and the crown and privy council relied on their voluntary cooperation to enforce its will in the shires.[8] Between 1590 and 1640 about twenty-five Cheshire families provided every deputy lieutenant, three-quarters of the sheriffs, more than a third of the justices, and the majority of the members of parliament representing the county.[9] There is a similar concentration of offices in the hands of the Lancashire county elite.[10] To give greater precision to the demands on both Lancashire and Cheshire, to their military potential, to their responses to these demands, and to the problems which they caused, each county will now be treated separately.

Lancashire's ability to meet demands

Lancashire, the sixth largest county in England, was predominantly pastoral in the sixteenth century and among the poorer of the shires, standing thirty-sixth in wealth of the English shires.[11] Historians see three distinct farming regions in the county: a mixed farming central zone from the Mersey to the Lune, a pastoral zone of the coastal plains, and a highland zone of mixed farming (and some mining). For the greater part of the century large tracts of mosses near the coast and along the three rivers, Mersey, Ribble and Lune, stayed undrained. Spinning and weaving supplemented agricultural earnings in the south and east of the shire, and mining did the same to the west and north, but Lancashire was generally regarded as poor.[12]

The author of a project for raising crown revenue in 1575 by first fruits of ecclesiastical offices thought the see of Chester, which included most of Lancashire, too poor to support a bishop.[13] Bishop Vaughan of Chester asserted in 1603 that it was common knowledge 'how little able the small revenues of this see is to defray the charges thereof'.[14] The lay subsidy roll of 1593 of the fifty-seven parishes in Lancashire shows a total tax collected of £1,038 9s 4d.[15] By 1625 the lay subsidy in the county had increased to £2,490 0s 0d[16] but it remained among the poorest counties of the nation. Its ship-money valuation in 1636, of £1,000, was the lowest per acre apart from Cumberland.[17]

Writers on sixteenth-century Lancashire generally call attention to the county's conservatism and slow rate of change, evincing the long survival of feudal forms of tenure and of the practice of retaining, as well as the fact that bad communications emphasised its remoteness from London.[18] William Camden, hardened traveller and topographer, admitted to being troubled in spirit 'with a kind of dread' as he approached the boundaries of Lancashire, but he (thankfully) pressed on, 'trusting in the divine assistance'.[19] Christopher Haigh may have exaggerated the isolation of Lancashire in writing that it 'was not quite part of England' and in stressing that Lancashire had its own structure of government in the duchy and palatine of Lancaster.[20] The historian of the duchy points out only two of the twenty-two palatine judges were indeed local men under Queen Elizabeth.[21]

From the geographical point of view Lancashire's lines of communication in the sixteenth century were not on the main north–south artery, which lay, rather, on the Yorkshire side of the Pennine chain, but were more directed north and west to Scotland, the Isle of Man and Ireland. Its trading connections were with Yorkshire, Northumberland and Durham rather than with London and the south, and overseas with Ireland, Spain and Portugal than with the Low Countries, France and Germany.[22]

Manchester was the county's largest town, notable in John Leland's time (1506–1552) for its two marketplaces and its one parish church. Liverpool, 'a paved town', had about six streets and was much frequented by Irish merchants. Warrington had a large market, but Wigan 'as big as Warrington was better builded', and had merchants artificers and farmers, but above all coal mines, nearby.[23]

In studying the social institutions of Lancashire from 1480 to 1660 Professor W. K. Jordan saw the county experiencing a rapid and continuous population increase in the sixteenth century, reaching by 1600 between 105,000 and 120,000 inhabitants, but his bias is towards the lesser figure.[24] Dr B. G. Blackwood argues that population growth in the seventeenth century was not continuous, and cites the evidence of the hearth tax assessments of 1664, which indicate a Lancashire population of 150,669. Clearly, the population increased, but whether or not the rate of growth was continuous appears to be controversial.[25]

To gauge the military potential of the county, and therefore its ability to meet governmental demands for the Irish wars, we look again at the muster returns. These exist for the 1560s, 1570s and 1580s, and in the years 1608, 1618 and 1625, so there is a notable gap in the evidence of muster returns for the county in the 1590s. J. Harland's *Lancashire lieutenancy* for the queen's reign ends in 1590,[26] and the Lancashire lieutenancy minute book runs from 1601 to 1640,[27] while Houghton's lieutenancy letter book covers the later period, 1625–1640.[28] The lack of county muster returns in the 1590s may indicate that in the north training, mobilisation and mustering of the militia were regarded as a luxury since there were so many demands for raw recruits for

Ireland. Muster returns exist for the 1590s for example in Kent, and for the last great mobilisation of home defence in 1599 against possible Spanish invasion in the south coastal shires.[29]

John Harland's collection of lieutenancy papers from the Shuttleworth, Harleian and local collections other than those noted show a copious mustering and arming of Lancashire men for Ireland as well as for the county's militia in the years before the last Elizabethan rebellion. In 1560 the general muster of the shire showed 3,993 able-bodied men; in 1569, 4,763; in 1574, 6,000; and in 1588, the Armada year, the deputy lieutenants certified that Lancashire could furnish 1,170 trained men made up of 700 calivers, 300 pikemen, 80 archers, 20 lances, 70 billmen, and in addition there were 265 horsemen. Known levies sent into Ireland from the county were: 50 archers in 1566, 100 footmen in 1574, 30 pioneers the following year, two dozen skilled artificers in 1576, and, unusually, in 1580 100 of the trained bands. Finally, in the decade 1580–1590, about 400 foot were ordered for Ireland, one levy of 100 being discharged in 1588.[30] Tudor Lancashire was always on a war footing and a higher proportion of its male population were soldiers than in any other shire.[31] But it must be recalled that the Elizabethan government expected every free and able-bodied man to keep arms and armour ready for use in every shire of the realm, and in that sense war preparations and defence measures were part of everyday life.[32]

The military organisation for raising levies and for raising of money to set them forth was not inherently different from elsewhere; the hundreds of the shire were administered by high constables and bailiffs acting under orders from the high sheriff and commissioners for musters.[33] In general, more men were levied in the more populous hundreds in south Lancashire.[34] The accustomed assembly places for soldiers levied in each hundred were: Wigan for West Derby and the Leyland hundreds, Manchester for Salford, Whalley for Blackburn, Preston for Amounderness and Lancaster for Lonsdale.[35] A levy of 100 men for Ireland in April 1602 was ordered to be divided in the following manner (allowing for dead pays): West Derby, 24, Salford, 24, Blackburn, 18, Amounderness, 19, Lonsdale 16, and Leyland 9.

An impression of the relative armed strength of the Lancashire hundreds to set against the quotas demanded in the last years of the queen's reign cannot be gained for the 1590s as full muster certificates are wanting, but the armed strength at the queen's accession is known hundred by hundred: Salford, 1,142, of whom 350 were trained; Lonsdale, 469, of whom 350 were trained; Amounderness, 582, of whom 300 were trained; West Derby, 672, of whom 430 were trained; Blackburn, 813, of whom 400 were trained; and Leyland is curiously given a figure of 46 armed and unarmed men, but 170 trained.[36] Under the year 1608 the county's lieutenancy minute book is lined to give the full military strength of every hundred under the headings of muskets, calivers, bills, archers and pikemen. Unfortunately, the clerk of the lieutenancy filled in only those of Salford and Blackburn, which two hundreds gave an armed total of 1,453, and for Amounderness he noted 224 armed men and 1,876 unarmed, and there his muster certificate ended.

Considering the financial charges incumbent on sending regular levies it is surprising not to find evidence of internal quarrels between the inhabitants of the six hundreds over the allocation of quotas. Perhaps the sheriffs and commissioners

Table 6   Quotas in the Lancashire hundreds of soldiers in the Irish war

Hundred	November 1594	December 1600	October 1601	April 1602	July 1602	Hundred total
Salford	14	5	21	24	7	71
Lonsdale	16	5	24	16	8	69
West Derby	24	8	36	24	12	104
Blackburn	18	4	27	18	9	76
Amoundenress	19	5	42	19	9	94
Leyland	9	3	0	9	5	26
Total shire levy	100	30	150	110	50	

followed long-formed precedents in their allocation of men and of the taxes necessary to furnish them.[37] There is much scattered evidence on how they divided up the demands from the privy council and though it is not complete in every levy the five occasions selected suggest equitable proportions. At times a shire levy seems to have been raised as a whole without any indication of division by the ancient hundreds; this was the case in January 1600, when the muster roll merely shows the dwelling places of the 200 then recruits.[38] Likewise, in 1598 Captain Edward Tarbock's indenture for 200 Lancashire men simply lists them by name without indicating either dwelling places or hundreds.[39]

Table 6[40] shows the hundred of West Derby furnishing the most men for Ireland on five occasions with the exception of October 1601, and invariably the small size of the hundred of Leyland is reflected in the numbers required from it.[41] More trained soldiers were being drawn out of the trained bands of the militia in the last years of the Irish war in order to raise the quality of raw recruits. West Derby, on account of its greater reserves of trained soldiers, had been asked to supply more than the other Lancashire hundreds.[42] The proportionate numbers of horse are much the same as the infantry proportions in the hundreds, except in the case of Amounderness and Leyland. In May 1602 eighty-nine horses were charged to be furnished and set out of Lancashire: thirty on West Derby, twenty on Salford, eleven each on Blackburn and Lonsdale, four on Amounderness, but thirteen on Leyland.[43]

From these particular demands on the separate hundreds of the county we turn to the annual levies on the county as a whole. Table 7 sets out these levies. During the period covered by the table there was no common commission of lieutenancy for Lancashire and Cheshire and therefore the privy council addressed its orders to the individual sheriffs and commissioners for the musters in each separate county.

Demands for large numbers of soldiers from the county tend to reflect the varying fortunes of Elizabethan armies in Ireland: Essex's expedition of 1599, Mountjoy's expeditionary forces of 1600, and the Spanish crisis of October 1601. To some extent the demands for smaller levies represent batches of reinforcements.[44]

The frequency of demands for soldiers from Lancashire suggests that the government took more account of the geographical position of the shire in relation to

Table 7   *Lancashire levies to Ireland*

Date	Number of foot	Number of horse	Note
October 1594	100	–	1
September 1596	47	–	2
April 1597	56	–	3
June 1598	200	1	4
January 1599	200	–	5
January 1600	200	–	6
June 1600	100	7	7
August 1600	50	–	8
December 1600	30	–	9
April 1601	40	–	10
August 1601	100	–	11
October 1601	150	12	11
December 1601 for			
January 1602	80	–	12
April 1602	100	–	13
July 1602	50	–	14
Totals	1,403	20	

1. PRO SP12/248/87.
2. *APC*, xxvi, 346; *APC*, xxvii, 21–28. These Lancashire troops joined up with forty-seven from Cheshire to form a single company – CCRO, Cholmondeley's letter book, DDX358/1–84, f. 33v.
3. *APC*, xxvii, 26–28. ·
4. *APC*, xxviii, 524–525.
5. *CSPD* (1598–1601), 151.
6. LRO, DDHE/61/13.
7. *APC*, xxx, 416, 436.
8. *Ibid.*, 566, 598.
9. *Ibid.*, xxxi, 23, these were reinforcements for Lough Foyle.
10. *Ibid.*, 318, further Lough Foyle reinforcements.
11. The original order of August 1601 was changed to an increased demand of 150 by October; the October number therefore is used for the total, not the August figure.
12. LRO, Lancashire lieutenancy minute book, LV/80, f. 3.
13. *Ibid.*, ff. 5, 6.
14. CCR, M/MP/13, a paper muster roll of the names of the Lancashire and Cheshire soldiers at the port of Chester in July 1602.

Ireland than its comparative poverty. Lancashire was asked to send infantry forces on thirteen separate occasions involving a grand total of 1,403 soldiers.[45] In this respect Lancashire stood fifth among the English shires in the number of infantry sent out in those years.[46] And in the earlier period of Irish rebellions, those of Shane O'Neill and of the Desmonds, Lancashire sent out 604 troops.[47] It was only in the small demands for the more expensive cavalry units that the Elizabethan government showed, perhaps, an awareness that Lancashire was not a wealthy shire. Overall, Lancashire was more heavily drawn upon for the Elizabethan Irish wars than the far wealthier shires of Kent and Northamptonshire.

Contrary to what one might expect, numbers under 100 men do not join up to make companies of 100 in Lancashire and Cheshire. More often than not Lancashire men joined forces with small levies from north Wales, for example, in August and December 1600.[48] On one occasion when Lancashire was twenty-two soldiers short at Chester, the commissioners for the musters combined the Lancashiremen with a similarly under-strength company from Lincolnshire.[49] By these cross-county arrangements the process of breaking down local loyalties of soldiers might have begun. Yet the captains, conductors and muster masters who organised Lancashire troops for Ireland were invariably local men. The privy council was usually content to leave such choice to the shires, but in the last decade of the reign there was an attempt to appoint muster masters from the centre. The council, for instance, pressed the Lancashire authorities to accept Hugh Done, an experienced soldier, as muster master of the county[50] in the place of Captain Lathom, the local choice in 1601.[51]

Considering the numbers sent from Lancashire to Ireland in the 1590s the evidence on the quality of the service is surprisingly thin in the local records. The Lancashire lieutenancy minute book, in bad condition and unfoliated, runs from 1601 to 1625. The letters from the queen, privy council, sheriffs and commissioners for musters reflect the same chain of command that can be seen for other counties, namely, the queen's letter of command to raise a specified number of troops to the county authorities, a following letter from the privy council elaborating the initial order, then orders from the commissioners for musters in Lancashire to the constables of the hundreds to translate the demand into a precise quota on each hundred.

Not found elsewhere are copies of 'A President [*sic*] for Preceptes', a form drawn up by the commissioners for musters for the convenience of the 'bailiffe of a hundred' to enable him to carry out the recruitment orders passed on by the high constable of the hundred. Blanks are left for the bailiff to fill in the number of recruits, the date of their assembly and the meeting place. The form is headed: 'These are in Her Majesty's name to require you that presentlie you deliver to the constables of the hundreds of — the no. — to be at —'.[52] The device was clearly a check on how the commissioners' orders were implemented, but no example of a completed bailiff's form has been found.

The same source confirms that the quality of some Lancashire recruits for Ireland was not up to the government's standard. When the August 1601 Lancashire levy assembled at Chester the commissioners returned eighty of them as unserviceable, and ordered the county to make up the numbers out of the trained bands.[53] Earlier, in 1594, the mayor of Chester had complained of the poor standard of armour sent with the Lancashire troops.[54] In their defence the commissioners for the Lancashire musters, Ralph Ashton and Richard Holland, explained to Lord Burghley how their men defaced their armour on the journey from Warrington to Chester and that the defects in their armour were not as great as Foulke Aldersey, the mayor, had made out. They had made it their business to go to Chester and there, after checking the allegation, found the Lancashire 'armours good and serviceable'.[55]

Half-heartedness for the Irish service was occasionally seen in the ploy of delaying the execution of privy council instructions when commissioners for musters asked for further clarification. In Lancashire the difficulty of immediate communication with London about precise instructions prolonged delays. In January 1599, when the Earl of

Essex was recruiting his 'army of Ireland', the Lancashire commissioners were ordered to have 200 men in a state of readiness. They received that order on 16 January but did not muster and view the assembled force at Wigan until 12 February. From Wigan on that date they wrote to Sir Robert Cecil to say that they 'could not proceed further for want of directions from your council which as yet we have not received'. The original letter of demand had promised that precise instructions would be sent to Richard Houghton, the high sheriff. Clearly, experienced commissioners such as Houghton, Ashton, Holland, Preston and Molyneux were well practised in viewing and sending troops to Chester and Liverpool, but they had not been given the precise date for their dispatch to the port.[56]

For a similar levy of 200 raised in the county the following winter of 1600, part of Sir Henry Docwra's Lough Foyle expedition, the long delays were not so much caused by lack of precise instructions as by contrary winds at Chester. The muster roll for that contingent shows the sheriff, Robert Hesketh, and his two main commissioners, Richard Holland and Ralph Ashton, were chiefly responsible for their muster and review. The conductors were local men, Robert Parker and Richard Assheton. The roll gives the full name of each soldier, his place of residence and the type of weapon he carried; under 'occupations' the spaces are blank but for three who are named as bricklayers. This levy allowed six dead pays in each hundred. Of those arms specified, the proportions are: forty pikes 'armed with corselets, pauldrons and morrions', twenty halberds, armed like the pikemen, twenty-four 'bastard muskets', eighty calivers, and every man carried a sword and dagger. Firearms predominated, indicating the increased use of muskets and calivers by the end of the century.[57]

While arrangements went smoothly in the recruitment and viewing of this levy for Docwra's expedition, there were misunderstandings and difficulties over coat and conduct money. The privy council had ordered the commissioners in Lancashire in January 1600 to have £400 collected and paid to the mayor of Chester towards the cost of apparelling the recruits on the grounds that 'the place is nerer unto you and may be done with lesse charge of the country'.[58] From the overall sum of the military taxes collected the commissioners deducted coat and conduct monies as a lump sum from the total. The privy council voiced its displeasure: 'In our letters we did particularly specify the several sums you were to receive out of the counties'. The council liked to see details of how much had been deducted for the coats, how many days' conduct money had been allowed and what allowances had been given the conductors. Otherwise, the council claimed, it could not ask the lord treasurer for a warrant to pay a generalised sum from the exchequer to Lancashire.[59] In June 1600 there was authorisation to pay Ralph Ashton, one of the Lancashire commissioners, £40 coat money, £33 6s conduct money, thereby indicating five days to have the levy assembled at Chester, and the sum of £3 8s as the conductor's fees.[60] Lancashire clearly did not succeed in its original plan of a blanket-type request for payment. The county authority may have genuinely feared that they would not be reimbursed for coat and conduct money from the exchequer, which was generally slow to repay the counties. Cheshire suffered a similar experience.

During the shirevalty of Sir Cuthbert Halsall, 1601, the county was in financial trouble with the privy council for buying up soldiers' uniforms which apparently had been brought back to England from Ireland by Captain John Baxter, a commissary for coats and victuals to the Lough Foyle soldiers. Baxter had been sent for to answer questions about his illegal trade at the council board; there he claimed the coats had been seized by the port officers in Chester and denied that he had received any money for them. The Lancashire sheriff, Halsall, had clearly bought up some of them, for a privy council letter scolded: 'we cannot allow of your doing or of any that shall go about to buy any of the provant apparel provided for the soldiers'.[61] That Halsall as sheriff may have been trying to save the county expense for future coat money is hardly in doubt. He may have been ignorant of the illegal source of the suits of apparel and it is unlikely that he was acting corruptly. Unlike some of the Kentish deputy lieutenants, there is no evidence against Halsall in Lancashire.[62]

At the period of heaviest demands on Lancashire, from June 1598 to June 1600, there were fears among the county's leaders that they were going to be ordered to raid the trained bands to meet the number of recruits. Sir Richard Molyneux, of great influence in Lancashire, wrote to Sir Robert Cecil on 19 March 1599 making it plain that Cecil had given special favour to Lancashire by agreeing that none of its trained bands were to be used for the Irish service. Molyneux wrote that he had made bold to declare this exemption at their last musters, that the soldiers were so thankful that they asked him in the name of the whole shire to present their thanks to Sir Robert Cecil. The good news was especially gratifying since they had heard that the trained bands of Cheshire had been for the Irish war.[63] Molyneux's letter of thanks also makes it plain that he did not have Cecil's direct permission for this exemption:

> though I received nothing concerning this matter from you [Cecil] my man wrote me that you had effected so much for us and I therefore presumed to declare it to the county, it standing at that time in such great fear.[64]

Sir Richard Molyneux may have had influence with Sir Robert Cecil to presume to act simply on the report of his man, but it seems certain that Cecil influenced the privy council to get this exemption for Lancashire.[65]

No particular class of persons in Lancashire appears to have sought exemption from military liabilities, as they did, for example, in the Cinque Ports and in parts of the City of London. The lawyers of the Duchy of Lancashire discharged their contributions in the year 1600 when asked to give a total of £75 to aid the setting forth of a levy for Ireland.[66] Resentment at military taxation did manifest itself among the inhabitants of Furness and Michael because tenants on crown lands there did not pay the same as the rest. The privy council ordered the commissioners to meet the stewards of the crown manors in the area and the spokesmen for the aggrieved inhabitants, to 'devise and set down some such order for the proportioning of the said taxes ... agreeable to equity and indifferency to bring both sides unto an agreement in the same'.[67] In view of the late Elizabethan government's dislike of the exemptions of privileged places it is unlikely that the crown tenants in Furness and Michael were able to continue in their inequitable tax contributions.

The gentry proved uncooperative in their traditional role of providing light horse. When in 1586 the county's justices of the peace were required to provide extra light

Table 8   Lancashire gentry furnishing horse for Ireland

June 1600	October 1601
Sir Richard Molyneux	Sir Richard Molyneux
Sir Richard Houghton	Sir Richard Houghton
Sir Cuthbert Halsall	Edward Tarbock
Edward Standish	Edward Standish
Richard Assheton	Richard Assheton
Ralph Ashton	Ralph Ashton
Richard Holland	Thomas Preston
	Edward Norris of Speke
	Richard Sherbourne
	James Anderton
	Robert Hesketh
	Richard Bold[73]

horse there was no reply.[68] By 1595 an increasing number of Lancashire gentry combined in groups of four, six and even eight to provide a single light horse.[69] To what extent this tendency resulted from the increased cost of fitting out calvalry in the 1590s, the poverty of the Lancastrian gentry, or evasion by the richer members is difficult to assess. Dr C. Haigh reckoned that the Lancastrian gentry formed a smaller proportion of the total population than in most other areas, 'having one gentleman for every 800 people'.[70] Dr B. G. Blackwood records 763 gentry Lancashire families in the year 1600, representing a higher proportion of such families than Yorkshire's 641 or Kent's 700.[71]

Whether numerous or not, the Lancashire gentry owed £200 in overdue payments for sending out horse to Ireland in the year 1600.[72] A comparison of the named gentry in Lancashire for the two occasions when they were asked to provide light horse for the Irish war, June 1600 and October 1601, clearly indicates that the numbers were far from a complete roll call of the wealthier families in the county (Table 8).

Most recalcitrant, however, were recusants expected to supply horse or contribute to their cost. They stand out in Lancashire as a group defying or evading government demands. When Lord Strange described his native county of Lancashire in 1583 as 'this so unbridled and bad a handful of England' he more than likely had the Catholic recusants in mind.[74] They have been much studied from the point of view of political and religious disaffection, but their reluctance to aid with cavalry levies to Ireland has not been much noticed. Recusancy was common in Lancashire, although Catholic gentry in the county were less numerous than hitherto supposed, at 28 per cent.[75] Puritans, also technically recusant, accounted for less than 15 per cent of the gentry, though in the hundred of Salford they outnumbered Catholics.[76]

Government pressure on recusants was always greater in times of foreign invasion scares, and the dangerous state of Ireland in the 1590s probably intensified this. South and west Lancashire, close to Ireland by geography and trade, meant that many in Lancashire were in touch with the Irish Catholic population; the dangers of these contacts were well appreciated in Elizabeth's reign.[77] It was said of south-west Lancashire that 'from Warrington all along the sea coast, all the gentlemen, except Mr. Butler, were of the Roman Catholic faction'.[78] Bishop Vaughan of Chester wrote to Sir Robert Cecil in 1602 of the district as 'the most corrupt place in Lancashire'.[79] The bishop's letters from 1598 to 1601 illustrate his difficulties in having recusants who refused to pay for the Irish service arrested. In January 1598 he reported that many chief recusants 'who were to be apprehended for non-payments' had gone to London seeking to procure their release from appearing before the ecclesiastical commissioners at Chester; he wanted Sir Robert Cecil to have an example made of some of them, so that his own authority in Lancashire would thereby be supported. The bishop saw little point in having them imprisoned in Lancaster gaol, 'for the prison is ill-kept; recusants there can go and come as they like to hunt hawk, and go to the horse races at their pleasure'.[80] In writing to Thomas Hesketh, Bishop Vaughan stated that despite the help of the sheriff, Richard Houghton, 'it is almost impossible to seize them [recusants] because they had so many kindred, spies and alliances'.[81] Houghton listed seventeen recusants who 'refused to contribute to the support of the service in Ireland' and who could not be found, except four who had been arrested: Edward Langtrey, William Anderton, John Asheton, and Elizabeth Tidesley.[82] Langtrey was later released from his obligation to furnish a light horse, 'in respect of his late reformation and conformity'.[83]

In recounting his problems to Cecil, Bishop Vaughan remarked that most recusants withdrew from their homes when his pursuivants were out in search of them, so that for three weeks' work he could only record three arrested.[84] During Sir Richard Molyneux's period of office as sheriff he had to enforce law and order against a recusant riot in which Bishop Vaughan's pursuivants were beaten up by the armed servants of the Norrises of Speke in February 1599.[85] When telling Cecil of what had been done at the special assize called to deal with the rioters, Vaughan said that it all took place in that part of the shire 'full of seminary priests and gentlemen recusants that harbour them'. He named Edward Earlston, William Blundell of Crosby, Henry Lathom of Mossborough and Henry Travis of Hardshowe.[86]

In another report Robert Hesketh, an active commissioner against recusants, added the Norris family of Speke to Vaughan's list of chief offenders among the gentlemen recusants of Lancashire.[87] Vaughan's final remark to Cecil expressed an opinion, not found elsewhere, that the recusants in his diocese 'have been much encouraged by our ill success in Ireland'. In expressing the natural fears of Cecil and the government at large of what would happen should England lose Ireland to Spain Vaughan may simply have been seeking to strengthen his own hand against the Lancashire recusants.[88]

From a list of February 1598, twenty-eight recusants, or the husbands of recusant wives, were to contribute towards the cost of sending horse to Ireland. The commissioners hoped to raise £280 in this way.[89] However, only seven of the twenty-eight paid a total of only £60.[90] John Bird, who had 'twenty-five years experience of Ireland', reported to Cecil that Edward Norris of Speke, worth £500 a year, had never been presented for his recusancy 'through fear of his greatness'.[91]

In September 1598 Vaughan received a batch of common form letters to send out to recusants asking contributions of £15 each to provide horse for the Irish war; five were asked for the full £15 and twenty were required to give £7 10s, each, and five of the latter category were widows of recusants.[92] The poor response to these letters so angered the privy council that the bishop was ordered to see all defaulters sent up under bonds to the council board to answer 'their contemptuous and unsubjectlyke behavyour'; the sheriff and all justices of the peace were to aid his commission on their arrest.[93]

Considering the number of Lancashire's recusants asked for contributions for the Irish war, it would appear that many escaped scot free. The bishop's visitation of 1598 detected 498 recusants for the diocese of Chester. By 1601 episcopal returns showed 754 recusants, and those of 1603 show almost 2,000 in the five deaneries of the Chester diocese.[94] Levies of horse and contributions to send them out were asked of the wealthier gentry among the recusants, yet their recalcitrant mood and their confidence in resisting government demands may have made recusants more noticeable in the military records of Lancashire than elsewhere.[95]

Lancashire, though poor, was asked to raise 1,403 infantrymen for Ireland, which at an average cost per head of £3 10s in the 1590s would have cost the county £4,910. Twenty horses and riders at £30 each would have cost an additional £600. Recusants proved reluctant to contribute to this part of the war effort. It is probably safe to assume that the quality of the men and arms supplied for the Irish service was not of the best on every occasion. In 1594 the mayor of Chester complained of the poor standard of armour sent with the Lancashire recruits.[96] Twenty-two recruits deserted from the October 1601 levy.[97] The levy of eighty in January 1602 from Lancashire was so bad that the commissioners at Chester turned them back; the privy council ordered Lancashire to make up the defects out of their trained bands.[98] In 1599 the Manchester magistracy was warned about recruiting disorderly persons and vagabonds.[99] And, finally, a report from Ireland commented that Lancashire soldiers were 'most faulty in desertion'.[100]

Cheshire's levies for Ireland

John Speed, William Smith and John Leland noted the industry, prosperity and independence of the people of the ancient palatine county of Chester. Speed, who mapped the shire, said it was forty-seven miles one way and twenty-six the other; but G. Ormerod stated that the county was thirty miles from north to south and forty miles from east to west. Leland noted the traditional independence and ancient survival of its gentry families, while Smith praised the sturdy virtues of its yeoman farmers and remarked upon their hatred of Scots. When sixteenth-century Cheshiremen referred to 'our countrey' they meant the county and not the nation at large.[101]

The county long continued to claim to be a palatine, but from 1536 the privy council asserted its authority over Chester and Cheshire.[102] By Elizabeth's reign Cheshire and Lancashire were under the lieutenancy of the Earls of Derby, until 1594. As mentioned in the introduction to this chapter, William, sixth Earl of Derby, who then succeeded did not get a commission of lieutenancy until 1607,[103] and in the absence of a commission of lieutenancy the privy council directed its orders to the high sheriff and commissioners for musters. The military demands from central government for musters, levies, trained bands and military and other taxes were based on the hundreds of the shire, as may be seen from the sole surviving lieutenancy letter book of the period, kept by Sir Hugh Cholmondeley's clerk.[104]

The county was divided into seven hundreds: Macclesfield, Bucklow, Broxton, Nantwhich, Northwich, Edisbury and Wirral. Their head or high constables and bailiffs were responsible to the high sheriff, commissioners for musters and justices of the peace for implementing government orders. The Cheshire hundreds contained many large parishes, each with a number of villages and townships, which arose from the small and scattered rural population of the county in the sixteenth century. Great Budworth, for instance, had thirty-four townships and Presbury thirty-two. A survey of 1669 indicated 400 townships divided between seventy-five parishes, nine of which were in the city of Chester.[105] Little confidence can be placed on a population figure arrived at on the basis of the musters; the highest muster return of 1595 gives a total of 4,000 able-bodied men, exclusive of the city of Chester, so that with a multiplier of seven, 28,000 may be too low as a population figure for the late sixteenth century.[106] Professor A. R. Myers reckoned the Tudor population of the city of Chester at about 4,000. Before his death in July 1980 Professor Myers was working on the Tudor period for the Victoria County History of Cheshire.[107]

The manpower base whence levies were selected for the Irish war may be, as usual, more reliably determined from the muster certificates; these indicate a smaller military potential than Lancashire's. In 1570, 1,640 men were mustered; in 1573, 3,000; in 1577, 1,640; in 1580, 3,000; and in 1595, 4,000.[108] For the last year Lancashire, by comparison, mustered 6,463 men.[109] Cheshire's round figures suggest conventional returns, hardly the precise figures of all able-bodied men from sixteen to sixty. Their 1580 muster certificate was sent in on printed forms; the practice was not general as the council did not send out printed forms on every occasion. The Cheshire justices described their 1580 certificate as a 'pye of squares'; they said the number of all 'able-bodied furnished men' was first given as 2,000, then at 1,000 because the 'armytriton in his unskilfulness hath sett down his figure of 1 in shewe lyke to the figure of 2'. The total of 3,000 therefore included this 1,000 plus the 2,000 unfurnished and untrained men of the shire.[110]

Yet Cheshire thought itself pressed hard for levies. The commissioners for musters in 1580 complained to the Earl of Leicester that in their small county the queen and non-resident nobles owned much of the land without contributing to the armed forces of the shire.[111] When preparing defences for the Armada the Cheshire justices complained that prices were rising so fast that the monies collected for these preparations would be insufficient.[112] In the 1590s, captains supervising the stores of arms and armour remained unpaid for five consecutive years; though warned by the privy council, the county's authorities were either unable or unwilling to pay up.[113] The council took little heed of the county's poverty pleas and in October 1594 directed the sheriff and commissioners that in addition to the 200 trained in April 1594 they were to keep 100 more well trained and ready armed for speedy service to Ireland if required.[114] In the 1590s the government was driven to ask that proportions of men from the trained bands be called out to fill up the drafts of conscripts for the Irish war. And,

Table 9   Cheshire levies to Ireland

Date	No. of foot	No. of horse	Note
October 1594	100	–	1
October 1596	47	–	2
April 1597	47	–	3
June 1598	150	–	4
January 1599	200	3	5
January 1600	100	–	6
June 1600	50	6	7
December 1600	20	–	8
April 1601	25	–	9
October 1601	25	11	10
August 1601	60	–	
December 1601 for			
January 1602	20	–	
July 1602	50	–	11
Totals	894	20	

1. PRO SP12/248/87, original order was for 200. Second order to train and keep in readiness for Ireland 100 men, PRO SP12/250/18.
2. This levy was to join the Lancashire contingent. Six dead pays were clearly allowed in the 100, hence 47 in each half. CCRO, Cholmondeley's letter book, DDX358/1, 33v.
3. *APC*, xxvii, 21–28.
4. CCR, CXX/358/1, 34.
5. Hatfield House, Cecil papers, 88/49, R; *APC*, xxix, 490.
6. *CSPD* (1598–1601), 377.
7. Hatfield House, Cecil papers, 88/49, R; *APC*, xxx, 416, 436.
8. *APC*, xxx, 566, 598.
9. *APC*, xxxi, 23, reinforcements for Lough Foyle garrisons.
10. *Ibid.*, 318. The original order for twenty-five in August was increased to sixty in October –

despite the deep-seated reluctance to draw upon the trained men of the counties, the ruling elites had to agree with government orders. Cheshire was no exception; some of its trained soldiers went with the 1594, 1596 and 1599 levies.

Cheshire, the natural hinterland of the port of Chester, shared the multiple burdens which the Irish war of the 1590s brought. Apart from fulfilling the privy council's demands for specific numbers of men and arms, as well as horse, the surrounding villages and parishes adjacent to Chester were liable for billeting levies from every shire of the realm.

Captains and conductors, who had lost men through desertion, were likely to call upon the same villages and parishes to make up their numbers.[115] With this in mind the numbers in Table 9 of the demands made on Cheshire may be considered but a part of the entire, and untold, contribution the county made to the war effort.

Cheshire was asked to provide soldiers for the war on twelve occasions over the period 1594–1602, nearly the same number of times as Lancashire, but fewer men were demanded. Less than 1,000 men over a nine-year period may not appear excessively demanding on a shire that had a prosperous reputation; the smaller geographical area of Cheshire may explain why Cheshire sent out 534 foot less than Lancashire; yet each county sent out the same number of horse, a possible indication of the greater prosperity of Cheshire gentry.[116] The gentry sending furnished horse in June 1600 were: Sir Hugh Cholmondeley, Sir Randall Brereton, Sir William Brereton, Sir Peter Leigh, Peter Warburton or Arley and William Brereton of Hanford.[117] In 1601 eleven gentry were asked: Sir Richard Brereton, Sir William Brereton, Sir Peter Leigh, Sir John Savage, Sir George Booth, Thomas Venables, Peter Warburton, Thomas Wilbraham, Thomas Holcroft, Richard Gravener and John Dutton.[118]

The heaviest demands on the county came between June 1598 and June 1600, reflecting crises in Ireland. The increase from twenty-five to sixty between August and October 1601, together with the demand for eleven horse, is a reflection of what was happening in other shires on the occasion of the Spanish landing at Kinsale.[119] In these last years of the war the complaints of the justices in Cheshire suggest that the Irish effort had denuded the shire of arms and armour and all other kinds of 'warlike necessaries'.[120] The county arsenals became a source of supply for these, understandably when the price of firearms had raised the cost of sending out a company by about 50 per cent compared with the earlier years of the reign, when firearms were not much used.[121]

The way in which the commissioners for the musters in Cheshire divided up the demands for men among the seven hundreds, and the rating on each for the money to have the soldiers equipped and sent out, is set out in Table 10. The evidence is not complete in the case of each levy, and differs from the Lancashire quotas in the hundreds in that military rates are given.

Unlike the lieutenancy records for Kent in the 1590s, those of Cheshire are disappointingly thin; nevertheless, from Cholmondeley's letter book the progress in mustering, equipping and sending out two levies from Cheshire, in September 1596 and in June 1598, can be followed in detail.[122] These two levies illustrate how Cheshire organised forces for Ireland.

On 27 August 1596 the queen wrote to the sheriff and commissioners for musters stating that it had become necessary to increase forces in Ireland: fifty able men were to be levied, mustered and put into a state of readiness with coats, armour and weapons. They were to be committed to the charge of an able captain, who would be designated in the privy council's instructions.[123] Cheshire appointed Sir Urian Leigh, a local man, the eldest of four sons of Thomas Leigh of Adlington in the hundred of Macclesfield.[124] In the letter of appointment Leigh is spoken of as 'a Gent of good reputation and knowne unto you'.

The council's directives elaborated the queen's order; they allowed three dead pays on the fifty, but wanted them armed in the proportion of twenty-three corselets with pikes, twelve calivers and twelve muskets, and because the winter season was approaching they wanted the soldiers to have 'coats of some mixed colour and well lined'. All were to be ready at Chester on the last day of September, or sooner should there be 'convenient shipping there for their transportation into the realm of Ireland'. They were to join up with another forty-seven from Lancashire 'to make one band', at the assembly place in Warrington.[125]

Table 10   Quotas of men and money in Cheshire hundreds

Hundred	March 1596	September 1596	June 1598	October 1601
Macclesfield				
men	25	9	25	12
rate (*£.s.d*)	£75.3.4	£25.2.0	£100.5.4	–
Edisbury				
men	16	4	16	7
rate (*£.s.d*)	£48.16.0	£16.16.0	£64.7.4	–
Nantwich				
men	21	7	31	10
rate (*£.s.d*)	£75.1.0	£24.19.6	£99.0.6	–
Broxton				
men	21	7	21	7
rate (*£.s.d*)	£69.1.0	£21.2.2	£90.13.2	–
Northwich				
men	20	6	20	7
rate (*£.s.d*)	£59.5.0	£18.14.0	£77.19.0	–
Bucklow				
men	24	7	24	10
rate (*£.s.d*)	£63.1.01	£21.3.4	£84.14.4	–
Wirral				
men	23	7	23	7
rate (*£.s.d*)	£60.7.8[1]	£20.15.6[2]	£81.3.2[3]	–[4]
Totals of men	150	47	160	60

1. This levy was sent out of Cheshire to aid Essex in his Cadiz venture at a cost to the county of £450 15*s* 0*d*. The commissioners noted 'this chardge was layd according to the mize', CCRO, Lieutenancy letter book of Sir Hugh Cholmondeley, DDX358/1, 26.
2. This levy went to Ireland under Sir Urian Leigh, who had been knighted by Essex at Cadiz. Stockings and shoes came to 4*s* 6*d* the man, coats at 16*s* each, conduct money 3*s* 4*d*. CCRO, Lieutenancy letter book of Sir Hugh Cholmondeley, DDX358/1, 35v.
3. The second largest levy to Ireland from the county. The commissioners reckoned the total cost to the county at £599 12*s* 10*d*. CCRO, Lieutenancy letter book of Sir Hugh Cholmondeley, DDX358/1, 45v.
4. No local evidence for this levy has been found; the numbers are counted from the indenture among the exchequer records – PRO E101/65/17 (a) signed by the conductor, Thomas Venables, and Thomas Ashton, the sheriff in 1601.

The sheriff and commissioners divided up the demand of forty-seven on the seven hundreds, and calculated for each hundred the sums of money the constables needed to levy.[126] Formal commands then went out from the commissioners to the constables to recruit the soldiers:

These shall be to will and command you that you be before us at Tarvin on Tuesday 28th of this month by nine of the clock in the forenoon and to bring with you one able and sufficient man, such a one as is knowne to be of good behaviour, not vagrant, nor of the baser sort for we are very strictly commanded that such be impressed for her gracious Majesty's said service in Ireland.[127]

The levying and collection of the military rate of £148 12s 6d to equip and clothe the twenty-three pikemen and twenty-four 'Shot' from the Cheshire hundreds were carried out between 10 and 18 September. We do not hear of the levy again until it came before William Brereton, deputy mayor of Chester, and Maurice Kyffin, the government's muster master, at the post of Chester, October 1596.[128]

From the muster master's report and the captain's muster roll, the one annotating the other, we learn that the company under Sir Urian Leigh passed muster, but not until the captain changed 'the men delivered out of Lancashire ... insufficient and defective' for 'voluntaryes of his owne follers'.[129] Sir Urian changed some of the Cheshire men not because they were insufficient but because 'the capten was desirous to have some of his owne friendes and tenants in their place'. Maurice Kyffin reported that this course of action had been permitted by him at the port 'because there was no corruption used therein by anye of his officers, and he the said capten assured us upon his creditt that there was none'.[130] The company, thus reconstituted largely of Cheshire men, was deemed 'exceedinge fayre', and in number four or five over and above the abatement of the six dead pays allowed, standing at thirty-four musketeers, thirty-eight pikemen, twenty-three calivers and seven officers. Among the officers were Captain Leigh's two brothers, Ralph and Thomas Leigh, the former lieutenant, the latter ensign, and his son, Thomas Leigh, sergeant. Ralph and one Thomas were later killed at the Yellow Ford in August 1598. The company lacked a surgeon but Sir Urian asked that the pay for one should not be deducted until he 'can provide himself of a skilful surgian'.[131]

From 'Payments to Sir Urian Leigh, Knight, capten of 100 footmen' it can be seen that he was given £3 2s 8d conduct money, 1d a mile per man for the sixteen-mile march from Warrington to Chester. For impressment money he received £15 8s and since he arrived with forty-seven men at Chester a day before the Lancashire men he was paid an additional £1 11s 4d for the day of 11 October. Further payments indicate the company was delayed on account of bad weather: 'for two weekes pay for the company beginninge the xii and endinge the xxiii of October, £46.13.4d. as well as £7.14s. for the officers'.[132] The last item shows that Leigh's company was held back a further week after 24 October 'by reasone this bande was the laste embarqued, £xx'.[133]

We pick up the progress of Leigh's company in Ireland on 13 November 1596, when it was reported that 'Sir Urian Leigh arrived at the Lord Deputy's camp at Rathdrum, 29 mls. s.w. of Dublin in Co. Wicklow bringing with him a prisoner from Dublin one of Feagh McHugh's followers'. Sir William Russell, then lord deputy, ordered Leigh's company to march to the garrison at Drogheda, twenty-three miles north of Dublin, where it remained until drawn out to fight with the lord deputy's field forces against Ulster the following autumn. It is a rare instance of where an English company can be followed through to military action in Ireland.[134]

The government's demand on Cheshire in June 1598 for 150 soldiers to reinforce defective bands in Ireland because of the continuance of the rebellion left similar records in Cholmondeley's letter book to those dealing with Sir Urian Leigh's company in 1596. The correspondence for the 150 suggested more urgency than in 1596. The queen's letter was sent to the commissioners on 13 June 1598, the privy council's directives on 18 June, the orders to the constables for men and money on 26 June, and the men were to be at Chester under the captaincy of Peter Warburton, a local man, by 9 July.[135] Half the force were to be pikemen, half 'shot' (the greater part of whom were to be musketeers); they were to be given training in firearms and the recruiters were not to admit 'anie rogues and vagabonds in the nombre of them'. The billeting, victualling and shipping had already been arranged between the council and the mayor of Chester, and hence no delays were to be allowed in the execution of the service.[136]

The recruits from the four hundreds of Nantwich, Wirral, Edisbury and Broxton mustered at Cobbler's Cross, near Tarpoley, on 4 July; and, on the same day, those from the other three hundreds at Knutsford. This was expeditious mustering since the orders went out to the constables on 26 June.[137] Captain Peter Warburton's part 'of the tripartite roll indented' shows that the full demand of 150 was mustered and viewed at Chester. The men are named by their hundred of origin, forename and surname, and divided into the proportion of weapons required by the council's orders.[138] The impression is one of an efficient piece of service, perhaps because the muster master was also their captain and conductor to Chester and because they were all Cheshire men.

To provide money for this levy the sheriff, Sir Edward Warren, and the commissioners for musters rated the sum of £599 12s 10d proportionately on the hundreds. They reckoned conduct money at 3s 4d for each soldier, a coat and cap for each at 16s, shoes and stockings at 4s 6d and hose and doublet at 14s. They paid Captain Warburton in two instalments of £20 and £30 as captain and muster master.[139] In these accounts no prices of weapons are given. This omission perhaps indicates that they were supplied out of the county's arsenal. If £599 12s 10d had been collected in military taxation, and the total expenditure on the levy a sum of £333 15s 0d, there should have been left in the hands of the commissioners for the county a sum of £265 17s 10d. There was nothing unusual or suspicious about a county having surplus funds from military taxation but for the fact that Cheshire had already been ordered to institute an enquiry into the misappropriation of military taxes in July 1596,[140] and twice after the Warburton levy, in December 1599 and June 1600.[141]

In ordering the enquiry and a 'true accompt to be yeelded', the privy council claimed in its letter of 26 July 1596 to Sir Hugh Cholmondley and the commissioners for musters in Cheshire that over the years from before the Armada crisis of 1588 sums of money had been levied on the Cheshire inhabitants 'for armour, weapons and setting forth of the souldiers', which came to the hands of 'certen persons which have not imploied the same to those uses'. The justices were to report on who had received sums of money 'for her majesties service these nyne yeres paste', how they used the money and what sums remained in their hands 'unpayed to the greate defraudinge and discontentment of the people'.[142]

The findings of the enquiry produced a series of complex financial accounts to 'prove' not misappropriation of public funds but non-payment of military taxes on the part of some unidentified persons in six of the seven hundreds, and to show a marginal overestimation. The total sum ordered to be taxed was £2,449 8s 6d, while that collected was only £2,190 12s 8d. Of this sum £2,140 7s 4d had been disbursed. Sir Hugh Cholmondeley and Sir John Savage held the balance of £50 5s 4d. Taxes unpaid amounted to £258 15s 10d, indicating the difference between the sum ordered to be taxed and that collected. Of that unpaid total, £39 12s 10d was owed from Macclesfield, £34 12s 8d from Nantwich, £18 12s 11 from Wirral, £8 19s 9d from Broxton, £41 12s 10d from Bucklow and £115 3s 10d from Edisbury. No account is given for Northwich hundred.[143]

The neat balancing of the totals contrasts with the clerk's methods of arriving at them – undated and random jottings of county taxes and expenses over the nine-year period, but not in chronological order; his omission of any accounts from Northwich, and his note of uncertainty under the Edisbury account, 'whether uncollected at the countrie or in the handes of the then justices of the peace wee can by no enquyrie learne,'[144] would all appear to cast suspicion.

The privy council was not satisfied. In December 1599 it wanted a further enquiry instituted. There was no reply;[145] it wrote again in June 1600 that the queen and her people were being defrauded by those who convert taxes to their own use, having been credibly informed of these abuses in Cheshire, and among 'gentlemen of honest reputation'.[146] The council wanted a full statement of what had happened to monies levied, who had received it, how it had been delivered and what portion had been detained, and it expected a speedy reply. The sheriff, Thomas Smith, and four commissioners, Sir John Savage, William Brereton, John Egerton and Thomas Wilbraham, replied to Sir Robert Cecil on 16 September 1600 with a schedule of accounts for the previous two years and a covering letter.[147] The schedule simply indicates that a sum of £19 15s 5d remained in the hands of Sir Edward Fitton from all monies received.

Under the heading 'for the service of 150 souldiers for her Majesties service of Irelande in July 1598' the sums given are different from those in Cholmondeley's letter book for the identical services in Cheshire. It is stated that £602 19s 6d was levied on the county and that £602 13s 8d was expended, and the balance of 5s 10d spent on the next levy for Ireland.[148] The Cholmondeley letter book gives £599 12s 10d as the sum levied; and from the items spent on each of the 150 soldiers of Warburton's company a total of £333 15s 0d can be calculated.[149] Both letter book and schedule agree that the county had £67 2s from the exchequer, but disagree on the amounts paid to Peter Warburton. The letter from the lord treasurer shows two instalments of £35 and £30 to be paid to Warburton, whereas the schedule sent in September 1600 gives instalments of £20 and £30 paid to Warburton, who 'nowe hath refused securitie for payment thereof'.[150] It seems possible that some misappropriation of public money had been going on among the Cheshire county officials in the 1590s, and that, as elsewhere, there was trouble over the payment of the muster master's salary.[151]

The demands for the men and money were not the only demands; Cheshire was an agricultural shire, famed for its cheese, butter and farm produce, hence it was much called upon by the army victualling contractors. While some complained of resulting food shortages, many may have profited by supplying victuals for the forces in Ireland. When the Earl of Essex was recruiting his Irish army of 1599 he told the privy council not to have the victualling contractors search remote counties for cheese and butter, such as Essex and Suffolk, but to have them take up these commodities in Cheshire, Lancashire and Wales, and thereby avoid decay of the goods on long inland journeys.[152] Such a victualling policy worked to the disadvantage of the county in years of dearth; there were grain shortages in 1596 and 1598 in the city of Chester. And as prices rose, so too did resentment at having to ship grain to feed the army forces in Ireland.[153]

The justices of Cheshire wrote indignantly on 12 October 1596 to the privy council of how Mr George Beverley, the government's victualling contractor for Ireland, had been sent into Cheshire by the lord deputy and council in Ireland 'to take up and transport from hence into Ireland 500 quarter bushels of wheat'. In unequivocal terms they pointed out the great scarcity 'of bread corn in all this country because of the continual wet that hath fallen over since April last'. A straight refusal to comply followed, which stressed that there was insufficient grain in Cheshire that winter to feed its own inhabitants. They wrote that in future demands of the same kind, the council must recall the 'pore estate of our countrey'.[154] George Beverley remarked to Sir William Knollys, comptroller of the Queen's household:

> The cheese of this Country [Cheshire] is a victual apt and ready to be shipped to serve the soldiers in Ireland, and heretofore hath usually been provided in the winter season, to serve the soldiers for their victualling in Lent, when beef and other victual faileth.[155]

In December 1600, Cheshire sent 600 quarters of wheat to Ireland, but that was among the lowest of the grain contributions. Somerset and Sussex, for example, sent 1,500 quarters each, Cornwall and Hampshire, 1,200 each; only Cambridgeshire and Huntingdonshire, at 500 quarters each, sent less than Cheshire.[156] These demands are a reminder that the Irish war not only cost the shires in men, money and arms, but that the army had to be largely fed out of England, a fact often emphasised by English captains from Ireland.[157]

The county of Cheshire gave signs of disenchantment with the government's demands in the 1590s. The impressment of troops was held in universal distaste. The county's negligence was noted in making irregular and improper returns to the exchequer of military taxes and expenditure. And there is other evidence of the county's reluctance to provide men and money. When loans were collected to support the army in Ireland in 1598, the contribution of £500 due from Cheshire was wanting.[158] Macclesfield wanted to take a stand on the privileges of its letters patent to gain exemption from *all* military services. This was refused in 1598.[159] In 1599 the inhabitants of the Wirral petitioned the privy council for a similar exemption because of their continual burdens with the passage of levies for Ireland.[160] On 30 November 1600 the council had to write to the sheriff and commissioners for musters in Cheshire about 'certaine townes and landes in that countie [which] doe refuse to contribute towards such publique chardges for post horses, carts and carriages'; the county was reminded that 'no pretence of charter or other privileges ought to free them in theis occassysons of her Majesty's services'.[161] In May 1601, Thomas Watson, an agent of the war treasurer in Ireland, complained to the privy council that carts used to convey munitions from the Tower of London to Chester, and which should have been sent to Dublin, were 'sold in various parts of Cheshire, and for mean prices'.[162]

The experience of raising troops, mustering and equipping them in Cheshire and Lancashire exhibits similarities and contrasts. The administrative system in both, under high sheriffs and commissioners for musters, worked as efficiently as in those shires which were under lords lieutenants. Though the personnel of the shirevalty changed annually, the office was circulated among a closely knit group of county gentry in both shires who continuously occupied the commission for musters. In Lancashire Sir Richard Molyneux stood out as the prominent commissioner, and in Cheshire Sir Hugh Cholmondeley.

Despite corruption in the military finances of both shires, an aspect of late-sixteenth-century public life from which no shire studied appeared totally innocent,[163] and rising resentment at the demands of the war, the amount of money and numbers of soldiers from both Lancashire and Cheshire made a considerable contribution to the national war effort; 1,403 foot from Lancashire and 869 from Cheshire. At an average cost of £3 10*s* to send a soldier equipped to Ireland their respective numbers would have cost the shires £4,910 10*s* and £3,041 19*s*; and to each sum must be added an approximate total of £600 each to send out horse. Coat and conduct money from the exchequer was normally in arrears, and their amounts never covered the full costs.

Clearly, neither shire sent out its bravest and best men, the majority being conscripts. Those from Cheshire appear to have had a better reputation. Lord Mountjoy, in writing to Cecil in June 1600 for reinforcements, suggested that they be raised in Cheshire, where the captain will be able 'to draw men of good quality to the service'.[164] There were more mentions of desertion among Lancashire men than Cheshire men.

Lancashire county authorities made more of their difficulties in communication with London than Cheshire's; however, more roads converged on Chester than north of the Mersey in the sixteenth century.[165] The county was small enough to be considered the hinterland to the city and port of Chester. In this sense Cheshire was subject to direct control from central government in a way Lancashire was not. The greater frequency of correspondence between the council and Cheshire was a measure of that control. The importance of Chester, towards which the national levies marched, gave the surrounding shire of Cheshire, through which many of them came, almost an equal importance as the chief port in the north for military operations.

Notes

1   For Welsh levies to Ireland see J. J. N. McGurk, 'A survey of the demands made on the Welsh shires to supply soldiers for the Irish War 1594–1602', *Transactions of the Honourable Society of Cymmrodorion* (1983), 56–68.

2   G. Scott Thomson, 'The origin and growth of the office of deputy lieutenancy', *Transactions of the Royal Historical Society*, 4th series, 5 (1922), 155.

3   *Cal. Carew MSS*, iv, 477, 'The note for Ireland of Sir H.S.', 1575.

4   *APC*, xix, 155, 156.

5   HMC, *Salisbury*, xi, 405; and see B. Coward, 'The Lieutenancy of Lancs, and Cheshire in the 16th and 17th centuries', *Transactions of the Historic Society of Lancashire and Cheshire*, new series, 19 (1967), 41; but the article ignores the Irish wars.

6   *APC*, xxiv, 256, 257.

7   F. R. Raines, ed., *The Derby household books* (Chetham Society, xxxi, Manchester, 1853), 23, 24, 84–88.

8   For the Lancashire county elite see J. Harland, ed., *Lancashire lieutenancy under the Tudors* (Chetham Society, xlix, Manchester, 1859), 1; B. G. Blackwood, *The Lancashire gentry and the Great Rebellion* (Chetham Society, Manchester, 1978), Chapter 1. For the Cheshire elite, see J. S. Morrill, *Cheshire 1630–1660* (Oxford, 1974); G. P. Higgins, 'County government and society in Cheshire c.1590 to 1640', MA thesis (University of Liverpool, 1973), 22; and P. J. Marriott, 'Commission of the peace in Cheshire 1536–1603', MA thesis (University of Manchester, 1974).

9   G. P. Higgins, 'County government and society in Cheshire c.1590 to 1640', MA thesis (University of Liverpool, 1973), Chapter 2, 'The county community'.

10 B. G. Blackwood, *The Lancashire gentry and the Great Rebellion* (Chetham Society, Manchester, 1978), Chapter 1; and C. Haigh, *Reformation and resistance in Tudor Lancashire* (Cambridge 1975).

11 R. S. Schofield, 'The geographical distribution of wealth in England, 1334–1649', *Economic History Review*, 2nd series, 18 (1965), 504; and P. R. Long, 'The wealth of the magisterial class in Lancashire, c.1590–1640', MA thesis (Manchester University, 1968).

12 J. Thirsk, ed., *The agrarian history of England and Wales, 1500–1640* (Cambridge, 1967), vol. iv, 80–89.

13 J. Strype, *Annals of the Reformation*, II (I) (Oxford, 1820–1840), 575–576.

14 HMC, *Salisbury*, xii, 669.

15 Lancashire Record Office (hereafter LRO), lay subsidy roll for 1593, DDF/2430, 3v.

16 LRO, Houghton lieutenancy letter book, DDN/1/64, 5.

17 W. G. Hoskins, *The age of plunder, 1500–1547* (London, 1976), Appendix 1, 245.

18 C. Haigh, *Reformation and resistance in Tudor Lancashire* (Cambridge, 1975), 46.

19 Cited in J. Parkes, *Travel in England in the seventeenth century* (London, 1925), 300.

20 C. Haigh, *Reformation and resistance in Tudor Lancashire* (Cambridge, 1975).

21 R. Somerville, *A history of the Duchy of Lancaster* (London, 1953), 470, 471, 473, 474.

22 W. K. Jordan, *The social institutions of Lancashire, 1480–1660* (Chetham Society, xi, 3rd series, Manchester, 1962), Chapter 1.

23 W. G. Hoskins, *The age of plunder, 1500–1547* (London, 1976), 16, 17.

24 W. K. Jordan, *The social institutions of Lancashire, 1480–1660* (Chetham Society, Manchester, 1962), 1–2, footnote 1.

25 B. G. Blackwood, *The Lancashire gentry and the Great Rebellion* (Chetham Society, xxx, Manchester, 1978), 3, 4, 29 and note 14.

26 J. Harland, ed., *Lancashire lieutenancy under the Tudors* (Chetham Society, xlix, Manchester, 1859).

27 LRO, lay subsidy roll for 1593, LV/80 (badly mutilated). This work may have been unknown to Harland in 1859 when he brought out the two pioneering volumes on lieutenancy for the Chetham Society.

28 LRO, Houghton lieutenancy book, DDN/1/64, not used by Harland for his second volume on Stuart lieutenancy in Lancashire.

29 L. Boynton, *The Elizabethan militia* (London, 1967), 198, 200, 206, 210.

30 J. Harland, ed., *Lancashire lieutenancy under the Tudors* (Chetham Society, xlix, Manchester, 1859), part i, 21, 22, 61, 62, 66, 67, 111, 132; part ii, 144, 164, 201, and notes 27, 215, 216, 226.

31 *Victoria county history*, Lancashire, ii, 223.

32 L. Boynton, *The Elizabethan militia* (London, 1967), 28, 33, 66–70.

33 The office of high constable, though much mentioned, has received little attention in recent local studies, but see H. B. Simpson, 'The office of constable', *English Historical Review*, 10 (1895), 625–641.

34 See map in J. P. Smith, *The genealogists' atlas of Lancashire* (Liverpool, 1930), 1. The numbers of freeholders in J. P. Earwaker, 'List of freeholders in Lancs. in the year 1600', *Lancs and Cheshire Record Society*, 12 (1885), 229–251.

35 LRO, lieutenancy minute book, LV/80, 608.

36 E. Baines, *History of Lancashire* (Manchester, reprint of the 1824 edn, 1968), 49; LRO, lieutenancy minute book, LV/80, 15.

37 Hundredal proportions of men and money are noted for the 1570s but only partly for the 1580s in J. Harland, ed., *Lancashire lieutenancy under the Tudors* (Chetham Society, xlix, Manchester, 1859), *passim*.

38 LRO, muster roll January 1600, DDH e/61/13 – Hesketh MSS.

39 PRO E101/65/28, 'Edward Tarbock, captain, indenture of the 19th July in the 40th yeare of Elizabeth'.

40 Figures based on J. Harland, ed., *Lancashire lieutenancy under the Tudors* (Chetham Society, xlix, Manchester, 1859), part ii, 234, 235, for the year 1594; and on the extant Lancashire muster rolls in the PRO E101.65.28. The latter, a box of exchequer records, documents not individually numbered, contains many of the tripartite indentures sent to the privy council.

41 See Table 7.

42 E. Baines, *History of Lancashire* (Manchester, 1968), 49.

43 LRO, lieutenancy minute book, LV/80, 11, 'Nombers of light horse within the county of Lancashire and who are charged to make the same', 21 May 1602.

44 See Table 7.

45 See Table 7.

46 See Chapter 3.

47 J. Harland, ed., *Lancashire lieutenancy in Tudor times* (Chetham Society, xlix, Manchester, 1859), part i, 22, 62, 65, 75, 76, 111–119, 132, 139–174. For a narrative account of the Desmond rebellion see J. J. N. McGurk, 'The fall of the noble house of Desmond, 1579–1583', parts, i and ii, *History Today*, 29 (1979), 578–585, and 670–675.

48 See notes 8 and 9 to Table 7.

49 *APC*, xxxii, 359–360.

50 *APC*, xxxi, 285. In 1598 Hugh Done petitioned Sir Robert Cecil for a captaincy in Ireland – HMC, *Salisbury*, viii, 317.

51 Lathom had previously been muster master in Lancashire, *APC*, xxxv, 335; and when employed at sea in 1596, the county asked if Richard Bridges, a servant to the Earl of Derby, could fill Lathom's place – Bridges acted later as a conductor of troops.

52 LRO, lieutenancy minute book, LV/80, f. 9, partly mutilated.

53 *Ibid.*, 2, 3, 4.

54 PRO SP12/240, 49, mayor of Chester to the sheriff and justices in Lancashire, 21 December 1594.

55 PRO SP12/251, 3, commissioners for musters in Lancashire to Lord Burghley, January 1595.

56 Hatfield House, Cecil papers, 59/64, the Lancashire commissioners to Sir Robert Cecil, 12 February 1599.

57 LRO, muster roll of 1600, DDH e/61/13 in the Hesketh of Rufford muniments. Robert Hesketh was son and heir of Sir Thomas Hesketh, Lord of Houghwick and Rufford. Richard Holland of Denton succeeded his father in 1573, aged twenty-four, was high sheriff in 1573, 1582, 1596; he died 1618. There are several Richard Ashtons/Asshetons at this period, for example of Middleton, of Downham and of Lever: see J. Harland, ed.,

Lancashire lieutenancy in Tudor times (Chetham Society, Manchester, 1859), part ii, 249.

58 *APC*, xxx, 25, 54, January and February 1600.
59 *Ibid.*, 119.
60 *Ibid.*, 450.
61 *APC*, xxxi, 256, privy council to Sir Cuthbert Halsall, 30 March 1601.
62 Halsall was high sheriff again in 1612. He was the natural son of Sir Richard Halsall of Halsall, but succeeded to the patrimonial inheritance – J. Harland, ed., *Lancashire lieutenancy in Tudor times* (Chetham Society, Manchester, 1859), part ii, 245, note 85.
63 PRO SP12/270/60, 'Sir Richard Molyneux to Secretary Cecil from Croxteth, 19th March 1599'.
64 *Ibid.*, Molyneux to Cecil, 19 March 1599.
65 Molyneux had been in trouble in 1597 with the privy council for negligence in not executing writs. *APC*, xxxi, 318, 354.
66 *APC*, xxx, 31, contributions from the lawyers.
67 *APC*, xxix, 561–562, the privy council.
68 L. Boynton, *The Elizabethan militia* (London, 1967), 88.
69 *Ibid.*, 182.
70 C. Haigh, *Reformation and resistance in Tudor Lancashire* (Cambridge, 1975), 107.
71 B. G. Blackwood *The Lancashire gentry and the Great Rebellion* (Chetham Society, xxv, Manchester, 1978), 5.
72 *APC*, xxx, 306.
73 *APC*, xxx, 440; *APC*, xxxii, 283. For brief biographical notices of many of the listed gentry see J. Harland, ed., *Lancashire lieutenancy in Tudor times* (Chetham Society, x/xi, Manchester, 1859), parts i and ii *passim*; F. R., ed., *The Derby household books* (Chetham Society, Manchester, 1853), 91–215; P. R. Long, 'The wealth of the magisterial class in Lancashire c.1590–1640', MA thesis (University of Manchester, 1968) shows that trade was more profitable than office holding, 147–157, 159.
74 Cited in C. Haigh, *Reformation and resistance in Tudor Lancashire* (Cambridge, 1975), 46.
75 B. G. Blackwood, *The Lancashire gentry and the Great Rebellion* (Chetham Society, Manchester, 1978), 28, relying on C. Haigh's and J. Bossy's work on recusant history.
76 *Ibid.*, Table 15.
77 J. S. Leatherbarrow, *Elizabethan recusants in Lancashire* (Camden Society, cx, 2nd series, London, 1947).
78 *Victoria county history, Lancashire*, II, 53.
79 HMC, *Salisbury*, x, 744, and ix, 18.
80 *CSPD* (1598–1601), 14, Vaughan to Cecil, 14 January 1599.
81 *Ibid.*, 7, Vaughan to Hesketh, 14 January 1599.
82 *Ibid.*, 7 and 8, Houghton's list of seventeen recusants.
83 *Ibid.*, 148, Vaughan to Cecil, 8 January 1599.
84 *Ibid.*, 7, Vaughan to Cecil, 19 March 1599.
85 *Ibid.*, 170, Molyneux to Cecil, 19 March 1599.
86 *Ibid.*, 389–390, Vaughan to Cecil, 31 January 1600 (n.s.).
87 *CSPD* (1598–1601), 466, Hesketh to Cecil.
88 *Ibid.*, 389, Vaughan to Cecil, 31 January 1600.
89 PRO SP12/266, 80, Vaughan's list, February 1598.
90 PRO SP12/270, 41, list of payments to Sir John Stanhope, treasurer of the chamber, 18 February 1599.
91 HMC, *Salisbury*, ix, 18, 19, Bird to Cecil, 11 January 1599.
92 *APC*, xxix, 220.
93 *Ibid.*, 300–301.

94   C. Haigh, *Reformation and resistance in Tudor Lancashire* (Cambridge, 1975), 330.
95   For the disarming of recusants in one shire, Kent, see J. J. N. McGurk, 'Lieutenancy and recusancy in Elizabethan Kent', *Recusant History*, 4 (1974), 157–170.
96   PRO SP12/250, 49, Foulke Aldersey, mayor of Chester to the high sheriff and justices of Lancashire, 21 December 1594.
97   *APC*, xxxii, 359–360.
98   LRO, lieutenancy minute book, LV/80, 3, 4, 7 January 1602 (n.s.).
99   W. E. A. Axon, *The annals of Manchester* (Manchester, 1886), 44.
100 *CSPI* (November 1600 – July 1601), 161.
101 W. Harrison, 'Leland's itinerary', *Transactions of the Lancashire and Cheshire Antiquarian Society*, 28 (1910), 40–58; G. Ormerod, *History of Cheshire* (London, 1882), vol. i, xliv;William Smith's account of Cheshire, *King's vale royal*, is edited from D. King's 1656 edition by G. Ormerod, *The history of the county palatine and city of Chester* (London, 1819), vol. i, 103–112.
102 J. Beck, *Tudor Cheshire* (Chester, 1969), Chapter 1.
103 B. Coward, 'Disputed inheritances: some difficulties of the nobility in the late sixteenth and early seventeenth centuries', *Bulletin of the Institute of Historical Research*, 44 (1971), 204–214.
104 CCRO, lieutenancy letter book of Sir Hugh Cholmondeley, DDX358, 1–84 (1595–1604). Sir Hugh Cholmondley, died 1601, was one of the two Cheshire deputy lieutenants under Henry, fourth Earl of Derby; commissioner for musters in Cheshire and Chester in the 1590s and escheator of the county in 1600.
105 J. Beck, *Tudor Cheshire* (Chester, 1969), 23.
106 CCRO, lieutenancy letter book of Sir Hugh Cholmondeley, DDX358/1, 28–29.
107 A. R. Myers, 'Tudor Chester', *Journal of the Chester Archaeological Society*, 63 (1980), 43–57.
108 CCRO, lieutenancy letter book of Sir Hugh Cholmondeley, DDX358/1, 1–11v; E. E. Rich, 'The population of Elizabethan England', *Economic History Review* (1950), 254.
109 CCRO, lieutenancy letter book of Sir Hugh Cholmondeley, DDX358/1, 28–29, where the Lancashire muster certificate is given with Cheshire's, 1595.
110 *CSPD* (1547–1580), 661, 679.
111 PRO SP/12/162, 12.
112 PRO SP/12/209, 98.
113 PRO SP/12/212, 27.
114 PRO SP/12/250, 18, to the high sheriff and justices of Cheshire, October 1594.
115 For examples, *APC*, xxx, 229, 230.
116 See Table 9.
117 *APC*, xxx, 440, Cheshire gentry furnishing horse, June 1600.
118 *APC*, xxxii, 283, October 1601.
119 See Table 9.
120 PRO SP12/230, 74, complaints of the Cheshire justices.
121 C. G. Cruickshank, *Elizabeth's army* (2nd edn, Oxford, 1970), 115–116.
122 CCRO, lieutenancy letter book of Sir Hugh Cholmondeley, DDX/358/1, f.33v. – 38; 44–46r.
123 *Ibid.*, f. 33v, copy of the queen's letter, 27 August.
124 Sir Urian was supposedly the hero of the ballad 'The Spanish Lady's Love'. He married Margaret, daughter of Sir Edmund Trafford, and in 1619 was one of the three deputy lieutenants of Cheshire. F. R. Raines, ed., *The Stanley papers*, vol. ii (Chetham Society, xxxi, Manchester, 1853), 100–101, notes; Angus Butterworth, *Old Cheshire families* (London, 1932), 99–102.

125 CCRO, lieutenancy letter book of Sir Hugh Cholmondeley, DDX358/1 34r and v, 10 September 1598.

126 See Table 10.

127 CCRO, lieutenancy letter book of Sir Hugh Cholmondeley, DDX358/1 35r, headed 'To the constables of...'.

128 The muster roll is dated 12 October 1596.

129 PRO SP63/194, 132–133, 'The muster rolle of Sir Urian Leigh his company mustered at Chester, 12th Octobris 1596'.

130 *Ibid.*, f. 133d, marginal notes by the commissioners William Brereton and Maurice Kyffin at Chester.

131 *Ibid.*, 133r, marginal note on the muster roll.

132 *Ibid.*, 233r and v, 13 September 1596.

133 *Ibid.*, 238 – payments, October 1596.

134 *Cal. Carew MSS*, iii, 252, 253, in Russell's journal (June 1594 – May 1597).

135 CCRO, lieutenancy letter book of Sir Hugh Cholmondeley, DDX358/1, f. 44r, the queen's letter under the signet; *ibid.*, f. 44v, the council's directives; *ibid.*, f. 45r, the commissioners' instructions; and *ibid.*, f. 47r, is a recommendation from the Earl of Essex that Captain Peter Warburton be muster master of the shire of Cheshire.

136 *Ibid.*, f. 45.

137 See Table 10 for the quotas on the hundreds.

138 CCRO, lieutenancy letter book of Sir Hugh Cholmondeley, DDX358/1, ff. 47 and 47, the muster roll.

139 *Ibid.*, f. 45v, 'the rates for the monie so supplie this service, 26th June 1598'; *ibid.*, 48v, a copy of the lord treasurer's letter, 10 July 1598, shows payments of £35 and £30 to Captain Warburton. The schedule in answer to the enquiry of September 1600, in Cecil papers, Hatfield, 88/49r, states these payments as £20 and £30.

140 *Ibid.*, f. 32r, privy council to Cheshire, 26 July 1596.

141 Hatfield House, Cecil papers, 88/50, the covering letter to the schedule from Cheshire, September 1600, referring to the privy council's letters of enquiry, December and June.

142 CCRO, lieutenancy letter book of Sir Hugh Cholmondeley, DDX/358/1, f. 32r, privy council to commissioners for musters in Cheshire, 26 July 1596.

143 *Ibid.*, ff. 40–41v, undated accounts.

144 *Ibid.*, f. 41v.

145 Hatfield House, Cecil papers, 88/50, privy council's letter, December 1599.

146 *APC*, xxx, 405, privy council to high sheriff and commissioners, 22 June 1600.

147 Hatfield House, Cecil papers, 88/50, 16 September 1600.

148 *Ibid.*, f. 49r, the schedule under 1598.

149 CCRO, lieutenancy letter book of Sir Hugh Cholmondeley, DDX358/1, f. 45v.

150 *Ibid.*, 48, and Hatfield House, Cecil papers, 88/49r and f. 48v, copy letter of the lord treasurer's letter to Cheshire, 10 July 1598.

151 L. Boynton, *The Elizabethan militia* (London, 1967), 106, 107, 180.

152 HMC, *Salisbury*, vi, 447.

153 *APC*, xxvi, 132, 133, 257; *APC*, xxx, 24, 25, 236.

154 CRO, lieutenancy letter book of Sir Hugh Cholmondeley, DDX358/1, 37, Cheshire to the privy council, 12 October 1596.

155 PRO SP63/202/part iii, no. 78, Beverley to Knollys, 23 September 1598 from Chester.

156 *APC*, xxx, 795.

157 PRO SP63/208, part i, no. 119, Captain Alford from Lough Foyle.

158 *CSPI* (1598–1599), 30, Irish council to the privy council, 21 January 1598.

159 *APC*, xxviii, 72.

160 *APC*, xxix, 593.
161 *APC*, xxx, 788, 789.
162 *CSPI* (1600–1601), 331.
163 See J. Hurstfield, *Freedom, corruption and government in Elizabethan England* (London, 1973), Chapter 5.
164 *CSPI* (1600), 232, Mountjoy to Cecil, 11 June 1600.
165 F. V. Emery, 'Communications circa 1600', Fig. 62, in *A new historical geography of England*, ed. H. C. Darby (Cambridge, 1973), 11.

PART II

Embarkation and transportation of troops to the Irish war

Our Marriners observe the sayling into Ireland to be more dangerous, not onely because many tides meeting, makes the sea apt to swell upon any storme, but especially because they ever find the coast of Ireland covered with mists, whereas the coast of England is commonly cleare, and to be seene farre off.

Fynes Moryson, *Itinerary*, vol. iv, 191

CHAPTER SIX

Chester, the chief military port for the Irish service in the 1590s

An overall view of the levies and the ports

The Elizabethan government knew how important it was to get companies of recruits quickly to their destination. It was essential to the efficient prosecution of the war that the ill-assorted levies of raw recruits be marched expeditiously from their assembly points the moment the companies were complete. When the raising of levies became frequent, leaders were appointed to see them safely to the port of embarkation; at times of large levies the commissioners for musters in the ports ordered conductors to stay with their men in port, to help keep order. On occasions the captain, under whom they were going to serve in Ireland, collected and led his new recruits out of the shires, acting in that capacity as a conductor. Whether a commissioned captain or not, the conductor was given a fixed amount of time to get his men to the port, and therefore a fixed allowance of conduct money from the county authority, which it later recovered from the exchequer.[1]

The frequency of levies to Ireland brought about a uniform set of procedures for their conduct to the ports, which were reiterated by the privy council to the officers of the lieutenancies. A particular set of instructions sent by Sir Robert Cecil to the Earl of Shrewsbury survive in the Talbot papers; these show that the many individual directives of the council had been brought together for the guidance of conductors to prevent abuses on the march.[2]

The first instruction is that a public warning be given to the assembled company informing them that after a recruit received the 'queen's purse money', and was placed under a conductor, he was not to run away, on pain of 'death as a felon according to the laws of the Realm'. The conductor was then to draw up a tripartite indenture showing the soldier's name, surname and parish, 'one part to be sent up hither with more speed than heretofore hath byn used, the other to be delivered unto hym, the third to remain in the country'. The conductor was not to postpone this duty until he was at the port, nor was he to alter the indenture. Most important, he was not to change any of the men or 'he will answer the same at his utermost peril'.

Should any soldier fall sick on the way, or get lame on the march, the conductor had to hand him over to the mayor of the next town they came to, or to a justice of the peace, with a signed report showing why he was unable to finish the march. Should any soldier on the march attempt to run away, 'he shall be followed with hue and cry as a felon,' and, if caught by the local constables, he was to be sent to gaol and tried at the next sessions of the peace in the county of his arrest.

When the conductor had delivered his men over to the authority of the mayor of the port he was to bring back with him 'ample certificate from the mayor of the port of the delivery over of so many soldiers as he doth receive in the county'. If it appeared from the certificate that men were wanting at the port for reasons other than sickness, the conductor should not only forfeit the gains in money he made but be committed to prison to 'remain there until we be advertised of his lewd dealings that some severe and exemplar punishment may be inflicted upon him'.[3]

These instructions were designed to prevent the fraudulent conductor lining his pocket at government expense to the detriment of the army. The indenture system could be manipulated by the conductor. He could sell freedom to his entire company once clear of the shire in which it was levied and arrive in Chester carrying only a muster roll. There he could procure, through agents, the men and arms he needed at the port for muster and review. The commissioners would review them as correct and duly inscribe the muster roll to that effect. The corrupt conductor could then pay off his agents, who in turn paid off the men, who went home to await another occasion to be soldiers for a few hours. If such a conductor was also a captain commissioned to recruit a company and lead them to Ireland he could repeat the ruse in Ireland, where he could try to get further payment from the treasurer-at-war for his fictitious company. The deception was easier in Ireland for on muster days there he could play the game with real soldiers hired from other companies or from among the Irish.[4] No case of such extreme fraud has been found, but lesser frauds abound. Chester, as the main military port for Ireland, had the reputation of being *spelunca latronum* – a robbers' cave.[5]

The government attempted to prevent fraud first by requiring more detailed information on indentures. From merely recording the soldier's name, his weapon and the parish or village from which he was levied, indentures of the late 1590s were expected to describe the soldier's appearance and the full equipment he carried.[6] This made detection easier should the conductor be suspected of changing his men. Second, by the 1590s the privy council began to appoint experienced captains as conductors to lead recruits all the way from the shires to Ireland. Captain Henry Hart, for example, was frequently employed as a conductor of levies. Such centrally employed captains were resented in the shires for they thwarted the wishes of the county authorities to choose local conductors. We have seen examples of this resentment, especially where captains were commissioned to conduct companies made up from men from more than one shire. Both measures, widening information on indentures and appointing well established captains as conductors, did not necessarily guarantee that levies would be perfectly conducted to the ports: abuses persisted until the end of the war.[7]

At the ports the mayors had authority to hire privately owned merchant vessels to transport the troops, their arms, victuals and impedimenta, though on occasion ships of the royal navy were used, for example for the levy of 2,000 men at Rochester in October 1601.[8] Ships' masters did not willingly abandon their trading interests to transport troops and bargained greedily to better 'the queen's price'. Adverse winds delaying the departure of levies, often for weeks, lowered men's morale and raised the

Table 11   Annual troop movements to the ports

Port	1594	1595	1596	1597	1598	1599	1600	1601	1602	Totals
Chester										
Foot	1,000	1,500	900	1,260	1,800	2,550	5,430	3,965	700	19,105
Horse	–	300	30	–	100	200	300	116	–	1,046
Bristol										
Foot	–	–	700	800	950	1,000	2,020	3,170	1,635	10,275
Horse	–	–	–	–	200	100	54	248	–	602
Barnstaple										
Foot	–	–	400	400	–	–	350	1,420	815	3,385
Horse	–	–	–	–	16	–	–	66	–	82
Plymouth										
Foot	–	1,553	–	–	1,750	–	–	500	–	3,803
Horse	–	–	–	–	50	–	–	–	–	50
Southampton										
Foot	–	–	–	–	500	–	–	–	510	1,010
Horse	–	–	–	–	–	–	–	–	–	–
Rochester										
Foot	–	–	–	–	–	–	–	1,600	–	1,600
Horse	–	–	–	–	–	–	–	–	–	–
Milford										
Foot	–	–	–	–	300	400	–	–	–	700
Horse	–	–	–	–	–	100	–	–	–	100
Weymouth										
Foot	–	–	–	–	400	–	–	–	–	400
Horse	–	–	–	–	–	–	–	–	–	–
Fowey										
Foot	–	–	–	–	300	–	–	–	–	300
Horse	–	–	–	–	–	–	–	–	–	–
Padstow										
Foot	–	–	–	–	–	–	–	–	100	100
Horse	–	–	–	–	–	–	–	–	–	–
Totals										
Foot	1,000	3,053	2,000	2,460	6,000	3,950	7,800	10,655	3,760	40,678
Horse	–	300	30	–	366	400	354	430	–	1,880

Compiled from privy council orders in *APC*, xxv–xxxii, *passim*, and additional evidence in the separate port tables following.

cost of transporting troops. The frequency of levies to Ireland in the 1590s multiplied such problems and forced the government to seek greater controls over shipowners and ships' masters and strengthen the authority of the mayors in the ports.

Earlier Irish rebellions, such as Shane O'Neill's in the 1560s and that of the Desmonds in 1578–1583, had given the Elizabethan privy council much practice in the logistics of transporting troops to Ireland. In this respect a 'plott' or plan drawn up on the occasion of the Desmond rebellion in 1579 for sending out 2,000 troops is of interest as a precedent showing 'in what shiers men may most commodiously be levied for the service of Ireland; the best places to embarque, and their landinge places in Ireland'. As we may expect, men from north Wales and adjoining shires went to Chester for Dublin; those from south Wales and bordering shires to Bristol for Waterford; and those from the West Country to Barnstaple, Padstow and Falmouth for Waterford.

The much larger troop movements of the years 1594–1602 show that the three ports most frequently used by the government were Chester, Bristol and Barnstaple.[9] In addition, Plymouth, Southampton and Portsmouth were used as reception ports for veterans from the Low Countries on their way to Ireland. And Haverfordwest, Holyhead, Ilfracombe and Beaumaris, though not used to launch primary levies, were frequently used as refuges whenever troop ships were blown back by bad weather; in that sense these western and smaller ports could be called secondary embarkation ports.[10]

Commanders in Ireland, particularly Sir George Carew in Munster, held forthright views on the West Country ports from which most of his troops came. 'Brystowe is a cursed port, for from other places passages are won ... from Brystow I never expect a packet,' he wrote to Mountjoy in August 1602.[11] He told Sir Robert Cecil on 20 August 1602 that the 'meetest place for the answering of all winds is Barnstaple or Padstow,' and condemned Ilfracombe as being 'too far within Severn'. The return trip was much easier. Noting the prevalence of the westerlies, Carew remarked that he had no trouble in finding winds or shipping 'to go from here [Cork] to England'.[12] Yet the crossing either way could still be difficult. Fynes Moryson, Mountjoy's secretary, complained of 'the tempestuousness of the Irish sea' and of mists on the Irish coasts.[13]

Similar expressions of difficulty in communication came from other commanders: Sir Henry Docwra at Derry, Sir Arthur Chichester at Carrickfergus and the lord deputy Lord Mountjoy did not seem to take account of the difficult operations in the ports. Some idea of the size of these operations is given in Table 11, which sets out the numbers of men and horses ordered to the ports between 1594 and 1602.

The annual totals of levies ordered to the ports confirm the considerable national effort to subdue the rebellion in Ireland, and the cumulative numbers demonstrate a massive burden on the chief ports of embarkation, though no single expedition from the ports to Ireland equalled in strength the Essex venture to Cadiz when 6,500 men sailed in 144 ships from Plymouth on 3 June 1596.[14] The cumulative totals indicate that the greatest pressure was on Chester and Bristol. Chester's total of infantrymen represented 47 per cent of all infantry levies and 55 per cent of the horse, and the port was used in each year of the war. Bristol was second in importance with 25 per cent of infantry levies and 32 per cent of the horse; Barnstaple and Plymouth accounted for 17 per cent of infantry and 7 per cent of the horse, which leaves the other six ports with 11 per cent of the infantry levies and 6 per cent of the horse. Rochester's single experience of launching an army of 1,600 arose because the privy council ordered the use of the royal ships conveniently at hand in the Medway.

The total of levied men sent to the ports is similar to the total of men previously ordered to be levied in the shires: the infantry total ordered to be levied from the shires of England and Wales was 37,203 and the grand total of infantry ordered to the ports is

40,678; the difference of 3,475 is largely explained by remembering that nearly 3,000 sailing from Plymouth had not then been ordered from the shires but were redeployed men in transit from the Low Countries to Ireland.

The near coincidence of these two totals suggests that the Elizabethan authorities did manage to get the required number of men *en route* to the ports. Whether or not the same numbers of men embarked at the ports is not always possible to test since muster rolls appear to have rarely been taken at the point of embarkation.

Chester

In 1588 Chester ranked as one of the main head ports in the kingdom. A national list of 7,000 mariners in the 1580s shows that seventy-four were of Chester and sixty-one of Liverpool, and in a national list of 1,383 ships of less than eighty tons, Chester had thirteen. By 1595, however, Chester stood only twelfth in a list of eighteen ports, indicating that by the late sixteenth century the port was beginning to decline from its former glory.[15]

Despite these national statistics Chester was nonetheless the most important of the north-west ports and exercised jurisdiction over all creeks, havens and member ports on the north Welsh and Lancashire coastlines, including Liverpool, and therefore from Barmouth round the coast to the Dee and Mersey estuaries and indeed along the north Lancashire coastline as far north as the estuary of the River Duddon.[16]

Trade with Ireland formed the basis of Chester's overseas activity, and by the 1590s accounted for two-thirds of its imports and almost all its exports. Dublin was clearly the most important Irish port for trade and the establishment of St Werberg's Church by Chester merchants in Dublin bespeaks the historical trading link between the two cities – St Werberg being the patron saint of Chester. Chester's local importance as the civil port for Irish trade was increasingly matched by its usage as a military port and base for the late Elizabethan government in the transportation of men, money, arms, victuals and, in a word, the sinews of war, to Dublin, Carrickfergus and the garrisons that were later established along the River and Lough Foyle in the north-west of the province of Ulster.

The increasing navigational difficulties at and near Chester's port meant that the military levies sent there often embarked from the Deeside harbours along the Wirral, or from Liverpool. In fact there were nine anchorages on the Wirral side of the Dee: Portpool, Shotwick, Burton, Denhall, New Quay, Neston, Gayton, Heswall and Redbank. Liverpool was then a creek of Chester and it was from there that the expedition of the elder Earl of Essex went to Ireland in 1573, and it also saw much of its sorry return.[17] Hilbre and West Kirby were also closely connected with Chester's trade; indeed, there was a customs house on Hilbre Island in 1582 and unbelievably ten alehouses as well. In the summer of 1600, when large numbers of soldiers left Chester for Ireland, they embarked from several harbours; Captain Humphrey Willis, one of the conducting captains of the force to Lough Foyle on board the *Angel* of Hilbre, wrote that his recruits were embarked at Neston, Hilbre, Liverpool and Chester itself on 22 April and that by 24 April they were still anchored awaiting the rest of the fleet at

Hilbre Island. However, the entire fleet sailed the following day and reached Carrickfergus on Belfast Lough on 27 April.[18]

The mayor of Chester was the key local official in the control of troops in the town, and his multifarious duties are reflected in his military papers in the 1590s.[19] His headquarters, known as the Pentice, stood beside St Peter's Church at the Market High Cross, where his gibbet was menacingly situated, a threatening spectacle to likely deserters. Whenever military levies were in port the mayor moved about with a bodyguard traditionally armed with halberds. Though a civilian, elected each October, the mayor acted much more like a military agent of the privy council when the levies were resident. His authority to act as such stemmed from his inclusion in the commission for musters and it was clearly a mayoral responsibility to supervise the levies until they had embarked.[20] His office called for powers of discretion and tact in dealing with the privy council, muster masters, captains, conductors of troops from the shires and the mayors of other ports, too. In every aspect of administering the levies in the port, the mayor, his deputy and disciplinary staff of sheriffs and bailiffs were much involved. It was the mayor's responsibility to provide billets for soldiers and ships for their transportation. He needed full powers to be able to deal with the unruly behaviour of conscripted men, who more often than not caused much unrest among the citizens.[21] An added responsibility was the collection and sifting of news for the government, an important task in wartime, and the already heavily burdened mayor had to provide post horses for the speedy delivery of dispatches coming out of Ireland to London; and, in the other direction, he had to supply post barques to send news, orders and indeed bullion to the Irish civil and military administration in Dublin. However, each mayor had these burdens only for a year; it may be significant that none of the mayors elected between 1588 and 1604 had a second term of office.

From October 1594 to July 1602 batches of soldiers and cavalry troops went to Chester on fifteen occasions, making it the busiest port for embarkation to Ireland; the grand total of soldiers involved was 1,046 cavalrymen and 19,105 infantrymen. Naturally, not all would have sailed or arrived in Ireland; some were discharged, others deserted and their numbers were not always filled up as they should have been.

The troops in Chester

The major rôle of Chester in the prosecution of the Irish war can clearly be seen from the numbers of men and horses which converged on the port to meet the demands of the army in Ireland. These are set out in Table 12.

The levy of 1,500 foot ordered to help Sir John Norris in April 1596 is illustrative of what could go wrong in moving large numbers of troops. When he was 231 men short of the total, the mayor of Chester reported that he had shipped 1,269 and that, of the rest, some had not passed muster, some were sick, some were in prison and some had escaped; and yet some of these deficiencies had been made up a week later as the mayor then reported that he had shipped 1,418. Of the 300 horse ordered from the clergy on that same occasion only half sailed with the 1,418 infantrymen.[22] It is not clear when the rest of the horse went to Ireland but thirty horse sent in the October levy were

Table 12 *Military levies in Chester*

Date	Number of foot (f.) and horse (h.)	Mayor responsible	Intended for:	Note
October 1594	1,000 f.	Foulke Aldersey	Sir William Russell's Ulster campaign	1
April/July 1596	1,500 f. 300 h.	William Aldersey	Sir John Norris, Ulster	2
October/November 1596	900 f. 30 h.	'Thomas Smith	Sir William Russell and Sir John Norris	3
April 1597	1,260 f.	Sir John Savage (died succeeded by Thomas Fletcher)	Sir Henry Bagenal's forces	4
July 1598	1,000 f. 100 h.	Richard Rathbone	Sir Samuel Bagenal for Lough Foyle	5
September 1598	800 f.	Richard Rathbone	Sir Richard Bingham in Connaught	6
January/March 1599	2,550 f. 200 h.	Henry Hardware	Earl of Essex's army	7
January/April 1600	2,800 f. 200 h.	Henry Hardware	Sir Henry Docwra's expedition to Lough Foyle	8
July/August 1600	2,000 f. 100 h.	Robert Brerwood	Lord Mountjoy, Dublin	9
December 1600	630 f.	Robert Brerwood (died succeeded by Richard Bavand)	Sir Henry Docwra, Lough Foyle	10
April/May 1601	830 f. 40 h.	Richard Bavand	Sir Henry Docwra, Ballyshannon	11
July/August 1601	830 f.	John Ratcliffe	Sir George Carew, Cork	12
September/October 1601	1,650 f. 76 h.	John Ratcliffe	Carrickfergus, 300 f., 26 h.; Lough Foyle, 700 f., 50 h.; Mountjoy, 650 f.	13
December 1601	655 f.	Hugh Glaseor	Mountjoy and Carew in Munster	14
July 1602	700 f.	Hugh Glaseor	Mountjoy's Ulster campaign	15
Total	19,105 f. 1,046 h.			

1. PRO SP12/268, 124, 125.
2. *APC*, xxv, 258–260, 262–265; *CSPI* (1592–1596), 342–343.
3. CCR, M/L/1/109.
4. CCR, M/L/1/117, 119, 121.
5. CCR, M/MP/L/1/ 151, 157.
6. CCR, M/MP/L/1/161–166; *APC*, xxviii, 153.
7. HMC, *Salisbury*, ix, 72, 89, 96, 106–108, 113.
8. PRO SP12/274/18; *APC*, xxx, 69, 91, 101–106.
9. HMC, *Salisbury*, x, 268–269; *APC*, xxx, 412–416.
10. *APC*, xxxi, 21–23; CCR, M/MP/11/1–14.
11. *APC*, xxxi, 315.
12. CCR, M/MP/12/1–22, muster rolls.
13. *APC*, xxxii, 233–239, 242, 260–262.
14. *APC*, xxxii, 474–478.
15. CCR, M/MP/13, muster book of the shire levies sent to Chester.

latecomers to the port from the 300 ordered in March 1596 (see Table 12). Likewise, in the levy of horse of September 1601, when seventy-six were supposed to be transported from Chester, only sixty-three were sent according to the government's reckoning.[23]

On three occasions levies of 2,000 and over were ordered to Chester: in January to March 1599, when the Earl of Essex organised his grand army; early in 1600, when Sir Henry Docwra assembled his expeditionary for the Foyle; and lastly in August 1600, when Mountjoy, Carew and Docwra needed massive reinforcement.[24]

An intractable problem in considering the veracity of these figures is how many men deserted and were not replaced before embarkation? Frequently, captains got their men on board in a hurry to take advantage of favouring winds and therefore did not have time to call a final muster at the quayside. Round numbers may also hide the fact that six dead pays in every hundred were beginning to be allowed but whether this prerequisite for the captain's benefit was permitted in the port or when they landed in Ireland is not made clear in the case of every levy.[25]

The shipping of troops followed a seasonal pattern: the end of April to October was the most favourable time of year for sailing to Ireland, as it still is, but the urgencies of the fortunes of war dictated that on four occasions at least the levies at Chester were sent out in the winter months. Clearly, crises in Ireland did not conveniently occur in the summer. In the theatres of warfare commanders generally tried to avoid winter campaigning with the exception of Mountjoy, an exception that partly explains his success. Bad weather and adverse prevailing winds delayed every winter expedition from Chester from 1592 to 1602. Docwra's embarkation enterprise for the Foyle and the reinforcements sent out in December 1600 and in December 1601 were particularly badly affected.

Chester in these years, city and port, was rarely without troops. Even when troops had been expeditiously embarked from the port the mayor of Chester still had to face the problem of returning sick, maimed and 'unserviceable soldiers', particularly from the north of Ireland after 1599, many of whom stayed to swell the problems of poverty in the city.[26] One of the very few advantages of being the principal embarkation port was that the mayor could rid the city of undesirable people by using them to fill shortages in the companies for the draft.

To illustrate the problems of assembly and launching of troops from Chester, the organisation of Sir Henry Docwra's army and expedition to the Foyle between January and April 1600 and the subsequent reinforcements sent to him may serve as a case study; despite the gaps in the main local source, the mayor's military papers, the recruitment, assembly and embarkation of Docwra's forces are strongly reflected in the major national sources.

The importance of planting garrisons at Lough Foyle had long been seen by the Elizabethan government and had been previously attempted by Edward Randolph, who launched the first great amphibious operation of the queen's reign, from Bristol to aid Sir Henry Sidney's expedition against Shane O'Neill in the autumn of 1566. The celebrated Humphrey Gilbert, then a captain in Derry with Randolph, was sent with the dispatch carrying news to the queen of the dreadful disasters which had taken place when the garrison's arsenal lodged in the cathedral blew up, destroying men,

144

munitions and victuals; the remnant of the army left by sea for Carrickfergus. For thirty years thereafter the strategic importance of the great inlet from the sea to Lough Foyle, dividing the territories of O'Neill and O'Donnell, was much discussed in the wars of Ireland, and though vital if Gaelic Ulster were to be reduced, nothing was actually done about reoccupying the area until Docwra's expedition.[27] The government had earmarked Docwra in the winter of 1600 for 'the most desperate assignment', as he would later describe his task. He was a veteran campaigner in the Netherlands and Spain and in Ireland under Sir Richard Bingham, the notorious governor of Connaught and the second Earl of Essex; Docwra was to achieve what Essex had merely talked about or was talked out of by Hugh O'Neill in 1599.[28]

In Chester, Sir Henry Docwra had to cooperate with Henry Hardware, the mayor, in supervising the levies that came in to form the backbone of his force. Some 3,000 foot and 200 horse were to be levied for him in the English and Welsh shires and directed to be at Chester by the last day of January 1600.[29] Their first destination in Ireland was to be Carrickfergus, where they were to pick up an additional 1,000 troops before continuing round the north Irish coast to put in at the Foyle. The privy council hoped that he would then have sufficient men to plant a further garrison at Ballyshannon, the key crossing point from Connaught to Ulster and much used by Hugh O'Donnell to maintain his areas of influence in north Connaught. All these hopes, even down to the strategic details, are reflected in Docwra's commission.

It was the mayor's task, together with the government's commissary for shipping, Robert Davies, to requisition enough ships. Henry Hardware and Henry Docwra were to act as commissioners for musters in receiving the men as they came in to Chester, checking the conductors' rolls, and in taking a view of the men, their armour, arms and noting their defects. The mayor was to take up his normal responsibility of seeing them dieted at 3*d* the meal and to give '2*d* a day to make up viii*d* by the day to every soldier to serve him for other necessary occasions'. The government was to see to their apparel by means of contract with clothing merchants, but the soldiers were not to be issued with these suits until they were safely on board.[30]

The government planned and hoped for an efficient amphibious operation to be launched with the first favourable wind. In practice, difficulties and delays beset the venture. There were complaints from some shires, notably those of Hereford and the Welsh borderlands, about difficulties in recruiting great numbers of able men so soon after Essex had recruited the same areas the previous year. Herbert Croft on behalf of Herefordshire wrote to Sir Robert Cecil 'to let this poor county be exempted' from the burdens of levying more soldiers.[31]

Lord Mountjoy, much involved in gaining support for the Lough Foyle expedition, reported from London that the name of Ireland, 'but principally Lough Foyle,' scared off recruits and that those already in receipt of impressment monies 'have quitted the service'.[32] Though all the soldiers were supposed to have assembled at Chester by the last day of January the levies were still coming in by mid-February and in depleted numbers. In these very first stages of the operation – the assembling, mustering and billeting – nerves began to be frayed as ill-feeling broke out between the commissioners for musters, especially between the mayor and the chief commander, Hardware and Docwra. The former accused the latter of refusing to accept men and armour from the shires because of minor defects and of unnecessarily delaying the departure of his troops; in turn the commander accused the mayor of not doing enough to keep order in his city and of not helping sufficiently in the muster and view of the soldiers.[33] Though it had long been customary for the mayor to act as a commissioner for musters in his own port, Henry Hardware refused to assist Docwra in this duty until he had received precise instructions from the privy council to do so. When desertion became rife the privy council put the blame firmly on the mayor's shoulders. Relations between the mayor and commander deteriorated even further so that henceforth at every stage in the proceeding each contradicted and criticised the other's work, or lack of it. To justify himself Hardware wrote to the privy council of how difficult it was to discern deserters at that time:

> many lewd and evil-disposed persons have shrouded themselves within this city under the name of soldiers and given advantage to divers for their escapes which hardly could be prevented despite vigilant watches appointed ... the soldiers did daily escape with those frequently in the markets being nothing different from them in attire.[34]

In a separate letter to Cecil he admitted to eighty deserters from the men at Chester; one of them he alleged had been caught for the second time trying to escape in women's clothing. He blamed the scale of desertion not this time on Docwra but on the conductors of the levies out of the shires. Eighty was of course an underestimate because by the end of February the council ordered 250 men to be raised in London and Middlesex to fill the vacancies 'of such as are run away at the port of Chester' and then in strong terms the council ordered the mayor to aid Docwra in keeping order, preventing any further absconders and quelling mutinous behaviour.[35]

The situation grew even worse. The privy council informed the mayor that in the interests of stopping desertion he was to allow Docwra to keep the conductors of the companies as helpers until embarkation and to pay them by the day. In normal circumstances these conductors would have handed over the men to their future captains but the latter came in slowly to their charge in Chester: though ordered to be there in time by their lord deputy, Lord Mountjoy, only half of them were present in Chester by 15 April.[36] According to one report ten captains and lieutenants of six companies were at Chester to aid in the embarkation but nine captains still had not come out of Munster; and, more seriously, Sir John Bolles, designated second in command to Docwra, was still in Dublin on the appointed date for departure, 15 April. Mountjoy became so anxious about the delays at Chester that he personally visited the city and reported to the council on the poor quality of the recruits – 'men unlikely to do Her Majesty any service in her wars' was his curt verdict. Those from Wales were 'most of them taken out of the prison or are boys,' he added.[37]

However, the mayor had stayed sufficient shipping to embark the men: thirteen sloops or hoys had been commandeered and a Flemish ship of 120 tons able to take 300 men, then anchored in the Dee, was pressed into service. Captain George Thornton, an experienced naval captain, had the general command of the convoy and he was given the protection of the queen's ship, the *Moon*, under Captain Thomas Button and two crompsters carrying small cannon.[38] Hardware claimed in writing to Cecil on 2 April that there was enough shipping stayed to transport both horse and foot if the commander, Docwra, would allow the shipowners to take on board as many as they were willing to carry; but Docwra resisted this, alleging that overcrowding in the ships would cause sickness and the force would arrive in Ireland unfit. Docwra's correspondence with Cecil gives a fuller picture of what was really happening in Chester: the ships' masters and the sailors 'were desperately bent to quit their barks', after not having been paid for three months and not having the liberty of following their own business – coerced as they were for the queen's service. And while the victualling ships had been loaded Docwra reckoned that there was sufficient only for 1,000 men, but the artillery and munitions were ready to be shipped; most of the captains had by then arrived and though there were still defects in most companies Docwra claimed he could make up the numbers from those that came out of Ireland and from deserters – though the latter were better worthy of punishment than entertainment, or rather their captains that allowed them to come over.[39] Buckhurst, the lord treasurer, doubted whether he should arrange payments to deserters to rejoin the ranks in the way that Docwra advised or whether they should simply be imprisoned as men destined to be hanged. The privy council was adamant that it should receive the names of those deserting, the names of parishes and villages they came from and the names of their conductors to Chester, and that this report should distinguish between 'those who had run out of Ireland to Chester and those that run away when they should go thither'.[40]

By 15 April the main body of the expedition was still in Chester, not delayed by adverse winds but by the need to lay aboard victuals and hay, oats and water for the horses, and this at a time of food shortages in Chester. Docwra appointed Captain Thornton to have victuals taken up on the Isle of Man as he anticipated further shortage when they arrived in Carrickfergus but Thornton came away from the Isle of Man empty handed, as the deputy governor of the island refused to deliver any victuals without immediate payment.[41] The expedition finally set sail on 24 April but without a final muster and review. Docwra assured Cecil 'from the shipboard' that the horses embarked were the same as those shown at the previous muster but he could not say the same of the infantry as he did not want to lose a good wind by further mustering on land. They arrived at Carrickfergus the night of 28 April. Henry Hardware wrote to the privy council with a sense of relief on the departure of Docwra and his men and added that he was sending in his accounts.[42]

A similar story of administrative muddle, private antagonisms and natural delays complicated the sending of reinforcements to Docwra's garrisons in December 1600. A Captain Henry Hart came from Lough Foyle to conduct 630 men from Chester. The privy council were surprised to hear from the mayor, Robert Brerwood, on 26 January 1601 that the reinforcements were still land bound 'considering how long the winds have continued lately good'. There were also at least twenty deserters at one attempted embarkation and in the end Hart's forces, ordered in December 1600, did not get to Lough Foyle until 10 March 1601.[43]

Captain John Vaughan's reinforcements of 830 foot and 40 horse for Lough Foyle ordered to Chester by 20 May 1601 seem to have proceeded much more smoothly and efficiently, even though in addition to the men and horses large quantities of accessories were also to be shipped out of Chester: tools, utensils, picks, shovels, spades, as well as three lasts of corn powder, one of cannon powder and ready-made sheds for storage. All were embarked on 25 May; they sailed the following day and arrived in Lough Foyle four days later. Furthermore, the muster master at the garrisons there reported them 'very sufficient and faultless' and Captain John Field, one of Vaughan's helpers at Chester, added that in his opinion 'never did supplies come in fuller numbers and better plight to this army'.[44]

But the final batch of reinforcements for Lough Foyle from Chester, ordered to be there by 20 October 1601, takes us back to the difficulties and delays experienced in the initial embarkation. Of the 1,650 foot, 700 were for Lough Foyle, 300 for Chichester's garrison at Carrickfergus, and the remainder for Dublin. At the muster held under the mayor, John Ratcliffe, and Captain Alford there were ninety men missing from the 700 destined for Lough Foyle alone and when Alford's contingent finally arrived at Lough Foyle he had 565, 135 short of the original number ordered. He blamed the mayor, who had not victualled the men in the city but had insisted on billeting them in the countryside about Chester, where desertion was more easily accomplished; and by so doing the mayor could disclaim responsibility, as then these soldiers were technically outside his jurisdiction.[45]

It was a moot point whether recruits who ran away at the port were strictly deserters from the army, for strictly speaking in martial law terms they had not yet begun active service.[46] In practice the warren of medieval back streets in Chester made the city an easy enough bolt hole for deserters; many citizens became adept at hiding soldiers 'until the ships be gone'. Some were caught, as is evident from the records of the quarter sessions courts – in 1601 there were twenty cases of desertion before these courts.[47] Vagabondage, thieving, general social disorder and desertion from the drafts are all allied, as well as forgery of passes from the forces; the quarter session records in Chester between 1600 and 1602 reveal a traffic in forged and corruptly obtained passports, which helped to disguise the scale of desertion out of Ireland, and the expense to which some went to avoid the Irish service. In the mayor's military papers some forty-three passes bear the signatures of Docwra, Chichester and Bingley to the standard formula: 'Permit the bearer a diseased soldier to return to the shire out of which he was pressed'. Chichester, from Carrickfergus, alerted the authorities to the large-scale disappearance of legally provided passports in his name, filched by one John Borretter of Otterspool of Liverpool, whom he wanted arrested on his arrival in Chester.[48] Of the 153 cases before the sessions in 1600 and 1601 at least forty involve soldiers' thefts and assaults in their billets, generally the inns and alehouses of the city. Card sharpers, pickpockets, forgers, hirers of men to take the place of soldiers in the musters – all the characters one meets in Elizabethan low life so vividly portrayed by Shakespeare – are to be met with in the quarter session courts in Chester. Faced with such imported problems into his city no wonder the mayor wished to get the levies embarked as soon as possible for the general peace of his citizens.[49]

The mayor's authority to have merchant vessels taken up needed full government backing to overcome the reluctance and, at times, downright opposition of ships' masters and owners to give their services at the queen's price. They considered soldiers unprofitable cargo and difficult to handle; they would have agreed with Adam Smith's later view that 'it appears evident from experience that man is, of all sorts of baggage, the most difficult to be transported'.[50]

This examination of the transportation of Docwra's soldiers through Chester illustrates the difficulties of what should have been a straightforward operation. Wind and weather upset government's plans and policies, tensions arose between the mayors of the port and the commanders sent to cooperate with them in the tasks of assembling, billeting and embarking troops to the theatres of warfare. One of the more serious results of all these difficulties was the high rate of desertion, so that fewer men actually arrived for service than had been originally intended by the government. Delays in port may have been serious from the government's point of view and yet they were no less productive of local problems for the mayoral authorities.

Thomas Smith, mayor in 1596, drew up a list of forty-seven shipowners whose vessels he could impress; but on the occasion of very large levies the mayor had to spread his net widely, calling on help from the dependent member ports such as Liverpool, a demand that did not improve their steadily deteriorating relationship in the last decade of the sixteenth century.[51] As the war effort gathered momentum the privy council sought more control over shipowners by appointing official government transport supervisors, a Robert Davies for Chester and dependent ports and John Goyce for the West Country ports and Bristol; in theory, therefore, central government could exercise greater control over the movement of troops by sea since one of the powers of these officials, often called captains and/or commissioners for shipping, was to transfer surplus ships to where they were most needed. Davies's certificate to Cecil on the shipping of Essex's contingents from Chester makes his apparently efficient organisation very plain: 'in Chester water 23 vessels for 1,500 men; in the river of Liverpool 9 vessels for 300 men; in the river Wyer 9 vessels for 500 and in the river of Formby 3 vessels for 200 men'.[52] Needless to say, neat organisation on paper representing government policy was frequently at the mercy of the elements, which played havoc with embarkation arrangements and proved a major obstacle in prosecuting the war; this is an underestimated factor in explaining the prolongation of hostilities over nine years. The difficulties caused by delays in shipping are much in evidence as contrary winds blew the ships back into port or, worse still, on to the north coast of Wales. Captain Dutton's minor expedition from Chester with ninety-four soldiers on 17 November 1596 may serve as an example. Four days later he was blown back on the coast near Holyhead, where his men caused much nuisance to the local justices for the next seventeen days. Meanwhile, an undisclosed number deserted with their arms, coats and equipment. The remnant put out to sea again on 10 December but they were back again in Holyhead on 13 December. By the time the privy council's order for the discharge of the levies that winter reached Holyhead, Dutton found that the remainder of his men had virtually discharged themselves before he had the order from the mayor of Chester and while he was still rounding up earlier deserters in Flintshire.[53]

Delays were often philosophically accepted; some mayors had men embarked unadvisedly in their haste to get them out of port; Brerwood of Chester, for example, told the privy council in January 1601 of how the ships had set off but were forced on to the Wirral and there embarked thrice. In the end the ships' masters were 'enforced to unship them' and he self-righteously added that 'any negligence or want of care in me I would rather die than deserve.'[54] Occasionally, the wind, oddly enough, was set fair at Liverpool but not at Chester. A levy in October 1596 that was meant to sail at the same time from both ports became divided as those from Liverpool got a head start out to sea.[55] And as Cecil once advised, if the wind was not exactly gale force troop ships could cross by tacking sail into contrary winds, as had been done from Bristol in September 1602.[56]

Mutinies in Chester were only occasional but desertion, as we have seen, was a constant problem. Few, it was reported in 1601, were ever recaptured by the constables of the city and its environs, 'so cunning they are in passing by all towns, bridges and highways'.[57] But that some were caught is shown by the examinations of about twenty deserters before quarter sessions courts in 1600–1601. The defendants' statements illuminate some attitudes to military service. Thomas Foxley, a Cornish man, stated that he was to serve under Captain Grimes but that because of a sore leg he was unfit for the service and paid the captain's lieutenant 45s for his discharge. John Holland of Denbigh said he was a 'supply soldier' and received 15s to go 'in another man's place' but because he demanded his coat from Captain Yelverton he was arrested for mutiny. Hugh Masterson of Thorne, Somersetshire, stood accused of stating that it was more profitable in Ireland to serve Hugh O'Neill, Earl of Tyrone, than the queen of England. Thomas Hoddy of Buckinghamshire said he deserted 'from a town in the Wirral' to go home and support his mother. Two Staffordshire men gave similar excuses for deserting.[58]

Chester mayors attempted to curb desertion. Henry Hardware, for example, let the privy council know in August 1600 of his zealous activities. When viewing troops with the commissioners for musters he read out to them the previous warning from the privy council that any of them who should run away or entice others to do so would be executed 'according to law' and others 'put into the galleys'. To prove his point the mayor had a group of former deserters, who were awaiting trial in Northgate gaol, brought out to the gibbet 'in show to be hanged', with 'ropes round their necks and standing uppon the ladder'. On the pleadings of their captains and colleagues, and on their own repentance, they were pardoned on the scaffold on condition that 'if any one man of their companies did either mutiny for apparel or run away, that they, together with these offenders should receive the extreme rigour of the law'. Henry Hardware assured the privy council that his firmness 'struck terror into their hearts', 'prevented the running away of whole hundreds' and 'has wrought much quiet in our city'.[59]

In addition to crimes of forging passports, the quarter sessions records give evidence of others imputed to soldiers in the city. Out of 153 cases before the courts in 1600 and 1601, thirty-eight indicate individual soldiers or groups of soldiers among the defendants. Thefts of clothes, purses, pewter and leather goods from landlords and landladies accounted for twenty of these cases.[60] Richard Browne, for example, stole from the White Horse, where he was billeted. Twelve cases involved assaults and brawls in alehouses and on the streets between soldiers and citizens.[61] Five soldiers from Norfolk, Nottingham and Rutland were suspected of murdering John Eaton, one of the sheriff's officers, but the accusation did not appear to result in a conviction.[62]

Edward Alexander, Captain Hart's lieutenant, was imprisoned in Northgate gaol for assaulting his landlady at the Crown.[63] A group of four Catholic recusants were arrested at the Saracen's Head in possession of psalters, 'the romane breviary', 'the romane catechisme' beads and crucifixes. Three of them had travelled from Leicester and one, William Leake, from Fleet Street in the City of London. He denied he was a Jesuit but was 'catholiquely affected and perswaded'.[64] The other cases were a mixture. William Shaw of Formby was accused of non-delivery of victuals at Lough Foyle and Thomas Elvinge was examined about horse saddles brought back to Chester from Lough Foyle. Two captains, Yelverton and Berkeley, were accused of selling arms to one John Swan when their companies were about to embark for Ireland. Robert Metcalfe of Preston admitted among other crimes that he came to Chester to make money 'among the horsemen in the city' as he was skilled 'at the newe cutt on the cardes'.[65]

Communications

Chester was particularly important in the transmission of intelligence to and from the various theatres of war in Ireland, especially with Ulster for the Lough Foyle and Carrickfergus garrisons, and the Dublin administration and the lord deputy relied much on the traffic with Chester for news of government orders. Chester became an important link between England and Ireland during every phase of the war, and the responsibility that fell on the mayor, of keeping letters, orders and instructions moving, greatly exceeded those he would normally have experienced in times of comparative peace. The mayor's military papers between 1598 and 1600 contain twenty-five letters to the privy council and to Cecil, and approximately forty copy letters and sets of instructions from the privy council to the mayor.[66] And in the Cecil papers between March 1598 and November 1600 there are thirty-three letters dated at Chester.[67] The mayor generally informed the privy council when levies were dispatched from the port and sometimes he wrote to the Dublin administration to say that reinforcements were on their way.[68]

Letters and packets of letters were often sent by Cecil and the council with trusted captains accompanying levies to Ireland.[69] But throughout the war years a 'post bark', as it was called, plied between Chester and Dublin.[70] In February 1599 another post bark was established at Holyhead, 'as well for serving the packet by land, as for entertaining a bark to carry over and return the packet'.[71] And after Docwra had established garrisons in the Foyle another post bark went to and from Lough Foyle to Chester.[72] John Francis, frequently referred to as 'the post of Chester' in the privy council records and Cecil papers, appears to have helped the mayor in dispatching letters to Ireland and to London. A letter of 24 October 1599 from Francis to Cecil illustrates some of the postal arrangements between London, Chester and Dublin. He said he had received Cecil's letter 'of the 22nd inst. this day'. It had thus taken forty-eight hours to get from London to Chester, an expeditious delivery. Cecil wanted to know if previous packets of letters had gone to Dublin. Francis confirmed that he had received these on 9 October, delivered them to 'Henry Aynsdale, owner of a bark of this river', and had taken Aynsdale's word that he would procure a certificate of their safe delivery at Dublin.[73] Aynsdale had set sail in his bark, the *Valentine* of Chester, on 12 October, but according to this letter from Francis of 24 October, the *Valentine* was reported at Chester to be still wind-bound at Beaumaris.[74] Francis hoped it had gone because at the time of writing there was 'a show of a favourable wind', and he further hoped it would 'by the grace of God be very speedily at Dublin'. Other news in his letter spoke of the activities of the post bark which had been established at Holyhead to ply to Dublin, for he said he knew of no other passage 'of late out of Ireland, saving the post bark which brought over two packets ... which arrived yesterday at Holie Head'. He hoped Cecil had received these, but 'yesterday' was 23 October and Francis's wish suggests a twenty-four-hour delivery from Holyhead to London, an exceptionally fast time for the period. Francis's hope was perhaps too sanguine.[75]

Other small ships, like Henry Aynsdale's, were apparently pressed into the government's postal service. Robert Harris, master of the *Katherine* of Hilbre, was hastened on to Dublin with letters in January 1598; he later demanded compensation since he had to sail with these letters 'before he was fully freighted'.[76] A privy council letter to Richard Rathbone, mayor of Chester in 1598, showed the government's anxiety to hasten its letters to Ireland; it asked whether any of its dispatches were delayed at Chester. If so, they were to be sent immediately to Holyhead, where 'they shall be sent by tyding and other paynes of rowing if necessary'.[77] At times of major crisis in Ireland, such as that of the Spanish landing at Kinsale on 2 October 1601, the privy council was understandably troubled in not hearing from there for five weeks.[78] The difficulties of distance and the erratic state of the posts were frequent talking points with many Elizabethan correspondents. Sir John Norris, for example, in writing to Cecil in March 1596, said his letters would carry 'so stale a date as makes me send them only to show they were written'.[79]

Nevertheless, there was a regular postal service to Ireland, horses and riders being maintained at post stages between London and Holyhead, via Chester; endorsements to letters indicate the stages *en route*: London, Barnet, St Albans, Brickhill, Towcester, Daventry, Coventry, Coleshill, Lichfield, Stone, Nantwich, Chester, Rhuddlan, Conway, Beaumaris and Holyhead. Moreover, some endorsements give a clear idea of the time taken. One example, a letter of Richard Rathbone, mayor of Chester, to the privy council, dated 23 March 1598, may suffice, but may not be typical of the speed of delivery:

For Her Majesty's affairs. To the right honourable the lords and others of her Majesty's most Honourable privy council; haste, post haste, post haste. At the city of Chester the 23 day of March at 6 in the evening, Richard Rathbone, mayor.
At Nantwich at 9 at night
At Stone at one of the clock past midnight
At Lichfield at five in the morning
At Coleshill between 7 and 8
At Coventry after 10 a clock in the morning
At Daventry past one in the afternoon
At Towcester past 3
Brickhill at 6

At St Albans at 10 of the clock at night
Barnet at 12 a clock at night[80]

Letters from the Irish council and from the lord deputy sometimes arrived at Beaumaris rather than Holyhead for dispatch to London. The authorities on Anglesey asked the mayor of Chester to obtain some allowance for their services in forwarding mail on the government's behalf.[81] When nothing was done by Chester the magistrates at Beaumaris enlisted the support of the lord deputy, Thomas, Lord Burgh (in 1597), to get the mayor of Chester to bring the matter to the notice of the lord treasurer.[82] A year later the mayor of Beaumaris, Thomas Bulkeley, reminded the mayor of Chester of his constant troubles and expense in sending mail to Ireland and to London 'without considerings the chardges', and that he must get authorisation for him from the privy council to have the charges defrayed by the government because the task 'as the state of things at this present standeth is like to be frequent'.[83] Bulkeley does not appear to have mentioned specific sums of money for these services, but a ship hired at Holyhead for Ireland cost £10 a month, and the annual charges in 1599 there for postal services was estimated by the privy council at £634 18s 4d.[84]

Communication between the privy council and the commanders in Ireland and vice versa was hindered by the difficulties of the sea passage. Changing circumstances in Ireland sometimes meant that events overtook privy council orders, making them irrelevant. For example, the overthrow of Sir Henry Bagenal in August 1598 made the council's orders to send Sir Samuel Bagenal, his brother, on an expedition to plant garrisons at Lough Foyle irrelevant and impossible to achieve.[85] Sometimes rapidly changing orders from the privy council caused confusion.[86] The double demand for large levies in October 1601 caught out John Ratcliffe, the mayor of Chester, who wondered if he was right in thinking that one of the levies was for Lough Foyle, or whether their destination should have been Waterford, since the Spaniards had put in at Kinsale in Munster. A privy council directive of 18 October told him to set his mind at rest and follow the original order to send 700 of the soldiers to Lough Foyle and 300 to Carrickfergus and to receive this 'for a playne and fynall dyrection'.[87]

Chester's relations with Liverpool

One particular complication for the authorities at Chester was the lack of cooperation from the mayors of Liverpool, who provided essential ships and billets for troops bound for Ireland. The privy council treated Liverpool as a dependency of Chester, a position resented and contested by the mayors and councils of Liverpool.[88] The fortunes of the levies ordered to Chester in 1596 illustrate the rivalry between the two ports.

In October 1596 the privy council ordered Thomas Smith, mayor of Chester, to provide sufficient shipping for 900 men from Yorkshire and north Wales, part of a levy of 2,000 intended to reinforce the army in Ireland, to see to their billets until the wind proved favourable and to provide enough victuals for their sea passage. His expenses were then to be reimbursed from the treasurer-at-war in Ireland, Sir Henry Wallop

(1579–1599), succeeded by Sir George Cary in that office (1599–1606). Both were posthumously accused of peculation, but merchants' complaints against Wallop aroused government suspicions in his lifetime.[89]

To ease the burden on Chester 300 soldiers of this levy were to be billeted and shipped from Liverpool, and Thomas Smith peremptorily stayed enough shipping at Liverpool for the purpose. William Moore, mayor of Liverpool, expressed great surprise to Smith that he should have made a general stay of shipping at his port without his consent.[90] In a further letter Moore wrote that he did not question the authority over Liverpool,[91] but he went on to refuse to have the 300, adding that 'Lerpoole is a desolate place in winter', and that her majesty's service would not be advanced in sending soldiers there.

It was hoped that the levy would be ready by 9 November, but by 10 November only 550 soldiers had arrived in Chester, and those out of Yorkshire came without any armaments.[92] By 12 November, Moore of Liverpool, still annoyed about the high-handed action of Smith of Chester in having ships stayed at Liverpool, wrote to say that if he could justify his action on the mere phrase 'commissioners without restraint' in the council's instructions, then he (Smith) might as well stay ships in London and ended by reiterating his refusal to take any soldiers.[93] Smith ignored this and replied to Moore on 14 November that he had already dispatched 100 Denbighshire soldiers under Captain Roger Billings and that he wanted them properly cared for in Liverpool until they embarked.[94] He sent precise orders on how Billings' company was to be fed and warned that '200 others would follow shortly'.[95] The *fait accompli* presented by Smith and the early incidence of a favourable wind saved further acrimony between the two mayors. Roger Billings reported that he and his men arrived in Liverpool on Sunday 14 November and embarked on *The Hope* of Liverpool on Tuesday 16 November. While in Liverpool each man had four meals at the rate of 4*d* the meal.[96] Smith wrote to the Dublin administration that ninety-four soldiers and six officers had departed before there was time to get a nominal roll and account of their arms, but did not doubt that their captain would perform that duty on his arrival.[97]

Within two weeks Liverpool billeted a further overspill of levies from Chester. Captain Price put up a Welsh company in the town on 6 December 1596; he had difficulty retaining his men and ten deserted.[98] The mayor of Liverpool appears to have had no objection on this occasion, but sent his bill to the mayor of Chester 'for the entertaininge of Captain Prees' companie'.[99] But he was not willing to cooperate any further; from the examination of one William Pye, it appears that the mayor refused to feed Pye and his companions and had them returned with a pass to Chester because they belonged to a different company, that of Captain Henry Malby.[100] Such actions drove the new mayor of Chester, Sir John Savage, to ask Lord Burghley in April 1597 whether or not Chester had any authority over shipping at Liverpool.[101] There was no reply.

The levy of December 1596 did not in fact go to Ireland; the troops were ordered back to their homes to remain in a state of readiness for future service.[102] The prevalence of westerly gales that winter made the privy council abandon the attempt. Weather conditions and the local quarrels of Liverpool and Chester must have proved as much a hindrance to the furtherance of the 'service of Ireland' as the activity of the enemy.

In April 1597 the privy council ordered these levies back to port together with an additional 560 recruits.[103] Aware of the imminent descent of soldiers, William Moore, mayor of Liverpool, implored Chester not to send any soldiers because of the poverty of the victuallers and the high prices and scarcities in Liverpool. He had, however, stayed three ships to aid in transportation.[104] The mayor of Chester, Sir John Savage, quickly replied that Liverpool had to stay further shipping, enough for an extra 560 men, but that he would send as few soldiers as possible.[105] Robert Moore, deputy mayor in Liverpool, taking up the battle, told Chester that it would be impossible to supply meals at less than 6*d* a time, and that the entire exercise could not be carried out at Liverpool without a special commission to purchase grain.[106] William Moore also wrote to say he needed proof of the mayor of Chester's authority.[107] The arrival of the soldiers ended the bickering, for both mayors agreed to ask the privy council for a special allowance to cover the expenses of victualling in port at the rate of 6*d* the meal in view of the high prices.[108] They cited the precedent of November 1594, a time of great scarcity, when the government had allowed 6*d* per meal. From Lord Burghley's instructions to disburse '£400, £500 or £600' and their receipts it appears that the increased allowance was permitted.[109] Altogether, 1,260 soldiers were sent to Ireland by the end of April, of whom Liverpool billeted and shipped 500. Behind them they left the mayors wrangling over the reimbursements of expenses.[110]

That Liverpool continued to share in Chester's work of sending out levies is clear from the mayor's military papers for the years 1598 and 1600, but numbers sent to Liverpool from Chester are not stated, nor is there any further evidence of squabbling; perhaps the Liverpool mayors, William Dixon and John Bird in those years, were more conciliatory characters than William and Robert Moore in 1596 and 1597. But in 1601 and 1602 trouble broke out again. Giles Brooke, Liverpool's mayor in 1601, put the city's case against what he called 'the abuses wherewith Liverpool hath for a few years, in the latter time of these last wars of Ireland, been pressed by our too near neighbour of Chester'. He asked the privy council in future to direct its letters 'as heretofore hath been accustomed, unto the mayor of this town,' which had not been done in the 1590s. Giles Brooke went on to claim that Liverpool could put up 1,000 foot and 50 horse at competitive rates by using the towns round about and could comfortably accommodate 700 'within our town ... at one time'. His letter catalogued the 'insults' of Chester to Liverpool 'over these four years past'. They 'term us to be a member of Chester ... challenge a superiority over us where it is evident that this is the chiefest port between us and the Land's End of England, Milford only excepted'.[111] The tune that Liverpool was a poor and desolate place had changed but not the reason for the basic antagonism between the ports. It is of interest that Liverpool had already begun to claim its own superiority as a port, resenting the commandeering of its ships, and having them sent out to Hilbre to await troops from Chester.[112]

In the following year, 1602, the mayor and burgesses of Liverpool continued to assert the greater convenience of their port for the transportation of troops to Ireland, using their own ships and sailing directly there and not from Hilbre at the behest of Chester. At length the privy council invited delegations from both ports to settle the problems of precedence and convenience between them. Hugh Glaseor, the mayor of Chester, sent his recorder, Robert Whitaby; no delegate was sent by Liverpool to the council's meeting in London. Whitaby maintained Chester's position as the head-port, arguing for the use of Liverpool's ships at Hilbre and Chester and pointing out that the carriage of men, arms, furniture, the habiliments of war and victuals from Chester to Liverpool 'will be of much more charge to Her Majesty than the conveying of their ships from Liverpool to Chester'. He went on to paint a picture of the havoc that would be caused by insolent and unruly soldiers robbing and spoiling the countryside if they were sent out of Chester. He went on to argue, perhaps unconvincingly from what is known of desertions in Chester, that if soldiers were not in fact shipped from Chester they would run away and 'disperse themselves as hath been often seen'. In a word, Whitaby argued against sending any further contingents to Liverpool; and Liverpool, by not having a voice there, lost the chance to make its case to the privy council. The lords of the privy council dismissed Whitaby with a decision to leave 'the course which hath been formerly used for the transport of soldiers from Hilbre to be continued until they shall show just cause to the contrary'.[113]

Arguments about precedence and superiority of jurisdiction between Chester and Liverpool were not settled by the privy council but by the gradual silting up of the Dee estuary, which gave Liverpool the upper hand from the late seventeenth century onwards into the modern age, when other factors marked the decline of the second port of the Empire which Liverpool had become in the nineteenth and early twentieth centuries. However, their rivalry in the matter of transporting troops into Ireland is an interesting and little-known aspect of their historic relationship.

Victuals and supplies

The transport of victuals was organised in much the same way as the transport of troops, the mayor having responsibility for procuring ships and sailors.[114] Large consignments of bread, wheat, rye, fish, beef, mutton, cheese, butter and beer were contracted from victualling merchants, whose main task was to buy up food in England and get it to the army's commissaries for victual in Ireland. The pressure of the Irish war helped to develop the contracting system between merchants and government in the supply of food to the army; this was more efficient than purveyance, the crown's right to commandeer goods and services for its own use, or a system of free enterprise where merchants working on their own account followed and sold provisions directly to the troops. Private victualling was much open to abuse, even the sale of goods to the enemy if he offered a higher price. Under contract, however, the merchant undertook to procure, transport and deliver various quantities of victuals to the army; he was paid half his bill on signature and gave the privy council a bond to guarantee his half of the bargain. The balance due to him was paid within six days of the privy council receiving a certificate from the mayor of the port that the food shipped was delivered and in good condition, and his bond became redeemable when he sent in his receipts from the army's commissaries of victuals on the delivery of the goods in Ireland.[115]

Merchants competed for contracts to supply individual garrisons, the army in whole provinces and occasionally the entire army in Ireland.[116] John Jolles and William Cockayne, for example, supplied victuals for 9,500 soldiers in the three provinces of Leinster, Connaught and Ulster in August 1601.[117] By means of the contracting system the government gained greater control of supplying the troops not only with food but with apparel and arms as well and, in theory, this extension of the contracting system in the last years of the war, approximately from 1598 to 1602, should have secured more efficient transit of these goods into Ireland. Stores of foodstuffs shipped with levies were forbidden to be broken into, despite long delays waiting on favouring winds, even should there be a time of dearth in the port, as happened in 1596 and 1597 in Chester.[118]

While victualling the troops in Ireland created a new market for a few years and benefited a few, the necessary bulk purchases of victuals in and about Chester led to food shortages and high prices. Foulke and William Aldersey, mayors in 1594 and 1595, were, for instance, concerned about the activities of William Beecher and George Leicester, agents of victualling merchants. In a time of serious shortage of food they had bought up so much corn, butter and cheese that they forced up prices in the environs of Chester even further. The mayor wanted them to go elsewhere for provisions, and would have liked the government to place curbs on the demands made by the army victuallers.[119] The government's intention in *The book of orders* to ensure fair distribution of food in time of famine appears to have had little effect on the situation in Chester.

The bad harvest 1595/1596 brought near famine conditions to Lancashire and Cheshire as elsewhere. Grain prices rose to 36 per cent above normal in 1595, in 1596 to a record 83 per cent above normal and in 1597 to 64 per cent above normal. The feeding of large numbers of troops in Chester, the collections for their 'sea victuals', and further provision of the whole army in Ireland caused a deep-seated resentment against the government's military demands.[120]

In April 1597 scarcity became acute in Chester when the privy council ordered fresh levies to the port. John Savage, the mayor, was surprised to read in his instructions that these soldiers 'maie bee victualled at a more easy rate than they were laste tyme'.[121] He wrote immediately to the council that prices were so high in Chester that to meet victualling requirements he would need supplies sent in from other parts of the country.[122] Thomas Lyniall was sent with the letter to act as Chester's agent to the privy council in obtaining further supplies; and, to ensure that he was fully briefed, John Savage gave him a draft of his letter to Lord Burghley and the council 'for your better understondinge of the contents hereof'.[123] Lyniall reported from London that the council had great sympathy with the obvious need of the city of Chester but could only suggest that the city import grain from Denmark.[124]

Thomas Fletcher, who succeeded as mayor on the death in office of John Savage, complained to Sir Robert Cecil of how the city of Chester had become impoverished because of the levies to Ireland and because of the war with Spain – 'a place wherewith the merchants had all their intercourse'.[125] It was a view with which the privy council had some sympathy, for later, in 1599, it supported the Chester merchants' request for a licence to ship 10,000 dickers of calf skins overseas and in so doing the council agreed that the Irish rebellion had damaged the city, 'being very much charged for the Queen's service'.[126]

With large numbers of soldiers, tons of victuals, thousands of coats and sets of arms and armour converging on Chester it is not surprising to find some merchants profiteering and smuggling, activities which were an almost natural accompaniment of war.[127] William Aldersey, mayor in 1595, stated that there was no merchant in Chester who could be trusted.[128] Agents acting for a victualling contractor in May 1595 came under suspicion of selling butter, cheese and corn at a profit in Chester instead of having these goods shipped to Ireland.[129] The governor of the Isle of Man, Peter Liyr, complained to the mayor of Chester in January 1597 about the treacherous behaviour of Chester merchants on his island.[130] Other merchants in Chester were examined in 1598 for exporting corn without a licence.[131]

There was also an illicit trade in apparel and arms, which were provided 'at Her Majesty's chardge for the souldiers'; in some cases it was suspected that the habiliments of war came back from Ireland to be resold in Chester.[132] Swords, daggers, rapiers, horses' saddles and on one occasion six horses were brought back to Chester by Captain Whyte's lieutenants; the reason was not given. When the privy council heard of the return of horse it wrote to the mayor of Chester, Robert Brerwood, on 4 August, 'wee doe not a littel mervaille that the Lord Deputie would give him [Whyte] leave to transport any horsses out of that realm consideringe wee doe send over thether horsse from hence to fill up the bands'.[133] The Irish war years gave rise to much disloyal trading in arms, which found their way to the Irish enemy. In 1597 merchants were interrogated in Chester over shipments of arms that went to Hugh O'Neill in Ulster. A certain Thomas Long was accused of having gone to Ireland with a consignment of muskets procured in Manchester and shipped through Chester to O'Neill.[134] In 1598 the privy council gave orders to stay consignments of arms and munitions at Chester and Bristol because of fears that they were intended for the enemy.[135] Severe warnings and reprimands were sent to the mayors of ports that the Irish were receiving arms and munitions which may have been bought at fairs at Chester, Bristol and London.[136]

The reality of this illegal and treasonable trade was also attested to by the high command and others in Ireland. William Saxey, chief justice in Munster, graphically described the crooked merchant's progress and profit when writing to Sir Robert Cecil in December 1599.[137] Sir Henry Docwra admitted that arms were embezzled at Derry and found their way to the enemy and back to Chester, where they were likely to be resold in a cycle of frauds.[138] The Company of Armourers, Gun-makers and Cutlers in Chester pointed out other disorders and abuses to the privy council in an effort to eliminate them. Many persons, they said, bought arms and armour from captains and others returning from Ireland, which were ostensibly old and unserviceable, but 'they trymmed and dressed them ... and re-sold them to the countries thereabouts,' to the undoing of the Company's proper trade, to the 'deceitfull utterance of olde armes for newe' and, 'which is the greatest offence, defraudinge her Majesties service'.[139] Opportunities for much greater frauds in financial deals multiplied from May 1601 on the introduction of a new debased coinage into Ireland in an effort to pay for the war at reduced cost.[140] To facilitate the movement of treasure and the payment of merchants, shipowners, the mayor and soldiers, an exchange was established in Chester. But the merchants used the difference in value between English sterling coin of the realm and the new Irish coinage to their own profit, a practice which the subsequent enquiry into the abuses in the exchange revealed.[141] The physical movement of treasure presented obvious security problems also. On one occasion the privy council was alerted in time to foil a plot by two Welshmen, John Salisbury and Peter Wynn, to steal £10,000 at Chester.[142]

In the privy council's registers for the Irish war years the number of warrants authorising the lord treasurer to have payments made to the mayor of Chester noticeably increases from 1598 to 1601.[143] The papers of William Knight, clerk to the mayor for Irish affairs, indicate as well the size of some of these financial transactions: £1,800 in 1595; £400 in 1596; £600 in 1598; £562 12s 10d in 1599; and £1,000 in 1600. These are but sampled items from those papers and do not indicate the full cost to the government for Irish services at Chester.[144] As is well known from the many petitions for payment of arrears for war and other services, the government of late Elizabethan England was slow to pay.[145] This is reflected in the way in which the mayor of Chester had on occasion to borrow money from wealthy citizens to meet the urgency of his creditors until government funds arrived. In 1601, John Ratcliffe borrowed £600 from Lady Mary Cholmondeley to help in victualling and transporting 1,000 foot and 76 horse.[146]

The tasks of the mayoral authorities in Chester were evidently multiplied in the war years and did not end when the levies set sail from the Dee estuary. We have seen some of the problems created by the government's demands to have troops billeted and transported and of their impact on the city and port of Chester. It may be significant of the attitude of the late Elizabethan government that the privy council commended and thanked the mayor for his work in the promotion of the 'service of Ireland' but on only three occasions, namely in 1595, 1597 and in 1601.[147] Sir John Savage was particularly singled out for his good government in having troops transported, especially since he 'saved some good part of Her Majesty's charges' and yet was able to give 'good satisfaction to all parties'. The privy council ended its gracious letter to Sir John with the wish that others would use similar care so that 'wee would bee less troubled in giving directions and the Queen's service better ordered than it is'.[148]

Notes

1 CCR, mayor's military papers, M/MP/8, 126, a list of twenty conductors in 1598 at Chester; five are designated 'captains'.
2 College of Arms, Talbot MSS, K, f. 30r, not dated but signed by Cecil.
3 *Ibid.* There are a number of such passes in the mayor of Chester's military papers, for example those of Gabriel Wethenhall and Jasper Rutter, constables of Nantwich, certifying that Daniel Storey of Lincolnshire was too ill to proceed to Chester, and signed at the request of his conductor, William Lilly – CCR, M/MP/10, 5, 2 July 1599.
4 *APC*, xxxi, 21–22; *CSPI* (1596–1597), 172.
5 *Ibid.* (1596–1597), 172; *CSPI* (1598–1599), 219.
6 CCR, mayor's military papers, M/MP/11, 5, 6, M/MP/7, 32, 35, M/MP/11, 1–14, examples of indenture from captains and from conductors.

7   For examples, see HMC, *Salisbury*, xi, 431; *APC*, xxxi, 21.
8   For the English merchant service see G. V. Scammell, 'Manning the English merchant service in the sixteenth century', *Mariner's Mirror*, 56 (1970), 131–154; J. J. N. McGurk, 'Rochester and the Irish levy of October 1601', *Mariner's Mirror*, 74 (1988), 57–66.
9   BL, Cotton MSS, Titus B, xii, 322.
10 *APC*, xxviii, 204, 529, 530; *APC*, xxxix, 65; *APC*, xxx, 758; *APC*, xxxi, 182, 205, for examples of weather-bound troops at Haverfordwest.
11 *Cal. Carew MSS*, iv, 316, Carew to Mountjoy, 25 August 1602.
12 *CSPI* (1601–1603), 475, Carew to Cecil, 20 August 1602.
13 Fynes Moryson, *Itinerary*, vol. iv, 19.
14 HMC, *Salisbury*, vi, 205–208; *Cal. Carew MSS*, iii, 178.
15 R. C. Jarvis, 'The head-port of Chester and Liverpool, its creek and member', *Transactions of the Historic Society of Lancashire and Cheshire*, 102 (1950), 69–70; D. M. Woodward, *The trade of Elizabethan Chester* (Hull, 1970).
16 J. Beck, *Tudor Cheshire* (Chester, 1969), fig. 1, p. 9.
17 J. A. Twenlow, ed., *Liverpool town books* (Liverpool, 1918), vol. ii, 120, 121, 147.
18 For the earliest accounts of the area in this respect see J. Leland's *Itinerary*, ed. Toulmin Smith (London, 1906–1908), vol. iii, 91, 92. And for Captain Willis' account *CSPI* (1600), 200, 209, and for a like account of a similarly normal passage to Ireland, HMC, *Salisbury*, xi, 24, 488.
19 CCR, the mayor's military papers are under M/MP; his assembly books A/B, his files M/F and the mayor's great letter books are M/L.
20 *APC*, xxxi, 86, 87, 295, 296; *APC*, xxxii, 70, 71, 126, 127, for examples of this.
21 CCR, mayor's military papers, M/MP/8, 8–15, for examples of the mayoralty in Thomas Smith in 1596.
22 Lambeth Palace Library, archbishop's clerical muster books, MS 2009, 64 and 68 – orders to the clergy; *APC*, xxv, 315, 326, 331–333; and see PRO SP63/186/82, 188.
23 PRO SP63/209/211.
24 See Chapter 3.
25 C. G. Cruickshank, 'Dead pays in the Elizabethan army', *English Historical Review*, 53 (1938), 93–97, but the author does not clarify the problem raised above.
26 CCR, mayor's military papers, M/MP/12, 34–45, are examples of sick passes signed by captains in Ireland for the sick and wounded to return to England.
27 PRO SP63/18, 41 – instructions to Edward Randolph, 8 July 1566; and for a narrative account see G. A. Hayes-McCoy, in *New history of Ireland*, eds T. W. Moody, F. X. Martin and F. J. Byrne (Oxford, 1976), 86.
28 Henry Docwra's *Relation and narration*, in *Celtic miscellany*, ed. J. O'Donovan (Dublin, 1849), 236, 237. The Gaelic source, *AFM*, vi, 11.2189, claimed that Docwra led 6,000 men first to Dublin but Docwra's own account is clearly the more accurate.
29 *APC*, xxx, 10, 12, 101–106, and for copies of his letters patent, Lambeth Palace Library, Carew MSS 621, 75.
30 *APC*, xxx, 54, 102.
31 HMC, *Salisbury*, ix, 420, Croft to Cecil, 29 December 1599.
32 PRO SP63/207, part i, 110, Mountjoy to Cecil, 16 February 1600 (n.s.d.).
33 *Ibid.*, 111, Hardware to the privy council, February 1600; PRO SP12/274, 92, the same to Cecil, 2 April 1600.
34 PRO SP63/207, part i, 111, Harware's complaints to the privy council.
35 *APC*, xxx, 69, gives 300 from London and Middlesex but *ibid.*, 255, shows payments to the conductor, Vincent Skynner, for 250 soldiers; for the council's orders to Chester see *ibid.*, 155, 156, 163, 164.
36 *APC*, xxx, 145, 146.

37 PRO SP63/207, part i, 106 Mountjoy to the privy council, 15 February 1600.
38 *Ibid.*, 15, the *Moon* was to be at Chester by 16 January.
39 *CSPI* (1600), 68, 69, Docwra to Cecil, 2 April 1600.
40 HMC, *Salisbury*, x, 108, Buckhurst to Cecil, 12 April 1600; *APC*, xxx, 245–246.
41 *CSPI* (1600), 121, Docwra to Cecil, 24 April 1600; HMC, *Salisbury*, x, 12, 136.
42 HMC, *Salisbury*, x, 136, Hardware to the privy council, 4 May 1600.
43 CCR, mayor's military papers, M/MP/11, 1–14, the muster rolls of the 630 reinforcements; *APC*, xxxi, 86, 87, 128, 141; *CSPI* (November 1600 – July 1601), 212, 26 March 1601.
44 *APC*, xxxi, 323, 324, 331–333, 337, 338; PRO SP63/208, part ii, 103; *ibid.*, part iii, 103, 15 Field to Cecil, 11 June 1601.
45 *CSPI* (1601–1603), 173, 174, Alford to Cecil from Lough Foyle, 19 November 1601.
46 J. R. Hale, ed., *Certain discourses military by Sir John Smythe* (Ithaca, 1964).
47 CCR, quarter sessions files, QSF/49, 91, 138, 142–144.
48 *CSPI* (1601–1603), 415, 416, Chichester to Cecil, 22 June 1602.
49 CCR, quarter sessions files, QSF/49 (1600–1601), *passim.* It is of interest that many of the names of the inns in Chester survive today as hotels and or public houses such as the Saracen's Head, the Crown, and the White Horse.
50 Cited by E. E. Rich 'The population of Elizabethan England', *Economic History Review*, 2nd series, 2 (1950), 247–265.
51 CCR, mayor's great letter books, M/L/1/109, i–iv; and 12, 81–85, for examples of ships taken up 1596–1599, and in the mayor's military papers, M/MP/12, 30, a list of ships, not dated, but in the 1596 bundle.
52 HMC, *Salisbury*, ix, 72, 89, 96, 106–108, 113, and for the list of ships' names used in the Irish service see the appendix to Part II.
53 CCR, mayor's military papers, M/MP/8/20, 36, 23, 26, 38, 56, 59, Dutton to Smith, mayor of Chester; and *ibid.*, 8/48, 49, 72, Dutton's notes on men and arms missing and correspondence to the deputy lieutenants of Flintshire. There are some duplicate documents of the incident in the mayor's great letter book.
54 HMC, *Salisbury*, xi, 24, and xii, 407.
55 HMC, *Salisbury*, vi, 436–437.
56 HMC, *Salisbury*, xii, 390.
57 HMC, *Salisbury*, x, 268.
58 CCR, quarter sessions files, QSF/49, 91, 138, 142, 143, 144.
59 HMC, *Salisbury*, x, 268–269, Hardware to the privy council, 7 August 1600; *APC*, xxx, 245, 246, April 1600.
60 CCR, quarter sessions files, QSF/49 (1600–1601), *passim.*
61 *Ibid.*, ff. 25, 28, 92, 94, 111, 113, 119, 132.
62 *Ibid.*, f. 132, assault and death of John Eaton, 16 January 1601.
63 *Ibid.*, ff. 12, 25, 28.
64 *Ibid.*, ff. 100–102.
65 *Ibid.*, ff. 24, 88.
66 CCR, mayor's military papers, M/MP/8, *passim*; CCR, mayor's great letter books, M/L/1, *passim.*
67 HMC, *Salisbury*, ix and x, *passim.*
68 CCR, mayor's military papers, M/MP/8, 18, 20, 33; M/L/1, 131, for examples.
69 *CSPI* (1601–1603), 365, Captain Vaughan; *ibid.*, 439, Oliver St John for instances.
70 *APC*, xxix, 591; *CSPI* (1592–1596), 493.
71 *CSPI* (1598–1599), 482, 'The stages of the new post laid for the service of Ireland' 24 February 1598 (o.s.d.). The post at Holyhead had a yearly allowance of £130.
72 *CSPI* (1601–1603), 412, 413.

73 HMC, *Salisbury*, ix, 377, 'Jo. Frauncis, Post of Chester, to Sir R. Cecil'.
74 CCR, M/MP/12/30 where the *Valentine* is stated of being of Liverpool, and for some of the activity of this ship in Docwra's service see *CSPI* (1601–1603), 190–191.
75 HMC, *Salisbury*, ix, 377.
76 CCR, mayor's great letter books, M/L/5, 244–246, January 1598.
77 CCR, mayor's military papers, M/MP/8/L/1, 148, 7 June 1598.
78 *APC*, xxxii, 437.
79 *CSPI* (1592–1596), 493.
80 *HMC, Salisbury*, ix, 113. The practice of marking official letters with 'haste', 'post haste' and 'For Life' even became common from the middle of the sixteenth century. See J. A. J. Housden, 'Early posts in England', *English Historical Review*, 18 (1903), 717.
81 CCR, mayor's military papers, M/MP/8/L/1, 12, William Sparowe to T. Smith, mayor, 12 November 1596.
82 *Ibid.*, 133, Thomas, Lord Burgh, to Thomas Fletcher, mayor, 12 May 1597.
83 *Ibid.*, 163, Thomas Bulkeley, mayor of Beaumaris, to Richard Rathbone, mayor of Chester, 20 September 1598.
84 *APC*, xxix, 590–592.
85 *APC*, xxviii, 578, 608–610, orders sent 16 and 23 July 1598.
86 For the confusions caused by Archbishop John Whitgift in implementing rapidly changing privy council orders for clerical levies see my 'The clergy and the militia, 1580–1610', *History*, 60 (1975), 207–208.
87 *APC*, xxxii, 287.
88 CCR, mayor's great letter books, M/L/1, and mayor's military papers, M/MP/8, which reflect the rivalry with Liverpool; R. Muir, *History of Liverpool* (London, 1970), 76–80.
89 CCR, mayor's great letter books, M/L/1, 109, 13 October 1596; *CSPI* (1596–1597), 413. For the case against Sir George Cary see H. Hall, *Society in the Elizabethan age* (London, 1907 edn), 126–132.
90 CCR, mayor's military papers, M/MP/8, 5, William Moore to Thomas Smith, 6 November 1596.
91 *Ibid.*, 6, the same to the same, 9 November 1596.
92 *ibid.*, 8–10, Smith to the privy council, 10 November 1596.
93 *Ibid.*, 13, Moore to Smith, 13 November 1596.
94 *Ibid.*, 14, Smith to Moore, 14 November 1596.
95 *Ibid.*
96 *Ibid.*, 17, undated account signed by R. Billings.
97 *Ibid.*, 18, Smith to the Irish council, 16 November 1596.
98 *Ibid.*, 52, list of soldiers 'who deserted with their arms' endorsed 'for Captaine Prees', 13 November 1596.
99 *Ibid.*, 57, Moore to Smith, 19 December 1596.
100 *Ibid.*, 58, examination of William Pye at Chester, 23 December 1596.
101 CCR, mayor's military papers, M/MP/1, 90, Sir John Savage to Lord Burghley, 18 April 1597.
102 *Ibid.*, 114 copy of the privy council's letter, 2 December 1596, to discharge contingents of men at Chester and Liverpool.
103 *Ibid.*, 121, the privy council to the mayor of Chester, 7 April 1597.
104 CCR, mayor's military papers, M/MP/8, 87, Moore to Savage, 16 April 1597.
105 *Ibid.*, 91, Savage to Moore, 18 April 1597.
106 CCR, mayor's great letter books, M/MP/L/1, 97, Robert Moore to Savage, 23 April 1597.
107 *Ibid.*, 98, William Moore to Savage, same date.

108 *Ibid.*, 100, the mayor to the privy council, 24 April 1597; and for the precedent of November 1594, PRO SP12/250, 35.

109 CCR, mayor's great letter books, M/MP/L/1, 127, Lord Burghley's instructions, 26 April 1597, and *ibid.*, 129, 131, receipts of money, sums of £400 and £600, from the treasurer-at-war's department in Ireland, 7 May 1597.

110 *Ibid.*, 57, 63, 104, 107, 110a, 110b, letters on reimbursements and receipts.

111 HMC, *Salisbury*, xii, 466.

112 R. C. Jarvis, 'The head-port of Chester and Liverpool, its creek and member', *Transactions of the Historic Society of Lancashire and Cheshire*, 102 (1950), 78, argues that the 'dependency of the Lancashire havens upon the port of Chester has got itself confused with the question of delimitation of the ports ... [an] entirely separate matter from dependency'. Yet, clearly, from the correspondence between Liverpool and Chester on Irish levies, Liverpool's dependency on Chester was resented and contested in the 1590s.

113 J. Touzeau, *The rise and progress of Liverpool 1551–1835* (Liverpool, 1910), 139–140, which summarises Whitaby's arguments, but from J. A. Picton's *Memorials of Liverpool* (Liverpool, 1873), 85, 86. It is surprising that the ancient rivalry between Chester and Liverpool which broke out again in 1602 is not mentioned in the Liverpool corporation records edited by J. A. Twenlow, *Liverpool town books* (Liverpool, 1936).

114 CCR, mayor's great letter books, M/MP/L/1, 89, list of victualling ships, 1597; CCR, mayor's military papers, M/MP/12, receipts for provisions put aboard, 1598.

115 CCR, mayor's military papers, M/MP/10, 3; CCR, mayor's great letter books, M/MP/L/1, 20, 161, examples of mayoral certificates. For the details of a typical contract for victuals see *APC*, xxix, 273.

116 *CSPD* (1595–1597), 21–23, merchant competition, and for a contract to supply the whole army see PRO SP63/211, 258, July 1602.

117 *APC*, xxx, 194, 196–203, 217, 294, 303, 394, 410, 553, 619, 623, 686, 724, 728, examples of payments to Jolles, Cockayne and John Wood, who supplied all the Munster garrisons in 1600 and 1601.

118 It was not until the late 1590s that the government shouldered the risks involved in sea transport – *APC*, xxix, 485–460.

119 PRO SP12/251, 61, the mayor to the privy council, 17 March 1595.

120 Cited in A. B. Appleby, *Famine in Tudor and Stuart England* (Liverpool, 1978), 112, 113.

121 CCR, mayor's great letter books, M/MP/L/1, 121, the privy council to the mayor, 7 April 1597.

122 CCR, mayor's military papers, M/MP/8, 81–83, the mayor to the privy council, 13 April 1597. This exchange of letters with the privy council is also found copied into the mayor's assembly books (1539–1624), CCR, AB/1.

123 CCR, mayor's military papers, M/MP/8, 84, 85, the mayor to Thomas Lyniall, 13 April 1597.

124 *Ibid.*, 92, Lyniall's report to the mayor, 19 April 1597.

125 HMC, *Salisbury*, viii, 298, Fletcher to Lord Burghley, 8 August 1598.

126 HMC, *Salisbury*, ix, 424–425, privy council's opinion on Chester's merchants petition, 'Endorsed, 1599'.

127 PRO SP/63/205/125; 206/59; 208, part i, 72, for examples.

128 CCR, mayor's military papers, M/MP/8, 2.

129 *Ibid.*, 1 and 1b.

130 CCR L/1/69, Liyr to the mayor, 13 January 1597.

131 *Ibid.*, 144.

132 CCR, quarter sessions files, QSF/49, 12, 24, 136, illegal sale of arms in 1600, 1601.

133 *APC*, xxx, 556, privy council to Brerwood, 4 August 1600.

134 PRO SP63/199, 107.

135 *APC*, xxix, 244.

136 PRO SP63/205, 125.
137 PRO SP63/206, 59.
138 PRO SP63/208, part i, 72.
139 *APC*, xxxi, 444–445.
140 *Ibid.*, 286; R. Bagwell, *Ireland under the Tudors* (London, 1890), vol. iii, 395–398, for the effects of the debased coinage on the army in Ireland.
141 *CSPI* (1601–1603), 506–511, 'Memorandum on the abuses in the exchanges'.
142 *CSPI* (1600–1601), 302; *APC*, xxxi, 191–192.
143 *APC*, xxxi, 18, 77, 88, 117, 363, 380, 423, 424.
144 CCR, mayor's military papers, M/MP/8/L/1, 73, 107, 111, 129, 131, 153.
145 Many examples may be found, for instance HMC, *Salisbury*, viii–xii, *passim*.
146 *APC*, xxxii, 323.
147 *APC*, xxv, 421–422; *APC*, xxviii, 115; *APC*, xxxi, 338–339.
148 *APC*, xxviii, 115, to Sir John Savage, mayor of Chester, 11 May 1597 – Savage died in his mayoralty year on 5 December and Thomas Fletcher was elected in his place on 9 December. See G. Ormerod, *The history of the county palatine and city of Chester* (London, 1819), vol. i, 200.

CHAPTER SEVEN

Bristol, Barnstaple and other western ports in the service of the Irish war

Bristol

Like Chester, Bristol was important to the late Elizabethan government in the provision of ships and as a base for the assembly and transportation of troops to Ireland. Military traffic in the 1590s gave employment to sailors, mariners and ships' masters whose normal trade with Spain and Portugal had been stayed because of the long war with Spain, but it is unlikely that the movement of men and the habiliments of war was as profitable a trade. Bristol's traditional Irish trade was with the southerly Irish ports of Waterford, Wexford, Cork and Youghal and with Galway on the Atlantic coast; timber, hides, linen and fish were its main Irish imports,[1] but with the intensification of hostilities at the end of the queen's reign the whole character of this traditional trade underwent a sharp change which was not entirely beneficial.[2]

Bristol had formerly been noted for its wealth in ships and in shipbuilding, but the mayor and corporation noted the decline of their port in a petition of 1595 to the privy council when they requested a lessening of contributions to government services, stating that their fleet had been reduced to 'eight or ten small ships'; that their shipowners and merchants were 'undone by the war' and that 'now this poor place' found the burdens of the Irish war too much to bear.[3] In an official list of ships built in English ports between 1581 and 1594 seven are of Bristol and twenty-five of London, which is a further indication of the port's decline.[4] By January 1598 Lord Burghley listed Bristol among the ports 'manifestly decayed in trade'. The citizens of the port blamed the evils of war, piracy and the greed of the London merchants in monopolising overseas markets.[5] In that crisis year of 1598 Bristol pleaded poverty and asked for a reduction in the military levies to be sent into the port, but none was then or later allowed. The government had long been inured to such pleas. An assessment of the port of Bristol by Jean Vanes concludes that there was no disastrous decline in Bristol's shipping at the end of the century; on the contrary, she sees an increase in the number of smaller ships trading in and out of the port in the 1590s but many of them owned in partnership.[6] Smaller vessels could overcome the problems of silting and tide and hence were able to come in the three miles from the mouth of the Avon to the city's harbour. The mayor and corporation enforced an Admiralty High-Court ruling barring ships of above 100 tons from the city's harbour; the larger ships anchored off the Avon at Hungroad three miles from Bristol, or off the Severn at Kingroad, near Portishead.[7]

Set between the rivers Frome and Avon with sheltered tidal harbours, Bristol was well placed for trade and shipping with Ireland. During earlier Irish rebellions Bristol had much experience in billeting and sending out troops, and appeared to have suffered much in the process. In 1566, 1569, 1579, 1580 and 1583 large levies for Ireland converged on the city and port. For example, Colonel Edward Randolph's 2,000 men set off from Bristol in July 1566 on an ill-fated expedition to Lough Foyle against Shane O'Neill's rebellion.[8] In August 1579 a riot of over 600 West Country soldiers caused the city to erect a gibbet in the High Street to strike terror into the rioters. Bad weather delayed the troops' embarkation for five weeks at a cost to the city of £483 8s 9d. In December 1579, 900 troops, who quickly departed, still cost the city £443.[9] And in July 1580, 500 soldiers were billeted in Bristol for nearly six weeks, causing frequent disorders and costing £1,160 for food, billets and the hire of ships. The city was reimbursed for these crown services from the exchequer, but normally after a long delay.[10]

During the 1590s Bristol was of much less importance than Chester as a staging post for the levies to Ireland. West Country ports were used to ease the pressure on Bristol as troops were sent to Barnstaple, Milford Haven, Padstow, Plymouth, Weymouth and Southampton. Perhaps as a result, few local records give evidence of troops in Bristol. There are no mayors' military papers and the passage of troops through Bristol to Ireland has left little mention in the mayor's court actions (1567–1761)[11] or in the quarter sessions files from 1595 to 1705.[12] And the great and little audit books were searched in vain for the years 1597–1601 for the city's expenses of sending out troops to Ireland.[13] The city chamberlain's accounts and the ordinance book of the common council note only minor expenses as evidence of troop movements, and then chiefly for the later seventeenth century.[14] This account, therefore, is mainly based on national records from which the full extent of Bristol's involvement in the transportation of soldiers to Ireland can be gleaned. The result is set out in Table 13.

Over an eight-year period military levies of horse and foot were sent to Bristol on fourteen occasions: the grand total of troops involved was 10,275 foot and 602 horse – the comparable figures at Chester were 19,105 foot and 1,046 horse on fifteen occasions.[15] On four occasions, levies of over 1,000 were ordered to Bristol, but none over 2,000 as had been the case in Chester. The majority of troops in Bristol were destined for the more southerly theatres of war in Ireland, hence the preponderance of levies sent to Sir George Carew, the president and military governor of Munster, but, like Chester, reinforcements were also sent to Sir Henry Docwra's garrisons at Lough Foyle in Ulster.[16] As with Chester, the largest levies were sent in the peak years of military action in Ireland: for Essex's army in 1599, Mountjoy's in 1600, the Spanish landing at Kinsale in 1601, and the aftermath and completion of the reconquest by the summer of 1602. And again like Chester, levies ordered to go to Ireland in the winter months, between November and March, had greater difficulty in getting there on account of the weather.[17] Delays increased desertions and expenditure and no doubt prolonged the war. Of the totals in Table 13 not all sailed to Ireland. The October 1596 levy of 700 foot (500 from south Wales and 200 from Gloucestershire) were sent home, partly because they had been unduly delayed in embarking in the first place and partly because a truce was made in Ireland during the late summer of 1596.[18]

166

Table 13   *Military levies to Bristol*

Date	Number of foot (f.) and horse (h.)	Mayor responsible	Intended for:	Note
May 1595	–	–	Sir J. Norris	1
October 1596	700 f.	W. Yate	Sir W. Russell in Dublin, but stayed	2
May 1597	800 f.	W. Yate	Sir H. Bagenal	3
June 1598	550 f.	W. Ellis		4
	200 h.	W. Ellis		
October 1598	400 f.	W. Ellis	Sir S. Bagenal in Dublin	5
January/March 1599	1,000 f.	J. Hort	Earl of Essex	6
	100 h.		Sir H. Danvers	
January/March 1600	1,200 f.	J. Hopkins	Lord Mountjoy	7
	18 h.		Sir G. Carew	
August/September 1600	600 f.	J. Hopkins	Sir G. Carew in Cork	8
	36 h.			
December 1600	220 f.	J. Hopkins	Sir H. Docwra, at Lough Foyle	9
July/August 1601	895 f.	W. Vawer	Sir G. Carew in Cork and Waterford	10
	40 h.			
October 1601	1,025 f.	W. Vawer	Lord Mountjoy and the Earl	
	208 h.	W. Vawer	of Thomond at Kinsale	11
December 1601/ January 1602	1,250 f.	W. Vawer/ R. Horte	Sir G. Carew in Cork	12
January 1602	835 f.	R. Horte	Cork – additional	13
July/August 1602	800 f.	R. Horte	Sir G. Carew and Sir G. Thornton	14
Totals	10,275 f.			
	602 h.			

1. PRO SP63/179, 65; BAO, account books for 1595 have perished, J. Latimer, *Annals of Bristol in the sixteenth century* (Bristol, 1900), 103.
2. *APC*, xxvi, 240, 243, 244; *Calendar of treasury papers* (1577–1696), 2, gives 750 men.
3. *APC*, xxvii, 24.
4. *APC*, xviii, 524, 529.
5. PRO SP63/195, no. 74b; *APC*, xxx, 240; *APC*, xxix, 237–240.
6. *APC*, xxx, 5, 6, 42, 51; HMC, *Salisbury*, viii, 487; HMC, *Salisbury*, ix, 68, 91, 96, 108.
7. *APC*, xxx, 42, 64, 65, 111, 113, 171, 140, 144; *APC*, xxix, 576.
8. HMC, *Salisbury*, x, 227, 264, 267–268, 294, 321, 322; and see Table 3.
9. *APC*, xxxi, 13, 14, 16, 20–23.
10. *APC*, xxxi, 315–318; *APC*, xxxii, 82, 83, 206.
11. *APC*, xxxii, 240–242, 294, 297; HMC, *Salisbury*, xi, 484.
12. *APC*, xxxii, 443, 444, 479; HMC, *Salisbury*, xii, 169.
13. *APC*, xxxii, 474–478.
14. *Cal. Carew MSS*, ix, 331, 335, 350. For the indentures of levies from south Wales to Bristol, PRO E101/66/19, 109–137, but they are incomplete for the years 1598 and 1600.

Like the mayor of Chester, the mayor of Bristol was beset with the problem of filling up gaps in the shire levies. In 1598 the mayor, William Ellis, was ordered to complete the numbers in the shire companies by drafting 'loose and idle persons in and about the city'.[19] In February 1600 John Hopkins, the mayor, certified that seventy soldiers had gone missing from over 1,000 ordered to the port. Furthermore, he complained that the deputy lieutenants of Pembrokeshire had failed to send their quota of 150 men.[20] The privy council took the deputy lieutenants of Pembrokeshire to task for this failure of duty. They had asked for exemption from the levy at the last moment:

> even when at the very date those men should have been at the Port you direct your letters unto us to excuse the levying of so great a number.[21]

Pembrokeshire appears to have got away with not sending any of the 150 men to Bristol.[22] But the privy council scolded John Hopkins for delays in not notifying the council earlier, for not noting the names, counties and other details of deserters in his port and for not telling them whether or not he had already filled up the vacancies.[23]

Despite the smaller overall scale of military operations in Bristol compared with Chester, the mayor, council and citizens experienced similar difficulties and problems in billeting, feeding and keeping levies of troops in order, as well as transporting them to Ireland. The mayor had continual troubles bargaining with shipowners, coping with delays and keeping order. Disorders were as common in Bristol as in Chester and caused as much anxiety to the mayoral authorities. The more serious outbreaks of riotous behaviour occurred when there were many soldiers in the port. The commissioners for musters in the city in 1601 pointed out to the privy council that the mayor should be empowered to deal with deserters and mutineers under military law, and that it was a pity in their view that military law operated only after troops had left England.[24] The mayor, William Ellis in 1599, was stoned by soldiers when he aided in quelling a fight as soldiers were being herded on board ship. The ringleader was tried and given a mock show of execution.[25] During 1601 it was said that the citizens of Bristol could not pass the streets in quiet at night because so many frays took place between the soldiers and citizens. Other reports claimed that citizens 'flew to arms' and beat the soldiers, driving many to take refuge in their transport ships.[26] And during the six-week delay in the departure of the last levy of the reign, from mid-May to the beginning of July 1602, outbreaks of violence between soldiers and citizens became a nightly occurrence. On 26 May the mayor and commissioners for musters had to quell a mutiny which broke out among the contingent from Gloucestershire. The ringleaders were arrested, a preacher sent to them in prison to prepare for execution, and the next morning with halters about their necks, all the troops standing by, they mounted the gallows; 'after they had said their prayers and expected no life', the commissioners ordered them to be untied and spared. It was reported that the example wrought much good and quiet in the city.[27]

The privy council was as anxious as the mayor to have soldiers embarked as quickly as possible since delays involved additional costs; its letters to the mayors of Bristol invariably urge them 'to use all means to hasten them away'.[28] A privy council letter ordering the shipping of 895 soldiers to Munster in July 1601 advised the mayor, William Vawer, to have the ships ready 'at King's Roade where they may be ready to set sail with the first convenient wind, for by the stay of shipping in Hunge-roads they lose the opportunity of the wind to the hindrance and prejudice of the service,'[29] and 'by that means occasion is given soldiers to escape'. The privy council was informed of local conditions and of the chief opportunity for desertion, delays caused by weather.[30]

168

There were complaints about desertion on ten occasions in privy council letters.[31] In December 1600 Captain Crompton, conducting 220 reinforcements from Bristol to Lough Foyle, ran into foul weather and was forced to put in at Haverfordwest, where a complete company from Gloucestershire and many of the Welsh deserted. Crompton complained to the privy council that these men were unfit to have been employed in the first place. The council sent on his letter to Lord Chandos, the lord lieutenant for Gloucestershire, with strict orders to have the deserting company hunted down.[32] This instance shows the difficulty of ascertaining the numbers of soldiers transported from the port actually to Ireland. The council's threats and reprimands to the mayors, the commissioners for musters and conductors of levies appear to have had little effect in stemming the losses. Council orders to the commissioners at Bristol in 1600, Edward Gorges, Samuel Norton, Hugh Smith and Nicholas Stallinge, alternated rebukes and encouragement. On 2 March 1600 the council wrote:

> we cannot but impute unto you some faults of slackness and negligence otherwise it was impossible for so many to escape through the country gone without any recovery or apprehension.[33]

In a further letter to the same commissioners of 16 March the privy council praised them and let them know of the council's awareness of their pains in ordering, disposing and in the embarkation of the men, for otherwise there would have been even more deserters.[34]

Bristol was troubled by deserters fleeing from Ireland, perhaps to a greater extent than Chester, especially after 1599 when hostilities were concentrated on Munster. The deserter with a counterfeit pass, purportedly licensing him to return to England, became a problem in most ports since he was difficult to detect among the vagrants posing as soldiers with feigned wounds who lived mainly by begging.[35] The problem of deserters became acute in 1599 and the privy council alerted all port officers that despite strict orders to commanders and captains in Ireland to allow no soldier to return without good reason, and then only with an orderly passport, 'there are daily very many that are suffered to come over' and most of them able and serviceable men.[36] To stem the flow of deserters from Ireland, port authorities were ordered not to disembark any soldiers without a strict examination of their passports, and to permit only those sick, maimed and with correct passes signed by their commanding officers to be landed. Any passes carried by able men were to be seized and sent to the privy council so that the captains signing such passes could be censured. Able soldiers returning without any licence were to be imprisoned until 'the occasion is ripe to see that they are imprested anew' and sent back to Ireland with the next shipping, because many of these soldiers 'do give forth very slanderous speeches to discourage others' from military service in Ireland.[37] Unlike Chester's quarter sessions records, Bristol's sessions books and other judicial records, such as the mayor's court actions, give no indication that these privy council directives resulted in the capture and trial of deserters returning from Ireland.[38]

The set of orders from the privy council in February 1599 appears to have had little effect on the problem of desertion. In exasperated tones the privy council wrote in

April 1600 to all port officers that 'this notorious disorder being grown to such an intolerable measure must cost some of them [the deserters] their lives by due execution of law' and that others must be put into the galleys'.[39] In June 1600 the privy council bitterly informed the Irish council in Dublin that they 'receiveth continually letters from Bristol ... of the daily return of able and sufficient soldiers in great numbers out of Ireland'.[40] And in August 1600 the lord deputy, Mountjoy, complained to Sir George Carew in Munster that the soldiers who continually flocked to Bristol 'must be out of your province of Munster'.[41] Carew was conscious of his responsibility. Earlier, in May, he had written to the mayor of Bristol to get him to stay the ship of William Williams, which was carrying many soldiers without passes. Although Carew had forbidden 'any soldier without a pass under my hand' to embark for England, many had evidently managed to do so.[42]

In the 1590s Bristol's chamberlain's accounts show how the city's vagrancy problems were complicated by such deserters and by the influx of Irish beggars. From 1596 the accounts record quarterly payments of 6s 8d to 'the beadle of the rogues', whose task it was to search out deserters and to differentiate them from the common rogues; to aid him he had a staff of assistants who were provided with ships. The common council also regularly appointed a second officer, 'the beadle of the beggars', who had the authority to ship Irish beggars back to Ireland at a cost to the city of a shilling a head for their passage.[43] There can be little doubt that Bristol was more affected than Chester by returning deserters who exacerbated the city's social problems.[44] On the other hand Bristol had, in the first half of the sixteenth century, attracted large numbers of Irish boys seeking apprenticeships – they may or may not have been an asset to the city.[45]

Another major burden on Bristol stemmed from the exercise of the government's right to hire ships and their crews to transport troops. As in Chester, ships were hired by the crown at the best bargaining price the mayor could gain, which in the 1590s was 8s per head for each man's passage to Ireland, which did not include his victualling on board ship. In 1596 the privy council protested to William Yate, the mayor, about his contracting with shipowners to carry soldiers at the rate of 10s a head; he was asked to renegotiate a better price with them.[46] This was probably achieved, for Yate was highly commended by the council in May 1596 for the efficient arrangements he had made in transporting and victualling 800 soldiers, which contrasted with the pilfering and waste of public money and goods occurring in other ports.[47] Not all mayors had the same success as Yate. On 9 December 1600 John Hopkins wrote to the privy council for advice on what rate to allow ships' masters, 'whether after the rate demanded at xs. a man, or according to Her Majesty's rates used heretofore'. The privy council gave him a simple rule of thumb, 'to choose that course which is most for the ease of her Majesties charge'. If the ships' masters and owners continued to make immoderate demands he was to let them know so that the queen could justly take their ships for her service. Hopkins was also told he had authority to impress pilots and to imprison them if they refused her majesty's service. He was reprimanded for overestimating victuals for the voyage because very many of the soldiers got seasick for 'the most part of the time of their passage, and do not spend their victual'.[48] Hopkins was not the only mayor to be berated by the privy council: William Ellis, mayor in 1598/1599, was censured in March 1598 for the delay of the levies and accused of slackness in not providing a ship to carry food to Cork.[49] Ellis earned further censure in March 1599 for ignoring John Goyce, the government's transport commissary appointed to help the mayor with the shipping, when embarking troops. Goyce's appointment and duties were similar to those of Robert Davies in Chester in commandeering troop ships, but on this occasion Ellis apparently did not want his help.[50]

Privy council orders to the mayors of Bristol were peremptory; they were ordered to provide the services of billeting, victualling and transporting the troops sent to the city and port. The mayor and corporation were expected to pay all the expenses incurred, to be later, and often much later, reimbursed when the privy council reminded the lord treasurer to issue warrants for repayments from the exchequer, or from the treasurer-at-war in Ireland. The council's registers proliferate with such reminders and warrants, and show some of the cost of the Irish war effort to the state.[51]

When the levies of 700 soldiers were in Bristol from October to December 1596, William Yate, the mayor, received £300 from Sir Henry Wallop, treasurer-at-war in Ireland, for their transportation.[52] The mayor told the privy council that this was £50 short, as he had contracted with the ships' masters to carry the soldiers for 10s a head. Moreover, the cost of billeting and feeding the soldiers (at 8d the day per soldier) for sixty-five days amounted to £1,516 13s 4d. Most of this expense had fallen on the city for, as the mayor was quick to point out, the captains of the companies had come with only seven days' impressment money to cover their stay in Bristol.[53] When the dispatch of the levy to Ireland was abandoned a warrant went out on 30 November to issue the mayor of Bristol a sum of £531 13s 4d to be used to send the levies home to Gloucestershire and south Wales. The mayor discharged the hired ships and stored the arms and armour of the soldiers. The entire and futile enterprise proved very costly to the city.[54]

In the winter of 1599–1600, when 1,200 soldiers were delayed at Bristol, the privy council appeared more sensitive to the mayor's financial difficulties and caused an advance of £800 to be sent him in April 1600. The balance of £1,798 10s 3d was paid to the mayor at the end of May. Later that year, in September, the mayor of Bristol had to meet the cost of feeding and shipping 600 infantrymen under Captain Patrick Arthur and thirty-six horses under Captain Arthur Hyde to be sent to Sir George Carew in Munster. The privy council ordered an advance payment of £500 in September for the mayor, but the full expenditure of £1,500 17s 10d was not fully reimbursed until 2 November.[55]

The financial difficulties of the government in the 1590s are well known; the delays in repaying the mayor of Bristol, among other government creditors, is one indication. Because the government was slow to pay, the mayor of Bristol had to borrow money from wealthy citizens to defray immediate expenses. In December 1600 the mayor, John Hopkins, borrowed £1,000 from one Cuthbert Gerrard to cover costs in sending out the reinforcements to Lough Foyle under Captain Crompton.[56] The expense of billeting and transporting this levy evidently did not cost as much as £1,000 for the mayor eventually received expenses of £456 7s 9d in January 1601.[57] In January 1602, there is further evidence of the government's straitened finances. It asked the mayor, aldermen and common councillors for loans to pay for victualling and shipping a large levy. The mayor was called upon for £100, each alderman £20 and the councillors for sums between £10 and £20. The total was £670. Those failing to pay were to have as many soldiers billeted on them as the mayor thought fit. A demand for a second loan was made in May of the same year.[58]

These loans were eventually repaid but their recovery entailed a journey by the city's chamberlain to London. Visits to London were expensive. One chamberlain in 1598 took twelve days to journey to London to obtain war expenses from the government, hiring horses at 2s a day, paying wages to servants at 6d a day, and their food and lodging at 6s 8d a day. He also paid the lord treasurer's secretary 10s 'for his pains in examining my accounts', which apparently took two days, 'for his charge was very much misliked, and evil taken by my Lord Treasurer'. The chamberlain obtained a sum of £1,160 8s 8¾d, which, 'thanks be to God could not be faulted in one half-penny'.[59]

Bristol, like Chester, was a place of banking and exchange and for sending treasure to Ireland, though its mint did not operate in Elizabeth's reign.[60] As at Chester, there is evidence of the precautions taken at Bristol for the transit of treasure to Sir George Carey, treasurer-at-war in Ireland. Carey's agent, Thomas Watson, drew up a description for the privy council dated 14 May 1601 of measures taken at the exchange in Bristol:

> That wereas Bristol being a place remote, far from the Treasurer himself, or any of his people of great trust, and far from your Lordships' eyes; and having appointed one Wilson to attend the exchange there, he hath in his discretion, for the safety of Her Majesty's treasure, made choice of Mr. Pitt, Chamberlain of Bristol, a man of good report and estate … the money to remain in Mr. Pitt's house, where his man shall confine himself to live, Mr. Pitt to keep a key to the chest, and his man the other.[61]

In December 1601 Wilson wrote to Watson of the lack of money at Bristol and of the arrival of creditors with bills of £460 and £800. He claimed to have pacified them and prevented them running up to the court in London. But rumours that there would be no money to pay such bills before March 'maketh men despair and at their wits end'. He added:

> You may be sure want of money will be a mighty hindrance to the army for there are now at least ten or twelve barques to whom monies are owing that would presently carry over all sorts of victuals for the army if these bills were paid … for want of money now they are not able to put to sea.[62]

Lack of money at the Bristol exchange to pay creditors at a critical time in the war, the period of the Spanish landing in Kinsale, was serious enough, but it was compounded by many abuses. A memorandum of abuses in Bristol alleged that merchants, trading on the difference between the English pound and the new debased coinage in Ireland, the Irish pound, made fortunes. They were said to have sold goods in Ireland at three times their price, despite the safeguards in the queen's proclamation setting up exchanges.[63] The long list of abuses of the merchants suggests that they had hindered the war effort, overburdening the exchange with excessive bills, punishing the army with excessive prices, and causing a distrust and 'distaste' for the new money.[64]

There were allegations and counter-allegations of abuses of public funds in Bristol during the war years. One mayor, William Ellis, for instance, was accused of charging the government for victualling Sir Henry Danvers' troops of horse in 1599 though he only provided ships for their transport. The abuse came to light when Sir Henry Danvers made a claim for their victualling at Bristol from Sir George Carey, the treasurer-at-war. But Danvers' troop of horse did not all arrive nor embark at the same time and Ellis may have paid for the feeding of the stragglers. The accusations against him were never proved.[65]

Customs duties in the port were another obligation which could be evaded. If true, the accusations made by Thomas Watkins, imprisoned at the instigation of the customer inward, John Dowles, suggest widespread evasion. Watkins wrote to the privy council and to Sir Robert Cecil enclosing lists of frauds practised in the Bristol customs from 1594 to 1599. One list comprising eight pages accused John Dowles of collusion with merchants to avoid paying custom dues; a second list told how Dowles sold bonds or contracts of employment so that within six years the queen was defrauded of £4,000; a third list outlined the abuses of John Andrewes, customer outward of the port of Bristol, and a final list exposed John Dowles' 'sinister dealings in deceiving Her Majesty of the prisage rents'.[66]

The government also suffered losses from disloyal trading in Bristol. John Bird, an informant in July 1599, claimed that at Bristol fair 'an extraordinary concourse of buyers of all kinds of warlike provisions for the strengthening of the Irish rebels' took place and, fancifully perhaps, asserted that the buyers were mainly Jesuits in disguise. Bird wanted the privy council to issue a proclamation signifying that no arms should be sold to anyone without bonds being taken of the buyers.[67] In Professor Willan's opinion, 'the only really satisfactory branch of Bristol's trade was the trade with the rebellious Irish'.[68] Considerations of disloyalty hardly disturbed the Bristol merchants' attempts to benefit from wartime conditions. Sir George Carew claimed that the seas around Munster were 'haunted with pirates which do ordinarily trade between Bristol and Cork'.[69]

Many aspects of Chester's experience in the Irish war years can be paralleled in Bristol. The mayor had similar problems in his dealings with the privy council, with shipowners, and with the levies in the port. Bristol, however, with more seamen than Chester, was ordered to provide seafaring men for the ships of the Royal Navy at Chatham. In August 1601, in answer to a government impressment order for seamen, John Hopkins, the mayor, sent up eighty-six to Chatham but said that he had kept back 120 mariners 'to take over the soldiers and furniture to Ireland'.[70] There was no such demand on Chester in the period. In most ports delays caused by unfavourable winds led to disorderly and mutinous behaviour and low morale among the waiting troops and encouraged desertion in the port. At times of scarcity, such as 1596 and 1599, prices rose. Whereas the mayor of Chester used Liverpool as an additional port for billeting and transporting surplus numbers of troops, the mayor of Bristol had no similar facility, but the numbers of soldiers he had to cope with were less.[71] Common to most ports were delays in winter levies and frauds in the musters and in the exchange.[72]

It is not surprising that Carew in Munster forecast that Ireland would cost England a greater price than it was worth,[73] or that Sir Robert Cecil should pray in October 1601: 'God in heaven send us rid of this continual vexation'.[74]

Barnstaple

Barnstaple, a member of the head port of Exeter, was well placed for communication with Ireland. In the ship money assessments of 1619 it ranked fifth among the maritime towns of the south and west.[75] The more celebrated ports of Plymouth, Falmouth, Southampton and Portsmouth were more important in coastal defence and the prosecution of the Elizabethan continental wars. Plymouth became more important as a staging port in the redeployment of veterans from the continent to Ireland. But, after Chester and Bristol, Barnstaple stood third in the transit of primary military levies to Ireland, transporting over 3,000 troops in five years. This activity gave sporadic employment to merchants, townspeople and sailors at a time when Barnstaple's export trade in cloth and tin, and import trade in wine, iron and wood, had declined.[76] And Barnstaple's patent to trade with West Africa was due to expire in 1598.[77] Like all the Devonshire and Cornish ports, Barnstaple's privateering had also declined by the 1590s. Only two privateers' vessels, the *Unicorn* and the *Prudence*, were operating in 1598, whereas earlier there had been as many as eight such ships active from the port.[78]

During the war with Ireland Barnstaple's town records give some glimpses of the military preparations in the port, but like Bristol's these are meagre.[79] They do show the same kind of problems met with in the busier ports – delays because of contrary winds, desertions in the port and from Ireland, and troubles in bargaining with shipowners. The government's anxiety to have troops expeditiously embarked in good order and in full numbers ensured the mayor of Barnstaple a regular correspondence with the privy council that few mayors of such remote towns experienced. The numbers ordered to the port are set out in Table 14.

The government used the port of Barnstaple on ten occasions over six years for sending out almost 3,000 infantrymen and less than 100 horse. As in the other ports, the October levies of 1596 were sent home and called back the following April.[80] As one would expect, almost every levy ordered to Barnstaple came in from the hinterland shires of Devon, Cornwall and Somerset, though in October 1601 Hampshire sent 100 men to Barnstaple. Captain Edward North, who was to receive the Hampshire men at Barnstaple for Ireland, complained that their conductor allowed seven of them to escape.[81]

The February/March 1600 levy of 200, though bound for Carrickfergus, was ultimately intended for Lough Foyle with the rest of Sir Henry Docwra's fleet from Chester. The mayor, Roger Beaple, reported to the privy council that all went well in embarking the levy for Carrickfergus because of the efficiency of their conductor, Captain Abry York, who accompanied them on the voyage. The ships were made ready with victuals, the men and their warlike equipment reviewed and found satisfactory, 'so that God continuing the wind fair, they will sail on Saturday till when they await a morning tide'.[82] Their departure time, however, did not coincide with those waiting at Chester, with the result that this levy of 200 from Barnstaple arrived in Ireland before Docwra's levies had left Chester.[83] And in December 1600 and in April 1601 Barnstaple transported 150 and 170 reinforcements respectively, for Docwra's garrisons then established in Lough Foyle.[84]

But Barnstaple advanced the government's service at Lough Foyle in other ways than in the transportation of levies and subsequent reinforcements. Barnstaple mariners were retained by Sir Henry Docwra, the commander at Lough Foyle, for patrol services in two crompsters according to his letter to the privy council in May 1600.[85] Privy council warrants also make it clear that it was from Barnstaple that the London victualler, William Webb, operated in transporting food to Docwra's garrisons in his own ship the *God Saviour*.[86] When Docwra needed more small ships to patrol the Foyle he suggested that Barnstaple would supply them. The privy council duly sent an order to the mayor, John Delbridge, for three small pinnaces of about twelve tons each, suitable for both rowing and sailing, to be bought from their owners 'at such reasonable prices and rates as the same may be worth'. The type and equipment needed for each boat was described in great detail, which suggests that the privy council was simply passing on Sir Henry Docwra's instructions to the mayor of Barnstaple.[87] The boats were to have 'a mayne mast, fore-mast, two small cables of 6 inches and a hallser of 4 inches, two good anchors of 200 lb. weight ... 12 oares or 24 foote and sailes with other tacklings'.[88]

Barnstaple also supplied ships for transporting levies from other ports; seventeen, for example, were ordered to be fully victualled and sent to relieve the pressure on shipping at Chester, but in the event only nine were actually sent.[89] And an unspecified number of Barnstaple ships helped in the movement of Sir Henry Danvers' troops of horse from Bristol to Essex's army in March 1599.[90]

From April 1601 until the end of the war Barnstaple was more concerned with sending forces to Munster to aid the military build-up to repulse the Spanish, and it is in its supplying of the war in the south that the importance of the port really lies. On 17 September 1601 John Delbridge, the mayor, wrote to Sir Robert Cecil when he heard the news of the Spanish fleet heading for Ireland: 'It is the first report that came of it to this place and it being of such importance I thought it my duty to inform'.[91]

Barnstaple's services in shipping troops and horses to Munster occupied the months of August to November 1601 when for the first time during the war levies of over a 1,000 were ordered to the port.[92] It was a period of strain and tension for the new mayor, George Stanberry, as is evident from his correspondence with the privy council and with Sir Robert Cecil, who had the main direction of the government's war effort. At first things went well. The Earl of Bath was sent to Barnstaple to aid Stanberry in the muster and view of the 975 foot and 66 horse ordered there in October 1601. He reported that most of the men had arrived by 20 and 21 October in reasonable order, many of them 'tall men well armed and willing to serve', and that their only fear was that they would arrive in Ireland too late to fight the Spanish. The captains who were to take charge of them to Ireland had not by then arrived in Barnstaple.[93] Mayor Stanberry wrote twice to Sir Robert Cecil, on 28 and on 31 October, with the same complaint about the captains' absence from the port.[94] Two weeks later Captain Patrick

Table 14   Military levies to Barnstaple

Date	Number of foot (f.) and horse (h.)	Mayor responsible	Intended for:	Note
October 1596	400 f.		Sir W. Russell in Dublin, but stayed	1
April 1597	400 f.	N. Downs	Sir W. Russell in Dublin	2
December 1598	16 h.	N. Downs	Sir A. Chichester at Carrickfergus	3
February 1600	200 f.	R. Beaple	Sir A. Chichester at Carrickfergus	4
December 1600	150 f.	G. Stanberry	Sir H. Docwra at Lough Foyle	5
April 1601	170 f.	J. Delbridge	Sir H. Docwra at Lough Foyle	6
September 1601	275 f.	J. Delbridge	The Earl of Thomond at Waterford and Kinsale	7
October/ November 1601	975 f. 66 h.		The Earl of Thomond at Waterford and Kinsale	8
January/February 1602	650 f.	G. Stanberry	Sir G. Carew at Cork	9
July 1602	165 f.	G. Stanberry	Sir G. Carew at Cork	10
Totals	2,985 f. 82 h.			

1. *APC*, xxvi, 243, 346, 406, 407.
2. *APC*, xxvii, 23–26; *APC*, xxviii, 599.
3. *APC*, xxix, 589.
4. *APC*, xxx, 41, 42, 102, 262, 388.
5. *APC*, xxx, 790; *APC*, xxxi, 23.
6. *APC*, xxxi, 296, 314, 318, 325, 326, 363; *CSPI* (1600–1601), 301, 365, 377, 380.
7. *APC*, xxxii, 71, which gives a levy of twenty-seven soldiers, but all subsequent references to the levy indicate 275; *ibid.*, 126, 127, 83.
8. *APC*, xxxii, 312, 313; HMC, *Salisbury*, xi, 454, 461, 490, 491.
9. HMC, *Salisbury*, xii, 13, 50, 51, 154.
10. HMC, *Salisbury*, xii, 277, 320.

Arthur began operations. By 6 November they were ready to sail. Of the sixty-six horse he chose fifty-three as 'able and sufficient', and forty of those he described to Sir Robert Cecil 'as good both men and horses as ever went into Ireland', but for the most part 'the men are ill-armed with swords, armour and pistols'. He remarked to Cecil that the 'foot are still here' when those sent to Bristol were 'no doubt in Ireland long since'.[95] It was on 8 November that Sir Anthony Cooke, the long-awaited captain, reported the embarkation of the infantry, 300 of them in the forenoon and the remaining 675 in the afternoon.[96] By 10 November, the mayor, George Stanberry, confirmed that 975 foot and 53 horse were under sail for Munster.[97] All three reports mention the unfavourable weather conditions which partly delayed the embarkations. The mayor was at great pains to exonerate himself from any blame for the long delays of the levies in his port, asking Cecil 'to clear our credits with the lords that no further imputation be made than we justly deserve'.[98]

An even longer delay of troops in Barnstaple occurred in January 1602, when 350 Devon men and 300 Somerset men were ordered to the port.[99] They were so poorly equipped that the commissioners for musters and the mayor selected only 400 of them, and these did not depart until the end of February.[100] At this time the mayor complained to Cecil of desertions: 'some of the men daily run away in spite of a continual watch by day and night'. A few were caught with hue and cry, and the mayor assured Cecil that these would be kept safely in prison.[101] Not until May 1602 did 200 more of the original 650 leave Barnstaple for Munster. The last levy of the reign was in July 1602. On 1 August 1602 the mayor had shipping ready for the 165 soldiers to be sent to Cork.[102] They were not unduly delayed, setting sail on 24 August, but were forced back to Ilfracombe by contrary winds where they were once more billeted, a mere seven miles from Barnstaple.[103] Sir George Carew reported their arrival in Waterford, though they had been intended for Cork, on 7 September 1602, over a month from their setting sail from Barnstaple.[104]

Communication between Barnstaple and London was a lengthy and difficult business. At one stage the mayor, Stanberry, suspected that privy council directions to him had been intercepted.[105] To improve communications between north Devon and London, the mayor and common council in Barnstaple established a 'foote poste' from Barnstaple to make connection with a foot post that left Exeter for London every Tuesday; in this way, it was claimed, the time of sending and receiving letters from and to London was cut from twenty days to eleven.[106] In common with Chester and Bristol, Barnstaple was used to forward letters from Cecil and the government to the lord deputy and Irish council. Cecil erroneously believed in 1601 that there had been a regular post bark or boat plying between Barnstaple and Dublin. Stanberry explained to Cecil:

> for post bark, here is none, as you suppose, but if it be your pleasure I will provide one to lie in readiness to answer all occasions hereafter … it will be very expedient during the time of this service.[107]

Sir George Carew considered Barnstaple one of the better ports for rapid communication with Munster, and in view of this and of the Spanish crisis at Kinsale it seems extraordinary that a regular post boat had not been instituted.[108]

Barnstaple collectors' and receivers' accounts in the 1590s give some indication of the presence of the levies in the port, and of the impact of war preparations on the town's treasurer. A recurrent item of expenditure from the town's treasury throughout the 1590s is payments to the constables for pressing men for the Irish levies and for pressing mariners for the ships to transport them; sums of £3 14s 4d, 9s, 6s 8d, 12s and 1s 6d are recorded for these services. On one occasion the town made a gift of 10s to certain soldiers pressed out of the town; on another a gift of 1s to a 'poor soldier that had his hand cut off'. In 1600 the town paid 3s 4d for sending several letters to Ireland, and in 1601 a gibbet was erected near the High Cross to deter would-be rioters and deserters, at a cost of 6d to the town's treasury. In the same year an unwanted Irishman was sent from Barnstaple to Ilfracombe for transportation back to Ireland at a cost of 2s 3d. To honour the arrival of Sir Robert Bassnett. the government's commissioner for musters, in 1599, Barnstaple put on a civic banquet costing 10s, and in the same year, Sir Arthur Chichester, the governor of Carrickfergus and future lord deputy of

Ireland, and a Devonshire man, was also honoured by an apparently grander banquet costing the town £1.[109]

These are petty sums. A more impressive measure of Barnstaple's services to the crown is the government's reimbursements to the mayors for the billeting, feeding and transportation of levies, though the sums involved reflect the comparatively small scale of these services. In 1598 payments of £390 and £100 were made; in February 1599, £300; in December 1600, £353 3s 7d and £150; in 1601, £81, £30 and £340. And in 1602 the mayor of Barnstaple's account with the government for Irish war services was closed with the larger payments, no doubt long in arrears as at Chester and Bristol, of £1,127 and £1,611 7s 6d.[110]

In other respects, too, Barnstaple does not compare with the more important ports in the transit of troops to Ireland. There are fewer mentions of disorders caused by troops in the town; there are few mentions of desertions in the port and apparently none from Ireland. But in common with all the ports dealing with Irish levies, Barnstaple received directives from the privy council to take precautions against the return to England of 'able and serviceable' soldiers out of Ireland.[111] Though Barnstaple's traditional trade was with Ireland there is no mention in the war years of disloyal trading, as had been the case at Chester and Bristol. Nevertheless, as an ancillary port for shipping troops to the south of Ireland, and in supplying ships to other ports, Barnstaple was important to the late Elizabethan government.

Other western ports and the Irish war

The English Channel ports from Falmouth to Portsmouth, vulnerable to threats and attempts at invasion from Spain in the post-Armada period, bore the main burden of the realm's defence measures.[112] When additional demands were made on them by the government for the Irish war, the port authorities were quick to point to their great charges for defence. Plymouth, Weymouth, Falmouth and Milford Haven made much of their undisputed vulnerability and the 'nakedness' they would experience if their ships and men were unduly called upon for 'the service of Ireland'. Nevertheless, as the Irish war effort stepped up from 1598 these ports became involved, though to a lesser extent than Chester, Bristol or Barnstaple.[113]

From Table 15, it may be seen that of this group of ports Plymouth and Southampton sent out the greatest numbers, and that they were concerned also with the redeployment exercises when veterans from Brittany and the Low Countries were brought back from the continent for service in Ireland. Milford Haven, Padstow, Fowey and Weymouth were involved in shipping small 'primary' levies: Milford 300 in 1598, 400 in 1599; Weymouth, 400 in 1598; Fowey, 300 in 1598; Padstow, 100 in 1602. Milford Haven stands out as more important in the shipping of horse levies than any other port in Table 15; in January/February 1599 it transported 100 horse and 50 carriage horses to Ireland (the latter, not being fighting forces, are not included). Milford Haven and Padstow were also concerned with what may be called 'secondary embarkations', along with Haverfordwest and Ilfracombe, as troop ships were blown back on their nearby coastal regions. Where secondary embarkations took place the numbers are not included since the initial embarkations took place from Chester, Bristol and Barnstaple. In this respect these four minor ports played an important additional role in the salvaging of men and equipment for crown services in Ireland.

‾Plymouth was the most important port of this group; all the Cornish ports and havens were administratively under Plymouth, and it was from Plymouth that the largest numbers of troops sailed to Ireland. The first levy, in March 1595, was a redeployment exercise when Sir Henry Norris conducted a force of 1,553 experienced soldiers out of Brittany under orders to have them sent to his brother, Sir John Norris, second in command under the lord deputy, Sir William Russell, in Ireland.[114] James Bagg, mayor of Plymouth, did not appear to have been unduly burdened with the levy

Table 15   Military levies to other ports

Date	Number of foot (f.) and horse (h.)	Port	Intended for:	Note
March 1595	1,553 f.	Plymouth	Redeployed troops from Brittany for Sir J. Norris in Waterford	1
July 1598	300 f.	Milford	Dublin: Earl of Ormond	2
August 1598	1,350 f. 50 h.	Plymouth	Redeployed from the Low Countries, first for Lough Foyle, but destination changed to Carlingford for Sir S. Bagenal and Colonel C. Egerton	3
October/ November 1598	500 f.	Southampton	Youghal	
	400 f.	Weymouth	Cork	
	400 f.	Plymouth	Cork	
	300 f.	Fowey	Kinsale	4
January/ February 1599	400 f. 100 h.	Milford	Waterford	5
October 1601	500 f.	Plymouth	Kinsale	6
December/January	510 f.	Southampton	Cork	7
1602	100 f.	Padstow	Cork	

Totals to each port:
Plymouth   3,803 f., 50 h.
Southampton   1,010 f.
Milford   700 f., 100 h.
Weymouth   400 f.
Fowey   300 f.
Padstow   100 f.
Total of all ports   6,313 f.
                     150 h.

1. PRO SP12/178/90, i, ii.
2. *APC*, xxviii, 524–530.
3. *Cal. Carew MSS*, iii, 281–283.
4. *APC*, xxix, 237–244, 255, 256.
5. *APC*, xxix, 543; *CSPD* (1598–1601), 159, 50 carriage horse from Milford.
6. HMC, *Salisbury*, xi, 425.
7. *APC*, xxxii, 476, 481 for Southampton, and *ibid.*, 444 for Padstow.

since Sir Henry Norris simply disembarked his sick men, sixty-three of them, and revictualled his ships in Plymouth for the remainder of the voyage to Ireland.[115] Norris claimed in writing to Lord Burghley from Plymouth on 13 March 1595 that 'if the wind had not been contrary they would have gone straight to Waterford'.[116]

The second large levy to Plymouth took place in August 1598. On 16 August, before the news of the defeat at the Yellow Ford had reached England, the government had already ordered a force of 2,000 recruits from the shires. Sir Samuel Bagenal was to lead 600 from Chester and Colonel Charles Egerton to lead 1,350 and 50 horse from Plymouth.[117] The government's intention was that they should be used to plant a garrison in the Lough Foyle area, and Egerton's force was to be made up of Low Countries veterans as well as new recruits. There were in fact many veterans, from the Earl of Essex's Cadiz adventure of June 1596 and from his islands voyage of the summer of 1596, already in Plymouth. Plymouth had been responsible for the embarkation of both Essex's ventures and saw their return; for instance, the spoils of Cadiz first came into the port of Plymouth.[118] Soldiers and sailors back from both ventures had orders to be maintained in Plymouth, Falmouth, Portsmouth and other channel ports against possible Spanish reprisals.[119]

The mayor of Plymouth, John Trelawney, and the commissioners for the musters began to exhibit the strains of organising Egerton's force of 1,350 foot and 50 horse during August 1598. Mayor Trelawney complained to the privy council of his problems in providing enough ships and was told that as vice-admiral of the Devon coasts he had wide powers to commandeer ships from Dartmouth and elsewhere. But he ran into difficulties in driving bargains with the shipowners, who demanded a rate of 2*s* the ton, besides wages and additional charges for victualling their ships' crews. Trelawney sent their demands to the privy council, which expressed annoyance at being sent 'so uncertain a demand ... we cannot guess what this charge may amount to'. They ordered the mayor to make no such agreement but to do what other mayors had done, that is to say, make an agreement either by the poll or by the tonnage, to include all charges for transporting the soldiers.[120] In the event the mayor agreed with the shipowners on a tonnage rate rather than the usual rate by poll which obtained in Chester and Bristol.[121]

The town of Plymouth was obviously feeling the financial strain of the levy. William Stallenge, Cecil's agent and servant in Plymouth, wrote to Cecil on 30 August 1598 that the mayor and inhabitants wanted more money, 'not being able longer to furnish the charge of the companies of soldiers to be shipped here'. He said the mayor had exhausted all possible means 'to procure money of the inhabitants', even to the extent of taking up money at interest, but that he could not obtain more than he had already disbursed.[122] Though Stallenge thought the mayor had overestimated the amount of shipping needed by taking up 1,000 tons, two of the commissioners for musters, Sir Ferdinando Gorges and Sir George Carey, wanted 300 or 400 more with which to transport the 1,350 men and 50 horse. Meanwhile accommodating the men was posing a problem. Of the thirteen companies, five were lodged in the town and the other eight in the adjoining parishes, but the military authorities wanted them all billeted in Plymouth, an impossible demand 'unless the inhabitants shall forsake their houses'.[123]

A serious state of tension grew up between the civic and military authorities in Plymouth. It appears, for instance, that mayor Trelawney did not inform Colonel Egerton, who was to conduct the levy, that Cecil had changed the intended destination from Lough Foyle to Carlingford. The new direction sent to the mayor in Plymouth on 22 August was clearly the result of the government's information on the state of Ireland after the defeat of the Yellow Ford.[124] Subsequently, on 13 September 1598, Cecil wrote to the commissioners at Plymouth demanding a full explanation of what had happened to his letter of 22 August giving the new direction for the levy: 'write to me, as you will stand to it, where the fault is, and let every ass bear his own burden'.[125] From Ireland on 9 October Colonel Egerton wrote to the privy council that he never received the letter but that he had since received a *copy*.[126]

The deteriorating relations between the mayor and the military authorities transmitted itself to the troops, leading to low morale and desertions, especially among the Somerset, Wiltshire and Hereford companies. The troops were insubordinate. A captain of one band, John Hales, angered by the mayor's refusal to supply his men with firewood, ordered his men to make firewood out of the town's stocks. Another captain, one Gibson, found the situation intolerable and went to the privy council with a catalogue of complaints about how the soldiers waiting in Plymouth were treated. Sir Ferdinando Gorges, Colonel Egerton and Captain Harris, the chief commissioners in the port, repeatedly wrote to the privy council about their difficulties, the delays, the defects in arms and armour, the lack of gunpowder and their shortage of money.[127]

The privy council replied, accusing both military and mayoral authorities of slackness in the queen's service; they were to take arms from the town's stores to make up defects and not put a new charge on the government by buying more; the council wanted to know what had become of the arms 'left in your custody the last year upon the return of the Earl of Essex'; as for powder, they had ten lasts, which was plenty, and, as for shipping, 1,000 tons 'in reason seems enough'; finally, as regards money, £600 was being sent from London with the mayor's brother, Robert Trelawney. Then, pointing to the real cause of all the trouble in Plymouth, the privy council berated the military authorities on the 'ill correspondence that is betwixt you and the town', otherwise they would surely have known of a matter of such importance as the change of destination for the levy, from Lough Foyle to Carlingford.[128]

The mayor of Plymouth's account for the services performed for this levy was settled with the government by two payments: one in November 1598, of £974 *2s 6d*, and another on 28 January 1599, of £172 *2s 8d*.[129] Egerton's soldiers had been allowed twenty days' victualling, ten of meat and ten of cheese and butter, with an allowance of *8d* a day to the infantrymen and *18d* a day to the cavalrymen. Their victualling ships were well supplied out of the West Country; they had stored on board cheese, meal, butter, peas, oatmeal, salt, sherry, brandy and enough beer to provide each soldier a quart a day for forty days. Three clerks accompanied the fleet to supervise victuals, ordnance and treasures.[130] One of the largest items of expenditure was for arms bought for the soldiers, amounting to £364 *13s 9d*, which suggests that either the privy council's directive to use the stores in the town had been ignored, or perhaps there were no arms in the stores left from the Earl of Essex's islands voyage of 1597.[131]

Egerton's fleet left Plymouth on 9 September, having been in port over three weeks. North-easterly gales drove them south to Youghal and Cork but, according to Egerton's report to the privy council, they reassembled at Waterford on 14 September, sailed for Dublin eleven days later and by 4 October put in at Drogheda. The sailors on one of his ships, the *Reindeer*, took over the ship after the soldiers had landed and pillaged its contents, including 'one hundred and four score and nine pounds of my money', flooded the ship and made off in a pinnace belonging to Sir Ferdinando Gorges, the *Little John* of Plymouth.[132]

Plymouth was less involved in the October/November levies 1598, when only 400 foot out of the 2,000 ordered to be raised by the government from the West Country and Midlands shires were ordered to the port. The government spread the burden over several West Country ports: 400 to Plymouth, 500 to Southampton, 300 to Fowey or to Padstow, 400 to Weymouth and 400 to Bristol.[133] The nearest port to the shire of origin of the recruits was used; hence, for example, Captains Digges, Caesar and Kemish were sent to Southampton to conduct Hampshire men; Captains Southwell, Cotterell and Dutton, Cornish men to Fowey. All captains and their soldiers were to be at the ports by 15 November.[134]

The mayor of Southampton, John Jeffreys, and the mayor of Weymouth and Melcombe Regis, John Moket, expressed the ability and willingness of their ports to billet and ship their contingents.[135] Plymouth's mayor, Martin Whyte, who had overall authority over the Devonshire ports, wrote to Cecil claiming he could provide food and ships for 500 or 600 soldiers, but in the event Plymouth was designated 400.[136] Fowey was considered more suitable than Padstow to embark the Cornish men though its mayor, Mr Mohun, tried to have the burden passed on to Padstow because his small and poor port had been greatly charged towards the expenses of fortifying Falmouth. Christopher Harris, deputy lieutenant of Cornwall, put Fowey's case to Sir Robert Cecil together with the objections of the shire to the demands of the Irish service. He complained that 300 recruits then to be raised from 'our poor country will be more burdensome than any charge that I have known heretofore, levies from Cornwall have seldom been more than a third part unto Devonshire, and now almost equal'.[137]

Southampton was ordered to embark the greatest number in October/November 1598. It was not in the flush of economic prosperity; Lord Burghley had noted that it was among the ports 'manifestly decayed'.[138] When asked to contribute ships to the navy in 1595 the port had pleaded its inability and appealed to Sir George Carey, Captain of the Isle of Wight, for help in meeting the quota of ships and mariners demanded.[139] Its rôle during the war years, like several south coast ports, was primarily defensive, a fact reflected in the records. The state papers are full of defence measures taken in Southampton, Portsmouth and the other ports vulnerable to attack from Spain; but the local records have left no trace of the transit of troops to Ireland in November 1598 or for the December/January contingent of 1602, and regrettably the mayor's records for the years 1590 to 1603 are non-existent.[140] A report to Sir Robert Cecil from one of the captains sent to Southampton, Charles Caesar, on 25 November contains rare mention of the transit of troops. He said that most of the soldiers had arrived by the appointed date (15 November) but that they were delayed a fortnight 'expecting a fair wind'. If shipping and victuals had been promptly provided they

182

could have sailed on 23 November, but all was not ready until two days later. The men had embarked and he hoped within two or three days 'to be landed in Ireland, where God bless our actions to His glory, our prince's honour, and our country's benefit' – unusual sentiments from an ordinary captain in the Irish wars.[141] This levy from Southampton was bound for Youghal in Munster to reinforce Sir Thomas Norris there.

The overall levy of 2,000 largely sent from these West Country ports in November 1598 was a near panic measure on the government's part when almost the entire province of Munster was in rebellion. Their individual times of arrival from the various ports in Ireland are not known, but Sir Thomas Norris, in charge in Munster, sent a message by the hand of Edmund Spenser, the celebrated poet, on his return to England from the ruin of his fortunes at Kilcolman, near Cork, after the destruction of the Munster plantation earlier that year. Norris said that 1,600 of the levy had put in at Cork and Youghal and 400 into Waterford. Reports of arrivals of troops in Ireland normally give different figures from those reported on embarkation, and Norris's therefore is unusual in that the numbers tally, but it is hard to believe that this levy did not suffer any desertions.[142]

None of the English Channel ports was involved in the embarkation of Essex's army of 1599, nor with the transportation of recruits raised to replace the many Low Countries soldiers sent to aid Essex in Ireland, though Thomas Heton, merchant of Southampton and customer of the port, was asked to supply 'three hundred tonnes of Beere, two hundred quarters of Mawlte and a thousand quarter of Oates' as part of the provisions for Essex's army.[143] Heton was the owner and builder of the ships the *Bevis* and the *George* used in the Irish service.[144] Milford Haven, however, transported 400 foot and 100 horse from south Wales as part of Essex's grand army. On the occasion of the Spanish landing at Kinsale Plymouth was used to send out 500 foot. And in the last levies sent through this group of ports, Southampton sent out 510 foot and Padstow 100 to Cork in December/January 1602.[145] At first the privy council asked the authorities at Southampton to have enough shipping prepared to transport 1,000 soldiers by 20 January 1602.[146] The mayor objected to this, pleading the poverty of the port, but said that he could arrange to feed, billet and ship half that number, which was agreed.[147]

The impact of the Irish war on this group of ports cannot be measured in terms of the numbers of troops embarked. They were important as centres for the collection and transmission of intelligence of enemy movements to the government; travellers to and from such ports as Plymouth, Falmouth and Southampton were frequently examined before the mayors; pinnaces were maintained for spying on Spanish and Irish ship movements, and post barks plyed to and from Padstow to Ireland.[148] For the benefit of the Irish service, fast-running posts were established to carry packets and letters to and fro between Plymouth and Falmouth, and by 1601 a like service was established between Plymouth and Padstow.[149] The Cecil papers of the time are full of letters communicating news from Ireland.[150]

The post boats were observed by the Spanish enemy. One Hortensio Spinola, on a mission to examine all the defences of the Channel ports, was induced to give the privy council an exact and detailed description of the position, ships, artillery and fortifications maintained at Plymouth, Dartmouth, Southampton, Portsmouth and Poole.[151] And the privy council registers for the late 1590s indicate the impact of the war in many other ways. At the time of Kinsale all the West Country ports were ordered to impress mariners and 500 were assembled at Plymouth and sent to Chatham for the manning of the queen's ships.[152] After the victory at Kinsale, Plymouth took in Spanish prisoners.[153] Weymouth, Portsmouth and Plymouth transported ordnance and munitions to Ireland.[154] At Southampton 'divers parcells of armour' were seized on board the *Elizabeth* of Southampton returning from Galway; its master, William Thompson, was arrested.[155] As Ireland became waste the army depended more on provisions from England; the West Country shires of Cornwall and Devon shipped surplus grain, 2,200 quarters of wheat, for instance, in 1600.[156] And in all these activities, the attentions of the piratical 'Dunkirkers' caused disruption and losses to the ships laden with supplies for the army in Ireland.[157] In this context it is worth recalling that piracy was an international menace. Merchants trading with Ireland went in terror of their lives and goods because it is generally agreed that the late Elizabethan government was unable to control the pirates around the home coastal waters. And yet as curbs began to tell against the Channel pirates, those less guarded shores of Wales and Ireland had a flourishing illegal trade, often in collusion or at least countenanced by some vice admirals on shore.[158]

Notes

1   D. B. Quinn and K. W. Nicholls, 'Ireland in 1534', in *A new history of Ireland, vol. iii, Early modern Ireland, 1534–1691*, eds T. W. Moody, F. X. Martin and F. J. Byrne (Oxford, 1976), 7, 8, 10, 36–37.
2   J. Vanes, ed., *Documents illustrating the overseas trade of Bristol in the sixteenth century* (Bristol Record Society, xxxi, Bristol, 1979), 14.
3   J. Latimer, ed., *Annals of Bristol in the sixteenth century* (Bristol, 1900), 1.
4   *CSPD* (1598–1601), 2.
5   PRO SP12/250/33.
6   J. Vanes, *The port of Bristol in the sixteenth century* (Bristol, 1977), 13.
7   For the ruling of the High Court of Admiralty, see R. G. Marsden, ed., *Select pleas in the Court of Admiralty* (Selden Society, ii, London, 1897), 187. And for a contemporary description of the port in 1568, see William Smith's in BL, Sloane MS, 2596, f. 77, and for a map see J. Vanes, *The port of Bristol in the sixteenth century* (Bristol, 1977), facing p. 8.
8   PRO SP63/18/41, instructions to Randolph, 8 July 1566.
9   HMC, *Appendix to the sixth report*, 74, 103.
10 Bristol Archives Office (hereafter BAO), mayor's miscellanea, MSS, 8029, f. 5.
11 I am grateful to Miss Close of the BAO for searching the mayor's court actions file.
12 BAO, sessions minute book, 1595–1705, erroneously 1605 on the spine, is unfortunately the only one of its kind in the BAO, and the indictments, recognisances, presentments, jury lists and judgements are all of the eighteenth century.
13 Before 1640 these audit books do not include income or expenditure from rates or loan transactions or accounts of money held by the city; many pages are blank for the 1590s.
14 D. Livock, ed., *City chamberlain's accounts in the sixteenth and seventeenth centuries* (Bristol Record Society, xxiv, Bristol, 1966), 100, 105, 106, 111, 123, 129.

15 Unlike the relationship between Chester and Liverpool, Bristol experienced no rivalry from Gloucester, which played the role of a river port supplying Bristol; see T. S. Willan, *Studies in Elizabethan foreign trade* (Manchester, 1959), 84.
16 See Tables 13 and 14.
17 *APC*, xxxi, 421; *APC*, xxxii, 87, 152.
18 *APC*, xxvi, 243–244.
19 *APC*, xxix, 485.
20 *APC*, xxx, 111.
21 *Ibid.*, 65.
22 Pembrokeshire did not send any levies to Ireland from 1598 to June 1600. See Table 3 'Infantry levies from Wales to Ireland, 1594–1602'.
23 *APC*, xxx, 111.
24 HMC, *Salisbury*, xii, 170.
25 J. Latimer, ed., *Annals of Bristol in the sixteenth century* (Bristol, 1900), vol. i, 15.
26 *Ibid.*
27 HMC, *Salisbury*, xii, 169.
28 *Ibid.*, 167.
29 *Ibid.*, 168.
30 *Ibid.*, 168.
31 *APC*, xxvi, 243, 244; *APC*, xxviii, 529; *APC*, xxx, 326, 396, 578, 671; *APC*, xxxi, 13, 14; *APC*, xxxii, 222.
32 *APC*, xxxi, 182–184.
33 *APC*, xxx, 139–140, the privy council to the commissioners, 2 March 1600.
34 *Ibid.*, 174, the same to the same, 16 March 1600.
35 F. Aydelotte, *Elizabethan rogues and vagabonds* (Oxford, 1913).
36 *APC*, xxx, 55–57, the privy council to port officers, 5 February 1599.
37 *Ibid.*, 56.
38 BAO, sessions minute books (1595–1705); mayor's court actions (1567–1761) and the writ books (1574–1836) give no evidence of cases in the 1590s. No quarter sessions records or coroners' court records survive until the eighteenth century.
39 *APC*, xxx, 245–246, the privy council to port officers, 13 April 1600.
40 *Ibid.*, 459, the privy council to the Irish council, 30 June 1600.
41 *Cal. Carew MSS*, iii, 424, Mountjoy to Carew, 12 August 1600.
42 *CSPI* (1600), 162, Carew to Cecil, 7 May 1600.
43 BAO, mayor's audits, ff. 31, 52, 66, 74, 77, examples of the quarterly payments in 1599 and 1600.
44 Bristol merchants brought in hundreds of Irish peasants as servants to England through the port in the early seventeenth century; J. J. Silke, 'The Irish abroad, 1534–1691', in *A New history of Ireland*, eds T. W. Moody, F. X. Martin and F. J. Byrne (Oxford, 1976), 600.
45 D. Hollis, ed., *Calendar of the Bristol apprentice book, 1532–1542* (Bristol, 1949), *passim.*
46 *APC*, xxvi, 339.
47 J. Latimer, ed., *Annals of Bristol in the sixteenth century* (Bristol, 1900), vol. i, 116.
48 *APC*, xxxi, 16–18, privy council to Hopkins, mayor, 15 December 1600.
49 *APC*, xxix, 353.
50 *APC*, xxx, 166. For the renewal of John Goyce's commission see *CSPD* (1598–1601), 159.
51 BAO, great audit book (1532–1785) is mainly concerned with record of payments of loans to and by the corporation and with charities, not with the mayor's military expenses.
52 *APC*, xxvi, 313, 338.
53 *Ibid.*, 339.
54 J. Redington, ed., *Calendar of treasury papers* (1557–1696) (London, 1868), vol. i.
55 *APC*, xxx, 113, 254.

56 *APC*, xxxi, 40.

57 *Ibid.*, 116, warrant to pay the mayor of Bristol, 28 January 1601.

58 J. Latimer, ed., *Annals of Bristol in the sixteenth century* (Bristol, 1900), 16.

59 *Ibid.*, citing the mayor's great audit book for 1598.

60 C. E. Challis, *The Tudor coinage* (Manchester, 1978), 8.

61 *CSPI* (November 1600–July 1601), 330, Watson's memorial to the privy council.

62 *CSPI* (1601–1603), 222, Wilson to Watson, 15 December 1601.

63 *CSPI* (1601–1603), 508–511, 'Memorandum on the abuses of the English merchants committed in her majesty's exchange', 4 November 1602.

64 *Ibid.*, 510.

65 HMC, *Salisbury*, ix, 96, 108, 111.

66 PRO SP12/274/57, i, ii, iii, February 1600. 'Prisage' was a customs duty or tax to the crown on imports and exports, originally applied only to the import of wine.

67 PRO SP63/205/125, July 1599.

68 T. S. Willan, *Studies in Elizabethan foreign trade* (Manchester, 1959), 86.

69 *Cal. Carew MSS*, ix, 125, Carew to the privy council, 14 August 1601.

70 PRO SP63/209/29, Hopkins to Cecil, 13 August 1601.

71 The overall numbers in Chester of horse and foot was 20,151, while those in Bristol came to 10,877.

72 Sir Anthony Cooke's experience in conducting a horse levy to Ireland February/March 1599 was especially troublesome and unparalleled at Chester – see HMC, *Salisbury*, ix, 111–112.

73 *Cal. Carew MSS*, iv, 169, Carew to Cecil, dated '1601'.

74 *Ibid.*, 156, Cecil to Carew, 19 October 1601.

75 S. R. Gardiner, *History of England* (London, 1883), vol. iii, 288, note.

76 T. S. Willan, *Studies in Elizabethan and foreign trade* (Manchester, 1959) 80, 82, 110.

77 *CSPD* (1598–1601), 16, a petition to continue that trade.

78 K. R. Andrews, *Elizabethan privateering* (Cambridge, 1966), 31, 32, 33.

79 J. R. Chanter and T. Wainwright (eds), *Barnstaple records* (Barnstaple, 1900); J. B. Gribble *Memorials of Barnstaple* (Barnstaple, 1830).

80 See Table 14, wherein the totals do not include the abortive levy of October 1596.

81 HMC, *Salisbury*, xi, 431, Captain North to Cecil, 15 October 1601.

82 HMC, *Salisbury*, x, 50, the mayor of Barnstaple to the privy council, 4 March 1600.

83 See the case study of Docwra's expedition from Chester in Chapter 6.

84 See Table 4.

85 *CSPI* (1600), 174, Docwra to the privy council, 11 May 1600.

86 *APC*, xxxi, 325, 326, 380, warrants to pay Webb, £200 and £81 6s 8d.

87 The detail and verbosity of Docwra's letters to the privy council and to Cecil are much in evidence in the *CSPI* (1600, 1601, 1601–1603).

88 *APC*, xxxi, 422–423.

89 *APC*, xxix, 365, 613–616.

90 HMC, *Salisbury*, ix, 96, William Ellis, mayor of Bristol, to the privy council, 9 March 1599, pointing out that the Barnstaple ships had not then arrived in Bristol.

91 PRO SP12/285/23, Delbridge to Cecil, 17 September 1601.

92 See Table 14.

93 HMC, *Salisbury*, xi, 443, Earl of Bath to Cecil, 23 October 1601.

94 HMC, *Salisbury*, xi, 454, 461, Stanberry to Cecil, 28 and 31 October 1601.

95 HMC, *Salisbury*, xi, 480–481, Captain Patrick Arthur to Cecil, 6 November.

96 *Ibid.*, 4, 7, Cooke to Cecil, 8 November 1601.

97 *Ibid.*, 490, Stanberry to Cecil, 10 November 1601.

98 *Ibid.*, 461, the same to the same, 31 October 1601. At the same time, the busiest one of his mayoralty, Stanberry was engaged in a feud with the Bishop of Exeter – *APC*, xxxii, 262–263.

99   See Table 14.
100 HMC, *Salisbury*, xii, 13, Stanberry to Cecil, 10 January 1602.
101 *Ibid.*, 50–51, the same to the same, 10 February 1602.
102 *APC*, xxxii, 434, 435, 443–444.
103 HMC, *Salisbury*, xii, 320, mayor to Cecil, 24 August 1602.
104 *Cal. Carew MSS*, iv, 331, Carew to Mountjoy, 7 September 1602.
105 HMC, *Salisbury*, xi, 461, Stanberry to Cecil, 31 October 1601.
106 J. R. Chanter and T. Wainwright, eds, *Barnstaple records* (Barnstaple, 1900), vol. ii, 215.
107 HMC, *Salisbury*, xi, 497, Stanberry to Cecil, 17 November 1601.
108 *CSPI* (1601–1603), 475, Carew to Cecil, 20 August 1602.
109 J. Chanter and T. Wainwright, eds, *Barnstaple records* (Barnstaple, 1900), vol. i.
110 *APC*, xxviii, 599; *APC*, xxix, 615; *APC*, xxx, 262; *APC*, xxxi, 102, 314, 325, 380; *APC*, xxxii, 363, 417, 418.
111 *APC*, xxx, 55, 56.
112 W. T. McCaffrey, *Exeter, 1540–1640* (Cambridge, Mass., 1958), 244ff.; M. Oppenheim, *The maritime history of Devon* (Exeter, 1968), 44–49.
113 *APC*, xxv, 277–278, for defences at Plymouth, 1596; PRO SP12/279/1 for complaints from Plymouth on inadequate defences; PRO SP12/272/25 for like complaints from Weymouth, and for a discussion of Milford Haven's defences, PRO SP12/259/11.
114 See Chapter 3 under 1595–1602.
115 PRO SP12/178/90, i, ii, Sir Henry Norris to Burghley, 13 March 1595.
116 *Ibid.*
117 *Cal. Carew MSS*, iii, 281–283, instructions for Sir S. Bagenal. The defeat at Yellow Ford had taken place on 14 August 1598.
118 *CSPD* (1595–1597), 202–203.
119 *Ibid.*, 271–275, 373, 457, 529–530.
120 *APC*, xxviii, 623–624.
121 *CSPD* (1598–1601), 85, 86.
122 *Ibid.*
123 *Ibid.*
124 HMC, *Salisbury*, viii, 344–345; *APC*, xxix, 73, 74.
125 *Ibid.*
126 *CSPI* (1598–1599), 284, Egerton's report of his passage to Ireland to the privy council, 9 October 1598, from Drogheda, near Carlingford.
127 *APC*, xxviii, 598, 599; *APC*, xxix, 73, 74, 81–83, 88, 89, 194.
128 *APC*, xxix, 121–124, the privy council to the mayor and commissioners.
129 *Ibid.*, 259, 503.
130 *Ibid.*, 84, 123.
131 *CSPI* (1598–1599), 284.
132 *Ibid.*
133 *APC*, xxix, 237–244; under Southampton 300 is a misprint for 500, which figure is given in the mayor's letter to Cecil, HMC, *Salisbury*, viii, 414–415, of 30 October 1598.
134 *APC*, xxix, 255–256, list of twenty captains.
135 HMC, *Salisbury*, viii, 408, 409, Weymouth; *ibid.*, 414–415, Southampton.
136 HMC, *Salisbury*, viii, 417, Plymouth.
137 *Ibid.*, 427–428, Harris to Cecil, 6 November, 1598. The demand on Devonshire for the levy was 400 recruits. Cornwall's shire musters had declined from 8,000 in 1596 to 4,000 in 1599. PRO SP12/273/91, 'Remembrances for Cornwall, 1599'.
138 *CSPD* (1598–1601), 2, 'Reflections by Lord Burghley', 2 January 1598.
139 *APC*, xxv, 162.

140 T. B. James and A. L. Merson, eds, *Third book of remembrance of Southampton 1514–1602* (Southampton, 1979) has no reference to these levies.

141 HMC, *Salisbury*, viii, 453–454, Charles Caesar to Cecil, 25 November 1598.

142 *APC*, xxix, 255, 256, 268. For Spenser's sixteen years of service in a minor official capacity in Ireland see Edmund Spenser, *A view of the present state of Ireland*, ed. W. L. Renwick (Oxford, 1970), 171–174.

143 I am grateful to A. C. J. Jones, deputy archivist, Southampton Record Office, for this reference and for help in searching the mayor's accounts.

144 For Heton's ships, *CSPD* (1598–1601), 129; T. B. James and A. L. Merson, eds, *Third book of remembrance of Southampton 1514–1602* (Southampton, 1979), editors' notes, 51, 53.

145 See Table 3.

146 *APC*, xxxii, 458.

147 *Ibid.*, 481.

148 HMC, *Foljambe*, 9, 89, 90–91; *CSPD* (1598–1601), *passim*.

149 *APC*, xxxi, 20, 418; *APC*, xxxii, 304.

150 HMC, *Salisbury*, viii, ix, x, xi, under letters from the mayors of ports.

151 *CSPD* (1598–1601), 178–179, Delcaration of H. Spinola, April 1599.

152 *APC*, xxxii, 136–137, 255; *CSPD* (1598–1601), 284.

153 PRO SP12/283/18, a list of thirty-seven living and three dead Spanish prisoners were put in at Plymouth, 13 December 1601.

154 *APC*, xxix, 260.

155 *APC*, xxx, 100–101.

156 *Ibid.*, 795.

157 HMC, *Salisbury*, x, 425, 426, 427, 431.

158 M. McCaughan and J. C. Appleby, eds, *The Irish Sea: aspects of maritime history* (Belfast, 1989).

Appendix
Ships in the service of the Irish war

The queen's ships[1]

Achates
Adventure
Amity
Bull
Charles
Crane
Defiance
Dreadnought
Foresight
Garland
Handmaid
Hope
Lion
Lion's Whelp
Merlin
Moon
Non-Pareil
Popinjay
Quittance
Revenge
Spy
Swiftsure
Tiger
Tremontana
Warspite

London[2] ships

Anne
Arcana
Benjamin
Charell
Daniel
Desire
Elizabeth of
    Hampton
Falcon
Flying Hart
Fortine
Hare
Hercules
Humphrey
Isaac
Marigold
Mary Katharine
Mayflower of
    Gillingham
Peter Bonaventure
Ruben of Lee
Samaritan
Swallow
Thomas
Triumph
White Hind

Chester and dependent ports

Chester
Angel[6]
Anne[4]
Bartholomew[3]
Brave[4]
Charity[5]
Curtlege[4]
Cuthbert[6]
Eagle[5]
Elizabeth[3]
George[5]
Good Luck[3]
Grace[5]
Grace of God[3]
Henry[5]
Hopewell[5]
John Abel[5]
Jonas
Luke[5]
Mary Magdalen[4]
Michael[4]
Primrose[6]
Speedwell[5]
Sunday[5]
William[3]

Liverpool
Bartholomew[6]
Eagle[6]
Elizabeth[3]
Ellen[3]
Falcon[6]
George[6]
Henry[6]
Hope[3]
Magull[6]
Marie[5]
Marie-George[6]
Michael[5]
Peter[6]
Phoenix[5]
Quest[5]
Saviour[3]
Stephen[3]
Valentine[5]

Hilbre
Bride[6]
Eagle[6]
Elizabeth[3]
Ellen[6]
George[6]
Harry[6]
James[6]
Jesus[6]
John[3]
Katharine[3]
Laurence[3]
Margaret[5]
Nicholas[3]
Sunday[6]
Toby[6]
Trinity[3]

Frodsham
Delight[3]

Gayton
Elizabeth[3]

Eastham
Trinity[5]

Northam
William[3]

Wallasey
John[3]

Heswall
James[6]
Mary[5]

Beaumaris

Bull[4]
Galleon[4]
Mary[4]
Searcher[4]
Sunday[4]
Suzanne[4]
Swallow[4]

Caernarvon

Grace[4]
Jesus[4]
Mary Mostyn[4]

Formby

Dragon[4]
Gregory[5]

Alt

Jesus[4]
Mary[5]
Michael[5]

Bristol

Adventure[8]
Exchange[8]
Flying Dragon[8]
Francis[9]
Gift of God[8]
Green Dragon[9]
Hopewell[9]
Madam[9]
Mary Fortune[8]
Minion[8]
Phoenix[12]
Pleasure[8]

Raven[9]
Rose[9]
True Love[9]
Unicorn[8]
White Lion[9]

Newport

Angel[12]
Content[6]
George[6]

Milford

Mary Tasker[13]

Barnstaple

Amity[9]
Falcon's Flight[11]
God Saviour[11]
Prudence[11]
Unicorn[11]

Plymouth

Antelope[10]
Arthur[13]
Christian[13]
Conqueror[9]
Crescent[9]
Dolphin[13]
Elizabeth Bonaventure[13]
Fortune[9]
Little John[12]
New Year's Gift[9]
Nicholas[13]
Plough[12]
Trinity[13]
Unity[13]

Weymouth

Francis[9]
Pearl[9]

Southampton

Bevis[13]
Elizabeth[10]
Flyboat[10]
George[13]
Minion[10]
Primrose[9]
Welcome[9]

Portsmouth

Advice[9]
Diana[9]

Fowey

Nightingale[13]
William & John[13]

Padstow

Honour[13]
Margaret[11]

Poole

Alice Bonaventure[11]
Eagle[13]
Unity[11]

Falmouth

Fortune[11]

Ships of Irish ports used[12]

George, of Waterford
Honey, of Drogheda
Hoy, of Dublin
Jesus, of Dungarven
Jolly, of Dublin
Jonas, of Dublin
Lord President, of Dublin
Margaret, of Wexford
Mary, of Lusk (nr Dublin)
Mary Fortune, of Waterford
Minion, of Carrickfergus
Peter, of Drogheda
Peter, of Dublin
Prosper, of Drogheda
Sunday, of Waterford

Total = 190

Notes

1 T. Glasgow, Jr, 'The Elizabethan Navy in Ireland, 1558-1603', *Irish Sword*, 7 (1965/1966), 291–307. From the time of the Desmond rebellion, 1579–1583, and to the end of Elizabeth's reign, a small royal warship remained in Irish coastal waters known as 'Her Majesty's Irish Galley'. It was mainly for the use of the lord deputy. The *Handmaid*, *Popinjay*, and *Tremontana* were used in this capacity.

2 Twelve of the twenty-four London ships listed were victualling ships in the Irish service. The *Isaac* was a small pilot ship. *CSPI* (1596–1597), 152, 242, 243, 281, 335, 338, 401, 402; *CSPI* (1598–1599), 83, 198, 215, 284, 406, 407; *CSPI* (1600), 105, 141, 208, 209, 254, 411; *CSPI* (1600–1601), 12, 53, 331, 332; *CSPI* (1601–1603), 23, 86, 303, 607; *CSPD* (1595–1597), 439, 455.

3 CCR, mayor's military papers, M/MP/12/30; CCR, mayor's great letter book, M/L/5/104; M/MP/28; M/ML/2; M/M/L/5, 244–250; M/L/1/111/15.

4 K. A. Wilson, 'The port of Chester in the late middle ages', 2 vols, unpublished PhD thesis (University of Liverpool, 1965), vol. 2, appendix C, 99ff., selected when the individual ships are known from other sources to have served in the Irish war of the 1590s.

5 HMC, *Salisbury*, ix, 86. Robert Davies, commissary for transport at Chester to Sir Robert Cecil, mentions these ships when organising the transportation of the Earl of Essex's army to Ireland, 1599.

6 E. A. Lewis, ed., 'Analysis of the extant port books of N. Wales', *Transactions of the Honourable Society of Cymmrodorion*, 12 (1927), *passim*. T. Glasgow, Jr, 'The Elizabethan Navy in Ireland, 1558-1603', *Irish Sword*, 7 (1965/1966), 291–307

7 I am also indebted to Dr J. C. Appleby, my colleague's *A calendar of material relating to Ireland from the High Court Admiralty examinations 1536–1641* (Dublin, 1992), for the identification of the names of some of these ships.

8 J. Vanes, *The port of Bristol in the sixteenth century* (Bristol, 1977).

9 HMC, *Salisbury*, vii, 446; *ibid.*, 449; HMC, *Salisbury*, viii, 452, 242, 258, 175, 236, 559, 503; HMC, *Salisbury*, ix, 503.

10 T. B. James and A. L. Merson, eds, *Third book of remembrance of Southampton* (Southampton, 1979), 456, 468, 273, note, 415, note.

11 PRO SP63/210, 50a, list of victuallers' ships, February 1601.

12 *CSPI* (1600), 105, 209, 208; *CSPI* (1600–1601), 53, 165, 425.

13 *CSPD* (1595–1597), 152, 411, 486; *CSPD* (1598–1601), 75, 155, 300, 427; *ibid.* (1601–1603), 85, 99, 140, 226.

PART III

Elizabethan military service in Ireland

Never by my consent shalt though train them up in wars. For he that sets up his to live by that profession can hardly be an honest man or a good Christian. Besides it is a science no longer in request than use. For soldiers in peace are like chimneys in summer.

William, Lord Burghley's advice to his son Robert Cecil on the bringing up of his family, cited in J. Hurstfield, *The Queen's wards* (1958), 257, from F. Peck's, *Desiderata curiosa* (1732–1735).

By concentrating on the service and welfare of the soldier in field and garrison and, considering his return, the relief measures taken for the sick and wounded, this part of the book attempts to follow the complete military fortune or otherwise of the common soldier. In so doing it is hoped to show that military service in Ireland in the late sixteenth century partook of some aspects of the 'military revolution' which was then beginning in Europe. Hence this section is *not* a history of the Nine Years' War in its military action as such, but rather deals with the pay, clothes, food, arms and armour necessary to maintain an army in late-sixteenth-century Ireland.

In almost any period of history the private soldier leaves but scant records of his life; more often than not his name or cipher on a muster list could be the sole document of his existence. However, his voice can occasionally be heard in petitions on his behalf, from his company captain's letters and dispatches, and indirectly in the many regulations sent by the privy council to govern his conduct, or again in the codes of military discipline issued by his chief commander. More directly we can hear of him from complaints about his behaviour from the civilian populace. At best the common soldier may get a mention in the dispatches and at worst his name may appear on a casualty list or simply as a statistic for fatalities.

His fortunes in the army in Ireland depended on: whether or not he was in the field army or in garrison; whether he originated from town or countryside; whether he was an impressed vagrant or a gentleman volunteer; whether or not he was an experienced veteran or a raw recruit; and most of all – whether he was English, Irish, Scots, or Welsh – the very quality and conditions of his life were largely at the mercy of his company captain.

The general condition of the Elizabethan soldier in Ireland was, by one accord, hard, cheerless and unprofitable, hence the Irish service was unpopular. In their accustomed requests to the privy council, perhaps not greatly exaggerated, captains wrote of service in Ireland as 'the most miserable war for travail, toil and famine in the whole world'.[1] Sir George Carew wrote about his soldiers in Munster that 'the travel and hard diet they endure passeth all the soldiers of Europe'.[2] Thomas, Lord Burghley, as lord president of the north, remarked that recruits going to Ireland needed 'two hearts putting into them'.[3] Hugh Bellot, bishop of Chester, writing to William, Lord Burghley, said that the Irish war had become so discouraging and fearful a prospect that 'better be hanged at home than die like dogs in Ireland' had become a common cliché in the city of Chester.[4] The Elizabethan troops scattered in garrisons throughout the island, many of them in remote places difficult to relieve, and those in the field army on the march were generally underpaid, undernourished, ill-equipped and often low in morale.

Some companies were considered unreliable because their Irish soldiers were sometimes secretly in sympathy with their fellow countrymen in the enemy ranks and liable to desertion; other companies, if all reports are to be believed, lived on the edge of voluntary disbandment, and there were cases of mutiny, such as the well publicised one at Dublin Castle in May 1590 when Sir Thomas Norris's men went armed to lord deputy Fitzwilliam to demand arrears and equal pay to that of newly arrived recruits. Troops, arms, money, victuals and munitions sent into Ireland in the 1590s were said to disappear 'as though in some Serbonian bog'.[5] The queen, the privy council and the high command might issue proclamations, orders, rulings, instructions and codes of discipline and articles of war (many clauses in the latter carrying the death penalty) and all to be carried out by a hierarchy of administrators – muster masters, clerks of the check, commissaries for apparel, for victuals, for arms and munitions – and yet rules were honoured in the breach or ignored as corruption and chaos at every level undoubtedly added to the many other factors in the prolongation of the war. The now generally recognised crises of the 1590s, particularly the outbreaks of plague, harvest failures and social unrest, began to expose the frailty of the military base on which Elizabethan power in Ireland was established, namely an army living a hand to mouth existence and at a distance from its precarious source of supplies. The war taxed England's resources. Desertions from the ranks, corruption in the higher commands and administration, and an unwillingness and often inability of the shires to support outgoing levies and returning disabled soldiers may very well present the tarnished side of the medal of a patriotic, self-confidently extrovert but not so merry Elizabethan England.

Notes

1 PRO SP63/202, part ii, no. 38, captains to the privy council, 18 May 1598.
2 *Cal. Carew MSS*, iii, 36.
3 PRO SP12/274/44, Thomas, 2nd Lord Burghley, to his half-brother, Sir Robert Cecil, February 1600.
4 *CSPI* (1592–1596), 489, 13 March 1596.
5 *CSPI* (1598–1599), ix, p. viii of the preface.

CHAPTER EIGHT

The maintenance of the army

Soldiers' pay and army costs

In theory, army companies in Ireland received a proportion of their wages each week and this was known as 'lendings'; the balance, known as 'full pay', was made up at six-monthly intervals. The treasurer-at-war was supposed to issue each week to captains the sum of money their companies were entitled to, from which the company clerk paid the individual soldiers.[1] The private's wages were 8d a day, reckoned for the year at £12 3s 4d; from this £4 2s 6d was deducted for two suits of summer and winter clothing, known variously as 'off-reckonings' or 'defalcations'.[2] In theory, the private soldier was left with annual wages of £8 0s 10d. By the system of lendings 2s 8d a week was paid to the soldier (£6 18s 6d per annum), and the balance of full pay, £1 2s 4d, was made up in two six-monthly instalments. The weekly lendings were intended as subsistence payments for the soldier's food and drink, from which, until reforms were introduced in 1600, he was also expected to pay for his gunpowder, match and repairs to his weapons.[3] Overall, the Elizabethan government provided sufficient money to meet the pay of the army, but treasure arrived from England at irregular intervals, making it impossible to pay the soldiers regularly by the week. Furthermore, whenever money did arrive, the system of payment was so open to abuse that both lendings and full pay were often in arrears, causing hardship and dissatisfaction. Thus payment of soldiers was a haphazard business and its collection by the private equally unreliable.[4] A number of officials were concerned with army pay: the treasurer-at-war, the muster master general, the clerk of the check, the auditor, the captain and the company clerk. In England commissioners examined the annual accounts of the treasurer-at-war. In Ireland the treasurer-at-war was responsible for the financial administration of all revenue received from England, and he made payments on warrants from the privy council, from the lord deputy and from the Irish council in Dublin. These warrants and the acquittances or receipts of the payees were his discharge against the crown for the allowances of his account.[5] Sir Henry Wallop acted as treasurer-at-war from 1580 until retirement in 1599; Sir George Carey succeeded him for the rest of the war and until 1606. Both were alleged to have made private fortunes at the queen's expense.[6]

The muster master's department was supposed to centralise all records of the number of men in the companies after field and garrison troops were mustered and reviewed, in theory, once a month by subordinate muster masters. Their rolls or returns were to record all absences on leave or sick leave so that these rolls would give the treasurer-at-war all the information he needed to reckon pay. Without accurate muster rolls on active service the government could not get value for money since they were the basis for the distribution of pay, rations and apparel. All distribution was the responsibility of the captain and the company clerk. That the pay of the common soldier should have been in the hands of the captains was considered 'a notorious abuse' by military writers such as Matthew Sutcliffe, and generally thought so by everyone but the captains.[7] But in theory the muster office kept a check on the captains. The muster master's deputies were to make inspections at irregular intervals and at short notice, to make it difficult for captains to fill up their bands by *ad hoc* hirelings. Had the muster office been permitted to work according to the rules it would have given the government an accurate account of the state of the forces in Ireland. In practice muster arrangements in Ireland were in a constant state of confusion. Though Sir Ralph Lane, muster master general from 1592, complained often to the privy council about the abuses of captains and put up schemes for reforming the musters and his own secretariat, he was himself under fire from the government's muster agent, Maurice Kyffin, who was sent to help Lane reform the musters in Ireland. Both wrangled and complained about each other's activities. Kyffin reported to Burghley of the confusions and corruptions among the muster officials themselves. And in practice, at the end of the line of administration in pay, the muster masters were at the mercy of the captains and their company clerks, who were frequently in collusion.[8]

The resident muster masters for the Derry garrisons under Sir Henry Docwra, Humphrey Covert and Anthony Reynolds, for the years 1600 to 1602 wrote vivid accounts of their hardships and ill-usage at the hands of the captains. Covert wrote to Cecil: 'the captains are most violently bent against my proceedings in the musters and daily myself and such as I use in this employment, are boldly threatened to have our throats cut'.[9] Only when Covert's zeal for the duties of his office cooled was he tolerated by Docwra and his captains until he resigned in June 1601.[10] Reynolds, his successor, on the other hand, tried too many tricks to outwit the captains in their frauds; he employed 'an intelligence' in each company and payed him 12*d* a week, so that he boasted to Cecil 'the captain shall not know his strength better than I do'.[11] Some of the muster returns Reynolds made of the Derry garrisons showed an uncomfortable discrepancy with those sent in by the commander, Sir Henry Docwra.[12] Eventually, the captains, angered by Reynold's methods, had him arrested, with the connivance of Docwra, on a trumped up charge of whoring with the preacher's maid; then his bi-monthly statistics ceased.

When his freedom was granted Reynolds appears to have given up the struggle to make honest returns and to reform abuses in Derry.[13] In their reports neither Covert nor Reynolds accused individual captains of fraud. Nor did Henry Bird, muster master in Newry who complained to Cecil only in general terms of disorders and abuses committed by the Newry captains.[14] And, in answering privy council criticism of captains in Munster for using will o' the wisps, who came and went bribed by a token payment from the towns on muster days, Sir George Carew told the privy council that 'so gross an error cannot escape the commissaries knowledge and therefore he must participate with the captains in that fault'.[15]

The muster officials lost the fight against the captains' abuses and many continued to profit from the fraudulent distribution of pay, food, clothing and arms. The captain appointed and therefore controlled all subordinate or junior officers: a lieutenant, ensign, sergeant, drummer, preacher, cannoneer, surgeon and about six corporals, the normal establishment of an infantry company.[16] A profiteering captain's company clerk, also his appointee and under his control, worked with him to circumvent the system of musters, checks and inspections. The common soldier's wages, food and clothing were the captain's responsibility, hence their lack was frequently laid at his door.[17] The captains in Ireland 'raised the arts of deception and corruption to a level of efficiency that has perhaps never been attained in any sphere since'.[18] Ideally, the company clerk should have cooperated with the muster master to save money and should have seen to it that justice was done to the soldiers. He was placed to expose abuses. Like all Elizabethan army officials, the duties of the company clerk were also thoroughly defined by military writers: in theory he should have been fully conversant with his company's list, since he was expected to record each soldier's name, his place of origin, and what equipment and clothing he had received from his home shire, so that he would be in a position to know what deductions had to be made from the soldier's wages. As company clerk he was expected to visit the sick and wounded, list their names and the place of their billets, and then to inform the muster master general of those unfit for service in his particular company. If he added more names than those genuinely unfit and was caught out he forfeited a week's pay. And when clothing was distributed it was his duty to see that no soldier was presented twice, on pain of a month's imprisonment.[19]

The basic unit then for all administrative and financial purposes was the company, and its captain the linchpin between the higher command and his soldiers. The captain was their leader in battle, skirmish and siege, their representative and defender with the higher command, and he was responsible for feeding, clothing and arming them. If the criticisms made of the captains in Ireland in the 1590s are to be believed, many of them became instead the exploiters of their men. It was said that 'only the common soldier shared with the Queen the honour of being a mere victim'.[20] Since only a rudimentary supervision of pay existed, some captains could swindle the government by maintaining fewer men than were officially on the list of their companies. Others, with little thought for the welfare of their men, economised on the services they were paid to provide or charged excessively for them. In the opinion of one observer, the queen would have been better off paying such captains £1,000 to keep out of the army.[21] The system lent itself to the making of illicit profits by both the nobly and base-born captains cheating their men and the treasury. The paper strength of the military companies considerably outnumbered the reality in the flesh. The military establishment was evidently corrupt and the mustering system inadequate and inefficient. Should captains retain part of the soldiers' pay, then their men came near to destitution if they did not resort to plunder and extortion. Billeting troops lent itself to extortion and soldiers on the move often went foraging, leaving it to their captains to arrange payments once they had gone. In effect, the military company was a private enterprise, and its captain an entrepreneur serving his own interests as well as the public service.[22] Central government failed as much in controlling the captains as it did in its attempts to reform the army's clerical staff.

The choice of captains was then crucial to the army's efficiency. In writing to Sir Robert Cecil, Sir John Dowdall, commander of Duncannon fort, Waterford, reported in January 1600 that a primary cause of all abuse in the army lay in the choice made of captains. Many of them, he said, were given office from favour not merit, and were unsuited for the leadership of soldiers, being:

> more inclined to dicing, wenching, and the like ... rather than spare a penny will suffer their soldiers to starve, as is daily seen in this kingdom, but others are gentlemen and worthy, yet fitter for the wars of the Low Countries and Brittany where quarters were in good villages than here on waste towns, bogs, or wood.[23]

Hugh Tuder, deputy to Maurice Kyffin, the muster agent in Ireland, had written of the captains in 1598 that they were 'rich in apparel to maintain their pride and lasciviousness, their drunkeness ... their carouses, their tobacco and tobacco pipes.'[24]

The privy council reserved the right to appoint captains, but their appointment was usually left to the commander-in-chief in Ireland, who was expected to know the relative merits of those applying for captaincies.[25] On one occasion Lord Mountjoy was accused of favouritism in his appointments but he defended his choice because those he picked were men of military ability.[26] Though the commander-in-chief had a free hand to promote lieutenants he sometimes bowed to petitions from his sub-commanders, giving them authority to appoint captains whenever vacancies occurred. He permitted Sir Henry Docwra, for instance, to fill his own vacancies at Derry, but refused the like facility to Sir George Carew in Munster.[27]

Absenteeism of many captains from Ireland became a serious problem from the beginning of the war. If a captain had a reasonable excuse to be absent he normally obtained a pass from his commander to return to England. Many though took unofficial leave, particularly in the period between Essex's failure and Mountjoy's appointment to supreme command.[28] Even at a critical time, the muster before the battle of Clontibret in May 1595, for instance, nineteen captains and officers are noted as absent in the muster lists.[29] In January 1598 Sir Ralph Lane, muster master general, told Burghley of the 'ruinous errors caused by the absence of captains from their charges in garrisons'.[30] Lord Justice Carey complained to Sir Robert Cecil in October 1599 that some captains stayed in England: 'If they will, or shall receive Her Majesty's pay, it is fit they should forthwith be commanded to their charge'.[31] The privy council assured Carey and the other justices of the Dublin council that they had warned all absentee captains to return without delay, and that they were not to be paid for the period of their absence.[32] But by November 1599 the Dublin council still complained to the privy council in England of the 'maim to the service' on account of absent captains.[33] Sir Geoffrey Fenton, the Irish secretary of state, in writing to Cecil in May 1601, said that it was not right that any captain should be absent 'when the service is like to grow hot in all places' and that he should dismiss all those captains attendant at court to their charge in Ireland.[34] When called before the privy council's board some captains swore that they had *no* companies in Ireland and others, it seems, were content

198

to sublet their companies as long as there was no need for their presence to watch over their profits.[35] Absenteeism, it was alleged by Sir Ralph Lane and the Dublin council, encouraged the soldiery to plunder the countryside, thereby spreading rebellion in their wake.[36]

The captains of the Pale had a particularly bad reputation for allowing their men in lieu of pay 'to spoil the subjects as if they were rebels'; spoliation appears to have been as prevalent in the Irish wars as elsewhere in the sixteenth century.[37] There are many instances of disorderly companies of soldiers taking out their anger on the peasantry and townsfolk whenever their pay, apparel or victuals were not forthcoming, inflicting on them the harassment which they were employed to do on the enemy. Complaints about the behaviour of the soldiery fell thick and fast on the Dublin administration and on commanders, especially after 1598.[38]

However, captains were not completely to blame for the poor state of the common soldier in Ireland. Many of the better sort, it was claimed, maintained strong companies 'out of their own purse and credit and have neither been repaid nor rewarded'.[39] Many captains, like St Lawrence, Dutton, Crofts and Leigh, went personally to the privy council to petition arrears of pay.[40] Mountjoy told Cecil in February 1601 that the army would never be strong until the queen paid well in money and victuals, stating that the 'incommodities that do arise from their lack hath lost the Queen far more lives than by the sword'.[41] Mountjoy, too, took the captains' part in their demands for an increase of pay and of the number of dead pays from six to ten, which was the customary dead pay allowance in the Low Countries. When Cecil received a request for this increase in July 1598 he simply put a cross against the item.[42] However, by 1599 pay was increased; the weekly lendings to soldiers went up to 3s 4d. In January 1600 Mountjoy suggested to Lord Buckhurst, the lord treasurer in England, that the soldiers be given the full pay of 4s 8d a week, which implied that dead pays for captains should also be paid at that rate.[43] Buckhurst's answer compromised advocating that soldiers be paid at the full rate of 8d a day and abolishing the dead pay system in Ireland from June 1600.[44] The captains had dead pays reinstated at the full rate of 8d a day in May of the following year and the survival of the system is demonstrated by the muster certificates of Anthony Reynolds, which show dead pay allowances being paid to captains in the Derry garrisons until the end of the war.[45] The attempt to have dead pays abolished was impractical because these payments were not merely bonuses for the captains but provided a fund from which the captains could support preachers, cannoneers and surgeons. And yet in Buckhurst's proposals for reform these positions were to be filled by gentlemen volunteers who were to be paid a shilling a day with no benefit to the captain.[46] Reynolds' certificates in 1601 indicate claims for 180 dead pays to subsidise sixty preachers and cannoneers, and in 1602 claims for 120 dead pays for forty preachers and cannoneers.[47] Whether many preachers were actually employed is doubtful; none was listed on the payroll in Munster in January 1600.[48]

The cavalryman needed higher pay than the infantryman to maintain his position. Not only had he to feed his horse but also a horseboy, who normally accompanied him on a native hackney or garron. Irish horseboys foraged for their masters and cleaned their arms and armour, and in these duties became the scourge of their own countrymen.[49] In 1590 a horseman's pay at 6¾d (9d Irish – see Chapter 7 for a discussion of the new coinage) a day was clearly inadequate. Sir William Fitzwilliam, lord deputy in 1591, set out the problem to Lord Burghley:

> No horseman is fed a meal under 3*d* sterling which taken out of his 6¾ sterling – being 9*d* Irish – by the day, there remaineth but ¾ sterling, or a penny Irish to feed his horseboy, his horse, and to furnish him of weapon and apparel, with armour.[50]

Sir George Carew, master of ordnance from 1590 to 1596, was much concerned in seeking an increase in pay for cavalrymen; he made representations to Sir Henry Wallop, to Fitzwilliam, to the Dublin administration and, when visiting the court, to the queen, but all to no effect.[51] When reporting his interview with the queen to the lord deputy, Fitzwilliam, Carew said that 'she replied as she pleased, but nothing was concluded'.[52] However, in 1598 the horseman's pay was increased to 8*d* (18*d* Irish) a day for one year, double what it had been in the early 1590s.[53] In Essex's army in 1599 there were three rates of pay: 800 horsemen were paid 12*d* a day, 200 more 15*d*, and 300 at 18*d* a day.[54]

The pay of the forces was obviously the most expensive item in war budgeting. To appreciate the greater costs of maintaining an army in Ireland some comparisons can be made. For instance, to meet the costs of one levy of 600 to Munster from England at the time of the Desmond rebellion to their discharge early in 1571 had cost the treasury some £7,300. To maintain an armed establishment in Sir Henry Sidney's time, for example 1558, of about 2,000 men the annual charge was almost £40,000. The total costs of Sir William Fitzwilliam's administration over a ten-year period as vice-treasurer ending in 1569 came to £348,000, and 90 per cent of this had to be met out of the English treasury.[55] By comparison, Sir John Perrot's scheme, in 1584, which the queen vetoed, of erecting seven towns, seven bridges and seven forts for the maintenance of a trained garrison of 2,000 foot and 400 horse was modestly estimated at a cost of £50,000 over three years.[56]

The hopes that Ireland would pay for its own conquest and government were false, as the Irish revenues from taxation, forfeitures, rentals and ecclesiastical fees never met the balance of expenditure – the administration of the war and of the government greatly depended on a flow of subventions from the English treasury. For instance, £40,000 was sent to the Irish exchequer in the late 1550s and as Elizabeth's reign progressed that figure was doubled and finally quadrupled by the end of the Nine Years' War. Cost became the predominant consideration in the government of Ireland. The primary policy had been ruling according to the common law of England in the pursuit of a unified sovereignty, but to achieve this military conquest became imperative in the late 1590s.[57]

Numerous lists of 'establishment of the army' and 'charges of the army' in the Irish state papers, in Moryson's *Itinerary* and the Carew papers indicate the various wages paid to soldiers between 1598 and 1602 and show beyond doubt that the pay of the forces was the most expensive item in the war. The point can be made by considering the payroll of Essex's forces in 1599 (Table 16).

The wages in Table 16 were those for the field army of the Earl of Essex, and did not include the pay of non-combatant administrators. The treasurer-at-war's fee, for

Table 16   *The pay of the Earl of Essex's Irish army, 1599*

Rank	Pay per day
Officers	
The lord lieutenant of the army	£10
Lieutenant of the army	£3
General of the horse	£2
Marshal of the camp	£1 10s
Sergeant major of the army	£1
Lieutenant of the horse	£1
Quartermaster	£1
Judge martial	£1
Auditor general	13s 4d
Comptroller general of the victuals	10s
Lieutenant of the ordnance	10s
Surveyor of the ordnance	11s 8d
Two clerks of the munitions each at	5s
Four corporals of the field each at	6s 8d
Four commissaries of victuals each at	8s
One commissary of victuals at	6s 8d
Carriage masters each at	10s
Total for the officers per year	*£13,127 16s 8d*
Horse (the pay of 1,300 horse divided into 26 bands)	
Captains of horse	4s
Lieutenant of horse	2s 6d
Cornets	2s
300 horsemen each at	18d
200 horsemen each at	15d
800 horsemen each at	12d
Total for the horse bands per year	*£31,408 5s 0d*
Foot (the pay of 16,000 footmen divided into 160 bands)	
Captains of each band	4s
Lieutenants	2s
Two sergeants, a drummer and a surgeon	12d
Ensign	18d
94 infantrymen and 6 dead pays each at	8d
Total for the foot bands per year	*£228,246 13s 4d*

Extraordinaries
£6,000 a year to be allowed by concordatum for spies, guides, messengers,
hiring of barques, keeping of prisoners, carriage of treasure, victuals and
munitions, buildings, repairs and rewards for services and necessaries
for the clerks

Sum total per year	£277,782 15s[1]

1. Fynes Moryson, *Itinerary*, vol. ii, 222–224. The editor of the *Cal. Carew MSS*, iii, 288–289
gives a similar establishment but wrote £5,000 a year for extraordinaries. In calculating totals the
exchequer used a set of tables as a ready reckoner, with divisions of the week into six days, the
month into three weeks and the year into thirteen months for companies of soldiers from 100 to
5,000; PRO SP12/250, 41, 42, for examples of these for the year 1594.

example, was 35s a day, and that of the muster master general 11s 6d a day. The president of Munster was designated an annual salary of £133 6s 8d and additional sums of £10 a week for his diet, 30s 6½d a day for his guard of horse and foot, and 14s a day for his provost marshal. The chief justice in the Munster council earned a fee of £100 a year, the second justice £66 13s 4d, an attorney of the council a fee of £13 6s 8d, and finally the clerk of the council an annual fee of £20. The total for the president and council of Munster came to £1,657 13s 9½d a year.[58] Connaught did not have a president and council but a governor; his annual salary was £100, and the payments to his establishment of justices, provost marshal and clerk amounted to an annual total of £909 12s 6d. Leinster or that part of its province lying outside Dublin and the Pale had a much lesser establishment to pay than either the provinces of Munster or Connaught – its annual wages came to £301 17s 8½d.

There was no establishment for the province of Ulster, which remained unsubdued in 1599, but provision for the garrisons on its borders at Dundalk, Drogheda, Newry, Carrickfergus and minor forts in Cavan, and for the then projected Lough Foyle garrisons, was thought to amount to £1,277 10s.[59] For the warders of forts and garrisons throughout Ireland, Fynes Moryson calculated a wage bill for the year 1599 at £3,031 0s 7½d. And for commissaries, pensioners and the almsmen, not mentioned in the sums above or Table 16, fees and pensions were thought to absorb about £2,385 8s 5½d. Fynes Moryson reckoned the yearly charge in all at £299,111 3 7d, whereby, he said, 'the heavy burthen of this yeeres warre in Ireland will appeare'.[60]

Yet such sums were still insufficient. Delays in the arrival of treasure brought real want to the common soldier; in January 1600 the Irish administration in Dublin told the privy council of how they borrowed over £6,000 and issued half-pay and half-victuals to eke out their resources.[61] Clearly, the London administration was increasing its grip on the Dublin council to control its expenditure.

No officer, not even the high-ranking president of Munster, had authority to issue warrants to pay for extraordinary expenses until the privy council's pleasure was known.[62] The lord deputy estimated in advance the expenses he was likely to incur under the heading of 'extraordinaries', which normally included such items as the cost of carriage for munitions, sea transport charges, the building of bridges and boats, the repair of forts, and rewards to spies, messengers and guides. The government in London tried to keep such expenses down. In November 1599 Sir Robert Cecil scrutinised a list of extraordinary charges from Dublin and advised the lord treasurer: 'I pray your Lordship do but cast your eye upon them, for I will pick good matter to stop many wild demands'. Against the item 'Governor of Atherdee, Governor of Killmallock' he wrote, 'A needless office'; against 'for works and reparations done upon Her Majesty's house of Kilmainham, £153-6-8', he wrote, 'A house of pleasure without Dublin, and therefore a superfluous charge'.[63] In contrast, commanders in the field wanted expenses increased in 1601; Mountjoy told the privy council that £6,000 was totally inadequate for extraordinaries when, for example, the repairs in one year to three forts alone at Philipstown, Athlone, and Maryborough had cost £900.[64] But there is no indication that the privy council allowed Mountjoy any increase on the £6,000 given to his predecessor for extraordinary expenses.

Queen Elizabeth and her privy council frequently complained of the vast financial burden of the Irish war. Sir Robert Cecil claimed that the queen would 'feele but small sence of victory' considering that during four years 1598–1602 Ireland cost £300,000 a year.[65] The Dublin muster officials reckoned that for the half year ending 30 September 1602 army charges came to £148,276 8s 2¾d, of which £113,349 3s 6¾d was paid out in wages and the remainder in clothing costs, but that, set against these outgoings, the queen saved £15,000 by the checks on 'lendings' and on 'apparell'.[66] For the whole period of the war the identifiable costs of maintaining the army in Ireland amounted to £1,845,696.[67] All this was a far cry from the days of Sidney, when in 1575 he offered to govern Ireland with only £20,000 from subventions from England; in any case his projection fell short of that since his government was £9,000 in debt by 1578. His victualling arrangements in the 1570s were no more successful than those of the lords deputy in the 1590s. By comparison, the army maintained in Brittany from 1591 on a smaller scale and for a shorter period cost the English treasury, £199,775 18s 1½d.[68] Growth in the numbers of levies sent into Ireland and the prolongation of hostilities, not to mention the effects of the overall 'price revolution', clearly meant that it was more costly to put a trained and equipped soldier into the field in 1600 than it did at the beginning of the queen's reign in 1558. And as the distinction between years of war and peace became blurred, so too did the former divisions between ordinary and extraordinary expenditure; the crown had to pay for the war from the same sources that paid the bills in peace time. With the frequent increase of troop strength, expenditure rose proportionately despite all efforts at retrenchment and reforms.[69]

Early hopes that the war in Ireland would pay for itself and that, once subdued, Ireland would yield a profit to the English crown proved illusory. The establishment and maintenance of garrisons and the support of a mobile field army under the lord deputy, expensive in themselves, were made more so by corruption in every aspect of military administration. In the final months of the war and just before her death Queen Elizabeth is supposed to have said to her court: 'I find that I sent wolves not shepherds to govern Ireland for they have left me nothing but ashes and carcasses to reign over'.[70]

And Mountjoy claimed in March 1601 that he could conduct a more effective war with 12,000 well fed and paid men than 'with sixteen thousand in pay as now they are'.[71]

We have seen some evidence of how fraudulent officers increased the costs of war and the misery of their soldiers; further evidence of this may now be seen in the provisioning and apparelling arrangements of the armed forces in Ireland.

Provisioning the soldiers

Providing sufficient victuals for the steadily growing number of troops in Ireland in 1590s proved a severe test of efficiency for the Elizabethan government and the victualling commissariat. The private soldier bought his food from the garrison stores out of his daily wage of 8d, but the government and the victualling commissaries were the agents responsible for buying, distributing and delivering bulk purchases of foodstuffs for garrison and camp. Many plans or projects to feed the army from Irish resources came to nothing, with the result that the soldiery had to be fed from England by means of victualling contracts made with merchants. Whenever supplies failed or distribution broke down the soldiers lived off the countryside.

Attempts to victual remote garrisons cut off from Dublin by the Irish enemy occasioned some of the bitterest fighting of the war. The sieges of Enniskillen in 1594, of the Blackwater fort in 1595, Armagh in 1598 and of Maryborough fort in 1599 all began after efforts to bring in supplies to those garrisons.[72] The garrison at Castlemaine, near Cork, was in straitened circumstances in October 1599 because the Irish would not allow the troops there to be victualled, according to one commissary's report to the Earl of Essex.[73]

The staple diet of the Elizabethan soldier in Ireland comprised loaf bread, biscuit, butter, cheese, peas or beans, oatmeal and beer, supplemented by rations of salted beef, dried cod, ling or herring. A typical food allowance for the soldier in 1598 consisted of a pound of bread or a pound of biscuit a day, half a pound of butter for three days, a pound of cheese for three days, and two pounds of salted beef, or eight herrings, or one large Holland ling shared between four men one day a week. Failing ling, one large 'Newland fish' or one and a half small Newland fish each was supplied each day.[74] Robert Ardern, a commissary for victuals in Munster in 1599, outlined a soldier's menu for the week:

1 lb. biscuit or 1½ lb. loaf of bread each day of the week. On Sunday, 2 lbs. salt or 2½ lbs. salt or 2½ lbs. fresh beef. Monday, 1 lb. Holland cheese. Tuesday ½ lb. of butter. Wednesday 1 quart of great oatmeal called cleas. Thursday 1 lb. of English cheese. Friday the third part of a large dried cod. Saturday ½ lb. butter. *Memo* The like proportion shall be served every second week; only in lieu of the 2 lbs. of beef on Sunday, 1 lb. bacon or 1 lb. of salt pork is to be delivered with one pint of pease.[75]

Bread, biscuit and cheese needed no cooking and were the obvious rations on long marches. The first and most important item to be supplied to the troops was bread – its quality was a variable, its quantity a 3 lb loaf every two days. Victuallers provided fish if they had no beef, but fish did not travel well and was not therefore a popular substitute. In May 1599, when writing to the privy council requesting further supplies of victuals, the Earl of Essex excluded fish on the grounds that 'it neither keepeth well, nor pleaseth the soldier, who by such victuals hath so much to provoke his thirst and no provision to quench it'.[76] In contrast, Sir Henry Docwra from Lough Foyle asked especially for 'Newland fish' though his men were seated in the best fishing waters in Europe and were well furnished with fishing equipment.[77] Docwra was well aware of this, for his five-page description of Lough Foyle, a valuable account of the area's topography and wildlife, particularly stressed the wealth of fish:

the mouth of the Lough is good fishing for cod, Culmore good for herring from August to September ... all along the Liffer excellently good for salmon from June to the end of August and all winter long the area is stored with the greatest plenty of fowl that I think any part of Christendom yields.[78]

The privy council made their irritation plain to Docwra for asking for 'Newland fish' to be imported; to them his letters must have read more like a sportsman's guide than the observations of a military commander. The council's practical response was to order fish nets, especially salmon nets, from the London merchants Jolles and Cockayne, to be sent to Docwra at Lough Foyle.[79] Yet Newfoundland fish continued to be brought to Lough Foyle. Ironically, in 1601, when a large consignment of it came to his garrisons, Docwra reported that his men refused to eat it; to avoid waste he would send it to Sir Arthur Chichester's men at Carrickfergus.[80]

Among proposals to keep down the charge of victualling, Nicholas Weston, the mayor of Dublin in 1598, suggested that the citizens of Dublin could feed 1,000 soldiers for the forty days of Lent with 'good Newfoundland fish ... delivered at their garrison places northward fronted upon the sea.' Despite the need to feed over 16,000 men in Ireland at that time, the privy council did not appear to have embraced the suggestion with any enthusiasm.[81]

A more common device for feeding the army from the land was for the field army, or for garrisons out on incursions, to plunder cattle from the Irish. Mountjoy, writing in 1600 of an incursion into the Wicklow Mountains against the O'Byrnes, described how he had 'spoiled and ransacked, swept away most part of their cattle and goods, burnt all their corn, and almost all of their houses'.[82] Docwra never failed to mention in his letters whenever his men took in spoils of cattle.[83] Much of the wealth of the native sixteenth-century Irish lay in their herds and such plunder necessarily embittered the warfare. Far from condemning the practice the privy council condoned and encouraged spoliation; in their instructions for setting up the garrison at Lough Foyle the privy councillors advised Sir Henry Docwra:

> If any prey of cattle or victuals be taken from the enemy we doubt not but you will see the same so ordered and expended for the use of the soldiers as the victuals provided by Her Majesty may be the more spared and stretched out to serve the army for a longer season.[84]

In most reports of engagements with the Irish enemy the taking of cattle is mentioned. When the private enemies of the Earl of Essex wanted to denigrate his Irish campaign they called his battles little more than cattle raids. It seems likely that the government counted on this occasional meat supply. After the victory at Kinsale the government reduced the soldiers' meat allowance of 2 lb a week to 1½ lb, but because of rising prices wanted the soldiers to pay the same rate as for 2 lb of meat. The captains and their soldiers, perhaps unappreciative of the fact of inflation, regarded the new measure as nothing more than yet another abuse on the part of the victuallers. Mountjoy wrote two sharp letters to the privy council on 8 and 24 March 1601 stating that unless the former rates and allowances were reinstated he could not prevent 'a general mutiny of the Army, in regard the soldiers are weak, and much enfeebled by the late siege of Kinsale'.[85]

In the last decade of the century prices of all kinds of commodities were rising at a time when the soldiers' wages were static.[86] The government noted how 'sea victuals', that is, those sent to the army, had risen in price from the year 1585 to 1595, wheat from 20s to 40s a quarter; beef from 12s 6d a hundredweight to 20s, ling from £3 a hundredweight to £5 5s, butter from 40s a barrel to £4, cheese from 28s per wey to 55s, malt from 15s to 26s and beer from 24s a tun to 36s.[87] A typical set of costs of the soldier's daily ration was reckoned at 1½d for bread or biscuit, ¾d for three ounces of butter, 1d for six ounces of cheese and ¾d for three-quarters of a pint of oatmeal. Delivery charges were calculated at ½d for each soldier, so that the cost of a single day's basic ration was 4½d, without meat or fish – over half a soldier's daily wage.[88] Captain Dawtrey in reporting to the privy council gave some prices of other foodstuffs in the army in the year 1598. Fresh beef was then 1d a lb, salt beef 1¼d a lb, bacon 3d a lb, herrings eight for 2¼d, peas 1d a quart and beer, 'very good and strong' at 4d for three quarts, was evidently good value for money.[89]

Beer was essential to the soldier's diet and health, for if he drank water he could easily fall victim to disease if he could not distinguish spring from surface water. The soldier's drink allowance drawn up by the privy council was, in theory, generous – half a pint of sack a day, a quart of beer and a quarter of a pint of whiskey or *aqua vitae* every second day.[90] A popular medicinal drink among the garrisons at Lough Foyle was a mixture of sack, liquorice and crushed aniseed balls, ingredients listed among the many items required by Sir Henry Docwra for his soldiers.[91] Fynes Moryson, who had a keen eye for eating, drinking and social habits, noted that the Irish 'have no beer made of malt and hops, nor yet any ale' but that they drank milk, beef broth and, when in towns, Spanish wine, which they called 'The King of Spain's Daughter' and 'usequebah or uisghbeagh', that is to say, whiskey or *aqua vitae*. Beer had to be imported along with other victuals.[92] In contrast Irish whiskey appears to have been more popular with the soldiery than the imported English drink, whenever they could afford to buy it.[93] Presents of Irish whiskey or of 'usequebahs' are mentioned by captains in writing to their friends in England.[94]

Inevitably, abuse crept into the sale of the soldiers' drink. Beer, for example, was delivered to Sir Henry Docwra's men in Derry at the contract price of £6 the tun and allegedly sold to the soldiers at £16 the tun. Another rumour said that the Derry captains converted the beer to their own use, 'whereby the soldiers were enforced to drink water'. There appears to have been no brewhouse at Derry and there is no mention of malt merchants delivering the raw materials for beer-making at Lough Foyle.[95] One muster master, Humphrey Covert, tried to eliminate the extortion in the sale of beer at Lough Foyle by having it first sold to the garrison's victuallers rather than to the captains. Covert then persuaded the commander, Docwra, to order his captains to pay their men 1d a day drinking money. Beer was then brought from the victuallers at 2d the quart. This arrangement gave the soldier the chance of at least a pint of beer a day, but was a far cry from the ideal drink allowance prescribed by the privy council.[96]

Once again, the gap between theory and practice was obvious; the fact that a system of provisioning had evolved by 1600 was no guarantee that it would work efficiently. Plenty of food and drink appears to have been supplied by the system of contracts, as is evident in the payments to the merchants by warrants from the exchequer. The Irish council noted in July 1602 the overall sum of £31,954 3s 4d which was to be paid to merchants contracting to provide food and drink for the soldiers for periods of three to six months in all parts of Ireland.[97] There was also a well defined commissariat for the delivery and distribution of food in each province where stores or magazines had been set up in the chief towns. If soldiers were on the move it became difficult to find communities large enough to quarter them, yet staples in the towns were the answer in the late sixteenth century. But problems, difficulties and complaints multiplied in the last years of the war about feeding the army.[98] The difficulties of transporting food by sea and the problems inherent in keeping food wholesome in a damp climate led to allegations of waste in the victuals sent out of England. One of the chief reasons for the appointments of muster masters to garrisons from 1599 was the prevention of such waste in the stores.[99] Generally speaking, the expenses of victualling the garrisons and mobile army were approximately 10 per cent of the total expenditure in Ireland in the 1570s and likely fluctuated between 15 per cent and 20 per cent in the 1590s, depending on the strength of the overall numbers in the army.[100]

The government made sufficient and generous contracts with the merchants to supply the army and was very concerned about waste, and irritated beyond measure when reports came to it from the Irish administration in Dublin, and from individual commanders, of a state of near starvation among the soldiery.[101] Mutual recriminations followed: Sir George Carey blamed the merchants for sending corrupt victuals and claimed that they made unreasonable gains;[102] the merchants blamed the captains for preventing them carrying out the proper tasks of the victuallers;[103] the captains blamed the government for lack of and arrears of pay; and finally the government put the blame for the poor state of the army on the Dublin administration, especially in the winter months of 1598/1599.[104]

Two of the more important London merchants at the heart of the controversy, John Jolles and William Cockayne, who had gained large contracts to feed the army in 1599, were anxious to clear their reputations from allegations of negligence and fraud made against them by George Beverley, the chief comptroller of army victuals, to both the Irish council and the privy council. Jolles pointed out on 29 July 1599 to Lord Buckhurst, the lord treasurer in England, that Beverley in Dublin could have no idea of what proportions or of what provisions had arrived in Cork, Galway, Newry, Carrickfergus or in any port other than Dublin for delivery to the various commissaries of victuals or about their condition and quality, and that therefore the allegations made against him and his staff were nothing but barefaced lies. From his own exact knowledge of what had been delivered to commissaries in three provinces of Ireland, he wrote, 'there is yet no want but good store of victuals … and enough to supply all wants that can justly be demanded'. Jolles went on to argue that his efforts were being undermined by Sir George Carey, who was furnishing certain captains with money to distribute to the soldiers so that they could buy food elsewhere than from the army stores or magazines, with the result that the commodities he had had delivered were inevitably decaying.[105] On a previous occasion, in May 1599, Jolles had sent a series of complaints to the privy council of how his staff of servants and under-officials were beaten up by captains and other officers when they demanded bills from them for the delivery of goods.[106]

The experience of Jolles and Cockayne as victuallers to the forces can be paralleled to those of Thomas Might and Thomas Sackford in the 1570s and though Might was victualler to about 1582 with a quarter of a century's service in that office he came to be distrusted and ended his days in debt.[107]

A major problem encountered in victualling the soldiers was the simple fact of delays suffered by the victualling ships from England because of the prevalence of westerly winds in an age of sail. Captain Kingsmill at Mallow near Cork, one of many who wrote much to Sir Robert Cecil from Ireland, said 'whatsoever is employed for the service here comes not directly from Bristol but must have six winds to blow before we can receive it'.[108] Few foodstuffs could be preserved for any length of time, so the poor state of much food on arrival aroused a string of complaints from the soldiers and the Irish council. One letter of complaint on 2 June 1599 said that in the four victualling ships then arrived in Dublin harbour all the cheese had perished.[109] Colonel Egerton from Carrickfergus pointed out that the soldiers there had had no delivery of victuals between May and October.[110] Sir Samuel Bagenal saw some of the soldiers of the Newry garrison 'fall dead in marching with very poverty and want of victuals'.[111] The Irish council said it grieved them to see the poor state of the soldiers, 'like prisoners half-starved for want of cherishing', and because they feared mutiny they borrowed £4,000 on bonds, lent their own money, and pawned their plate.[112]

Sir George Carey continued to complain that victuallers were gaining by selling corrupt food to the army.[113] In November 1599 the privy council wrote to the Irish council telling them to institute a full enquiry, to appoint an officer with every commissary of victuals in the ports and towns to be present at the view of victuals to find out where the faults lay, and to have Robert Newcomen, then chief comptroller of victuals, sent to England 'with all his books and reckonings'.[114] Subsequent reports revealed abuses on the part of the merchants, the bad state of some victuals in some garrisons, abuses practised by some captains through their company clerks in selling the soldiers short rations,[115] the obtuseness of victuallers in not declaring proper rates for the issue of victuals[116] and the extraordinary revelation that some captains conveyed provisions *out* of Ireland and had them sold at La Rochelle.[117] One Captain John Baynard, who wrote to the queen in December 1599 listing twelve abuses in the army, indicated that the soldier would rather have 2s in money than 5s worth of the victuals that came out of England.[118] William Jones, the commissary for musters in Munster, made the same point to Sir Robert Cecil,[119] as did the Irish council to the privy council on 10 December 1599.[120]

The queen and council appear to have done everything possible to ensure that the army was fed; victualling contracts were made for all levies going to Ireland, and in Ireland the victualling commissariat was organised in each province and centred on the government's stores in towns and garrisons. The system was similar to the chains of military *étape* created by French occupation forces in Italy and the Netherlands.[121] But all the time they had to struggle against widespread dishonesty and the westerly winds which made the passage to Ireland difficult and often disastrous to the cargoes. The judgement of Sir John Fortescue, the historian of the British army, that no sovereign of England neglected the soldiers 'more wantonly, wilfully, and scandalously than Elizabeth' is not borne out by a comprehensive study of the privy council's records.[122] The huge contracts for food supplies seen in the warrants for payments to merchants and the near state of starvation of so many soldiers are difficult to reconcile if the practical difficulties in getting the food to the soldiers and the ubiquitous practice of fraud are ignored. It was no fault of the government that some of the years of greatest military activity in Ireland, from 1596 to 1601, coincided with years of exceptional dearth of grain in England following bad harvests. The year 1596 was a disastrous one, with an average price of 83 per cent above the norm for grain; there was panic legislation with widespread near starvation and a real threat of rebellion in many parts of England in 1597 and 1598.[123] Though the government tried to cover up some of the reasons for price increases by blaming private traders in grain, its very exports to Ireland increased dearth at home. By the end of the century the government's need to supply grain to the Irish military effort seems to have become a priority, overriding the need to stabilise food prices in England. Riots broke out over corn prices in Sussex in March and April 1597; in Oxfordshire the riots were serious and there were widespread disturbances in Norfolk; most depositions make it clear that hunger was the chief cause.[124]

Despite all the government's efforts, the army in Ireland from 1598 to 1599 was not well victualled. The evidence of the Irish state papers of a hungry and discontented army is strong and the cause is clear – profiteering and corruption. It was said of Sir Thomas North's company in December 1596 that they were 'miserable, unfurnished, naked, and a hunger-starven band', and that many of his soldiers died wretchedly at Dublin, 'some whose feet and legs rotted off for want of shoes'.[125] Dublin reported to the privy council in January 1598 that the 'lamentable state of the army doth not a little grieve us'.[126] Captain Atherton wrote to the Earl of Ormond from Carrickfergus in January 1598 of the great lack of victuals in the garrison.[127] The privy council was told in February 1598 that 'such is the universal scarcity here of all kinds of victuals, as, in many parts of Leinster and the English Pale, the common people are already driven to eat horseflesh'.[128] Sir Geoffrey Fenton spoke of a nation 'already entered into famine'.[129] In Newry the garrison mutinied for lack of food in February 1598, and when a paymaster, James Carroll, was sent to them from Dublin the soldiers would have torn him to pieces but for the intervention of their officers.[130] Fynes Moryson wrote that the common English soldiers in 1599, 'by poverty of the war ... by the late defeats, by looseness of body, the natural sicknesses of the Country were altogether out of heart'.[131] The whole sorry scene is further evidence of an inglorious phase in the history of this war in Ireland.

The soldiers' clothing

Shire levies were provided with clothing, either in the county of origin or when the soldiers were on the point of embarkation. There was no such thing as a national uniform in the sixteenth century, though soldiers from the same shire would, as a rule, be fitted out in much the same way. Infantrymen were frequently dressed in motley or russet, a practice in which the military historian, Sir Charles Oman, saw an early instance of 'adaptation to environment', or camouflage, since Ireland, like England, was then much afforested.[132] On occasion the cavalry were issued with red cloaks in the classical tradition. One of the earliest mentions of 'red coats' is the description by Philip O'Sullivan Beare of an English force arriving in Munster, 1582, during the Desmond rebellion.[133] A preference for red coats or cassocks began to appear during the O'Neill war; English soldiers under Marshal Sir Henry Bagenal were surprised to find themselves confronted by Irish troops in red coats 'like English soldiers'. The explanation lay in O'Neill's loyal period when he had been given six English captains to train six companies for the queen's forces, and no doubt the red coats which surprised Bagenal's men at Clontibret in 1595 had belonged to that loyal period.[134] In 1599, when the clergy had to raise cavalry for Ireland, Archbishop Whitgift decided that his horsemen should be dressed in tawney or blue, which he said had been the custom. But throughout the war years there was no pressure put on clothing contractors to provide suits of a standard colour and there appears to have been but two sizes provided: 'large' and 'small'.[135]

Sir John Harrington, who served under Essex in 1599, left one of the fullest descriptions of a private soldier's clothing and the cost then of the various items: a winter coat of Kentish broadcloth lined with cotton (17s 6d); a canvas doublet with white linen lining (12s 6d); a pair of Venetian breeches lined with linen (13s 4d); two shirts with bands (8s); three pairs of ox-hide shoes (7s); and three pairs of kersey stockings (8s). During the summer he was issued with two pairs of shoes and a pair of stockings and a hat (3s).[136] Nicholas Weston, the mayor of Dublin in 1598, described the apparel for an officer and its cost:

> a cassock lined with bays and trimmed with silk lace (18s.6d.); a doublet with silk buttons (12s.); two shirts and two bands (7s.9d.); three pairs of neat leather shoes (5s.3d.); three pairs of kersey stockings at 2s.2d. the pair; broadcloth Venetians with silk lace (12s.6d.); and a felt hat coloured with a band (4s.6d.).

Weston calculated that the winter apparel of an officer could have been made in Dublin for £3 7s and his summer wear for 17s 11d, and the common soldier's winter apparel for £2 13s 8d and his summer's at 14s 4d. Weston was of the opinion that much money could be saved in clothing the troops – 19s on an officer's clothing and 15s 8d on the common soldier's if they could be clothed from the City of Dublin rather than by the London merchants, Babington and Bromley. He reckoned that £780 on every 1,000 soldiers could be thereby 'saved to Her Majesty's coffers'. But nothing came of his plan, which was perhaps an unreliable under-bid to get the custom for Dublin.[137]

The privy council repeatedly urged the shire authorities to fit out their levies generously with clothes other than coats, but the general tendency was to give the recruits the minimum official clothing allowed by the institution of 'coat money', of which the counties paid only a quarter and the government the rest. Shire authorities knew that the soldiers would be given further clothes on their arrival in Ireland. Once there, as for any army fighting overseas, clothing was issued twice a year, for winter and summer. During the 1590s the supply of suits was mainly in the control of merchant clothiers under contract to the crown. The distribution of the suits to soldiers was done by the captain and his company clerk; the common soldier was again at their mercy for the clothes on his back. Despite efforts on the part of the government to reform distribution, many captains retained control over a lucrative source of additional income.[138]

Some captains had the welfare of their men at heart and wrote to Sir Robert Cecil about the hardships their soldiers had to suffer in Ireland. Hugh Mostyn, a Flintshireman with twenty-seven years' service in Ireland, was typical of the better captains. He wrote from Connaught to say his men were 'in a cold country, under a cold climate, where no relief is, but what they carry with them'. It was his greatest wish that every shire should send out troops to Ireland with:

> one blanket, one rough sheet, four pair of spare shoes, three pairs of stockings, two spare shirts, and all of which will be bought for 20*s* of money or thereabout; it would be better for the soldiers to want their blue coats than these necessities.... the country where I was born when they do send me for Ireland, do usually give xx*s*. each soldier to drink, which is better to be bestowed as aforesaid.[139]

Mostyn's is one among many such letters to Sir Robert Cecil. Sir Henry Brouncker painted a miserable picture of the state of his forces, blaming the lack of clothing and victuals on Cecil.[140] William Jones, a Munster commissary, told Cecil in 1600 that the soldiers there were as poor in apparel 'as the common beggar in England', and though it was mid-winter they had not yet received their suits, and many had not got the previous summer's clothing allowance.[141] Sir Arthur Chichester, the commander at Carrickfergus, wrote to Lord Mountjoy on 14 May 1601 about the extremities of his garrison: 'we are in as great want of clothes as of money, and of them both more than ever I formerly saw in the Queen's wars'. He pointed to the difficulty in keeping men in discipline, saying that it was unreasonable 'to inflict punishment where dues are so long withholden'. However, he added that 'their daily employment, some killing, and a little booty puts them out of minding of these wants many times'.[142] Hugh Tuder, an experienced muster official on Maurice Kyffin's staff before 1598, spoke of the captains 'rich in apparel' and of the 'nakedness' of many soldiers.[143] The Irish council also spoke of the 'poverty and nakedness' of many troops arriving in Dublin.[144] Captain Francis Stafford, who went to Chester to conduct a contingent, complained of the Buckinghamshire men as the 'worst apparelled' and of the Londoners dressed in 'London cassocks made of northern cloth, which by wet doth so much shrink that they will this winter stand them in little stead'.[145]

The reasons for the poor state of the common soldier's clothes are similar to those which applied to his food. Delays in the deliveries of suits, maldistribution when they arrived, and frauds perpetrated by the clothiers, commissaries for apparel and the captains lay at the heart of all the troubles over clothing the troops. From 1598 until the end of the war two London clothing merchants, Uriah Babington and Robert Bromley, won the main contracts with the crown to provide summer and winter suits. Other merchants, whose trade they had cornered, such as James Quarles and William Holliday, accused them of pocketing vast sums of public money.[146] Holliday alleged that Babington and Bromley had defrauded the crown of £27,000 between 1597 and 1600 by the simple device of supplying only two-thirds of the number of suits originally contracted. He accused them of giving the captains money instead of clothes, 24s for instance instead of a winter suit, for which the crown had already paid them 40s. They thus made an unjust profit of 16s on each suit. Holliday reckoned that when these London clothiers had contracted to clothe 1,000 men only 600 received suits, and that the money which should have clothed the remaining 400 they shared out with the captains.[147]

Even if Holliday's testimony against Babington and Bromley was biased there is other evidence to show that the two were not above board in their contracts with the government. The Irish administration claimed in 1598 that the merchants had delivered only 2,500 suits for all the forces in Ireland and that they were forced to share out all available supplies so that every soldier would get something, at a time when the merchants reported they had supplied all the forces for the winter.[148] In May 1599 William Beecher, a wealthy London citizen and former associate of Babington and Bromley, informed on them to Sir Robert Cecil. He claimed they owed him £4,000 and that they had promised him 'a third share of the profits of any business they may have from the Queen'.[149] Cecil took no action on this information, probably because Beecher had himself come under severe criticism from the privy council in 1594 because of his underhand dealings in clothing the troops in the Low Countries.[150]

Further evidence was offered by John Bryde, an employee of Babington and Bromley, who wrote to the privy council that his employers had sent him to Bristol to persuade the mayor to certify the shipment of a larger number of suits than had in fact been sent to Ireland, and he went on to say that, should he be allowed to examine the merchants' accounts and the port books at London, Bristol and Chester, he would be able to prove all his allegations against Babington and Bromley.[151] In a law suit of 1616 brought against the heirs and executors of Babington and Bromley counsel for the crown brought to light that these merchants provided only 6,300 suits of apparel for 12,000 soldiers in the winter of 1599. Nothing had been done about their frauds at the time and their contracts to clothe troops in Ireland were annually renewed until 1606.[152]

The privy council said it was ready to believe that the clothiers were profiteering and that muster masters, commissaries and captains had their mouths silenced by bribes.[153] Lord Mountjoy was ordered to carry out a full investigation into the supply of apparel to his troops but there is no evidence that he did so.[154] In view of the distress caused to so many soldiers by the lack of proper apparel and the fact that the government was aware of the frauds, it is extraordinary that it did not pursue the enquiry. Lord Buckhurst seems to have gone on depending on Babington and Bromley to supply clothes for the army despite the complaints against them.[155] The details of their frauds were exposed only in 1616, when the crown sued the merchants' executors for the recovery of misappropriated funds: this law suit implicated many, from the treasurer-at-war, Sir George Carey, down to minor officials, in the fraud. The government was not willing to suspect that Carey, a trusted servant of the crown and a relative of the queen, could be part of the fraud.[156] The case against Carey was said to have been unprecedented in the history of peculation. He sounded sincere enough in the turmoil of Essex's failure in Ireland and the bankruptcy of the Irish administration when he wrote to Cecil: 'I find the perils and hazards such, that I protest unto your honour that I never had a quiet night's rest sithence I first came into this cursed land'.[157]

Accounts of the military companies remained unsettled that year, 1599, and every department of the administration was in confusion; the short supplies of apparel and its poor quality were but symptoms that all was not well with the army or its administration in Ireland. The previous treasurer-at-war, Sir Henry Wallop, had outlined a scheme in July 1597 whereby the soldiers could be clothed in Ireland with garments of Irish make, which, he claimed, would be 'far better cheape' and more durable than those sent out of England. He suggested Irish frieze coats, and especially the Irish mantle, which kept the soldier dry by day and gave him shelter by night when billets were poor, and Irish linen shirts, would cost less than 30s an outfit.[158] The government was not sympathetic to the idea, and Lord Burgh, lord deputy in 1597, disapproved of Wallop's scheme on the grounds that Irish clothes, though cheaper, would be made by rebels who would then receive 'Her Majesty's good coin' to buy arms and munitions to maintain their rebellion.[159]

The respective merits of the Irish frieze mantle and the English broadcloth cassock were long debated but the privy council did not believe that English soldiers could carry an Irish mantle and still be able to fight. In any case the Irish mantle had a bad press as a fit garment for theft and was much decried by Edmund Spenser in his famous *View of the present state of Ireland* (1598). Though sound in itself, Wallop's proposal to clothe the soldiers with such mantles had an ulterior motive: had it been agreed to, it would have entailed large sums of money being sent to Ireland to make the purchases there, and as treasurer-at-war he was allowed a percentage of monies carried to Ireland by him.[160] Lord Burgh made a different suggestion to Lord Burghley in September 1597 of how savings could be made in clothing the soldiers: by having the garments made of 'coarser and cheaper stuff', or by 'suiting the foot [infantry] but once a year in the winter', except for 'stockings and shoes which must be oftener furnished'. He added: 'nothing can be better than to provide the apparel out of England'.[161]

The question of clothing the soldiers in Ireland in Irish materials, frieze stockings and brogues was raised again in 'The Humble Requests of the Captains' in May 1598, which emphasised the superior merits of the Irish frieze mantle.[162] In his marginal notes to these requests Sir Robert Cecil wrote opposite the word 'mantle': 'our difficulty in this article is, that by this means our English shall become in apparell barbarous, which hath hitherto ben avoided'.[163]

Captain John Baynard advised the queen on the adoption of Irish-made garments for the troops.[164] And the Earl of Essex favoured them, claiming his troops would keep their health much longer if English cassocks and shoes were replaced by Irish mantles and brogues.[165] Under the weight of opinion the government relented in 1600 and gave orders to the clothiers to issue either a mantle or a long broadcloth coat and also recommended the use of brogues instead of shoes, though it was not stated whether or not these items should be of Irish or of English make.[166]

Some measure of reform was brought into the distribution of suits of apparel by Lord Mountjoy, who in 1600 instructed the clothing merchants Babington and Bromley to have apparel shipped to several convenient ports in Ireland and not all to

Dublin, so that there would be a minimum of delay in distribution to the outlying garrisons.[167] But the scheme tackled only one of the many problems. Abuses continued mainly because the captains were able to keep final control over the soldier's food and clothing allowances. The reports of Humphrey Covert and Anthony Reynolds, muster masters at Lough Foyle, indicate the stranglehold of the Lough Foyle captains over their men's necessities of life.[168] The privy council commented on the fraudulent dealings of the captains: 'we do plainly perceive that divers of the captains there do wholly convert Her Majesty's pay into their own purse.'[169] Though general criticisms of the captains as a body are very frequently made, it is of interest that not a single captain seems to have been punished for the neglect of his men, nor a single one named for frauds in depriving men of their coats in Ireland.

The weight of evidence, however, suggests that the common soldiers were the victims of their superiors' dishonesty. It is not difficult to see how frauds were carried out; supplies came out of England at irregular intervals because of the difficulties of the sea passage, arrangements for feeding and clothing the soldiers were not settled into a routine, and the numbers to be fed and clothed were constantly changing. And the trust reposed in the main clothing contractors, Babington and Bromley, seems to have been badly misplaced.[170] The government appears to have done all it could to see that the soldiers were properly and sufficiently fed and clothed; the debt left by the queen of £17,864 to her successor 'for the apparel of the forces in Ireland' may be viewed as one measure of the crown's efforts to look after its forces in Ireland in the late 1590s. But, even so, these efforts were not enough; the general state of the army was one of corruption, discontent and suffering.[171]

Notes

1   *CSPI* (1598–1599), 146–150, 'The humble requests of the captains of Ireland', 18 May 1598, illustrates the system of payment and its weakness.
2   From *defalcatio*, medieval Latin, to scale down, deduct.
3   See Chapter 9 under 'Arms and armour'.
4   J. W. Fortescue, *A history of the British army* (London, 1899), vol. i, Book II, Chapter iv.
5   *Calendar of patent rolls, Ireland* (1558–1560), 120–121, shows, for instance, how Sir William Fitzwilliam as treasurer-at-war balanced his accounts.
6   Instructions to Sir George Carey on appointment as treasurer outline the ideal execution of the office – *Cal. Carew MSS*, iii, 290–292, 22 March 1598. For the exposure of Carey's frauds in the office see H. Hall, *Society in the Elizabethan age* (London, 1901), 128–132. And for the accusations against Sir Henry Wallop, *CSPI* (1596–1597), 413.
7   C. G. Cruickshank, *Elizabeth's army* (Oxford, 1970), 143.
8   For the difference between Lane and Kyffin, *CSPI* (1598–1599) 12, 13, 43, 71–73, 96, 97, 152. For complaints of Lane's negligence, *Cal. Carew MSS*, iii, 268, and iv, 63. Lane presented a full account of two and a half years' service to Cecil and wanted to be exonerated from all blame: *CSPI* (1598–1599), 491.
9   *CSPI* (1600–1601), 284, Covert to Cecil, 22 April 1601.
10   PRO SP63/208, part ii, no. 17, no. 103 (May 1601) and no. 16 (June 1601) are Captain Covert's letters describing his difficulties to Cecil.
11   PRO SP63/209/62, Reynolds to Cecil, 5 September 1601.

12 *Ibid.*, 62b. For abstracts of Reynold's muster certificates *CSPI* (1601–1603), 60, 61, 102, 179, 189.
13 *CSPI* (1601–1603), 214, 215.
14 *CSPI* (1600–1601), 27, Bird to Cecil, 22 April 1601.
15 *Ibid.*, 162, Carew to Cecil, 25 January 1601.
16 PRO SP63/209, 244b, 'The pay for a bande of a 100 footemen', 14 December 1601.
17 *CSPI* (1598–1599), 208, allegations of Hugh Tuder, servant to Maurice Kyffin, made against the captains. *Ibid.*, 443–445, criticisms made in general of the captains in Ireland by Sir Robert Cecil in his 'Observations on the condition of Ireland'.
18 C. G. Cruickshank, *Elizabeth's army* (Oxford, 1970), 139–140.
19 BL Cotton MSS, Galba, C, viii, ff. 238b–239b, Captain Thomas Digges' (died 1595) view of the ideal company clerk. Digges was muster master general of the English forces in the Netherlands 1586.
20 J. E. Neale, 'Elizabeth and the Netherlands, 1586–1587', *English Historical Review*, 45 (1930), 373–396.
21 *CSPI* (1596–1597), 172, memorandum, unsigned, not dated.
22 G. Parker, *Europe in crisis 1598–1648* (Glasgow, 1979), 73ff.
23 *Cal. Carew MSS*, iii, 353–355.
24 *CSPI* (1598–1599), 209.
25 *CSPI* (1596–1597), 59.
26 *CSPI* (1600), 503.
27 *Cal. Carew MSS*, iv, 137, Carew's complaint on the matter to Mountjoy, 1 September 1601.
28 *CSPI* (1599–1600), 192, 193, 212, 248.
29 The muster lists at Clontibret published in *Irish Sword*, 2 (1957), 368ff.
30 *CSPI* (1598–1599), 43, 72.
31 *CSPI* (1599–1600), 192, 193.
32 *Ibid.*, 212.
33 *Ibid.*, 248.
34 *CSPI* (1600–1601), 358.
35 *CSPI* (1599–1600), 255, 424.
36 *CSPI* (1600), 442, 505.
37 *Cal. Carew MSS*, iii, 260–265, 'Declaration of the present state of the English Pale of Ireland … June 1597'.
38 *CSPI* (1598–1599), 62, 68, 208, 297, 429–430, 433, 436, 444, instances of complaints in the year 1598–1599.
39 *Cal. Carew MSS*, iii, 354.
40 *APC*, xxx, 215, 389, 483, 550, 610–611, 780, captains' petitions in 1600.
41 *CSPI* (1600–1601), 175, Mountjoy to Cecil, 4 February 1601.
42 PRO SP63/207, part ii, 115, 'Humble requests of the captains of Ireland', with marginal notes by Sir Robert Cecil.
43 *Ibid.*, part i, no. 76, 'Certein pointes necessarie for the armie in Ireland', Mountjoy to the privy council, January 1600.
44 *APC*, xxx, 415.
45 PRO SP63/208, part ii, no. 84, in a memorandum concerning the new coinage, 20 May 1601.
46 PRO SP63/207, part i, no. 7, 'Consideration touching Ireland causes'. A document of forty-three points in the script of Thomas, Lord Buckhurst, January 1600.
47 PRO SP63/209, 62a,b, certificates of July/August 1601; *ibid.*, 197a,b, certificates of October/November 1601; PRO SP63/212, 18, certificates of August 1602.
48 PRO SP63/207, part i, no. 8, William Jones, commissary for Munster to the privy council, 6 January, from Youghal.

49 C. Falls, *Elizabeth's Irish wars* (London, 1950), 37, 41.
50 *Cal. Carew MSS*, iii, 55, Fitzwilliam to Burghley, 18 June 1591.
51 *Ibid.*, 18, 19, 41, 53, 54.
52 *Ibid.*, 58, Carew to Fitzwilliam, 18 July 1591.
53 PRO SP63/202, part iii, no. 144.
54 Table 16.
55 C. Brady, *The chief governors: the rise and fall of reform government in Tudor Ireland, 1536–1588* (Cambridge, 1994), 136.
56 PRO SP63/123, no. 52; PRO SP63/127, no. 35; PRO SP63/153, no. 67.
57 Wallace T. MacCaffrey, *Elizabeth I: war and politics, 1588–1603* (Princeton, 1992), Chapter 2, which draws heavily on my PhD thesis findings, J. J. N. McGurk, 'The recruitment and transportation of Elizabethan troops and their service in Ireland, 1594–1603', PhD thesis (University of Liverpool, 1982), and for the comparisons see N. Canny, *The Elizabethan conquest of Ireland: a pattern established, 1565–1576* (Hassocks, 1976), 155.
58 Fynes Moryson, *Itinerary*, vol. ii, 222–228.
59 For the failure to establish an Ulster presidency see N. Canny, *The Elizabethan conquest of Ireland: a pattern established, 1565–1576* (Hassocks, 1976).
60 Fynes Moryson, *Itinerary*, vol. ii, 229.
61 *CSPI* (1599–1600), 386.
62 HMC, *Salisbury*, ix, 115–116, Dudley Norton to Cecil, 24 March 1599.
63 PRO SP63/206, 16, A book of concordata, November 1599.
64 PRO SP63/209, 53 – Mountjoy to the privy council, 3 September 1601.
65 J. MacLean, ed., *The letters of Sir Robert Cecil to Sir George Carew* (Camden Society, London, 1864), 147–148.
66 PRO SP63/212, 37, 30 September 1602.
67 BL, Lansdowne MSS, 156, ff. 253–258, Irish costs differentiated; S. Ellis, *Tudor Ireland: crown, colony and the conflict of cultures 1470–1603* (London, 1985), 269–274.
68 *CSPD* (1595–1597), 8.
69 R. Schofield, 'Taxation and the political limits of the Tudor state', in *Law and government under the Tudors*, eds C. Cross *et al.* (Cambridge, 1988), 230ff.
70 F. Chamberlain, *The sayings of Queen Elizabeth* (London, 1923), 308.
71 PRO SP63/208, part I, no. 122.
72 PRO SP63/203, 77, Captain Thomas Reade to Cecil, 14 March 1599.
73 PRO SP63/205, 205, commissary for victuals to Essex, 12 October 1599.
74 *Ibid.*, no. 26, 16 April 1599, 'the allowance of victual for everie soldier servinge in the realme of Ireland'.
75 *Cal. Carew MSS*, iii, 350.
76 PRO SP63/205, no. 54, Essex to the privy council, 9 May 1599.
77 *APC*, xxx, 11, 12, items from Lough Foyle, 'netts for fyshing of sondry sortes'.
78 PRO SP63/207, part vi, no. 84, i, ii, iii and 85. A description of Lough Foyle enclosing three sketch maps of Derry, Lifford and Dunalong – *ibid.*, no. 84, i, ii, iii.
79 *APC*, xxxi, 348.
80 *CSPI* (1600–1601), 209–215, Docwra to the privy council, 9 March 1601. His 10½-page letter is fully transcribed by the editor of the calendar.
81 PRO SP63/202, part iii, no. 123, Weston to the privy council, 22 October 1598.
82 *CSPI* (1600–1601), 178.
83 In thirty of Docwra's letters to the privy council and to Cecil from 1600 to 1602, cattle, sheep and horses taken from the Irish are mentioned in about half of them: *CSPI* (1600–1603), *passim*; *APC*, xxx, xxxi; and in HMC, *Salisbury*, ix, *passim*.
84 *APC*, xxx, 103, 'Instructions as to the Plantation at Lough Foyle'.
85 Fynes Moryson, *Itinerary*, vol. iii, 124, 142, Mountjoy to the privy council.

86 E. H. Phelps Brown and S. Hopkins, 'Seven centuries of the prices of consumables compared with builders' wage-rates', *Economica*, no. 92 (November 1956), 296–314, see fig. 1, p. 299.
87 *CSPD* (1595–1597), 101.
88 *APC*, xxix, 272.
89 PRO SP63/202, part ii, no. 53, Dawtrey to the privy council, 31 May 1598.
90 *APC*, xxxix, 70.
91 *APC*, xxx, 11.
92 Fynes Moryson, *Itinerary*, vol. iv, 200.
93 *Cal. Carew MSS*, iii, 8, 77, 79, 175.
94 HMC, *Salisbury*, ix, 232, 243, 313, 434.
95 *CSPI* (1600–1601), 112, 113, answers to questions raised in the privy council concerning the government of Lough Foyle under Sir Henry Docwra, unsigned, but dated December 1600.
96 *Ibid.*, 113.
97 *APC*, xxx, 194, example of a warrant to pay John Wood, merchant, £2,417 3s 9d, and *ibid.*, 724, payments of £10,000 to William Cockayne and John Jolles, merchants supplying the army in Ireland.
98 PRO SP63/211, 93, 24 July 1602.
99 PRO SP63/208, part ii, no. 38, Humphrey Covert, muster master at Lough Foyle, to the privy council, 22 April 1601, reporting measures taken to prevent waste of food and clothing in the garrisons.
100 BLCott MSS Titus B, xiii, ff. 185, 186; PRO SP63/95, 2–4, and PRO SP63/205, *passim*.
101 *CSPI* (1598–1599), 59, 165, 334, 340: *Cal. Carew MSS*, iii, 354, 355; *Cal. Carew MSS*, iv, 427, 429, in which the misery of the soldiers is stressed.
102 *CSPI* (1599–1600), 26, 278, 350.
103 *Ibid.*, 35, 36.
104 *Ibid.*, 276.
105 PRO SP63/205/119, Jolles to Buckhurst, 29 July 1599.
106 *CSPI* (April 1599 – February 1600), 35, 36 and 45.
107 Jon G. Crawford, *Anglicising the government of Ireland, 1556–1578* (Dublin, 1993), 299–300.
108 PRO SP63/205, 148, Kingsmill to Cecil, 22 August 1599.
109 PRO SP63/205, 75, Irish council to the privy council, 2 June 1599.
110 *CSPI* (1598 – March 1599), preface, lxix.
111 *Ibid.*, 476.
112 *Ibid.*, 357.
113 *CSPI* (April 1599 – February 1600), 278, 350.
114 *Ibid.*, 276.
115 *APC*, xxxi, 122–125.
116 HMC, *Salisbury*, ix, 116, 316.
117 *CSPI* (January 1598 – March 1599), 462, report endorsed by Cecil, 'Captains that steal from Ireland'.
118 PRO SP63/206, 116, 'The opinion and advice of Captain John Baynard', December 1599.
119 *CSPI* (April 1599 – February 1600), 484, Jones to Cecil, 17 February 1600.
120 *Ibid.*, 310–312.
121 G. Parker, *The army of Flanders and the Spanish road 1567–1659* (Cambridge, 1972), 88.
122 J. W. Fortescue, *The history of the British army* (London, 1899), vol. i, 146, and *CSPI* (1599–1600), 45, 68, 107, 300, 347, 379, 393, 469, examples.
123 W. G. Hoskins, 'Harvest fluctuations and English economic history, 1480–1619', *Agricultural History Review*, 12 (1964), 28–46, see Fig. II, p. 39.

124 *CSPI* (1595–1597), 316–320, 342–345, 401; *APC*, xxvii, 55–56.
125 *CSPI* (1596–1597), 194–195.
126 *CSPI* (1598–1599), 2.
127 *Ibid.*, 11, Atherton to Ormond, 5 January 1598.
128 *Ibid.*, 62, Dublin council to the privy council, 27 February 1598.
129 *Ibid.*, 68, Fenton to Cecil, 28 February 1598.
130 *Ibid.*, 59, Richard Wackely to Sir Ralph Lane, 19 February 1598.
131 Fynes Moryson, *Itinerary*, vol. ii, 273.
132 Sir Charles Oman, *A history of the art of war in the sixteenth century* (London, 1937), 385.
133 Philip O'Sullivan Beare, *Historiae Catholicae Iberniae Compendium* (Lisbon, 1621), ed. and trans. in part by M. J. Byrne, *Ireland under Elizabeth* (Dublin, 1903), 27.
134 *CSPI* (1592–1596), 322, an early mention of red coats, later known universally as the characteristic English military colour.
135 Lambeth Palace Library, miscellaneous musters, MS 247, f.118. Note that 'coat' is used to indicate full suits of clothing in sixteenth-century military parlance.
136 Sir John Harrington, *Nugae antiquae*, ed. T. Park (London, 1804), vol. i, 17.
137 PRO SP63/202, part iii, 123, 'a plot for furnishing the provant apparel by Nicholas Weston, mayor of Dublin and five others of the inhabitants of the said city for the good of the soldier, and the great relief of the now decayed citizens'. For other Weston commercial ventures see J. C. Appleby, 'The fishing ventures of Nicholas Weston of Dublin', *Dublin Historical Record*, 39 (1986), 150–155.
138 *APC*, xxix, 238; and, for a typical warrant to pay a clothing merchant, PRO SP12/267, 43, docket to pay £2,443 16s 8d for winter apparel for ten bands of men, and £627 6s 8d for summer apparel.
139 PRO SP63/202, part iii, 185, Mostyn to Cecil, November 1598.
140 *CSPI* (1598 – March 1599), 37–39, Brouncker to Cecil, 22 January 1598.
141 *CSPI* (April 1599 – February 1600), 483–484, Jones to Cecil.
142 *CSPI* (November 1600 – July 1601), 357, Chichester to Mountjoy, 14 May 1601.
143 *CSPI* (1598 – March 1599), 209.
144 *Ibid.*, 357.
145 *CSPI* (January 1598 – March 1599), 286.
146 HMC, *Salisbury*, vii, 202, 203.
147 HMC, *Salisbury*, xi, 535, 536.
148 *CSPI* (1598–1599), 464.
149 HMC, *Salisbury*, ix, 178–179, Beecher to Cecil, 23 May 1599.
150 *CSPD* (1591–1594), 25.
151 HMC, *Salisbury*, xvi, 75–77.
152 H. Hall, *Society in the Elizabethan age* (3rd edn, London, 1888), 127.
153 *CSPI* (1599–1600), 442.
154 *Ibid.*, 442.
155 HMC, *Salisbury*, ix, 253, Buckhurst to Cecil, 30 July 1599.
156 H. Hall, *Society in the Elizabethan age* (3rd edn, London, 1888), 125–130.
157 *CSPI* (1599–1600), 466.
158 *CSPI* (1596–1597), 359.
159 *Ibid.*, 381, 383.
160 *Ibid.*, 413.
161 *Ibid.*, 299, 392.
162 PRO SP63/202, part ii, 18 May 1598.
163 *Ibid.*, part iii, 55, 'Errors to be reformed in Ireland', 1598.
164 PRO SP63/206, no. 116, 'The opinion and advice of Captain John Baynard to the Queen', December 1599.

165 PRO SP63/205, no. 109, Essex to the privy council, 15 July 1599.
166 *CSPI* (1599–1600), 310.
167 PRO SP63/207, no. 72, 'Instructions for the Lord Mountjoy, 1600'.
168 PRO SP63/208, part ii, no. 17, report from Lough Foyle, 22 April 1601; PRO SP63/209, no. 114, report from the same, 30 September 1601.
169 *APC*, xxx, 807.
170 HMC, *Salisbury*, viii, 162; HMC, *Salisbury*, ix, 253.
171 For the queen's debts to King James, which included £60,000 incurred on the Irish exchange during the debasement of the Irish coinage, see BL Additional MSS, 36, 970, ff. 17; BL Lansdowne MSS, 151, ff. 76–86.

CHAPTER NINE

The Elizabethan soldier at war

Strategy and tactics

There was no permanently paid standing army in Ireland in Elizabeth's reign. The nearest approach to such in the 1590s consisted of the soldiers in the manned forts or garrisons in or around the centres of Gaelic resistance, intended to be 'a bridle upon the Irish', and captained by a cadre of literate younger English gentry sons, distinct from the administrators and colonisers, with a natural interest in military strategy and tactics and authors of reform tracts. The same men were often troublemakers with the Irish enemy and when they had fought their battles, skirmishes and sieges, often with brutality, they were left unrewarded. Many were likened to frontiersmen, caught up in local Gaelic politics, marrying into their families, learning Irish, acquiring small estates and large debts around the fortified places they had defended during the war. Sir Henry Docwra's captains in their forts along the Foyle and those of Sir Arthur Chichester at Carrickfergus are representative of the cadre in Ulster – many of them to be the later servitors of the plantation era, such as Brooke, Cole, Hamilton, Leigh, Blaney and Brett, to name but a few.[1]

Many of long service in Ireland, like Captain Thomas Lee, recently described by Hiram Morgan as 'a soldier, marauder, squatter, debtor, poseur, pamphleteer, mediator, conspirator and jailbird', advised that at the initial stage of setting up a garrison 'the soldiers must be ready to fight for the ground where they purpose to set down and that obtained they are to expect daily assaults'.[2] 'To ring Ulster with forts' became a virtual cliché among military advisers – the province being regarded as the fountain head of all rebellion and the chief source of O'Neill's power in the war. All strategists agreed on the importance of a strong garrison at Lough Foyle as one of the most effectual measures to divide O'Neill from O'Donnell, hem in O'Neill and cut him off from Scottish support.

Francis Jobson, who had surveyed parts of Ulster in Sir William Fitzwilliam's time, recommended in 1598 sending an army of 11,000, of whom 2,000 would be cavalry, into Ulster and described eight different places for placing the garrisons; Jobson went on to point out that the greatest wealth of Ulster was in its herds of cows, horses and goats, that the people were most savage, and that when there he was in hourly danger of losing his head, which his colleague cartographer,[3] Richard Bartlett, actually did before finishing mapping Donegal.[4]

Captain Mostyn, who had twenty-seven years' military service in Ireland, advised an army of 13,000 foot and 2,000 horse with enough supplies for six months and all to be distributed over various parts of Ulster to cut off the rebels, to lift their cattle and to 'bring the whole issue to the cruelty of famine'. And by placing horsemen in the garrison he advised sudden raids from several quarters.[5]

Sir Ralph Lane, the muster master, stressed the need for competent commanders, those experienced in the 'plots and draughts' of the Irish, whose general martial skill, order and discipline 'for strong fights, both of horse and foot' were not to be underestimated, and recommended Coleraine and Belfast as well as strong camps in Leinster as the best places for garrisons. Lane reiterated what many another captain had said – that they must break their sleep who will do good service in Ireland.

That O'Neill's men made an elusive enemy is evident in contemporary writings and that they were well equipped with arms, armour, horse and ammunition in the final stage of the war is equally clear. They were also more conversant with the terrain of wood, bog and bush which they made work for them in skirmish, ambush and siege – their favourite tactics, rather than the set or pitched battle.[6] Fynes Moryson described how 'they dare not stand on a plain field but always fight upon bogs and passes of skirts of woods' and if their opponents began to retreat Moryson commented that the 'Irish were swift and terrible executioners … never believing the enemy to be fully dead till they have cut off their heads'. And should the Irish be forced to give ground they disappeared into the undergrowth, where pursuit was not recommended since they doubled back and slayed the unwary. Even Lord Mountjoy, the greatest of the Elizabethan commanders in Ireland, observed that when it came to hand-to-hand combat it was the Irish who usually prevailed. And though Moryson admits that they took slowly to firearms, nevertheless, by the end phase of the war, he conceded that they were well experienced in 'managing their pieces'. However, they were unable to march in an orderly fashion or to assault fortified garrisons or indeed to fight on an open plain – the latter being one of the major causes of their final defeat at Kinsale.[7]

Captain Nicholas Dawtrey almost at the beginning of hostilities, in May 1594, suggested three well placed garrisons at the Foyle, Carrickfergus and Blackwater, 'inclosing Tyrone in a triangle', would put a finish to the war in three years.[8] He was right about the placements but wide of the mark in his timing of the end of the war. Needless to say, there was much contemporary contradiction regarding the military capabilities of the Irish enemy.

By the beginning of the war there was little trace of earlier English influence in Ulster except for the small isolated and widely separated garrisons at Carrickfergus, Olderfleet (now Larne), Carlingford, Newry, Monaghan and a precarious and desultory presence in Maguire's castle at Enniskillen. By the end Mountjoy's captains had hedged Ulster about with a line of manned forts from Derry, south along the Foyle to Castlederg, across the south-west borders of Tyrone at Newtonstewart, Omagh, Clogher and Augher, and along the river Blackwater at Armagh, Mountjoy and Charlemont, thus completing a line of military communication around Ulster from Derry to Carrickfergus. Those established along the Foyle by Sir Henry Docwra were the most influential achievement in the subjugation of Ulster, or as Docwra put it himself 'the most desperate assignment'.[9] This Yorkshire captain, in one sense the founder of the modern city of Derry, could be considered one of the unsung victors of the Nine Years' War, overshadowed as he was by the brilliance of Mountjoy and the ruthlessness of Chichester. The lodgement and maintenance of his forces in garrisons along the Foyle from May 1600 could also be considered the most important single disposition in the strategy of reducing Ulster. Raids upon the enemy from the security of the camps were more profitable in that they secured 'preys of cattle' and according to Docwra more enjoyable than the labour of building forts where they had to fight for every stick and stone.[10] Many of his men became workshy, some actually breaking their spades and shovels.[11] Great numbers fell prey to sickness. In his grandiloquent letters to Cecil and the privy council, Docwra took every opportunity to include a veritable shopping list requesting not only more men but building materials, tools, arms, victuals, even fish and outrageously to Cecil's eyes 'a gallon of ink' on one occasion to write his exceptionally long letters. His men had hardly been established six months along the Foyle when the queen let it be known that she was unwilling to charge the shires with more levies when it was clear that 'to raw men such a place will rather serve now for a grave than a garrison'.[12]

The Derry fort and others along the river, like Lifford, Dunalong and Culmore, were erected under the supervision of Docwra's Dutch engineer, Joyes Everard, and his deputy surveyor, Thomas Rookewood. They are likely the cartographers of the series of remarkable military maps of these forts (e.g. Figure 1).[13] Many monastic and ecclesiastical buildings were destroyed in their erection or converted to military purposes, notably those at Derry and Donegal. The number of ships on the Foyle on the map shown in Figure 1 may represent the river's traffic, not just those provided for defence, since Docwra, in all his extensive writing, mentions only two ships retained by his garrison for river defence: *The Grace of God* of Newcastle and the *Samaritan* of London, as the *Peter* of Drogheda and the *Hoy* of Dublin had been discharged.[14] The prominently marked gallows on the Derry map was certainly used by Docwra in hanging hostages when pledges broke down; for example, he told the privy council in August 1601 that he was keeping some McSwiney hostages 'to be martyred' *in terrorem*.[15]

Derry and Lifford were the two main garrisons established by Docwra's forces in a line of others along the Foyle from the estuary at Culmore up to Strabane; they aimed to keep O'Neill and O'Donnell apart. Those around Carrickfergus on Ulster's eastern seaboard became bases for incursions to the shores of and across Lough Neagh into the O'Neill ancestral heartlands of County Tyrone. And from Ballyshannon and Beleek at the Atlantic outfall of the Erne detachments of troops would move out to fortify and garrison fording points over the Erne to put barriers between O'Donnell and O'Rourke, his ally, and thereby prevent their traditional routes into north Connaught. If they did not always succeed in keeping O'Donnell at home in Donegal they served to harass him when he returned laden with spoil.[16] And in the final stages of the war the additional forts with small garrisons established by Mountjoy on the southern borders of Ulster, at Charlemont, Mount Norris and, one named after himself, Mountjoy, helped to link up with those already established by Docwra and Chichester and were all of sufficient strength to support one another in a ring round the north. It was this strategy which was instrumental in the mopping-up military operations against O'Neill in his final fifteen-month resistance movement which ensued on his defeat at Kinsale.

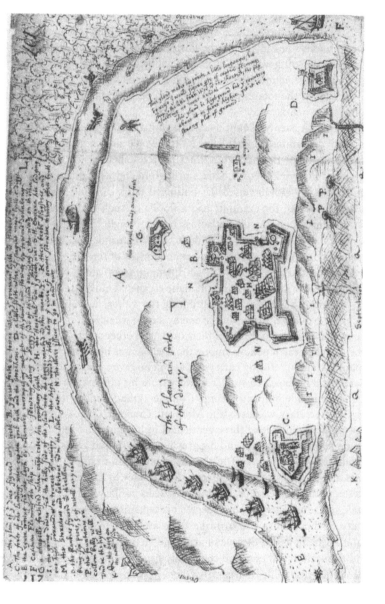

Figure 1 Map of the fort at Derry. Probably drawn by Joyes Everard and Thomas Rookewood, and taken from Sir Henry Docwra's reports. (Reproduced with permission of the Public Record Office, London.)

We are not here concerned with numbers of soldiers in these garrisons. Suffice it to say that Mountjoy increased the numbers surrounding Ulster. Fynes Moryson, his secretary, noted how on seven separate occasions he redistributed soldiers to meet the needs of incursions, skirmishes and battles between November 1600 and May 1603.[17] From time to time within that period Mountjoy withdrew small bodies of soldiers to augment his mobile field army in making his 'northern journeys' into O'Neill's lands.[18] After Kinsale, Moryson's army lists of April 1602 show a renewed concentration of soldiers in and around the Ulster borderlands, approximately 1,000 in the east, 1,500 in the south-west, 2,000 along the Foyle, west, and *circa* 3,000 in the series of forts from Donegal to Ballyshannon and along the Erne river and loughs, in all about 45 per cent of the total infantry forces and 34 per cent of the total cavalry then in Ireland.[19]

In isolating the Irish enemy Mountjoy had the notable advantage of sea power to support his land operations, particularly in the Foyle and notably at Kinsale. Whenever overland routes for victualling forts proved dangerous he used ships to send in provisions to Carrickfergus, Lecale, Carlingford and whenever apt, in a land of loughs and rivers, his captains used flat-bottomed boats carrying armed men to launch attacks. Chichester, for example, had a flotilla of such craft under Captain Hugh Clotworthy for his raiding parties across Lough Neagh.[20] Docwra had armed boat patrols on the Foyle and Henry Folliott, his commander at Ballyshannon, maintained armed boats and barges on the river and loughs of the Erne. Docwra also had a prison ship in the Foyle under Captain Fleming, from which McSwiney Ne Doe, one of his notable prisoners, made a dramatic escape.[21] Unlike previous military commanders, Mountjoy made his men fight during the winter; he employed them in surprise attacks, he had them cut down the enemy's corn when ripe, destroy it when sown, burn out their stores and drive off their cattle and other stock – he was a firm believer in the scorched earth policy. Among the Irish he was noted for his meanness in granting pardons and in refusing parleys. In action he gave a personal lead careless of his own safety and he expected similar bravery from his officers. Dr Latware, his chaplain, was killed beside him and George Cranmer, grand-nephew of the famous Marian martyr, his secretary, was also slain; Moryson, Cranmer's successor, suffered a severe thigh wound, as did at least three gentlemen of his immediate entourage. His favourite horse was shot under him and his greyhound shot dead at his stirrup. The chief commander clearly put himself in the firing line as an example to his men – these incidents told by Moryson also illustrate the accuracy of the Irish marksmen.[22]

Like Leicester in the Netherlands, Mountjoy issued a military code of discipline to improve morale and administration; he expected his captains to swear in his men with oaths of loyalty to the colours and to make them aware of regulations. Desertion carried the death penalty, as did the sale of arms and victuals to the enemy, as well as cowardice and fornication – these were commonly listed capital offences in military codes, but Mountjoy also added harbouring rebels, breaking rank and sleeping on sentry duty.[23] When Cecil and the privy council complained that Mountjoy was not doing enough about desertions he roundly replied that he had recently hanged sixteen and that if they in England would also do the same he would have better men in Ireland. And yet, Mountjoy was not as severe or as sadistic in his government of the army as Sir William Russell (1593–1596) had been, whose journal is littered with entries on the execution of soldiers.[24]

The ordinary soldier was certainly in constant danger, whether in garrison or with the mobile field armies, and he was almost always in a state of physical discomfort from the wet climate and hard labour at siege works and fortifications in garrison or exhausted by exacting marches in difficult terrain on 'journeys', as the Elizabethans called attacks on and skirmishes with the enemy. Mountjoy often demanded a ten-mile march a day. It was not the fixed battles but the small-scale skirmishes and sieges which characterised Irish warfare in the sixteenth century; these operations required fit and alert troops in mobile company units ready to improvise offensive and defensive action, but where corporate discipline and collective movement mattered less than intelligent initiative and familiarity with a variety of weaponry.

The war was not a glorious one but for students of strategy it provides much variety of military engagement, from the medieval-type siege and even what turned out to be a trial of strength between two leaders such as took place between Hugh Maguire and Sir Warham St Leger near Cork in February 1599, to the more formal battle, such as at the Yellow Ford, and to the more sophisticated skirmish which also combined naval and land operations, as at Kinsale. (In the trial of strength, which in fact had begun as a skirmish, St Leger shot Maguire with his pistol, through the body, but Maguire drove his lance into his opponent's skull – both died of their injuries.) The Irish ambush of the English marching column was of frequent occurrence, two of the most notable being the disaster suffered by Sir Conyers Clifford in the Curlew Mountains and the annihilation of Sir Henry Harington's forces in the Wicklow Mountains.[25] The tide of Irish military success in skirmish, ambush, sorties and surprise attacks on English arms began to turn with the determination of Mountjoy and the Elizabethan government to make a total conquest; Mountjoy had learned from his predecessor's mistakes – he would meet Irish tactics with equal ingenuity and above all he would concentrate his forces on invading and subduing Ulster.

In that final phase of the war all passages into Ulster from the south were hotly contested, not only that across the river Blackwater but also through the Moyry Pass, an area that saw some of the most prolonged close fighting of the war in September and October 1600. All dispatches mention foul tempestuous winds and weather and exceptional rainfall. William Farmer, the surgeon with Mountjoy's troops, wrote 'the weather was most inconstant, rain, boisterous winds, storms, tempests, the tents often overthrown, rent to pieces'.[26] Nicholas Dawtrey said he had never seen such rain in Ireland these thirty-seven years, so that he could never say 'all the clothes on my back were ever dry'.[27] He added that the Irish defence works of the pass were so expertly erected that it would not have been easy for swine to get through, let alone armed men.[28] While other reports play down the general effects on the soldiery of those two months of fighting in the passes of southern Ulster, Dawtrey was exceptionally blunt in his letter when he spoke of many horses dying and of the many sick and wounded men and of the difficulties of keeping a fire in the camps. Although 'he plied his troops with whiskey and wine I could not keep them from dropping with the country disease' (i.e. dysentery). He believed that the 'extremity of the weather killed more men than the enemy'.[29]

The centre of military operations necessarily switched from Ulster to Munster during the winter of 1601 with the Spanish landing at Kinsale on 23 September 1601. The whole enterprise is much commented upon in recent histories; suffice it to say here that it was much more than a single siege and battle, as the whole campaign around Cork and Kinsale from that September to Christmas is illustrative of every type of military engagement – small-scale defensive action against Spanish and Irish sorties, skirmishes and assaults on fortified bases, the full-scale siege of a major castle and walled town aided by naval bombardment, and a formal pitched battle at the end.[30]

The most effective and cruel means of shortening hostilities was the devastation of crops and this was systematically used from 1599 to 1602; the strategy was universally recognised as a legitimate method of warfare. The Earl of Essex's Munster 'journey' of mid-May to mid-July 1599 was undertaken to destroy all the local crops so that the Irish lords of the area could not feed mercenaries brought into Munster from Connaught.[31] O'Neill and O'Donnell also used this tactic, destroying crops on lands surrounding garrisons planted in Ulster, and on his incursions into Munster, O'Neill burnt out villages, stores of corn and plundered cattle. The greatest practitioners of the scorched earth policy were Mountjoy, Chichester and Carew. George Flower, one of Carew's captains in Munster, wrote of burning corn in the fields and drowning cattle on MacCarthy's lands in Cork.[32] The Irish annalists noted Mountjoy's methods and described how his soldiers used 'harrows, pracas, scythes and sickles to destroy ripe and unripe grain'.[33] English and Irish writers describe the results of the policy in equally graphic detail. Moryson, for example, commenting on the final drive into O'Neill's own lands, on one journey of about twelve miles between the two places mentioned, says: 'We found everywhere men dead of famine ... one O'Hagan protested unto us that between Tullogh [Tuallaghoge] and Tome [Toome] there lay unburied a thousand dead'.[34] Famine and widespread destruction were particularly noted by those captains who after the war were to possess estates. Mountjoy expressed some squeamishness about the effects his methods had on the civilian population. He wrote to Carew from Ulster in July 1602: 'We do now continually hunt all their woods, spoil their corn, burn their houses, and kill so many churls as it grieveth me to think that it is necessary to do it'.[35]

Sir Calisthenes Brooke, distinguished for his bravery, applied for a transfer to the Netherlands claiming he was not fulfilling his proper calling as a soldier in the Irish war which, he said, required huntsmen not professional soldiers.[36] Other captains and commanders, such as the Binghams in Connaught, Chichester at Carrickfergus or Carew in Munster, had few qualms about such actions against civilians. Wasting the enemy's resources and hinterland was based on the counter-revolutionary principle that if fish live in water as rebels live among the people the way to kill the fish is to dry up the water.

The strategy worked because it denied food to the Irish while the English forces could be supplied out of England, though the expense of maintaining the army in this way in the last years of the war was so great that the government was forced to debase the Irish coinage to support the war effort. Some historians see this debasement as a fitting end to the Elizabethan exploitation of the island, when 'shillings Irish were struck which contained no more silver than an English three-penny piece passing as a groat Irish'.[37] In one other respect the English forces had a complete advantage – the Irish were never able to challenge or disrupt English seapower in any significant way. Their only major disruptive naval challenge came from the pirate fleet commanded by Grace O'Malley, which made shipping difficult on the Atlantic seaboard of Connaught until 1598. English naval power was effectively used to plant garrisons, to aid in raising the siege at Kinsale, and to send in supplies, reinforcements and the habiliments of war via Lough Foyle, Belfast Lough, Carlingford and Dundalk for the northern garrisons, the ports of Dublin, Waterford and Cork for those of the south, and Galway and Limerick for the western outposts.

Many of the features of the Irish war were commonplace in European warfare. Mountjoy and his commanders took hostages, ignored offers of truce, destroyed crops, especially in areas where rebels were harboured, and generally deprived the enemy of food and shelter. Their light flying columns of troops soon became the equal of the Irish in mobility in hunting out and harrying pockets of resistance. In Ulster especially these operations were based on a network of garrisons and fortified blockhouses which the Irish, apparently lacking in artillery, could not storm. By such methods did Mountjoy, the last Elizabethan lord deputy, unlike his predecessors, concentrate on destroying O'Neill's chief power base in his Tyrone homelands. In so doing he spared neither himself, his men, nor, above all, the Irish.

Arms and armour

The Elizabethan soldier who carried out the reconquest did so with the new infantry weapons of the time: muskets, pikes, calivers and, to a lesser extent, small cannon. The celebrated English longbow was obsolete by the end of the sixteenth century. English writers in their lists of Irish weapons mention the bow, which they certainly used to deadly effect at the battle of the Curlews in 1599.[38] Archers, as a classification of trooper in the muster rolls, disappear by 1595, when the privy council ordained that they should no longer be enrolled in the companies.[39] Firearms, or 'weapons of fire', revolutionised warfare; more than half the infantry carried guns and in the muster lists are collectively termed 'shot'. The pike was the major defensive weapon but was carried by less than half the infantry; it was a stout shaft of wood, usually ash, twelve feet long or more and tipped with a sharpened iron blade; its traditional functions were to resist cavalry charges and to hold off enemy pikemen. The physically strongest men in the company carried or 'trailed the pike'. As well as firearms and pikes, swords and daggers were used and with the round shield or target these became the characteristic weapons in hand-to-hand fighting. O'Neill's forces were equally adept in the use of all these weapons, as is attested to by the military writers of the time, but Irish kern seemed to have also specialised in the use of the dart, thrown with great accuracy to disconcert horses and unarmed men.

The transport of artillery posed problems for mobile field forces. Communication by road was notoriously bad, especially in Ulster; Sir Henry Bagenal, for instance, tried to use field cannon at the Yellow Ford in August 1598 but had to abandon them in the boggy ground on his retreat.[40] Mountjoy made better use of smaller field artillery with pieces like the 'falcon' and the 'robinet' in his sorties into south Ulster across the Blackwater in July 1601.[41] Larger cannon, however, was still effective in its traditional role of attacking or defending fortifications. Given time to make strategic gun emplacements and plenty of shot, cannon proved decisive at a number of sieges. Contemporary maps all illustrate the successful English use of cannon. George Bingham's cannoneers were in action at the siege of Maguire's castle at Enniskillen in February 1594 and his musket fire from emplacements across the Erne and from longboats on the lough itself to the rear of the castle gave supporting fire.[42] This map is by the soldier/artist John Thomas and his other map, of the Battle of the Erne Fords, Belleek near Ballyshannon, fought on 10 October 1593, shows English musketeers enfilade Maguire's positions while infantry with sword and buckler or targets lead the assault across the ford; Maguire's hired galloglasses, Scots mercenaries, may also be seen with their characteristic weapon, the axe.[43]

The pictorial maps in Thomas Stafford's celebrated *Pacata Hibernia* are also illustrative of the successful use of cannon, for instance the Earl of Essex's siege of Cahir Castle in May 1599, a siege which the queen in her disillusionment with Essex's Irish venture dismissed as of no great matter, 'to have taken an Irish hold from a rabble of rogues'.[44] The Earl of Thomond's and Sir George Carew's attack on Glin Castle near Limerick, July 1600, also illustrated, shows the drawing up of saker and falcon to batter the walls. Stafford's description of the siege tells how Captain George Flower led the assault, of how many of the defenders leaped from the battlements into the river and of how Sir George Carew, 'a man that knows well how to manage great artillery', despite his skills had many difficulties in getting the cannon to fire.[45] Carew's success at what proved to be the last big siege of the war, Dunboy Castle on Bantry Bay, Cork, in June 1602, clearly shows the importance of cannon in Fynes Moryson's map of the siege. The inscription tells how the ordnance was brought in by sea and drawn up to within firing range of the barbican. Then, in his account of the military action, he wrote of how:

> our forces encamped within musket shot of the castle, but not within sight of the castle, a
> rising ground lying between the Camp and the Castle, so as the great shot from the castle
> flew over the camp without doing any hurt.

After a two-day battery Carew's men assaulted the breach and possessed part of Dunboy, but before they were masters of it all fighting continued within the walls for a day and a night. In the capture Carew took a demi-culverin, two sakers, a brass falcon, five minions and an iron falcon used by the Spanish and Irish in the long defence. Moryson then described how the castle was destroyed: 'nine barrels of powder taken in the castle were imployed to blow it up, lest any Spaniards or rebels might after make use of it'.[46]

All sixteenth-century weapons had disadvantages. The pike, while excellent in defence, required an exceptionally strong soldier to use it offensively and without the support of 'shot' the pikeman was vulnerable to the enemy's missile fire. The caliver and musket were much better as offensive weapons but their effective range was comparatively short and the rate of fire slow. Barnaby Rich reckoned that though the caliver had a range of between 350 and 400 yards it was only effective up to 300 yards, and he estimated that its rate of fire could vary between ten and forty rounds an hour. The heavier musket was more effective over 300 yards; it could fire heavier balls which could shatter armour, but it needed a support or rest and it had an even lower rate of fire than the caliver.[47] Firearms were of little use in heavy rain; both sides in the battle of the Moyry Pass in 1600 abandoned their pieces 'for neither side could take fire in the rain' and were forced 'to betake themselves unto their swords'.[48]

Firearms had not entirely superseded older weapons. The Irish, for example, employed Scottish archers at Clontibret in 1595. O'Donnell's men used javelins when they retook Enniskillen in the same year; Captain John Fuller was killed in that engagement by a throw of a javelin[49] and near Derry Sir Henry Docwra was wounded by a javelin.[50] O'Clery's *Life of Red Hugh O'Donnell* gives a very detailed account of the types of weapons used by the Irish. At the Yellow Ford they had 'plenty of broad-shouldered darts, and broad green spears, with strong handles of good ash. They had straight, keen swords, and light shining axes.' In the battle for the Curlew Mountains, between Sligo and Roscommon, O'Clery speaks of O'Donnell's forces as having:

> loud-sounding, straight shooting guns, and ... strong bows ... and bloody venomous javelins ... strong keen edged swords and polished thin edged battleaxes, with large headed, smooth narrow lances ... and long smooth spears.[51]

The spears and lances were probably pikes, but it is of interest that axes, javelins and bows were still in use. The primitive nature of some weapons mentioned in these Irish sources may give a misleading impression of an ill-equipped Irish soldiery. In fact this is far from the case. Carew thought some of the Ulster soldiers who fought against him in Munster in 1600 to be 'the best furnished men for the war, and the best appointed we have seen in this Kingdom'.[52] The Earl of Essex in writing to the queen acknowledged the Irish were more skilful in handling their weapons than the English.[53] Others said that O'Neill's men were a better-trained force than the queen's, as good marksmen as France, Flanders or Spain could show, and 'came as little short of the English for proportion and provision as they were for the skill and use of arms'.[54]

From English muster lists it is clear that firearms were carried by about 60 per cent of the company, pikes and halberds by 40 per cent. In the 1596 levy for Ireland the 'shot' amounted to half the total. One in four of these were armed with muskets and the other three with the light caliver; the other half of the total were pikemen and a few halberdiers.[55] The general tendency throughout the war was not only to increase the proportion of firearms against pikes but also to increase the light calivers as against the heavier muskets. A muster list made before the battle of Clontibret of Sir Henry Bagenal's force in 1595 illustrates this tendency and also shows how the proportions between weapons could vary between companies. Here firearms predominated, making up approximately 65 per cent of all the companies, against 35 per cent pikes and halberds, but between companies a wide variation can be noted which was likely due to availability of particular weapons, or the lack of them at the muster and review. Many of the soldiers in the muster were comparatively untrained recruits and perhaps for that reason there is no mention of swords, which required much skill in fighting at close quarter. The halberd, not yet an exclusively ceremonial weapon, was used by the commander's bodyguard and to protect ensigns carrying the colours.[56] There is no mention of the bill, with its hooded blade and spike, which resembled the halberd and was likely obsolete. Carew, master of ordnance, remarked in 1590 on the futility of the government sending him 'old brown bills' and 'long bows': he told Burghley that these weapons 'are held in such scorn, that unless I should sell them to the farmers of the Pale ... I am in despair to utter them'.[57]

A more experienced force than that mustered at Clontibret drew up a three-lined battle formation under Sir Conyers Clifford and fought in the Curlews on Sunday 5 August 1599. The vanguard, led by Sir Alexander Ratcliffe, had 385 men with firearms and 186 'armed', that is with pikes; Lord Dunkellin commanded the 'battle' line with 256 'shot' and 165 'armed'; and Sir Arthur Savage led the rearguard with 344 'shot' and 160 'armed'.[58] Pikes, halberds and targets, collectively called 'armed', were in about the same proportions as at Clontibret.

Mountjoy's muster at Dundalk in 1600, however, shows the proportion of pikes and targets, 'armed men', at 42 per cent. By the following year, when Mountjoy mustered near Newry in June 1601, there were 291 pikes, 112 targets, 635 calivers and 125 muskets in his total force of 1,250, a proportion of 39 per cent 'armed men', 3 per cent lower than in his muster of the previous year.[59] The preference for the lighter firearm can be seen in the orders sent to the ordnance officers in London to dispatch to Ireland 1,000 calivers as against only 100 muskets.[60]

Arms arriving from the shire levies were never enough. The Dublin council wrote to the privy council in May 1598 asking for good quantities of weapons to be speedily sent. They calculated that:

> By the death and running away of soldiers, and by their selling and embezzling their arms, as well to the rebels as to the country people, and through weapons being broken, lost and consumed there cannot but be a great want of the same.[61]

The Earl of Essex reminded the privy council that 'when reinforcements come over they bring arms ... for here in service the arms decay faster than the men'; he added that the stores were so diminished as to be of little help to any new levy.[62] Lord Mountjoy advised the privy council to have '3,000 especial good swords, broad and basket-hilted provided ... for those swords sent out of the counties with the soldiers are nothing worth'.[63]

Joshua Aylmer, in reporting a skirmish near Cork in April 1600 to Cecil, tells him how a company of infantry lacking firearms and armed only with sword and pike encouraged the enemy so much that the whole force would have been overthrown had not the horse troops come to the rescue, and 'in that fight we lost thirty horses'.[64]

Mountjoy pointed out to the privy council what happened to a soldier if he broke his firearm. If his captain did not have an allowance for broken arms, he would turn him into a pikeman, and 'so our shot prove very few, and our pikes many more than we have use of'.[65] Sir Arthur Chichester complained about defective guns sent to him, reiterating Mountjoy's opinion of arms from the shires. He particularly blamed conductors of troops out of Yorkshire who bought cheap arms in Chester, 'not thinking of the loss and danger it brings unto us who are to adventure our lives with them'.[66]

Was it the government's fault that arms were often wanting? Contracts with arms suppliers appear to have sufficiently covered the numbers in the levies sent over to Ireland, and yet the ordnance office in Dublin continually sought additional arms and munitions and commanders constantly petitioned for more supplies. Military operational failure was often put down to bad arms or lack of them. Sir Henry Docwra's Lough Foyle garrisons, for instance, occasionally blamed their lack of success on the want of good arms.[67]

Infantry forces of 'shot' and 'armed men' formed the bulk of the fighting forces. Cavalry, potentially the principal arm and most powerful force on the battlefield, never achieved prominence in late Elizabethan Ireland. Its heyday would be in the future, with Oliver Cromwell and the New Model Army.[68] The heavily armed knight on a charger was clumsy and expensive; chargers were likely scarce, having to be well fed and exercised and their riders extremely skilled, for the use of the lance on horseback was 'a thing of much industry and labour to learn'.[69] Cavalry fully armed are hardly mentioned in the 1590s because their place was gradually taken over by the light horse or demi-lance, so called because their chief weapon was still the lance or horseman's staff.

In Ireland the cavalry was arranged in troops of a hundred, fifty and twenty-five, and at times bands as small as ten or twelve are mentioned in accounts of raids and skirmishes such as those undertaken by Docwra's scattered garrisons into Donegal, Innishowen and north Tyrone.[70] But the smaller units of horse are also mentioned in the many army lists throughout Carew's papers and in Fynes Moryson's *Itinerary*.[71] There were far fewer cavalry forces than infantry active in Ireland. In muster lists, totals of 1,200 horse and 14,000 foot are typical. The army list of 1595, for example, shows 657 horse to 4,040 foot.[72] In the field army under Mountjoy in 1601 there were 124 horse to 2,150 foot,[73] while in the great concentration of forces at Kinsale there was but a total of 857 horse as against 11,800 foot.[74]

Small bands of horsemen were vulnerable to a resolute square pike formation and when the enemy chose uneven terrain an old-fashioned cavalry charge could prove disastrous. Occasionally, as at Kinsale, charges were successful where the Irish had been driven on to open ground and there forced to fight on English terms. The well known woodcuts in John Derricke's celebrated *Image of Irelande* (1581) (see Figure 2) show English cavalry using the lance underhand, in contrast to the Irish, who used it overhand; they show the horseman's lance resembling the pike in length and head, but as thicker at the butt and bored through at the butt end to take a leather thong for fastening on to the arm.[75] By the 1590s a proportion, ideally a third, of the cavalry units carried firearms, variously termed harquebusiers, argualiters, pistoleers or petronels, and collectively known as 'shot on horse'. Mountjoy's ordinances issued in February 1600 state that 'a third of the horse be shot-on-horseback', so that 'the meanest horses will be as serviceable as the greatest'.[76] By the end of the sixteenth century the arquebus had a standard bore or calibre and the phrase then in use 'arquebus of calibre' soon became abbreviated to caliver.[77] Calivers or handguns were an early form of the matchlock with a snaphance and, because one type was held against the chest, they

Figure 2   A woodcut from John Derricke's Image of Irelande *(1581) – Sir Henry Sidney's army in battle with an Irish force.*

became known in England as petronel from the French *poitrinal*.[78] The smallest handgun, the pistol, became more versatile with the development of the wheel-lock, which did away with the need for match. Some of these horsemen carried three such pistols, 'two in cases and one at the girdle, or at the hinder part of the saddle.'[79] And all cavalrymen carried a sword and dagger as a secondary means of defence. Like his colleagues on foot with a musket or a caliver, the shot on horseback also needed 'a flash and touchbox for his piece' and a bullet bag at his girdle, the ancestor of the bandolier.[80] When the horseman came face to face with the enemy he could either charge into the mêlée or engage him from a short distance with his shot, wheeling away to reload and returning to fire.[81] This, at least, was the theory, which rarely had the chance to be tested in practice for only on a few occasions, such as at Clontibret and Kinsale, did the Irish accept the challenge of the open battlefield.[82]

The army had no means of making gunpowder in Ireland. All supplies had to be imported from England. Its manufacture and supply came under the control of the ordnance office. Licensed powder makers had to import sulphur, but saltpetre was made from lime, ashes and earth treated with animal excrement; there was a plentiful supply of charcoal, the third essential ingredient.[83] In 1599 powder makers contracted to supply the government 100 lasts of gunpowder a year at 7*d* the pound, and any surplus was authorised to be sold to private merchants at 10*d* the pound.[84]

Shipping and distributing gunpowder to Ireland caused problems. Delays in transport, careless storage in the ships and bad weather conditions meant that consignments of powder and match arrived in Ireland wet, rotten and therefore unusable. Sir Henry Docwra, for example, checked the unloading of munitions in Derry from the *George* of Chester to find the match and powder wet and deficient.[85] There was often insufficient powder sent and accidental powder explosions further reduced the valuable commodity. Stocks of powder ran dangerously low. On one occasion, for instance, there was not a single barrel of powder in Dublin while forty-four cart loads were waiting to be shipped from Chester.[86]

The private soldier was expected to buy his own gunpowder. The soldier knew that the more powder he used the less money he would have for life's necessities. When the Earl of Essex wanted a free issue of gunpowder the idea was dismissed as being against all reason, equity, good order and justice.[87] Some captains were strongly against the custom of their men having to purchase their own powder. One of them said it turned brave men into cowards. Another claimed that the practice made the soldier unwilling to burn powder 'because he by that means thinketh he should starve his belly or his back'.[88] Buckhurst agreed in January 1600 to give soldiers in Ireland free issue of powder when about to go into action.[89] In Mountjoy's time there was also occasional issue of free powder for training sessions as well as for battle. A satisfactory state of affairs was finally reached in 1601 when the privy council decided that the private soldier would not in future have to bear the cost of gunpowder or replace arms lost on the field of battle.[90]

The safekeeping of stores of munitions in Ireland was aided by restricting storage to 'common halls or town houses of cities or towns' and reserving issue only to authorised army personnel.[91] But this did not prevent abuse. James Perrot claimed in his *Chronicle* that this proclamation would have done much to prevent an illicit trade in powder 'if it had byn well observed ... but nyther proclamacion nor lawes will prevyale unlesse they be well executed'.[92] Captains and other officers were accused of taking out barrels of powder on pretence of immediate service, then selling or pledging it so that official stocks were sometimes empty, putting soldiers in danger of their lives. At Clontibret Captain Nicholas Merriman ran short of ammunition and powder, so he had to send out a detachment of pikes 'to charge uppon Tyrone's shot'. In that battle the Irish were said to have expended fourteen barrels of powder or 1,400 lb to the English ten barrels.[93] Dublin's corporation records noted in the same month that two companies of recruits marching out of the city were 'taken with a Scarborowe warninge [apparently a contemporary expression for any sudden movement] ... all unfurnished for powder and shot'.[94]

In every war human error can cost lives; accidents with gunpowder were frequently reported from the Elizabethan forces in Ireland. In May 1598, for example, Captain Wilton's men at Enniscorthy in Wexford, facing the rebel forces of Owney O'Moore, were devastated when one Goldwell 'wolde not give them pouder tyll he sawe wheather theare weare cause of service or not'. O'Moore, observing the confusion, attacked 'so that the soldiers coming thick together to receive pouder, it fell on fire and so was consumed'. O'Moore pressed home his advantage and 'before ten of the clocke before noone thear was slayne of the Queene's souldiers 309 and the rest putt to flight to save themselves'. The English force was almost wiped out; William Farmer, a surgeon with the army, in reporting the incident said that there were only 400 men in the

Enniscorthy garrison.[95] At the Yellow Ford in August 1598 a soldier went to fill his flask from the open powder barrel with a lighted match in his hand; the inevitable explosion which followed helped to cause the retreat and rout.[96]

The absence of match could be almost as troublesome. In August 1601 Sir Henry Docwra's planned excursion to link up with Mountjoy's into the heartlands of Tyrone had to be called off when it was discovered that no match had been provided. In his *Narration* Docwra recalled the embarrassment:

> I called for the clerk and asked him the reason. He told me he had it not, Now (says I) did you not tell me you had 60 barrels: I told you (said he) that I had 60 barrels: of powder, and so I had, but of match you ask me nothing.[97]

The clerk's literal following of instructions led to the expedition's failure to meet up with Mountjoy, followed by sharp criticism from the lord deputy and privy council. Docwra made amends by the successful capture of Donegal castle and abbey from O'Donnell but the powder magazines blew up in the abbey and killed about thirty of Docwra's men in the newly established garrison.[98]

The most devastating and spectacular explosion of gunpowder occurred in Dublin on Friday 11 March 1597, when a consignment of 140 barrels from the Tower of London blew up on the quayside, leaving dead 126 'men, women, children and fifty of these were strangers'; many merchant houses in Wood Quay and Winetavern Street were obliterated. The mayor's enquiry into the cause ruled out sabotage but John Allen, the chief clerk of munitions, was shown to have displayed negligence in having the barrels transported up to the castle; apparently his porters were on strike and the forced labour engaged included children. The immediate cause was accidental, likely the result of a horse's hoof striking sparks from the cobbled quayside into single-shelled casks. The city council computed the losses at £14,076, which the state revenues could ill afford – the restoration work was incomplete ten years later, as is evident from John Speed's map of Dublin *circa* 1610. Two leading merchants and two aldermen were questioned by the council on alleged gun-running activities to O'Neill, who had sympathisers among all ranks of the Dublin citizenry.[99]

The greatly increased use of firearms hastened the obsolescence of heavy armour. In a guerrilla war in which the skirmish rather than the set battle was the most characteristic action the soldier needed to be lightly accoutred. Little armour was worn other than morions or helmets, 'well stuffed' for comfort, and cuirasses made of layers of oxhide to protect the chest and back. The traditional metal corslet, the body armour of the pikeman, was more rarely used. Pikemen wore the corslet, a metal shell for the torso, pauldrons, vambraces and tasses, metal plates protecting shoulders, arms and thighs, and gauntlets for the hands and wrists. Captains rightly considered such a weight of armour to be an encumbrance.[100] These items of armour continued to be supplied but often lay unused. Humphrey Covet, muster master at Lough Foyle, told Cecil in December 1600 that 'no headpieces or armours for footmen be now, or hereafter sent to Lough Foyle, because they are never worn ... but negligently scattered and buried in the soil of every quarter'.[101] Captain Dawtrey reported in February 1601 that it was a common fault that no pikeman in Ireland 'weareth curates and morions'.[102] The well known war of words between military writers of late Elizabethan England on the relative merits of the longbow and the gun had its counterpart in the argument about protective armour,[103] but it would seem that soldiers in Ireland decided for themselves upon the lightest possible body protection when in action. Sir George Bourchier, master of ordnance in 1594, asked Lord Burghley's permission to exchange or sell 1,000 corslets 'of an old fashion'.[104] Sir Urian Leigh wanted to abandon the morion or steel helmet in favour of caps for his Cheshire company of 1596. Leigh regarded morions 'as needless' but he was persuaded by the Cheshire commissioners to use the helmets.[105]

By comparison with the English, the Irish soldier wore little or no armour, yet it is clear from Irish accounts of engagements that they too wore the morion and some of their cavalrymen wore chain mail over padded jackets in the same manner as the English light cavalry. In 1600, for example, an Irish ambush was detected when the sunlight glinted off their morions.[106]

Reports of fighting illustrate the effectiveness of some body protection and the foolhardiness of its absence. Dermot O'Connor, an Irish captain, said he saved his life from a musket ball by taking it on his target – the old-fashioned shield still had a use outside hand-to-hand combat in a sword fight.[107] O'Sullivan Beare's report of a duel between Rory O'Donnell, the younger brother of Red Hugh, and an unnamed English sergeant described how the sergeant's jerkin of oxhide 'whether owing to the toughness of the leather, or some spell' saved him for a time until O'Donnell forced him into a river and held him under water at pike point until he drowned.[108] Sir Henry Bagenal at the Yellow Ford, having raised his visor, was struck in the face by a bullet and was killed.[109] Sir Henry Docwra was luckier to have survived a head wound from the cast of a javelin because he was wearing his helmet.[110]

Armoured or not, soldiers inevitably died. William Farmer, the army surgeon, wrote of Sir Henry Norris's fatal wound: 'shot into the leg and all the bones broken, which came to a gangrene whereof he died'. In his account of the battle of the Moyry Pass, September 1600, Farmer dwelt on some of the injuries with a professional interest:

> Sir Oliver Lambert was shott in the syde, Sir Christopher St. Lawerence in the neckbone, Captaine Gainsford in the hypp, Captain Rush in the bellye, Captain Harvey in the kne pan, four or five lieutenantes hurte and one slayne. Sir William Godolphin had his horse braynes dasht in his face.

Later, at Carlingford, November 1600, Farmer noted further injuries: Sir Henry Danvers was shot 'in the thygh', Captain Handford 'in the rynes of the back'; Captain Trevor 'in the arme', and Sir Thomas Norris died 'of an apoplexie which grew in his head after a wound'.[111]

Accurate contemporary accounts of battles are rare; the vanquished were seldom in a position to commit to writing a version of what they thought had gone wrong, even if they knew. The victorious, for their part, tended to exaggerate their success and were more concerned with the fact of their victory than the method of its achievement. War in any period can be seen as a competition in which the participants seek to inflict maximum suffering on each other. Military histories which ignore this central fact to concentrate on the glories of victories in arms or to explain away defeats on the battlefield do not give the whole story. For many of the soldiers the experience of injury or death was probably a more pressing reality than the elation of victory. While precise figures are difficult to obtain it is thought that casualties from hostilities, disease and inadequate medical care were high in the last years of the Irish war.

Notes

1 J. J. N. McGurk, 'The recruitment and transportation of Elizabethan troops and their service in Ireland, 1594–1603', PhD thesis (University of Liverpool, 1982), appendix ii, 550–578, a list of captains in which the servitors have been identified. A. J. Sheehan, Head of the Arts Computing Unit at Queen's University, Belfast, subsequently compiled a more complete database of such captains.

2 BL Additional MSS 33743, f. 97d, Lee's 'Discoverie, recoverie and apologie of Irelande', and see H. Morgan, *Tyrone's rebellion* (London, 1993), Chapter 7.

3 PRO SP63/202, part iv, no. 83.

4 J. H. Andrews, 'Geography and government in Elizabethan Ireland', in *Irish geographical studies*, eds N. Stephens and R. E. Glassock (Belfast 1970), 181.

5 *CSPI* (January 1598 – March 1599), cited in the preface, xv.

6 *Ibid.*, xvi.

7 For Moryson's close observations of Irish fighting men and their methods see his celebrated *Itinerary*, vols ii and iii.

8 *CSPI* (1592–1596), 247.

9 For Docwra's appointment see Lambeth Palace Library, Carew MSS, 621, f.75, 'Letters Patent to Sir Henry Docwra'.

10 H. Docwra, *Relation and Narration*, ed. J. O'Donovan (Dublin, 1849), 239.

11 *CSPI* (1600–1601), 160.

12 *CSPI* (1600), 417.

13 PRO SP63/207, part vi, no. 84, i, ii, iii, military maps of Derry, Lifford and Dunalong.

14 *Ibid.*, no. 64.

15 *CSPI* (1601–1603), 21.

16 *CSPI* (1600), 202, 260, 265, 279, 291, 305.

17 Fynes Moryson, *Itinerary*, vol. ii, 253.

18 *Ibid.*, 343, 359, 431, 432.

19 *Ibid.*, vol. iii, 11, 12–14 and vol. iii, 151, percentages calculated on Moryson's lists.

20 *CSPI* (1601–1603), 63, 64, 396–397.

21 *CSPI* (1600), 280, 313 and see Docwra's vivid description of McSwiney's escape to Cecil, PRO SP63/207, part iv, no. 97, 29 August 1600.

22 Fynes Moryson, *Itinerary*, vol. ii, 269 and throughout vol. iii; see also a modern biography by F. M. Jones, *Mountjoy: the last Elizabethan Deputy* (Dublin, 1958) especially Chapters 7 and 12.

23 *Cal. Carew MSS*, iii, 502–505, Mountjoy's military code, and for a typical military oath of loyalty BL Additional MSS 30, 170, f.35.

24 *CSPI* (1600), 94, 351, 505, and for Russell's Irish journal, *Cal. Carew*, iii, 226ff.

25 *Ibid.*, 14–16, 18, 33, 36; *CSPI* (1598–1599), 227–229, 241, 253–254, despatches after the Yellow Ford; and see Trinity College, Dublin, MS 1209/12, for a map of Harington's defeat 1599. The main military actions of the war are to be found in C. Falls, *Elizabeth's Irish wars* (London, 1950) and in G. A. Hayes-McCoy, *Irish battles* (London, 1969).

26 W. Farmer, *Chronicles of Ireland 1594–1613*, ed. C. Litton Falkiner, *English Historical Review*, 22 (1907), 119–120.
27 *CSPI* (1600), 531, Dawtrey's report to Cecil, 28 October 1600.
28 *Ibid.*
29 *Ibid.*, 533.
30 The fullest single contemporary account of Kinsale is Fynes Moryson's *Itinerary*, vol. iii, 40–92; there are about twenty-three other contemporary accounts of the action. The best modern history is J. J. Silke, *Kinsale: the Spanish intervention in Ireland* (Liverpool, 1970).
31 *Cal. Carew MSS*, iii, 307.
32 D. MacCarthy, ed., *Life and letters of Florence MacCarthy Mór* (Dublin, 1867), Chapter 8 and 242–243.
33 *AFM*, vi, 2187; *praca* was an Irish term for a spiked harrow to uproot weeds.
34 Fynes Moryson, *Itinerary*, vol. iii, 208.
35 *Cal. Carew MSS*, iv, 264.
36 Cited in E. Spenser, *A view of the present state of Ireland* (1596), ed. W. L. Renwick (Oxford, 1934, reprint 1970).
37 M. Dolley, 'Anglo-Irish monetary policies, 1172–1637', *Historical Studies*, 7 (1969), 58.
38 *CSPI* (1599–1600), 91, 113–114.
39 C. Oman, *A history of the art of war in the sixteenth century* (London, 1937), 384.
40 *CSPI* (1598–1599), 242, Captain Kingsmill's dispatch from that battle.
41 Fynes Moryson, *Itinerary*, vol. ii, 408.
42 BL Cotton MSS, Augustus I, ii, 39.
43 *Ibid.*, 38.
44 T. Stafford, *Pacata Hibernia* (London, 1810 facsimile edn), illustration facing p. 76, reproduction about half the original and for the queen's comment; *Cal. Carew MSS*, iii, 315, the queen to Essex, 19 July 1599.
45 T. Stafford, *Pacata Hibernia* (London, 1810 facsimile edn), 115, 116, and for another account of the siege at Glin, *CSPI* (1599–1600), 260.
46 Fynes Moryson, *Itinerary*, vol. iii, illustration facing p. 288, and p. 285 for Moryson's account. Other descriptions of the siege are in T. Stafford, *Pacata Hibernia* (London, 1810 facsimile edn), vol. ii, 283, and in P. O'Sullivan Beare's *Historiae Catholicae Iberniae Compendium* (Lisbon, 1621), vol. iii, Chapters 8–12 (the author's uncle, Donall O'Sullivan Beare, defended Dunboy with the help of the Spaniards).
47 Barnaby Rich, *Pathway to military discipline and practise* (London, 1587), cited in H. Webb, *Elizabethan military science: the books and the practice* (Madison, 1965), 93.
48 *CSPI* (1600), 524ff., 'The Lord Deputy's Journal of his journey unto the north', 28 October 1600, endorsed by Sir Robert Cecil.
49 Philip O'Sullivan Beare, *Historiae Catholicae Iberniae Compendium* (Lisbon, 1621), ed. and trans. in part by M. J. Byrne, *Ireland under Elizabeth* (Dublin, 1903), 81.
50 H. Docwra, *Narration*, ed. J. O'Donovan (Dublin, 1849), 242.
51 M. O'Clery, *The life of Red Hugh O'Donnell*, ed. P. Walsh (Dublin, 1948), vol. i, 175, 176.
52 *Cal. Carew MSS*, iv, preface, lxii, footnote.
53 T. Stafford, *Pacata Hibernia*, 43.
54 For some English captain's opinions of Irish soldiers see *CSPI* (1596–1597), 27, 38, 151; *CSPI* (1598–1599), 38, 338, 507.
55 *APC*, xxv, 262.
56 L. Marron printed Bagenal's muster lists in *Irish Sword*, 2 (1957), 368ff.
57 *Cal. Carew MSS*, iii, 40, Carew to Burghley, 26 July 1590.
58 S. O'Domhnaill, 'Warfare in sixteenth century Ireland', *Irish Historical Studies*, 5 (1946), 29–54.
59 Fynes Moryson, *Itinerary*, vol. ii, 334–336, 403.

60 *APC*, xxx, 374.
61 *CSPI* (1598–1599), 138.
62 *CSPI* (1599–1600), 30.
63 *Ibid.*, 448.
64 *CSPI* (1600), 113.
65 *CSPI* (1600–1601), 441.
66 *CSPI* (1601–1603), 207.
67 *CSPI* (1599–1600), 227, 228; *CSPI* (1601–1603), 25, 126, 144, 155, 164.
68 D. Murphy, *Cromwell in Ireland* (Dublin, 1883), 434, 435.
69 *Cal. Carew MSS*, iii, 365, Mountjoy's ordinances, February 1600.
70 PRO SP63/208, part ii, 19; PRO SP63/207, part iii, 133; PRO SP63/208, part iii, 12, mentions of cavalry action in Docwra's letters, June 1600 – June 1601.
71 *Cal. Carew MSS*, iii, 127, 288; *Cal. Carew MSS*, iv, 92, 93, 296; Fynes Moryson, *Itinerary*, vol. ii, 345–348, 431, vol. iii, 40, 41, 146, 249, 338.
72 *Cal. Carew MSS*, iii, 127–128.
73 *Cal. Carew MSS*, iv, 92–94.
74 Fynes Moryson, *Itinerary*, vol. iii, 40–43, 'The Lyst of the Army at Kinsale the twentieth of November 1601'.
75 J. Small, ed., *The image of Irelande by John Derricke, 1581* (London, 1883), plate ix, for example.
76 *Cal. Carew MSS*, iii, 365, Mountjoy's ordinances, February 1600.
77 J. Fortescue, *A history of the British army* (London, 1899), vol. i, 101–103, 137.
78 C. Oman, *A history of the art of war in the sixteenth century* (London, 1937), 84–87.
79 Cited in H. Webb, *Elizabethan military science: the books and the practice* (Madison, 1965), 117.
80 J. Fortescue, *A history of the British army* (London, 1899), vol. i, 137.
81 C. Oman, *A history of the art of war in the sixteenth century* (London, 1937), 86.
82 *CSPI* (1592–1596), 320ff. for the battle of Clontibret; and for the use of cavalry at Kinsale see *CSPI* (1601–1603), 240ff.
83 *Calendar of patent rolls, Ireland*, ii, 188, for licences to make gunpowder for the ordnance department of the Tower of London.
84 C. G. Cruickshank, *Elizabeth's army* (2nd edn, Oxford, 1970), 127.
85 *CSPI* (1601–1603), 25.
86 *CSPI* (1600–1601), lxi.
87 *CSPI* (1599–1600), 380.
88 PRO SP63/202, part ii, 38.
89 *CSPI* (1599–1600), 380.
90 *APC*, xxxii, 337.
91 *Cal. Carew MSS*, iii, 120.
92 James Perrot, *The chronicle of Ireland, 1584–1608*, ed. H. Wood (Irish Manuscripts Commission, Dublin, 1933), 110.
93 G. A. Hayes-McCoy, *Irish battles* (London, 1969), 124–128.
94 J. T. Gilbert, ed., *Calendar of the ancient records of Dublin* (Dublin, 1891), vol. ii, 349–350.
95 William Farmer, *Chronicles of Ireland 1594–1613*, ed. C. L. Falkiner, *English Historical Review*, 85 (1907), 108.
96 Philip O'Sullivan Beare, *Historiae Catholicae Iberniae Compendium* (Lisbon, 1621), ed. and trans. M. J. Byrne, *Ireland under Elizabeth* (Dublin, 1903), 110.
97 H. Docwra, *Narration*, ed. J. O'Donovan (Dublin, 1849); and *CSPI* (1600–1601), 426; *APC*, xxxii, 181–189, the privy council's rebuke to Docwra.
98 *CSPI* (1601–1603), 92–95, Docwra to the privy council, 28 September 1601; *ibid.*, 97–99, Docwra to Cecil, report of the Donegal disaster.

99 C. Lennon, 'Dublin's great explosion of 1597', *History Ireland*, 3, no. 3 (1995), 29–34, for a popular account of the event.

100 G. A. Hayes-McCoy, *Irish battles* (London, 1969), 62, 92, 110ff., 124, 127.

101 *CSPI* (1600–1601), 113, Covert to Cecil, December 1600.

102 *Ibid.*, 183, Dawtrey to Cecil, 9 February 1601.

103 M. J. D. Cockle, ed., *A bibliography of English military books 1642 and of contemporary foreign books* (London, 1900) is the best guide to contemporary military writers, and for selected arguments and counter-arguments see J. R. Hale, *The art of war and Renaissance England* (Washington, 1961), *passim*.

104 *CSPI* (1592–1596), 230, Bourchier to the privy council, 10 April 1594.

105 PRO SP63/194, 133d, Sir Urian Leigh's muster roll and letter; Mountjoy's instructions of 1600, PRO SP63/207, part i, 72, January 1600.

106 P. Walsh, trans. and ed., *O'Clery's life of Red Hugh O'Donnell* (Dublin, 1948).

107 *Ibid.*, 167.

108 Philip O'Sullivan Beare, *Historiae Catholicae Iberniae Compendium* (Lisbon, 1621), ed. and trans. M. J. Byrne, *Ireland under Elizabeth* (Dublin, 1903), 137.

109 *Ibid.*, 111.

110 Docwra, *Relation and narration*, ed. J. O'Donovan (Dublin, 1849), 229.

111 W. Farmer, *Chronicles of Ireland*, ed. C. Litton Falkner, *English Historical Review*, 85 (1907), 113, 115, 118, 119.

Casualties and welfare measures for the sick and wounded of the Nine Years' War

In official military histories of sixteenth-century warfare wherein arms, strategy and logistics necessarily predominate, the human cost in combatants, the sick, wounded and dead are comparatively neglected. In every sixteenth-century campaign, in Ireland as elsewhere, disease was a greater killer than battle wounds. Army surgeons and field hospitals tried in vain to cope with both. For those who survived, welfare measures were taken in England when they returned from Ireland, but there was an attempt made to rehabilitate the sick and wounded in Ireland.

At the end of the war, virtually co-terminus with Queen Elizabeth's death on 24 March 1603, demobilisation was anticipated with dread in many ports and shires; some of the soldiers had been vagrants whose return was not expected. Others had performed honourable service and came back wounded to their native parishes sorry witnesses of the horrors of war. Some went home unpaid and others were unable to take up their former employment. The shires were burdened with paying pensions for maimed soldiers and the steady increase of masterless returning men added to the problems of poverty and vagrancy at a time when such problems strained the meagre resources and nascent shire poor law administration. By May 1602, as the war in Ireland was nearing its close, the privy council claimed it was the Irish war, not the conflict with Spain in the Low Countries or in France, which had impoverished England. The Irish conquest went on for nearly nine years largely because of Gaelic resistance in Ulster, which was then at its peak, and equally because the Elizabethan government had ploughed too much in men and money to lose sovereignty over Ireland. Whether the Elizabethan reconquest vindicated the human and material loss of the war is not the purpose of this chapter; it sets out rather to examine some aspects of the casualties, as well as the provision of care for the sick and wounded both in Ireland and on their return to England. Provision for those returning to the Welsh shires remains to be researched.

Casualties in Ireland

A combination of inadequate and bad food with the 'raw and waterish' Irish climate and often poor lodgings in garrison brought on 'the disease of Ireland', most likely a general term for ague and dysentery, which singly or together became the lot of many a

240

soldier after a couple of months in the country.[1] One soldier wrote to Lord Burghley that his health had not stood up to the diet; he had been seasick on the voyage and had fallen victim to dysentery because he slept on the hard ground.[2] His experience was typical. Captain Nicholas Dawtrey wrote to Cecil on 9 February 1601 that his cavalrymen had not been able to endure even a month's ill weather, some of them dying of agues and fluxes, others lying sick, hurt and impotent. 'I gave them passport,' he wrote, 'for they were good for nothing but to hang upon their master's beef-pot and buttery'.[3] An anonymous writer of a scheme to defeat O'Neill, sent to Sir Henry Brounker on 12 March 1598, mentioned that O'Neill 'has a friend that never yet failed him, the disease of the country, fatal, as you know to all of our nation at their first lying in camp'.[4] O'Neill was wont to say that his best captains were Captains Hunger, Toil, Cold and Sickness.[5] Many dispatches from Ireland mention that sickness killed more newly arrived recruits than the sword. Patrick Barnewall, in writing to Cecil on 10 August 1600 from Dublin, said 'if their garrisons at first be in places far from relief, they fall into sickness and disease, and so drop away, or are sent back again to England'.[6]

Outbreaks of sickness among the soldiers were generally attributed to a change of diet and air and the 'foulness' of the Irish weather, to which all kinds of maladies were attributed. Ignorance of the first principles of hygiene and the excesses of the soldiers were more likely reasons.[7]

Of all the large-scale levies of soldiers that went to Ireland, those to Lough Foyle under Sir Henry Docwra suffered the most from outbreaks of disease. Dysentery and typhus, it now appears, struck the Derry garrisons within six months of their landing there.[8] Of a landing force of nearly 4,000 there were hardly 1,500 fit men remaining a year later; in the next six months, from September 1600 to March 1601, the loss of men from disease seems to have continued.[9] Docwra attributed the cause of the sickness to the 'distemperature of the air ... which exceedeth all credit to such as feel it not,'[10] but the Irish annalists were probably closer to the truth when they wrote of the state of Docwra's soldiers:

> they were diseased and distempered in consequence of the narrowness of their situation [i.e. overcrowded] and the old victuals, the salt and bitter flesh meat they used, and from the want of fresh meat, and other necessities to which they had been accustomed.[11]

While Docwra wrote of 'seas of sick men daily increasing ... some by counterfeiting, some by hurts and other casualties by the hand of God', the privy council was of the opinion that lack of exercise and idleness were the real reasons why so many of Docwra's men fell 'into sundry diseases'.[12]

Even well fed garrisons in Ireland often suffered from what the Elizabethans called 'the looseness of the country disease, or flux'. Dysentery was liable to break out in any camp that stayed in one place for more than a fortnight because of ignorance of the basic principles of hygiene.[13] As an antidote to dysentery Docwra laid in stores of 4,000 lb of liquorice and 1,000 lb of aniseed to make medicinal drinks, but they do not appear to have worked. Fynes Moryson suggested that the flux did not affect the Irish because their favourite drink was 'usequebah' or whiskey.[14] And it was a disease that did not greatly affect Lord Mountjoy's field army; except at the siege of Kinsale, he generally kept his men on the move, thereby reducing the incidence of camp diseases. Bad food, a wet climate and poor lodgings appear to have been the chief causes of much sickness among the Elizabethan forces in Ireland.

Medical attention to the battle wounded had by all accounts improved, but much depended on the speed with which the wounded were removed from the field to the surgeon. Captain Hugh Mostyn, who claimed twenty-seven years' experience of fighting in Ireland, vividly described in November 1598 the fate of the wounded in battle. He had often seen soldiers attending to the 'carriage of their wounded comrades', an act of mercy that involved further peril, 'for the longer they be carried, the more danger and trouble shall be with them'. He went on to say:

> when they are hurt ... unless the wounded man be able to shift for himself, or have great friends in the camp (which every common soldier hath not) he is but lost, and so the longer they are forth, the more will increase their wounded men ... and hinder the service.

He recommended that a hospital be established on the grounds that if soldiers saw their wounded fellows going to 'warm beds to surgery' there is no doubt 'but each soldier will put forward his best foot, and show himself most valiant'.[15]

Any assessment of numbers wounded and killed in the war is likely to be inaccurate. Contemporary reports of killed and wounded on both sides tend to exaggerate the losses of the enemy. The Irish annalists, for example, tend to use vague phrases like 'a great number were killed' and 'hundreds lay slain on the field of battle', and similar phrases can be found in English reports of Irish losses.[16] When numbers of killed and wounded are given they tend to be round figures, which may justly be suspected as inaccurate. We might have had more accurate figures of casualties if a clerk of casualties, mentioned in 1595, had kept a tally throughout the war. But Sir Robert Napper, chief baron in the Dublin administration, saw no use for the office and recommended to Lord Burghley in March 1595 that the 'office of clerk of casualties be suppressed'.[17] There is no further mention of such a clerk and there are no surviving casualty figures that he might have drawn up.

Sometimes the number of English casualties was deliberately concealed. O'Sullivan Beare wrote that it was an English custom to conceal their own dead and expose their slain enemies in public places.[18] Sir Ralph Lane, the muster master general, wrote to Lord Burghley after the English defeat at Clontibret in 1595 that 'more men were hurt in the late service than was convenient to declare'.[19] Serious histories of the war agree that loss of life from hostilities was less than from sickness, but we shall probably never know the exact figures of losses, or the numbers sent back to England or rehabilitated for service. Contemporary dispatches of skirmishes, battles and sieges give some numbers of the killed and wounded. Table 17 sets them out. We can be more confident of the numbers of officers killed or wounded, for they were usually named. Of the 475 captains who served in Ireland during the O'Neill war over sixty-five were killed or died of wounds in Ireland and about fifty were seriously wounded, which suggests that captains were more active in military engagements than some reports would have us believe. Very often mentions of Irish rebel losses give a single figure for the killed and wounded. Finally, no adequate figures were recorded for Irishmen who died fighting on the English side. Fynes Moryson, for example, dismisses such Irish losses. In his account of the skirmish at Monaghan in July 1601 he wrote:

> Captain Esmond ... was sorehurt ... and forty or fifty of our side slain. We cannot learn that any English were among them so as we account our loss to be no more than the taking of the Captain.[20]

The figures in Table 17 give an idea of the casualties suffered on both sides in twenty-eight major engagements, but are not comprehensive. We do not know how many Irish were killed and wounded by Sir Arthur Chichester's sorties from Carrickfergus in the course of the war, or how his own forces suffered. And during the post-Kinsale scorched earth policy of Mountjoy there are no figures for the various acts of devastation then carried out. Moreover, after the battle in the Curlews in Connaught, August 1599, there is little mention of military action from that province.

At the outset of the war the struggle to possess Enniskillen, and other fording points on the River Erne, such as Belleek and Ballyshannon, occasioned much loss of life: on the three major engagements, seventy-four English were killed and eighty-nine wounded. Among Hugh Maguire's attacking forces almost half his men were lost, though by May 1595 his soldiers retook Enniskillen, slaughtering the fifteen remaining English soldiers in the garrison.[21] At Clontibret, one of the fiercest battles of the war, the English claim to have lost but thirty-one killed and 109 wounded, while the Irish claimed to have accounted for 700 English dead. Irish losses reported vary between none and 400.[22] Lieutenant Tucher's report from the battlefield of 100 enemy slain and many hurt is the figure used in Table 17.[23]

The worst disaster to befall any single garrison in the war happened to Sir John Chichester's forces near Carrickfergus when O'Neill's Scottish allies wiped out 180 men from a garrison of not more than 250.[24] Lieutenant Hart, who was present, saved his life like thirty others by swimming over the River Olderfleet (Lough Larne). He listed the names of the officers killed and wounded:

> *Officers slain:* Sir John Chichester, his lieutenant, and both his sergeants. Captain Rice Mansell, his lieutenant and both his sergeants. Lieutenant Price, both his sergeants and his drum. Lieutenant Walsh, his ensign, sergeants and drum.
>
> *Officers hurt:* Captain Merriman, Lieutenant Hill, Lieutenant Hart.[25]

His report outlined how many of the casualties occurred because they lacked powder: 'our shot were beaten into the battle ... the enemy came so closely with their horse that they killed our men within two pikes' length of our battle'. Sir John Chichester, the governor of the garrison, tried to rally his men 'because they would not stand', but he was shot in the leg, 'whereupon he took his horse, and coming down the hill was shot in the head, which was his death's wound'. After their commander's death 'the soldiers utterly dismayed ... dissolved the battle; Captain Merriman and Lieutenant Barry did with their horses take the river and swim over into the Island Magee'. It was reported

Table 17   Numbers killed and wounded on each side in main engagements

Date	Place	English side		Irish side		Notes
		Killed	*Wounded*	*Killed*	*Wounded*	
May 1593	Belleek, Ballyshannon	3	20	300	–	1
June 1594	Enniskillen	56	69	200	–	2
May 1595	Enniskillen	15	–	–	–	3
May 1595	Clontibret	31	109	100	–	4
November 1597	Carrickfergus	180	40	–	–	5
August 1598	Yellow Ford	1,300	60	300	400	6
May 1599	Wicklow Mts	200	–	–	–	7
June 1599	Ardee	8	–	–	–	8
August 1599	Curlew Mts	241	208	200	300	9
April 1600	Cork	–	10	98	120	10
July 1600	Glin Castle, Limerick	11	21	80	–	11
August 1600	Carriagfoyle	–	–	32	–	12
September 1600	Kilmallock, Cork	17	6	120	80	13
October 1600	Moyry Pass, Dundalk/Newry	200	400	400	300	14
November 1600	Carlingford	20	60	200 killed and wounded		15
March 1601	Tyrell's Island, Westmeath	14	21	37	40	16
May 1601	Lifford	1	–	40	–	17
May 1601	Dunnalong	5	2	200 killed and wounded		
July 1601	Benburb	26	79	200 killed and wounded		18
September 1601	Monaghan	50	–	39	–	19
September 1601	Newry	10	30	–	–	20
September 1601	Newtonstewart	50	–	–	–	21
September 1601	Derry	40	–	–	–	22
September 1601	Donegal	29	–	many	–	23
November 1601	Kinsale (a sortie)	3	10	21	–	24
December 1601	Kinsale (a sortie)	40	–	50	–	25
December 1601	Kinsale (siege)	1	6	1,200	800	26
June 1602	Dunboy (siege)	80	7	134	–	27
Totals		2,631	1,158	5,991 (Irish and Spanish, killed and wounded)		

– indicates lack of information.

Kinsale figures include Spanish on the Irish side.

1. *CSPI* (1592–1596), 163–166.
2. Philip O'Sullivan Beare, *Historiae Catholicae Iberniae Compendium* (Lisbon, 1621), ed. and trans. M. J. Byrne, *Ireland under Elizabeth* (Dublin, 1903), 72; *CSPI* (1592–1596), 262.
3. *CSPI* (1592–1596), 317, 319.
4. *Ibid.*, 321, 322, 327, 331.
5. *CSPI* (1596–1597), 441–446.
Table notes continued opposite.

that Captain North's horse was shot under him three or four times. Captain Constable was taken prisoner after receiving a head wound. Captain Merriman was shot through the shoulder. Finally, Hart summed up the losses: 'The number of our men that were lost in my judgement were about nine score, and there were hurt between thirty and forty, most of which recovered'.[26]

At the Yellow Ford the English had their highest losses of the war in a single set battle, but the numbers engaged were large for the period: Sir Henry Bagenal commanded about 4,000 foot and 320 horse; O'Neill by Irish accounts had 4,050 foot and 600 horse and by English estimates 6,000 to 8,000 men. It is not clear whether the English loss of 1,300 included about 300 Irish who deserted to the winning side. In the battle fourteen English captains were among the dead, a measure of the seriousness of the defeat.[27]

Sir Henry Harington, the commander in the Wicklow Mountains in May 1599, explained his heavy defeat to the Dublin council by blaming the cowardliness of his infantrymen 'who would never once couch their pikes or offer to strike one stroke for their lives'. He tried to minimise the casualties by pointing out, 'no captain lost but Captain Wardman; and Captain Loftus hurt in the leg but I hope without danger'. Loftus later died of this leg wound.[28] Captains Atherton, Mallory and Linley, all participants in Wicklow, wrote fuller reports than Harington's, giving the full measure of the disaster; all corroborate that over 200 of their men were killed out of about 450

Notes to Table 17 continued
6. Accounts of the Yellow Ford listed in G. A. Hayes-McCoy, *Irish battles* (London, 1969).
7. *CSPI* (1599–1600), 81–82, 83–91, and for a map showing the action in the Wicklow Mountains, TCD, Library MS 1209, 12.
8. *CSPI* (1599–1600), 67.
9. *Ibid.*, 113–114; and for an Irish account of this battle see D. Murphy, ed., *O'Clery's life of Red Hugh O'Donnell* (Dublin, 1893), 211–213.
10. T. Stafford, *Pacata Hibernia* (unedited and not dated), 54, 59.
11. *Ibid.*, 54, 59.
12. *Ibid.*, 129.
13. *Ibid.*, 150.
14. Fynes Moryson, *Itinerary*, vol. ii, 305–306.
15. *Ibid.*, 342.
16. *CSPI* (1600–1601), 203.
17. *Ibid.*, 190, 338, 364, 365.
18. PRO SP63/208, part iii, 83i.
19. Fynes Moryson, *Itinerary*, vol. ii, 437.
20. *CSPI* (1601–1603), 65.
21. *Ibid.*, 102.
22. *Ibid.*, 60.
23. *Ibid.*, 98, 99
24. F. Moryson, *Itinerary*, vol. iii, 31–32.
25. *CSPI* (1601–1603), 219.
26. *Cal. Carew MSS*, iv, 179–200.
27. T. Stafford, *Pacata Hibernia* (unedited and not dated), vol. ii, 525–527.

because of the cowardly retreat of so many pikemen.[29] Mallory reported that Captain Loftus's sergeant, who led a loose wing of pikes and shot, 'quite forsake us ... and ran away to our place of garrison'.[30] Captain Lindley was alone in stating that 'they were beaten back by the bitterness of the weather,'[31] but he did blame the beginning of the rout on Captain Loftus's men 'who quite their places in the battle'. Lindley said that forty-four of his own men were killed and at that point in his report he condemned Captain Loftus for his own inactivity in the battle, and mentioned that Irishmen in the companies of the English 'never took their horses, nor made any service that day'.[32]

Sir Conyers Clifford's defeat in the Curlew Mountains, August 1599, was generally put down to the inexperience of his raw recruits and to the ambush tactics of the Irish. Clifford had 1,496 men in three regiments of 571, 421 and 504. Of the ordinary soldiers, 231 were killed and 196 wounded, and of the officers, 10 were killed and 12 wounded.[33]

Between the battle in the Curlews in August 1599 and Kinsale in November/December 1601 the battle, or series of skirmishes and battles, to secure the Moyry Pass in September/October 1600 caused the heaviest casualties.[34] Most accounts of the month's fighting there agree with William Farmer that the 'outrageous weather,' 'great storms of winds and tempests' and 'continual raining for the space of five days' greatly hindered Mountjoy's progress.[35] But the same reports do not agree with Farmer's casualty figures. Those given in Table 17 are from Fynes Moryson, who was present with Mountjoy. Farmer, a surgeon with the English forces, may or may not have been in the Moyry Pass. In the first serious skirmish on the night of 20 September 1600 Farmer said the English lost but one man and six or seven hurt, whereas of the enemy 'many were slain'. On 22 September 'Captain Dawtry's lieutenant slew two of them [the Irish] with his own handes,' and Sir Henry Danvers' troops slew another two and took Murtagh McShane prisoner. For the main fight, on 2 October, Farmer reckoned 30 killed and 130 wounded on the English side and over 500 of the Irish killed and wounded, and for the battle which engaged Sir Charles Percy's regiment Farmer said that they 'killed 500 of the common sort besides 14 of the chiefest gentlemen' whereas only Sir Robert Lovell was killed on the English side. Moryson's casualty figures and Farmer's are clearly at variance with one another.[36]

The single English casualty noted for the siege of Kinsale, one John Taylor, cornet to Captain Richard Graeme, mentioned in at least three accounts, more than likely refers to the action of Christmas Eve 1601 and surely not the ten-week period of the siege as a whole, in which hundreds, if not thousands, died of cold, disease and hostilities.[37] Sir George Carew's letter to Cecil reporting events at Kinsale suggests that one English death was a grotesque misrepresentation. He wrote:

> Kinsale was brought at so dear a rate, as (while I live) I will protest against a winter siege, if it may be avoided. I do verily believe that at that siege and after (the sickness were gotten) we lost above 6,000 men that died.[38]

The Irish annalists state that Irish losses were not great,[39] but English accounts agree that they had accounted for 1,200 dead and about 800 wounded of the enemy. O'Sullivan Beare wrote that the English had about 15,000 men at the beginning of the siege but that 8,000 perished by the sword, hunger, cold and disease.[40] As for the final battle, O'Sullivan claimed O'Neill lost but 200 foot and the English three noblemen, suggesting once again that English losses in the final battle were slight.[41]

Sick and wounded

Men wounded in battle were supposed to be treated by army surgeons, though there was little they could do beyond cauterisation of wounds to prevent infection and, more commonly, amputation. Each captain was supposed to employ one in his company. In the absence of a surgeon the soldiers knew that if they were hurt they would have no skilled medical attention. It is clear from complaints in many dispatches that not every captain employed a surgeon during the war.[42] A physician or 'chirurgeon' was obtained for military forces in one of two ways: either he was sent by the Company of Barber Surgeons in London, which in return for its charter's privileges was required to send a medical officer and assistants to forces serving overseas, or he was impressed by a particular captain, who was then responsible for his pay and seeing to it that he carried out his duties.[43] The military surgeon possessed neither rank nor distinction; in recruiting warrants he is invariably classed with drummers, fifers, armourers, smiths and carpenters. Like the common recruit, he had no love for military service. In 1598, for example, when six surgeons were taken up for the Irish service, one bought his discharge for £6 and it is likely that another escaped by providing a substitute.[44] During the greater part of Elizabeth's reign the normal pay for a military company's surgeon was 12*d* a day; by about 1590 this sum was increased to 20*d*.

From 1595 a surgeon general of the army was instituted and one William Kelly was appointed at a stipend of 2*s* a day, which was raised by means of a benevolence from the captains, 2*d* from some, 1*d* and ¾*d* from others. When Kelly died in 1597 the same allowance was continued to his successor, William Newton.[45] This system of paying the surgeon general was unsatisfactory, and the privy council decreed in 1599 that the surgeon general was to receive one man's pay out of every company in Ireland. A soldier's pay was 8*d* a day and since there were then about eighteen companies in Ireland the surgeon general would receive 12*s* a day, three times that of a captain's pay, but out of this the surgeon general had to pay his assistants.[46] This new system of payment in Ireland had long been the custom in the Low Countries, but many captains complained about the deduction of a man's pay from company funds to pay for a surgeon who they claimed was rarely present.[47]

The gap between what was administratively and humanely desirable, a surgeon to each company, and the general lack of surgeons in practice during the Irish war is clear. The Lough Foyle and Ballyshannon garrisons provided places for only two surgeons each for between 3,000 and 4,000 men. Each was to have three assistants, to be paid from the surgeon's stipend, at 10*s* a day each.[48] William Jones, the commissary for musters in the whole province of Munster in 1600, wrote to the privy council in January 1600 in terms which suggested that there was not a single surgeon in his entire province: 'If an allowance went to some skilful chirurgeon … he might do some good when the camp were in the field, and appoint some men of skill as his deputies in the garrisons'.[49]

Henry Bird, a commissary for musters in Ulster, in writing to Cecil in November 1600, bemoaned the fate of so many sick and hurt men lying in the garrison in Newry 'without officers or others to attend them,' adding, 'it would have grieved any Christian heart to see so many perish for want of looking onto'.[50]

However, under Mountjoy's general administration of the army the general care of the sick and wounded seems to have improved. Fynes Moryson's 'Lyst of the Army ... to be a direction to the Treasurer-at-Wars for the payment thereof from the first of April in the years 1600' states that sixteen surgeons were to be paid; the surgeon general, not named, was to be paid £5, and the lord deputy's doctor of physick also £5 a week. The remaining fourteen surgeons were to be dispersed 'in the provinces and garrisons at thirty or forty shillings a peece the week'.[51] Considering that the total number of foot was 14,000 and the cavalry 1,200, the number of surgeons to be paid would appear to have still been very inadequate and, in any case, there is no clear evidence that sixteen surgeons were actively employed in their posts from 1600 to the end of the war.[52]

Nevertheless, from letters and reports sent to Cecil and the privy council it is clear that Mountjoy cared for his sick and wounded soldiers. Captain Nicholas Dawtrey, for instance, described to Cecil how Mountjoy sent sick and hurt men to the nearest towns 'to get their health or recovery', and that often he sent his own 'surgeon, fissiones [physicians] and divines to be sure of their estate ... to give them both bodily and ghostly comforts,' but that no soldier was given these facilities except 'by his exact warrant'.[53]

When questioned by the privy council about the numbers of sick and hurt men he kept sending to Dublin, Mountjoy sent a reply by Captain Sir Oliver St John:

> As for soldiers dismissed and remaining in Dublin, they are sick and are come with their Captains' leave, either to the hospital for their recovery or for their passports [to England] if they be irrecoverable, which in that case I grant to none but such as the surgeon, physician, or mustermaster do certify me to be utterly unserviceable, and most of them I view myself before.[54]

Military hospitals were regarded as a necessary investment for the army in Ireland. They reduced the numbers of sick and wounded returning to England, who roaming through the countryside of England and Wales were a positive discouragement to recruitment. Seasoned captains knew that those soldiers who had weathered their first bout of dysentery were worth three raw recruits.[55] Captain John Baynard lamented the waste of 'sick and hurt soldiers that have dies in the open streets merely for the want of some succour'.[56]

Buckhurst and Cecil wanted military hospitals set up in each of Ireland's four provinces 'by the allowance of a soldier's pay out of every band' and that the 'house rents, reparations and bedding appertaining to the said hospitals be borne and provided by the Queen's Majesty'.[57] Mountjoy set down 'Certain points necessary for the army in Ireland, offered to their Lordships'; he gave more detail on the provision of hospitals:

That there be several hospitals maintained, at Cork for Munster, and at Dublin and Drogheda for Leinster, every hospital to have two overseers that shall be honest householders in the towns, a Master that must be a surgeon or a physician, a servant and four women to attend the sick and hurt men, and a hundred beds furnished for them. The Overseers to have nothing for their pains, the Master at 5s *per diem*, his servant 12d. four women at 6d. the peece, and this entertainment to be levied upon the army rents, reparations, and bedding to be defrayed by her Majesty.[58]

The only hospitals which were established for the army were at Dublin, Derry and at Cork; no mention is made of one for Drogheda or for Connaught. Though much discussed before Mountjoy's time, the army hospital in Dublin does not appear to have been established until May 1600,[59] and in the course of its operation it appears to have been inadequate to cope with the numbers of sick and wounded sent there, for many returned untreated to England during the last years of the war.[60] The hospital at Cork was necessitated by the nearby siege of Kinsale in the winter of 1601. And that at Derry was a response to mass illness among the Derry garrisons in the autumn of 1600.

The Derry hospital was situated in the centre of the great fort next to Docwra's own house; it is frequently mentioned in his many letters and in the *Narration* of his services at Lough Foyle.[61] It was built 'within the walls of an old church, fitted out with 28 beds, far too few to take the sick and wounded men who flooded into it'. Docwra ruefully remarked, 'I do not know that the best hospital in London cannot contain the sick men in the army'.[62] Even such a small hospital proved a struggle to establish. Docwra assumed that his soldiers would willingly work at its construction, but instead they had to be compelled under threats to complete the work. And there was an early lobby, successfully resisted, for using the hospital as an ammunition dump.[63] When it came into use it was sensibly suggested that soldiers suffering from infectious diseases 'of whom the tenth man doth not recover' should be separated from the wounded 'of whom there is greater hope of recovery'.[64]

The charge of governing the Derry hospital was given to an overseer and an unspecified number of assistants. There was certainly one surgeon in the Derry garrisons, for his signature, 'Thomas Dowghton, surgeon', appears on lists of sick and wounded men discharged from Lough Foyle together with Sir Henry Docwra's signature, but whether or not Dowghton was the master of the hospital is not known.[65] The assistants working in the hospital were to be paid 4*d* a month, 'allowed from every man's pay to maintain it'. On the basis of eighteen companies at Derry of 150 each the monthly contribution for the pay of the assistants and upkeep of the hospital would have been £45, but the Lough Foyle companies were under-strength after September 1600 so that the full allowance for the hospital was probably rarely met.[66] Nevertheless, Docwra seems to have taken some pride in the Derry hospital. Nearly every aspect of his administration came under official censure but he always roundly defended his military hospital.[67]

While there was some provision, even though inadequate, for the care and treatment of the sick and wounded on the English side, we know little or nothing of how the sick and hurt fared on the Irish side. One report of 'intelligences that came into the English camp' after the battle of the Moyry Pass in October 1600 claimed that O'Neill's wounded man must have two 'whole men at the least to carry him' and that to avoid weakening his forces he left his wounded in their cabins, where they had 'no other salves applied to their sores more than their country salve, butter'.[68] Another report, from Sir Griffin Markham, suggested that O'Neill 'so heavily armed his men with drink' that, being senseless, they hardly noticed their hurts.[69]

The treatment of the dead on both sides, when bodies were not recovered for burial by their friends, indicates some of the brutality of the age and the ferocity of the war. Decapitation of the killed seems to have been a common practice from the frequent mentions of 'heads brought into camp', of 'heads sent up to Dublin' and of 'heads sent' to commanders as evidence of soldiers' victories in skirmishes and battles. Many of the slain Irish had their heads sent to Dublin for public exposure on the gates of the city. One Thomas Ball was paid £15 for the gruesome carriage of seventeen heads of the followers of Feagh McHugh O'Byrne to Dublin in December 1596.[70] And when their leader was eventually captured and slain his head was sent to the English court, it greatly angered the queen that 'the head of such a base Robin Hood was brought solemnly into England.'[71] Lord Burgh, lord deputy in 1597, complained that the air about Dublin was 'so thick corrupted' with 'the heads daily brought in'.[72]

The English treated their own dead with some respect. The bodies of notable commanders were returned to England for honourable burial. The corpses of Lord Burgh and Sir Henry and Sir Thomas Norris 'were embalmed, and were rowled up in cearclothes and carried over into England to be buried'.[73] But scant respect was paid to English corpses by the Irish. After the capture and killing of Sir Conyers Clifford in the Curlews the Irish sent his head to Red Hugh O'Donnell as an earnest of their victory.[74] It was said of the mayor and citizens of Limerick that when the constable of Limerick Castle had been killed they cut off his head 'and played at football with it'. It was reported that the same citizens had killed a lord justice and buried his body with other Englishmen in their cellars.[75] O'Clery wrote about the aftermath of the Yellow Ford when Irish soldiers returned to the battlefield 'and proceeded to strip the people who had fallen ... and to behead those who were severely wounded there'. Whether this was an act of mercy, revenge or for loot is not clear.[76] Looting the war dead was a common practice on both sides. Fynes Moryson mischievously described the looting of the Spanish dead by the English after Kinsale:

> And in general among the dead bodies many were found to have spells, characters, and hallowed medals, which they wore as preservations against death, and most of them when they were stripped, were seen to have scars of Venus warfare.[77]

It would seem that the ordinary Elizabethan soldier was condemned to a grim fate in Ireland. If he escaped death in battle he might easily succumb to sickness and could expect 'no succour or relief generally of the inhabitants, although they hold amongst themselves that charity is a great merit'.[78] And the provision of surgeons and hospitals was clearly inadequate for the large numbers of sick and wounded. It is hardly surprising that the raw recruit dreaded the very name of Ireland, went reluctantly to serve there and often deserted to fly back to England and even, at times, to the enemy. To those who returned honourably to England we finally turn.

Provision for the relief of disabled soldiers in England

Despite the strictures of that notable historian of the army Sir John Fortescue on the queen's lack of care for the sick and wounded men who faithfully served her there was a steady improvement in their treatment during the war.[79] Sick leave with pay was beginning to be allowed; if a soldier had to return to England he was kept on the muster roll and as long as he came back to his own company within three months with a certificate from a justice of the peace or from a high constable he was paid during his absence. However, from the many petitions to have ordinary arrears of pay made up we see that sick pay was not the norm. On one occasion, for example, the privy council advised the lord deputy in Ireland that a wounded captain who had returned to England for treatment should not have his pay stopped.[80] The government's interest extended to the care of disabled soldiers too. From 1593 disabled soldiers and sailors, because of their increasing numbers, became recognised for the first time as a distinct category of poor deserving relief. Sir Robert Cecil drew up the preamble to the first of three Acts of parliament to help disabled soldiers and sailors.[81] The 1593 Act for the Relief of the Poor emphasised that, like the lame, blind, diseased and impotent poor, maimed soldiers and mariners were incapable of earning a livelihood and therefore dependent on alms and relief. The preamble reads:

> It is agreeable with Christian charity, policy and the honour of our nation that such as have adventured their lives and lost their limbs or disabled their bodies ... in the defence and service of her Majesty and the state should at their return be relieved and rewarded.[82]

The date 1593 coincided with the beginnings of the war in Ireland, but what was probably instrumental in the passing of the Act was the queen's annoyance at the appearance of wandering soldiers in London. It was said in 1593 that 'the Queen is troubled whenever she takes the air with these miserable creatures'.[83] It was suggested in the House of Commons in 1593 that since parliament had provided money for the wars it should also provide money for the relief of those deprived by war of the means to relieve themselves, 'who cry upon us daily in the streets'.[84]

At the committee stage of the 1593 bill Sir Thomas Cecil, the member for Northampton, suggested that maimed soldiers could well be provided for from a tax on inns and alehouses. If the 60,000 such hostelries were to pay a noble (6s 8d) annually, the £20,000 a year so raised would support five guest houses for twenty maimed soldiers each, giving each soldier an annual pension of £10 as well as providing a salary of £20 a year to the governor of each guest house. His figures were contested and the lavish provision derided by many, including Sir Walter Ralegh, who said it was not fitting that the 'most beggarly people of the land should be charged with so onerous provision'.[85] Sir Robert Cecil argued that if parliament showed the way the charitable and well disposed in all the shires of the realm would remember the maimed soldiers in their wills and alms.[86] But in the end all schemes for raising funds for the 'maimed and impotent soldiers' were rejected in favour of a parish rate.

The justices of the peace of each country were to organise the fund for the relief of the genuinely maimed in war and from their own members appoint treasurers to pay out pensions to those who qualified. A parish rate not above 6*d* and not below 1*d* was to be levied on subsidy men assessed at 40*s* in lands, or £5 and above in goods. Counties of less than fifty parishes were to be assessed in groups of parishes to be determined by their justices of the peace. And the Act was to apply to all soldiers maimed since 1588 and to those who would be maimed in the future.[87] In the subsequent Acts for the Relief of the Poor, of 1597 and 1601, it was claimed that the previous rates were insufficient to provide for the increasing numbers of returning wounded soldiers. By the 1597 Act the rates were raised to not above 8*d* a parish and not below 2*d*; in London the limit was extended to 2*s* a parish but the average was not to exceed 8*d* a parish.[88] And by the 1601 Act the rate was further raised to an average of 6*d* a parish, and the London limit to 3*s* a parish.[89] In 1598 an order in the House of Lords laid down a scale of contributions from the clergy and nobility for the same fund: 40*s* from archbishops, earls, marquesses and viscounts, 30*s* from bishops, and 20*s* from every baron.[90]

A set of accounts of the rates levied and collected from the parishes and townships of the hundreds in Cornwall for the maimed soldiers' fund shows how the system was supposed to work. A weekly rate of 2*d* on each parish and a quarterly rate of 2*s* 3*d* was collected by the churchwardens, remitted to the high constables of the hundreds, who in turn passed the money to the treasurer of the fund, an elected justice of the peace. The arrangement appears to have been a typical implementation of the Acts of parliament.[91]

It was not long before there were complaints that this legislation was not being carried out.[92] In 1598 some justices of the peace were sending the wounded from place to place, to where they had been impressed or to where they had been born, and refused to sign their certificates, thereby forcing them to be treated as vagabonds and common rogues.[93] The Act of 1597 had ordered that in those cases where there were insufficient funds to provide for a maimed soldier in the shire where he had been impressed, he was to be sent to the county where he was born or which he had last inhabited. The government soon discovered that this rule was confusing and led to the failure of either county to provide relief. To clear the confusion Sir Robert Cecil brought in an amendment to the Act in 1601 to the effect that the maimed soldier was to be relieved only in the shire where he was born for, as he said, 'only in a man's country either charity, kindred or commiseration will breed pity'.[94]

Insofar as it is known there was only one hospital founded in England exclusively for disabled soldiers; it was built in Buckinghamshire to house thirty-six 'maimed unmarried soldiers' from the town of Buckingham or the three hundreds of Buckinghamshire. The licence to have the hospital erected also gave authorisation to the shire to purchase land for their maintenance, but it was not to spend more than £200 a year in such purchases.[95] In addition, Lord Burghley showed his personal concern for ex-soldiers by endowing a hospital for thirteen poor men of Stamford Baron in Northamptonshire, particularly for those who had been honest soldiers and were unable to work.[96]

Most towns, especially the cathedral cities and the two ancient university towns, had almshouses. Some ex-soldiers petitioned for rooms in them through influential friends and sometimes the privy council ordered a particular trustee of an almshouse to provide a disabled soldier with the next vacancy.[97] Occasionally provision was made for retired soldiers of long and distinguished service by appointment to a sinecure, such as the post of gunner in the Tower of London offered to Stephen Langdon as a reward for his services,[98] or the oddly incongruous post of 'guider' in the Dunstable almshouse offered to Barnaby Danvers who had 'lost both his legs'. The Earl of Bath indicated that there was a vacancy as the former 'guider' of Dunstable was in St Albans gaol 'for foul murder'.[99]

Distinguishing the genuinely maimed soldier from the rogue was a major problem. The government's confining of relief to soldiers in their home counties was to enable local communities more easily to separate the genuinely maimed in war from malingerers, rogues and vagabonds, and to detect those who went about with counterfeit certificates. The Act for the Relief of the Poor of 1597 had made those caught passing themselves off as wounded soldiers punishable as rogues and vagabonds.[100] A spate of government proclamations in the late 1590s against beggars posing as disabled soldiers indicated that the problem greatly increased with the demobilisation of soldiers from Ireland.[101] Edward Hext, the treasurer for the maimed soldiers' fund in Somerset in 1597 sent a counterfeit pass to the privy council claiming that the relief provided by the Act was an encouragement to soldiers to desert and 'find such swete by this statute as they are become continual travellers by counterfeit passports'.[102]

In January 1598 Lord Burghley reflected on the 'discommodities uppon dissolving of soldiers'; if left in Ireland, he thought, they would make waste or provoke new rebellion, or return to England to live disorderly.[103] In September 1598 a special proclamation was issued against idle, able-bodied rogues exacting money in London and near the court on pretence of having been wounded in the wars.[104]

The identification of genuine soldiers in need was all the more important when the available funds ran short, as happened in the last years of the reign when the number of sick and wounded returning from the war increased.[105] This may be seen from the increased number of petitions to the privy council for pensions for disabled soldiers: fourteen in 1595, twenty-seven in 1596/1597 and forty in 1599.[106] Edward Hext may not have exaggerated when he informed the privy council that there were 300 to 400 wandering soldiers 'in a shire, and though they go by two and three in a Company, yet all or the most part in a shire do meet either at fair or market, or in some Alehouse once a week'.[107] Hext may well have been referring to demobilised soldiers at large and not simply the returning disabled, but as we have seen it became increasingly difficult to differentiate the deserving from the counterfeit wounded. It is doubtful if all the necessary pensions could be paid at the statutory rates. Petitions to the government, to high-ranking commanders and to captains on behalf of illiterate soldiers increased.

The government tried to limit the problem in England by putting pressure on the lord deputy and the Dublin council to relieve the wounded with pensions payable in Ireland and not to send them home for such relief. In the case of Anglo–Irish soldiers the government intended that they should stay permanently in Ireland; judging by the few lists of pensions granted by the Dublin administration in the last years of the war, it appear to have supported the privy council's wishes.[108] In the case of Mark Le Strange, the privy council referred his petition to Lord Mountjoy: 'he hath been a long suitor unto her Majesty for a pension … since he has long service in Ireland … we have

253

thought it most convenient to return him unto you'.[109] And in other cases referred to the lord deputy the privy council seemed determined to shift responsibility to the Irish administration:

> considering the great ocasions her Majesty hath daily more and more to expend her treasure, both by reason of the unnatural wars in that kingdom and the charge she is put unto for the defence of the realme, it is not time (as you can judge) to move Her Highness in this kind of suits.[110]

But, in general, helpless soldiers were sent back to England without hesitation. In Derry, for example, Sir Henry Docwra and his surgeon Thomas Dowghton signed a list of forty-two sick and wounded men to be sent back to their homes; their signed certificates survive in the mayor of Chester's military papers.[111]

Chester, the chief port of embarkation, was also the chief point of re-entry to England. It would have been a natural place for a hospital such as the one founded in Buckinghamshire, but there is no evidence that the city of Chester had one during these years. Instead, the mayor had authority to pay small sums of money to hasten the wounded out of the city to their places of birth or impressment so that they would not mope about the streets of the town and discourage fresh levies. Such payments proliferate in the mayor's books in the years 1597 to 1602. For example, in the years 1597 and 1598 *ex gratia* payments were made by the mayor and common council to:

> Richard Evans, soldier, with one arm, xiid.
> To a lame soldier of London, xiid.
> To three Yorkshire soldiers, ii sh. each.
> To a poor soldier having a canker and a pox, xiid.
> To a sick soldier of Cherry Norton, xiid.[112]

Since county justices of the peace, through their treasurer of the maimed soldiers' fund, were responsible for disbursing relief to the returning wounded soldiers, one might expect quarter sessions rolls to contain evidence of the pensions paid from the county fund, but not all do. For instance, throughout the published Staffordshire quarter sessions rolls there is no mention of such a fund in the years 1595 to 1603.[113] In Kent, on the other hand, the sessions rolls for the 1590s show much activity on the part of the justices of the peace for the relief of the 'military poor', disabled soldiers and their dependants.[114] It may be indicative of the Elizabethan aim of streamlining administration that the rate for the maimed soldiers' fund was levied at the same time as that for gaol money, but it may also reflect the prevalent association of poverty and crime. The assessments on the parishes of the north division of the lath of Aylesford towards both funds were settled at the mid-summer quarter sessions at Canterbury in 1595, where a rate of 20*d* a week for gaol money and of 19*d* a week for the maimed soldiers' fund were agreed.[115] Treasurers to administer the fund were elected at Easter each year from among the justices, the first two being Michael Sondes of Throwley and Timothy Low. Sondes did not want the post and wrote indignantly to Sir John Leveson saying the office was 'thrust upon him'.[116] Later sessions rolls, from 1600, show treasurers still being appointed for the fund and for the county's stock.[117]

Presentments of grand juries and high constables of the hundreds show that more persons were being presented for defaulting in their payment of gaol money than for not contributing to the maimed soldiers' relief fund.[118]

Pensions paid in Kent varied in accordance with need: an annual pension of £4 was awarded John Bishopenden at Canterbury in 1601.[119] Five pensions were granted at the Maidstone sessions, varying in amount from 6s to 10s, to be paid each quarter year.[120] Nicholas Crampton, 'disabled in the wars of Ireland', was awarded a £6 annual pension; he was paid this for two years; six years later he petitioned the privy council to bring pressure to bear on the justices in Kent for four years' arrears of pension and its continuation. The privy council wrote the Kentish justices a sharp rebuke but we do not know if it resulted in redress for Crampton and perhaps his case may have not been a deserving one.[121]

The Lancashire rolls give evidence of similar activity on behalf of wounded soldiers. For the year 1601 the Lancashire justices chose James Assheton and John Braddel to be treasurers of the fund in the Manchester area, and William Traves and James Banks for the Lancaster, Preston and Ormskirk areas, succeeded in the following year by James Holt and John Fleming. In their sessions the justices in Lancashire ruled that the treasurers of the maimed soldiers' fund 'shall make the high constables of the hundreds their deputies to distrain for the sums taxed on the parishes,' and that if any place becomes vacant in an almshouse a wounded soldier can there be relieved so that 'the collecting for him will cease'. Fines of 10s were to be imposed on churchwardens who failed in their duty of collecting the money and fines of 40s on defaulting constables; such fines were themselves to be paid into the maimed soldiers' pension fund.[122] The inhabitants of Dalton in Furness were ordered to collect 18d a week for John Wilson, a wounded soldier; Preston was ordered to give 2s a week to Henry Bushell; Wigan 12d a week to Thomas Owen; Ormskirk a similar sum for Thomas Cookson. Annual pensions were also granted: 40s to John Whitston and £3 6s 8d to Thomas Parre, both of Ormskirk. When the justices of the peace met at Preston they could not decide which parish Michael Lea belonged to, but they took order that his immediate need as a maimed soldier be relieved by a collection made by the ordinary overseer of the poor in Preston.[123]

Wiltshire quarter sessions show larger pensions granted there and give more detail about their recipients. In 1599 a pension of 50s was granted to William Shiler, who had served under Captain Edward Digges in Munster, and the same was given to Thomas Willis, who had served under Captain Edward North. Both soldiers presented certificates signed by William Waad, clerk of the privy council. In September 1600, the Wiltshire justices granted Henry Venn a £5 pension for 'his hurt and services' in the Irish wars. At the 1601 sessions they struck off eight pensions and ordered the treasurers of the fund to make payments only to those pensioners present in person at the next sessions.[124]

An important part of the work of the sessions had to do with restoring lapsed pensions and fulfilling requests from the privy council for pensions for ex-soldiers. The Wiltshire quarter sessions records provide many instances of all these functions. And as the Wiltshire certificates generally name the captain under which a soldier was wounded, the part of Ireland in which he served is fairly easy to find out by identifying the captain's garrison or company from the army lists.[125] Robert Bungey, for example, who received a pension of £5, had served under Captain Charles Egerton and Sir Samuel Bagenal, colonel of foot, in 1599 in Ulster; Thomas Logett had been a foot soldier of Captain Dillon's company in Kilkenny; Christopher Strong had served as a cavalryman under Sir John Chamberlain at Lough Foyle; and John Dankett had served under Sir Arthur Savage in the garrison at Carrickfergus.[126]

As in other shires, some of the petitions to the Wiltshire justices for pensions were supported by privy councillors and other eminent noblemen. King James himself ordered the Wiltshire justices to grant a pension to Richard Somner, a gunner who became deaf 'by the noise of the cannon shot'; the order was signed by Sir Julius Caesar. Somner was granted twenty nobles.[127] Sir Walter Ralegh signed John Duckett's certificate; Duckett was given 20s 'present relief' and a pension of £5 a year.[128] In the shire of Kent Sir William Cobham, the lord lieutenant, supported soldiers' petitions;[129] in Cheshire and in Wales Robert, Earl of Essex signed certificates.[130] And the commanders in Ireland, Lord Mountjoy, Sir George Carew, and Sir Arthur Chichester, frequently signed certificates for aged and wounded soldiers' relief. In this way humanitarianism fleetingly united the common soldier and the great ones of the realm.

Some soldiers of exceptionally long military service petitioned the monarch directly. Thomas Westroppe wanted to resign his pension of £18 a year for life for his long military service in Ireland for a thirty-one-year lease of lands to the value of £30 a year.[131] George Smith petitioned King James for a pension saying he had served thirty-three years in Ireland and in Denmark and that he was at Cadiz and the Island of Rhe. Smith's petition was referred to the Wiltshire justices, who allowed him 20s to help him on his journey out of the county to an unspecified destination.[132]

Some idea of the considerable petitioning in these years is given in an appendix which collects 189 petitions for pensions and alms rooms, the restoration of lapsed pensions, arrears of pensions and requests for an increase of pension recorded in the state papers and the privy council registers.[133]

Worcester quarter sessions records show that relief was sometimes extended to the dependants of wounded soldiers. Anne Nash of Burdley in Worcestershire petitioned for her weekly allowance of 2s, which had not been paid to her for over a year, her husband having been 'pressed for a soldier in Ireland' and presumably wounded in action.[134] Margaret Glover of Ripple in the same county petitioned the justices that her daughter had married Richard Sanders, who was taken up for Irish military services 'from whence he has never returned to the utter undoing of his poor lame distressed wife and children'. The quarter sessions court awarded her 4d a week.[135]

A maimed soldier needed to stand up for himself and petition for relief if he was to receive it. Richard Coitte petitioned the Worcestershire sessions court himself as 'a lame and impotent soldier' having been drafted many years ago to Ireland; 'by lying on the ground he had fallen into great lameness' and he now wanted a pass to let him go to King's Hospital in London to be treated.[136] John Sampson stated to the court that he had been a soldier in Ireland under Queen Elizabeth 'for the full term of eight years' and that he had been wounded many times. The court granted him 13s 6d.[137] Henry Cotterell, a maimed soldier living in London, petitioned the Worcester justices that since the charges to go to Worcester every quarter for his pension were very great, he would be much helped if his allowance could be paid every half year.[138]

Until 1601 the justices continued to send maimed soldiers back and forth between the places of their birth and their impressment to avoid the burden of paying pensions. The Hertfordshire justices were reprimanded by the privy council in 1599 for refusing a pension to Edward Gouldhurst, having sent him to Middlesex where he was born:

> It is not unknown to you that it resteth in the choice of the party hurt or maimed to be relieved either in the place where he was borne or the county out of which he was impressed.

Their letter continued with the well known complaint that there were too many wounded soldiers in and around London at that time, and the Hertfordshire justices were peremptorily ordered to see to Edward Gouldhurst's needs.[139] We have seen that the Act of 1601 for the relief of the poor was amended to stipulate that such as Gouldhurst in future would be relieved in the place of their birth.[140]

The concern of the late Elizabethan government for the maimed and wounded does not appear to have been continued into King James's reign. Captain Sir Oliver St John, who had been wounded in Ireland, raised the matter in the 1604 parliament on behalf of wounded captains; many of his class had spent their fortunes, their best means and their time to do her majesty's service there and the wounded among them were deprived and not rewarded after the queen's death. In peacetime these men were forgotten and were likely to perish from want.[141] Many perhaps did not regard wounded captains as deserving of public assistance since it was generally recognised that many of them had profited by Irish lands, but some did not prosper.[142] Having survived the war, they found equal difficulty in surviving the peace.[143]

Notes

1 *CSPI* (1596–1597), 148, 263.
2 PRO SP63/44, 49.
3 *CSPI* (1600–1601), 182.
4 HMC, *Salisbury*, ix, 100.
5 PRO SP63/202, part iv, no. 75, a discourse on Ireland, unsigned, 1598.
6 *CSPI* (1600), 341, Barnewall to Cecil, 10 August 1600.
7 *Ibid.*, 243, 406, 415, 455, 473, 489, 531, 532, mentions of bad weather as a cause of diseases in one year.
8 PRO SP63/207, part v, no. 2, Docwra to Cecil, 2 September 1600.
9 This proportion is deduced from Covert's muster certificates, PRO SP63/208, part ii, no. 17, and the needs of reinforcements at Derry in December 1600 as set out in April 1601, *APC*, xxxi, 21–23, 315.
10 PRO SP63/202, part v, no. 2, Docwra to Cecil, 2 September 1600.
11 *AFM*, vol. vi, 2209.
12 *APC*, xxx, 578, privy council to Docwra, 10 August 1600.
13 P. Logan, 'Pestilence in the Irish wars: the earlier phase', *Irish Sword*, 7 (1966), 285–288.
14 Fynes Moryson, *Itinerary*, vol. iv, 192, and for his description of Irish drinking habits, *ibid.*, 197.

15   *CSPI* (1598–1599), 385–386, Mostyn to Cecil, November 1598.

16   *AFM*, vi, *passim*, and many reports throughout the eight relevant volumes of the *CSPI*.

17   PRO SP63/178, 118, 118i, Sir Robert Napper to Lord Burghley, 26 March 1595.

18   Philip O'Sullivan Beare, *Historiae Catholicae Iberniae Compendium* (Lisbon, 1621), ed. and trans. M. J. Byrne, *Ireland under Elizabeth* (Dublin, 1903), 122.

19   *CSPI* (1595–1596), 163–166.

20   Fynes Moryson, *Itinerary*, vol. ii, 437.

21   *CSPI* (1592–1596), 163–166, 317, 319.

22   G. A. Hayes-McCoy reconstructed the action of the battle in *Irish battles* (London, 1969), 87–105.

23   *Cal. Carew MSS*, iii, 109–110, Lieutenant Tucher's report, 1 June 1595.

24   *CSPI* (1596–1597), 441–443, Lieutenant Hart's report, 4 November 1597.

25   *Ibid.*, 442–443.

26   *Ibid.*

27   *CSPI* (1598–1599), 224–229, 231–233, 236–238; Fynes Moryson, *Itinerary*, vol. ii, 216–217, which gives 1,500 soldiers killed.

28   *CSPI* (1599–1600), 58, 59, Harington to the lord chancellor Loftus, 29 May 1599. Captain Loftus was the chancellor's son.

29   *Ibid.*, 83–91, captain's reports in July 1599.

30   *Ibid.*, 88, Mallory's report.

31   *Ibid.*, 89, Lindley's report.

32   *CSPI* (1599–1600), 91.

33   *Ibid.*, 113–114, 'A note of the army under the command of Sir Conyers Clifford, at the Curlews, Sunday, the 5th August 1599', endorsed by Sir Robert Cecil 'this shows how many are slain'.

34   Table 17.

35   William Farmer, *Chronicles of Ireland 1594–1613*, ed. C. Litton Falkiner, *English Historical Review*, 85 (1907), 117, 118.

36   *Ibid.*

37   Three lesser known accounts of Kinsale by participants are: Folger Shakespeare Library MS X. d. 393, ff. 10–16, a historical commonplace book, *c.* 1625; William Farmer, *Chronicles of Ireland 1594–1613*, ed. C. Litton Falkiner, *English Historical Review*, 85 (1907), 125; and *A letter from a souldier of good place in Ireland* printed pamphlet of 25 March 1602, written at Cork 13 January 1602 and signed 'I.E.' This last account is reproduced in A. Kinney, *Historical documents of the age of Elizabeth* (Connecticut, 1975), 345–360.

38   *Cal. Carew MSS*, iv, 305, Carew to Cecil, 11 August 1602.

39   *AFM*, vi, 2, 283.

40   Philip O'Sullivan Beare, *Historiae Catholicae Iberniae Compendium* (Lisbon, 1621), ed. and trans. M. J. Byrne, *Ireland under Elizabeth* (Dublin, 1903), 145.

41   *Ibid.*, 147.

42   H. J. Webb, 'English military surgery during the age of Elizabeth', *Bulletin of the History of Medicine*, 15 (1944), 261.

43   *Ibid.*

44   *Annals of the Barber Surgeons of London*, ed. S. Young (London, 1890), 320–321.

45   *CSPI* (1600–1601), 241–242, 'Concerning the defalcations out of the army in Ireland, for preachers, physicians, surgeons and cannoneers'.

46   *APC*, xxx, 107, 108.

47   *CSPI* (1600–1601), 241, 242.

48   *CSPI* (1599–1600), 396.

49   *Ibid.*, 383, 384.

50   *CSPI* (1600–1601), 26.

51   Fynes Moryson, *Itinerary*, vol. ii, 295.

52   There is no mention of such a number of surgeons employed in the four volumes of the *CSPI* dealing with the army between 1600 and the end of the war.

53   *CSPI* (1600), 532, Dawtrey to Cecil, 28 October 1600.

54   *Ibid.*, 505, 'several answers to be made by Sir Oliver St. John … as he shall find occasion in speech, either with Her Majesty or with their Lordships', October 1600.

55   *CSPI* (1599–1600), 350.

56   *Ibid.*

57   *Ibid.*, 377, 396.

58   *CSPI* (1599–1600), 448. H. J. Webb, 'English military surgery in the age of Elizabeth', *Bulletin of the History of Medicine*, 15 (1944), 261–262, is clearly inaccurate in stating 'there was seldom more than two surgeons assigned to the entire army', and that there was 'but one army hospital in all of Ireland', p. 262. He is also wrong in stating that Sir Henry Docwra wrote to Lord Burghley in September and December 1600 – Lord Burghley died in August 1598, and Webb means Sir Robert Cecil, his son and successor.

59   Nicholas Weston, mayor of Dublin, put forward a hospital scheme in October 1598 and reckoned it would cost the city £1,000 a year – *CSPI* (1598–1599), 296–297. Mountjoy sent £150 to the Dublin corporation for the hospital in May 1600 – *CSPI* (1600), 209.

60   *CSPI* (1600), 334, 341, 449; *CSPI* (1600–1601), 165, and see under 'Sick and wounded'.

61   PRO SP63/207, part vi, no. 84, Docwra's map of Derry.

62   *CSPI* (1600), 113; *Cal. Carew MSS*, iii, 374–376, for a list of provisions for the Derry hospital.

63   *Ibid.*

64   *CSPI* (1600–1601), 113.

65   CCR, mayor's military papers, M/MP/12, f.38, list of discharged soldiers signed by Thomas Dowghton and Sir Henry Docwra.

66   *CSPI* (1600) 406.

67   Between March 1599 and 1603 Docwra wrote over fifty letters to London: understandably one of the items he requested for Lough Foyle was 'writing paper – one reame, and incke – one gallon', *CSPI* (1600), 95.

68   *CSPI* (1600–1601), 29.

69   *Ibid.*, 121.

70   *CSPI* (1596–1597), 214.

71   *Ibid.*, 300.

72   *Ibid.*, 315.

73   William Farmer, *Chronicles of Ireland 1594–1613*, ed. C. Litton Falkiner, *English Historical Review*, 85 (1907), 115.

74   *CSPI* (1599–1600), 332.

75   *CSPI* (1600), 13.

76   P. Walsh, ed., *O'Clery's life of Red Hugh O'Donnell* (Dublin, 1948), 183, 185.

77   Fynes Moryson, *Itinerary*, vol. iii, 55.

78   *CSPI* (1599–1600), 350, Captain John Baynard's address to the queen, endorsed '1599 December'.

79   J. W. Fortescue, *The history of the British army* (London, 1899), vol. i, 157.

80   *APC*, xxxii, 194.

81   J. R. Kent, 'The social attitudes of members of parliament, 1590–1624', PhD thesis (University of London, 1971), 41.

82   35 Eliz., c. 4 (1593), from the preamble to the Act.

83   PRO SP12/244, 125.

84   BL Lansdowne MSS, 73, f. 130–130v.

85 The debate is rehearsed in J. R. Kent, 'The social attitudes of members of parliament, 1590–1624', PhD thesis (University of London, 1971), 46–48.
86 BL Lansdowne MSS, 73, f. 130v.
87 35 Eliz., c. 4 (1593).
88 39 & 40 Eliz., c. 17.
89 43 Eliz., c. 3.
90 PRO SP12/244, ff. 118, 119.
91 PRO SP12/288, 73/75, maimed soldiers' fund in Cornwall.
92 PRO SP12/244, f. 125.
93 *Ibid.*
94 BL Stowe MSS, 362, f. 223v.
95 *CSPD* (1598–1601), 13.
96 J. R. Kent, 'The social attitudes of members of parliament, 1590–1624', PhD thesis (University of London, 1971), 37.
97 J. J. N. McGurk, 'Casualties and welfare measures for the sick and wounded of the Nine Years War in Ireland, 1594–1603', *Journal of the Society for Army Historical Research*, 68 (1990), appendix, 'A register of relief awarded disabled and aged soldiers from petitions 1593–1603'.
98 *CSPD* (1598–1601), 388.
99 *APC*, xxxii, 366.
100 39 & 40 Eliz., c. 17.
101 P. L. Hughes and J. F. Larkin, *Tudor royal proclamations* (New Haven, 1964–1969), vol. iii, nos 740, 745, 762, 779, 796.
102 R. H. Tawney and E. Power, *Tudor economic documents* (London, 1924), vol. ii, 343.
103 *CSPD* (1598–1601), 2.
104 PRO SP12/268, 54.
105 J. J. N. McGurk, 'Casualties and welfare measures for the sick and wounded of the Nine Years War in Ireland, 1594–1603', *Journal of the Society for Army Historical Research*, 68 (1990), appendix, 'A register of relief awarded disabled and aged soldiers from petitions 1593–1603'.
106 *APC*, xxviii–xxxii (1597–1603), 125, 251, 420–429.
107 R. H. Tawney and E. Power, *Tudor economic documents* (London, 1924), vol. ii, 345.
108 *CSPI* (1599–1600), 240; *CSPI* (1603–1606), 125, 251, 420–429.
109 *APC*, xxxii, 142.
110 *Ibid.*, 143, and for examples earlier in the war, *APC*, xxv, 386 and 391.
111 CCR, mayor's military papers, M/MP12, f. 38, list of forty-two soldiers discharged from Lough Foyle garrisons, 6 March 1600.
112 F. J. Furnival, *English entries from the mayors' books, Chester, 1597–98* (Early English Texts Society, no. 108, London, 1897), 168–171.
113 S. A. H. Burne, ed., *Staffordshire quarter sessions rolls* (William Salt Library, Stafford, 1931–1936), vols i–iv, *passim.*
114 This aspect is not noted by P. Clark in his *English provincial society from the Reformation to the Revolution: religion, politics and society in Kent, 1500–1640* (Hassocks, 1977).
115 BL Additional MSS, 41137, f. 182. This manuscript is Lambarde's original of the Eirenarcha, which went through seven editions by 1610. See W. Holdsworth, *History of English law* (London, 1945), vol. iv, 118.
116 SRO, Sir John Leveson's letters and papers, D593/S/4, 39, 10, 17 August 1595.
117 KAO, quarter sessions records, Q/SR/1.
118 KAO, quarter sessions records, QM/SB/80, 142 (i–iv), samples of presentments.
119 KAO, quarter sessions records, QM/SR/2m, 2d. no. 10, Canterbury, Ephiphany, 1601.
120 KAO, quarter sessions records, QM/SM/35.
121 *Ibid.*, 176, 246.

122 J. Tait, ed., *Lancashire quarter sessions records, 1590–1606* (Chetham Society, lxxvii, Manchester, 1917).

123 *Ibid.*, 252, 253, 261, 272, 275.

124 HMC, *Various collections, vol. i, Wiltshire quarter sessions rolls*, ed. W. D. Macray (London, 1901), 69, 70.

125 Army lists in *CSPI* (1595–1602); *Cal. Carew MSS*, iii, iv; and in Fynes Moryson, *Itinerary*, vols ii and iii.

126 HMC, *Various collections, vol. i, Wiltshire quarter sessions rolls*, ed. W. D. Macray (London, 1901), 70, 71.

127 *Ibid.*, 77.

128 *Ibid.*, 85, 86.

129 SRO, Sir John Leveson's letters and papers, D593/S/4, 11, 8.

130 HMC, *Salisbury*, ix; J. H. R. Bennett and J. C. Dewhurst, eds, *Quarter sessions records in Cheshire* (Record Society of Lancs & Cheshire, xciv, London, 1940), 46.

131 PRO SP12/276, 8, not dated.

132 HMC, *Various collections, vol. i, Wiltshire quarter sessions rolls*, ed. W. D. Macray (1901), 99.

133 J. J. N. McGurk, 'Casualties and welfare measures for the sick and wounded of the Nine Years War in Ireland, 1594–1603', *Journal of the Society for Army Historical Research*, 68 (1990), appendix, 'A register of relief awarded disabled and aged soldiers from petitions 1593–1603'.

134 *Calendar of the quarter sessions papers (1591–1643)*, ed. J. W. Willis Bund (Worcestershire County Records, Worcester), 345.

135 *Ibid.*, 76, 77.

136 *Ibid.*, 345.

137 *Ibid.*, cited in the introduction, p. cxlviii. It is by no means clear that there was such a thing as a 'full term' of service in Ireland. Sampson may mean that he was in Ireland for the full duration of the O'Neill war.

138 *Ibid.*, introduction, p. cxlviii.

139 *APC*, xxix, 235.

140 43 Eliz., c. 3 (1601).

141 *Commons Journals*, 1 (1604), 153, and see J. E. Neale, 'The Commons Journals in the Tudor period', *Transactions of the Royal Historical Society*, 4th series, 3 (1920), 136–170.

142 W. Notestein, H. Simpson and F. H. Relf, eds, *Commons debates, 1621* (New Haven, 1935), vol. ii, 403–404. W. K. Jordan did not distinguish the military poor as a separate category. The chief concern of his work was private charitable benefactions in his *Philanthropy in England 1480–1660* (London, 1959); *The charities of rural England 1480–1660* (London, 1961); *Social institutions in Kent, 1480–1660* (Ashford, 1961); and *Social institutions of Lancashire, 1480–1660* (Chetham Society, 3rd series, ii, Manchester, 1962).

143 See J. J. N. McGurk, 'Casualties and welfare measures for the sick and wounded of the Nine Years War in Ireland, 1594–1603', *Journal of the Society for Army Historical Research*, 68 (1990), appendix, 'A register of relief awarded disabled and aged soldiers from petitions 1593–1603'. The author is grateful to the Society for permission to use that article as the basis of this chapter.

Conclusion

This book has been concerned with the Elizabethan effort to fight the Nine Years' War in Ireland; indirectly that effort illustrated the continuing centralising policy of the crown as it clashed in both islands with provincial interests and autonomies. On the Irish side those who have studied late Gaelic Ireland show how the Gaelic revival of the fifteenth century was far from worn out and of how the lordships were in the process of absorbing smaller political entities into larger territorial principalities, such as Hugh O'Neill's in Ulster. The war lasted so long because the crown was financially weak, Elizabeth I vacillating between firm policies of conquest and compromises with O'Neill, vetoing what would have been expensive plans for conquest on the part of her ministers, but not her treasurer, and of not facing up to the realities of the dangers from Ireland until O'Neill's victories and the threat from Spain spelt out the imminent loss of Ireland to the crown. Neglect, muddle and compromise, combined with spasmodic outbreaks of brute force, characterised Elizabethan policy in Ireland until the final conquest was undertaken in the last years of the reign and the Irish for their part were forced into a desperate resistance with the help of Spain. Elizabethan arms, strategies and seapower were successful but the souring of English–Irish relations for contemporaries and descendants left an embittered legacy.

In studying the details of the Elizabethan efforts at home to maintain military forces in field and garrison in Ireland we have seen how the demands of the crown for soldiers were answered reluctantly in the English and Welsh shires. The taxation to have them sent out was resented and conscripted soldiers showed their attitude to the war by frequently deserting. And yet despite the lack of enthusiasm for the Irish war, and with no tradition of an organised standing army or general staff, and with hand-to-mouth financial provision for the needs of large-scale land and sea operations, Ireland was painfully reconquered, if not permanently pacified, between 1594 and 1603. Was the Elizabethan government stronger and more centralised at home because of the demands of the Irish war?

These demands certainly gave the Elizabethan government opportunities for imposing its will on the shires, towns and ports and, on the whole, central government gained ground against provincial autonomies, liberties and past exemptions. The recruitment, the organising and transporting of such large levies necessarily demanded some degree of uniform and central control and, because of the relentless regularity of these demands in the 1590s, the Elizabethan state began to impinge more heavily on the daily lives of the queen's subjects than ever before. The government had ever been able to get its way in demanding support for overseas levies to quell the many minor local rebellions which were a feature of Irish history in the Tudor century. The military establishment in Ireland varied in strength as crisis followed crisis but this and the civil administration in Dublin and the Pale seemed to require rigorous supervision in the prevention of corruption, self-interest and aggrandisement on the part of the New English, who were rapidly adopting a colonial mentality. Earlier in the century Machiavelli, in his *Arte della guerra*, had noted the tensions and contradictions inherent in the civil and military life:

> many are now of the opinion that no two things are more discordant and incongruous than a civil and a military life. But if we consider the nature of government we shall find a very strict and intimate relation betwixt these two conditions.[1]

The civil administration involved in mustering, recruiting, arming, billeting and transporting these levies to Ireland in the 1590s has clearly engaged the interest of more than the purely military historian; the demands of war can hardly be divorced from the society on which it was inflicted. These demands, moreover, highlighted the government's bureaucratic, financial and administrative problems in retaining the sovereignty of Ireland. How did the queen and government manage to avert a major clash with the nation at large over these constant demands of the war in the final decade of the reign? The short answer must be that there was a general consensus in the nation with the queen's and council's commitment to the safety of the state, as the military struggle in Ireland was partially motivated by the continual Spanish threat to England's security.

Ireland's open seaboard invited Spanish intervention in much the same way that queen and council supported the Dutch rebels in their struggle against their Spanish masters. For the Irish, what had started as a rebellion, and mainly in the north in the early 1590s, had become a war of liberation by 1598. And, at Kinsale in 1601, the hostilities in Ireland had taken on an international aspect when Elizabethan forces fought out their last land battle with the Spaniards, hence in that context the Irish war could be seen as part of the continuing war with Spain, after the failure of the Armada of 1588.

Maybe too it could be argued that the queen avoided a major clash with the nation because, unlike her successor, she used the prerogative sparingly, kept factions at court under control, and maintained 'a precarious balance' between the demands of the crown and the temper of the nation, though the Irish war almost upset that balance. There was a crisis in the shires over the thorny question of sending out the trained bands, statutorily exempt from overseas service.[2] Former rights in this respect were ignored in the Irish emergency when on a number of occasions the queen and council ordered the shires to raid their trained bands. The widespread character of the rebellion, its strength under O'Neill's charismatic leadership and the direct invasion threats from Spain dictated that the Elizabethan government pursue a forward policy towards the shires and ports in raising, billeting and transporting troops for the prosecution of the war. Near the end of 1598 the Dublin council warned its English counterpart:

> this rebellion is now thoroughly sorted to an Irish war, whose drifts and pretences are, to shake off all English government, and subtract the kingdom from Her Majesty, as much as in them listeth.[3]

The crisis facing England in Ireland then was just as serious as the crisis facing Spain in the Netherlands; similarities are sometimes drawn, since the enemies of state centralisation reacted in much the same way during their respective revolts. Within England the policy of centralisation, accentuated by the burdens of the Irish war, was deeply resented because these burdens were heavy and frequent and not so much because the localities thought them constitutionally wrong, although some areas, like the Cinque Ports, Stannaries and some chartered towns, cited their past exemptions to the privy council in an attempt to be freed of military taxation and other demands for the war.

From the assessments for military taxation studied, it appears that the governing elites in the shires and merchant dynasties in the ports were far from open-handed in declaring their ability to pay for the Irish war. In the 1601 parliament Sir Robert Cecil saw little change in the prevailing system of taxation in which the rich were under-assessed and the poor squeezed *secundum sanguinem*.[4] In parliament the gentry were loud in their support for the queen and council's Irish war policy but in their home shires they proved unwilling to pay for it. Many wondered how it came about that Ireland was costing so much.[5] Cecil bemoaned that that 'land of Ire has exhausted this land of promise'.[6] His papers showed £4,326,923 expended from taxation and the sale of lands, and he claimed that that revenue was £651,131 short of the charges of war. O'Neill's rebellion is there listed as costing £1,934,000, whereas the previous major rebellion there, that of the Desmonds in 1579–1583, had cost but £254,960.[7] Sums of money raised from the gentry, clergy and recusants were small compared with the costs of the war in the decade 1588–1599: an average sum of £6,000 a year had been collected. Fines and miscellaneous payments brought the treasury about £7,000 in the year 1600, £9,000 in 1601 and £8,500 the following year – peak years of hostilities in Ireland.[8] The lay subsidy of 1601 brought in £80,000 and the clerical subsidy of the same year about £20,000. The totality of these do not compare when we consider that Mountjoy's expenditure between April 1601 and March 1602 was estimated at £322,502. By comparison, in the much longer period 1574–1588 the cost of the Irish administration was estimated at £490,000, of which £370,000 had to be found by subvention from England.[9] However, when the army in Ireland was finally paid in debased coin or 'mixt money' in the last years of the reign and in James I's time to September 1604 the integrity of the crown was called into question, as it was apparently saving millions by the device of debasement.[10]

The fears of the government of a strong reaction to the exceptional demands of Ireland for money and men can occasionally be seen in the preambles of the queen's letters and those of the council to the shire authorities, lords lieutenant, sheriffs and commissioners for musters. Resistance drove the government towards well known financial expedients other than debasement of the coinage, such as the sale of crown lands, the increase in rents for the farm of the customs, the revival of benevolences and loans on privy seals. Heavy war costs also meant that the queen was not lavish in bounties to loyal servants. The Irish war created but few new offices; the main ones were the treasurer-at-war and the muster master. These offices required a large staff in Ireland and a number of lesser posts dependent on them in England, such as the shipping commissioners and provost marshals in the ports. But like so many Tudor officials their salaries were inadequate, so it is not surprising that they were almost expected to use their ingenuity to make profits out of their offices.

The difficulties of raising funds and the constraints the crown had to operate under led to frustration in the prosecution of hostilities. It was not a coincidence that after 1599 privy council directives to train the home militias became less clamorous; in 1601 the shires were ordered only to train the militia, the home defence force, on two days once a year; the year coincided with peak military action in Ireland, which necessitated economy at home in the interests of saving gunpowder and arms and armour for Ireland.[11] William Knollys, uncle of the Earl of Essex, expressed his fears to Cecil in May 1599 about the dangerous effect Ireland would have on this country, likening it to a consumption, 'and it cannot but so infect England as it may grow into the like danger'.[12] Other correspondents, like a John Petit, wrote of Ireland 'as a plague sent to the English when one considered how many good men had been slain there,' the cost it 'has been and is' and the numbers of soldiers sent 'to finish those wars and cannot end them'.[13] Financial straits and price inflation had made the sinews of government creak just when a strong 'forward' policy was required, and this war was conducted at a distance in an age of sail against an elusive and resourceful enemy and where geography, culture and social differences as well as corruption and disloyalty among English administrators hindered any quick solution. Slow progress left the Elizabethan state virtually bankrupt.

The conclusion can hardly be avoided that Ireland was by the end of the reign *not* a low priority, as it had been earlier, but was considered important enough by queen and council to impel them to great expense in men and money to retain sovereignty of the island. It is surprising then that some former historians of Tudor England have played down the Elizabethan effort to regain Ireland in the 1590s – more recent historians do not.[14] We have seen the determination in the writings of the queen, the chief secretary, the privy council and those of high command in Ireland itself to carry out a conquest despite all difficulties. The logistical exercise of recruiting, assembling and transporting 40,678 infantrymen and about 2,000 horses on the part of central and local authorities – especially those in the ports, where soldiers were an unprofitable cargo – and to get the majority of them into mobile field armies and garrisons throughout Ireland was in itself a remarkable achievement. To arrive at an assessment of what economic and social effects the Irish war had on the English and Welsh shires, apart from needing a further volume, may also well prove to be intractable, as the assessment and collection of taxation shire by shire would need further investigation, and the war expenditure noted here in general terms would bear further enquiries; again, revenue and expenditure in years of peace would have to be isolated from war years, itself a difficult task in a period of endemic warfare and when late Elizabethan England and Ireland were both on a war footing.

The hopes often expressed by Elizabethan writers that the Irish war would pay for itself and that the government of Ireland would be self-supporting were dreams, even though the Irish fighting on the English side may be said to have paid in part for their own conquest. Such hopes are generally to be found in the rhetoric of would-be colonisers, who used the dangerous situation as a bargaining point to get constant supplies out of England and from which not a few enriched themselves. As may be seen from the goodly number of captains who became servitors, land greed and a developing colonial mentality towards the country had clearly begun before the great influx of Jacobean planters.

By comparison with other theatres of war, few did well out of the Nine Years' War. Most of the profits were made not by junior military men and gentlemen volunteers manipulating dead pays and muster rolls but by those who took on lucrative army contracts. The treasurer-at-war and the muster master general had large resources at their disposal. The majority who sought position and profit in Ireland frequently found neither, but hardship and frustration instead, so it is small wonder they turned to exploit the government and, if captains, their own men, their political masters, military commanders and at times the civilian population.

Contemporaries and historians are agreed that one of the main factors militating against a proper settlement of Ireland after the conquest was that the disbanded soldiery remaining were unsuitable as colonists and unlikely agents of English law and order; their record in acts of brutality, mutiny and pillage would appear to bear out this conclusion. In the context of sixteenth-century warfare, there was nothing to choose in merciless barbarity and acts of devastation between English and Irish soldiers. Personal profit making in Irish lands was encouraged by the government after the war, but to what extent the expectations of military captains seeking land were fulfilled needs further research. One commentator, Patrick Tipper, claimed in 1604 the cause of all disorder in Ireland arose from the misgovernment of the English, who 'are not only English but military men who delegate to inferior officers' and that they sold their lands 'bestowed by the late Queen Elizabeth' and so conveyed the money out of Ireland to the impoverishment of the country. Understandably, Tipper recommended the removal of all the military to relieve the financial burden on both countries.[15]

What the queen's ordinary subjects thought of the Irish war was not given written expression but their desertions and reluctance to provide men, horses and money were eloquent enough; so too are the few records of disloyalty, treasonable conduct and such like from the courts martial and quarter sessions. The Elizabethan soldier certainly understood his oath 'to do all loyal true and faithful service unto the Queen', an oath he took when he entered into pay, but to what extent he felt bound by this in Ireland, where he may not have been paid, is an imponderable question.[16] Furthermore, his monarch's legal sovereign rights over a country not his own may well have been too intangible a concept for him to risk life and limb away from home. In the end it was such reluctant soldiers, lifted from their farms and villages in the cause of a war, many hardly understanding what they were fighting for, who helped to make a military conquest of Ireland in the last days of the queen's reign, when the nation at large was weary of an old woman's government.

Demobilisation at the end of the war was anticipated with dread in many ports and shires; some of the soldiers had been vagrants or criminals out of the gaols, whose return was not expected. Others had performed honourable service and came back wounded to their native parishes sorry witnesses to the horrors of war. Some went home unpaid and others were unable to take up their former employment. Shires were burdened with paying pensions for the maimed and the steady increase of masterless returning soldiers added to the problems of poverty and vagrancy in a decade when these problems strained the meagre resources of a nascent poor law administration.

By May 1602 the privy council admitted it was the Irish war, not the conflict against Spain in the Low Countries or in France, which had impoverished England;[17] but they claimed they had ploughed too much in men and money into Ireland to lose control over it at the end of the day.[18] Early-seventeenth-century descriptions of Ireland leave the impression that the peace secured by 1603 was more the peace of exhaustion on both sides than the *Pacata Hibernia* the queen would have desired.[19] The war did not provide a long-term solution. In view of the minor rebellions of 1603, 1609 and the major one of 1641 and the subsequent Cromwellian conquest there is a tragic irony in Sir John Davies' comments of 1612:

> we may well conceive the hope that Ireland, which heretofore might properly be called the land of Ire ... will henceforth prove a Land of Peace and Concord and that in the next generation the Irish would become English in heart and tongue so that the Irish Sea would be the only difference between the countries.[20]

And was not Mountjoy, realist though he was, unduly optimistic when he wrote that 'Ulster may easily be made one of the quietest countries of Ireland'?[21] Some of his captains who stayed in Ireland as planters did little to conciliate the Irish during the Jacobean settlement as they and the Old English became steadily alienated from the government of the New English. Hence, in the long term, the Elizabethan reconquest of Ireland was an expensive failure in that it left a smouldering foundation for future national resistance to the exercise of English political power in church and state.

In the context of late-sixteenth-century Europe's increasingly powerful monarchies, who relied on larger armies, better fortifications, more sophisticated firearms and amphibious military operations, higher taxation and tighter central controls over government, religion and law, it was almost inevitable that the Elizabethan state would finally undertake a costly programme of military conquest to bring about a fragile peace. One of the effects of the war was to remove the Old English community, who to some extent had acted as a buffer between the Gaelic Irish and the New English, and this heightened the religious divide and hardened New English policies against the Irish. In its own way this partially explains the eventual success of the Catholic reformation in the seventeenth century and the emergence of a nationalist ideology forged in opposition to all things English; this reformation also began to replace deeply rooted provincial attachments with a new emphasis on Ireland as a fatherland based on a common Catholicism. While O'Neill's appeals to faith and fatherland had little impact on the Old English at the beginning of the war, such emotions would become part of the growing ideology of the native Irish in the next generation.

Notes

1   N. Machiavelli, *Arte della guerra*, ed. and trans. J. Mazzoni and M. Casella (Florence, 1929), 265.
2   *APC*, xxvi, 4.
3   *CSPI*, vii (January 1598 – March 1599), 305.
4   J. E. Neale, *Elizabeth I and her parliaments, 1584–1601* (London, 1957), 414.
5   PRO SP12/269, 6, 19.
6   HMC, *Salisbury*, x, 345.
7   HMC, *Salisbury*, xv, 2.
8   PRO SP12/270, 36; PRO SP12/271, 108; PRO SP12/286, 56.
9   *Cal. Carew MSS*, i, 484; iv, 503–504.
10 M. Dolley, 'The Irish coinage, 1534–1691', in *A new history of Ireland, vol. iii, Early modern Ireland, 1534–1691*, eds T. W. Moody, F. X. Martin and F. J. Byrne (Oxford, 1976), 412–415.
11 *APC*, xxxi, 406.
12 HMC, *Salisbury*, ix, 188–189.
13 PRO SP12/273, 7, J.P. (alias John Petit) to Peter Halins, October 1599.
14 See under the bibliography, A. L. Rowse, L. Stone and W. T. MacCaffrey, but not in the latter's final volume of his trilogy on Queen Elizabeth, *Elizabeth I: war and politics 1588–1603* (Princeton, 1992), where he takes into account recent researches.
15 HMC, *Salisbury*, xxiii (addenda, 1562–1605), 201–203.
16 BL Harleian MSS, 168, f.109b, 'The oath to be ministered unto soldiers upon their entering into pay'.
17 H. Spencer Scott, ed., *The journal of Sir Roger Wilbraham* (Camden Society, London, 1902), 50.
18 *CSPI* (1600–1601), 125.
19 T. Stafford, *Pacata Hibernia* (unedited reprint, 1810), 3.
20 Sir John Davies, *A discovery of the true causes why Ireland was never entirely subdued ... until ... his majesty's most happy reign* (London, 1747), 281.
21 *CSPI* (1601–1603), 81.

Select bibliography

Manuscript sources

Unless otherwise stated the sources here listed are large collections of letters, papers, and reports concerned with the late sixteenth and early seventeenth centuries.

Bodleian Library, Oxford

Ashmole MSS: 781, 840, 1144
Carte MSS: 57, 58, 131
Rawlinson MSS: 657, 754
Tanner MSS: 458
Wood MSS: 504

Bristol Archives Office

Bristol ordinance book and common council minutes: BAO/04026, 04352, 04264, 04441
Mayor's court actions (1567–1761) and mayor's writs (1574–1836)
Mayor's great audit books (1599, 1600, 1601, 1604)
Mayor's miscellanea: BAO/8029, 5, 6
Sessions minute book (1599–1605)

British Library, London

Additional MSS: 11, 32, 33, 34, 41, 137, 162, 177, 370, 473, 574, 907, 4792, 4793, 5495
Cotton MSS:
    Augustus I, ii
    Galba C, viii
    Titus B, X–XIII
Harleian MSS: 168, 357, 594, 1291, 2093, 3292, 7004
Lansdowne MSS: 156, 159, 276
Sloane MS: 2596
Stowe MSS: 145, 362, 422

Cheshire County Record Office

Lieutenancy letter book of Sir Hugh Cholmondeley (1595–1604): DDX358/1–84
Meyer collection: DDX43
Private sessions file: 10 Eliz. I to 44 Eliz. I (gap in the file, 1591–1602)
Quarter sessions book: no. 4, QJB/1–3, for 1593–1608

City of Chester Record Office

Mayor's assembly books: A/B/1
Mayor's files: M/F/30, 31
Mayor's great letter books: M/L/1, 11, 109, 112–117, 119–122, 127; M/L/2, M/L/5
Mayor's military papers: M/MP/7, 8, 9, 10, 11, 12, 13
Quarter sessions files: QSF/49, 1–153 for the years 1599–1601
Sheriff of Chester's files of writ: uncatalogued and damaged

College of Arms

Talbot MSS: K, L, M, N, including the letters and papers of Gilbert, 7th Earl Shrewsbury

Folger Shakespeare Library, Washington, DC

MS collection X. d. 393, formerly 4444, dealing in part with Kinsale, microfilm sent with thanks

Hatfield House, Hertfordshire

Cecil papers: 24–67, 70–73, 133–143, 177–179

Kent County Archives, Maidstone

Quarter sessions records: Q/SR/1–5; Q/SM; QM/SB/145
Scott lieutenancy papers: U1115/04–013

Lambeth Palace Library, London

Archbishop's clerical muster book: MS 2009
Carew MSS: 615, 620, 621, 624, 632
Fairhurst collection: MS 2004–2008
Miscellaneous musters: MS 247
Twysden book of musters, Kent: MS 1392
Twysden lieutenancy papers: MS 1393

Lancashire Record Office

Houghton lieutenancy letter book: DDN/1
Lay subsidy roll for 1593: LRO/DDF/2430

Lieutenancy minute book: LV/80
Muster roll of 1600: DDH/61

National Library, Dublin

Blackwater valley description, 1602: MS 2656, 8
Lodge's MSS: M5037–9
Mayor of Waterford (1601): MS 4637

Public Record Office, London and Belfast (NI)

Declared accounts: 165–168, merchant contracts for 1599 and 1600
Exchequer records and accounts: E 101/65/5, 17, 19, 27, 28 – shire musters
Maps: M/PF 50, 72, 81, 86, 98, 117, 133, 311, 335, mainly of Ulster forts and garrisons
Port books: E 190
State papers:
    Domestic, addenda, SP 15
    Domestic, Elizabeth, SP 12
    Ireland, Elizabeth, SP 63

Staffordshire Record Office, William Salt Library, Stafford

Extensive collection of Sir John Leveson's letters and papers, 70 boxes: SRO D593/S/4– (Irish
    interest from S/4/22–70)

Trinity College, Dublin

College lands: MUN/P/23/–
Description of the north of Ireland with inset plans: 1209/14–
Harrington's Wicklow defeat: 1209/12–
Pynnar's survey of Derry: 864–
Selection of Docwra letters: MS 845–

Printed primary sources (record publications)

Acts of the privy council of England 1542–1631 (1890–1907), 32 vols
Analecta Hibernica (Irish Manuscripts Commission, Dublin, 1930)
Baines, E., *A history of the county palatine and duchy of Lancashire*, 5 vols, ed. J. Croston
    (Manchester, 1888–1893)
Ballinger, J., ed., *Calendar of Wynn papers* (Aberystwyth, 1926)
Bateson, M., ed., *Records of the Borough of Leicester*, 3 vols (Cambridge, 1899–1905)
Batho, G., ed., *Calendar of Shrewsbury and Talbot papers*, vol. ii (Derby, 1971)
Beacon, R., *Solon his follie* (Oxford, 1594)

Bennett, J. H. E. and J. C. Dewhurst, eds, *Select Cheshire quarter sessions records 1528–1760* (Record Society of Lancashire and Cheshire, 1940)

Brownbill, J., ed., *Calendar of Moore MSS* (Record Society for Lancashire and Cheshire, London, 1913)

Bruce, J., ed., *Diary of John Manningham, 1602–1603* (Camden Society, London, 1868)

Burne, S. A. H., ed., *Staffordshire quarter sessions rolls*, vol. iii (1594–1597) (Stafford Record Society, 1933)

Calendar of Carew MSS preserved at Lambeth Palace Library, 6 vols (1867–1873)

Calendar of state papers, domestic, 1547–1625, 12 vols (1856–1872)

Calendar of state papers, Ireland, 1509–1603, 11 vols (1860–1912)

Calendar of state papers, Scotland, 1589–1603

Calendar of state papers, Spanish, 1485–1603, 17 vols (1862–1964)

Calendar of state papers, Venetian, 1509–1603, 9 vols (1867–1898)

Camden, W., *Britannia sive ... Angliae, Scotiae, Hiberniae...* (1586), trans. R. Gough, 3 vols (London, 1789)

Campion, E., *A Historie of Ireland* (1571), ed. R. G. Gottfried (New York, 1940)

Chanter, J. R. and T. Wainwright, eds, *Barnstaple records*, 2 vols (Barnstaple, 1900)

Churchyard, T., *A generall rehearsall of warres* (London, 1579)

Clapham, J., *Certain observations concerning the life and reign of Queen Elizabeth*, eds E. and C. Read (Philadelphia, 1951)

Collins, A., ed., *Letters and memorials of state from the De L'isle and Dudley papers* (London, 1746), vol. ii, 137

Collins, A., ed., *Letters and memorials of state*, vol. iii (London, 1746)

Cox, J. C., ed., *Calendar of the records of Co. Derbyshire, 1558–1896* (London, 1899)

Cox, J. C., ed., *Three centuries of Derbyshire annals*, 2 vols (London, 1890)

Curtis, E., ed., *Calendar of Ormond deeds*, vols iii–iv (1413–1603) (Dublin, 1935–1943)

Curtis, E. and R. B. McDowell, eds, *Irish Historical Documents* (London, 1936)

Davies, J., *A discovery of the true causes why Ireland was never entirely subdued ... until his majesty's happy reign* (1612), facsimile reprint, ed. H. Morley (Shannon, 1969)

Derricke, J., *The image of Irelande* (1581), J. Small's edn (London, 1883)

Desiderata curiosa Hibernica; or a select collection of state papers (Dublin, 1772)

Devereux, W., *The lives and letters of the Devereux Earls of Essex*, 2 vols (London, 1853)

D'Ewes, S., *Journal of all the parliaments* (London, 1693)

Dictionary of national biography (DNB), ed. L. Stephen and S. Lee, 22 vols (2nd edn, London, 1908–1909)

Digges, T., *An arithmeticall militare treatise, named stratioticos* (London, 1590)

Docwra, H., *Relation and narration* (1614), ed. J. O'Donovan (Celtic Miscellany, Dublin, 1849)

Dymmock, J., *Treatice of Irelande*, ed. R. Butler (Irish Archaeological Society, ii, Dublin, 1843)

Edelen, G., ed., *William Harrison's description of England* (Folger Shakespeare Library, Ithaca, 1968)

Edwards, R. D. and M. O'Dowd, *Sources for early modern Irish history, 1534–1641* (Cambridge, 1985)

Farmer, W., *Chronicles of Ireland*, ed. C. Litton Falkiner, *English Historical Review*, 85 (1907)

Fisher, F. J., ed., *The state of England anno domini 1600 by Sir Thomas Wilson* (Camden Miscellany, 3rd series, xvi, London, 1936)

Freeman, A. M., ed., *Compossicion booke of Connacht* (Irish Manuscripts Commission, Dublin, 1936)

Freeman, A. M., ed., *Annals of Connaught* (Dublin, 1944)

Furnival, F. J., *English entries from the mayors' books, Chester, 1597–98* (Early English Texts Society, no. 108, London, 1897)

G. A. Hayes-McCoy, *Ulster and other Irish maps c. 1600* (Irish Manuscripts Commission, Dublin, 1964)

Gilbert, T. J., ed., *Calendar of the ancient records of Dublin* (Dublin, 1891)

Goodman, G., *The court of King James I*, vol. i (ed. J. S. Brewer, 1839)

Gribble, J. B., ed., *Memorials of Barnstaple* (London, 1830)

Hamilton, C. L., ed.,*The muster master by Gervase Markham* (Camden Society, London, 1975)

Harrington, J., *Nugae antiquae*, ed. T. Park (London, 1804)

Harrison, W., *Description of England*, ed. F. J. Furnivall (London, 1877)

Hayes, J. R., *Manuscript sources for the history of Irish civilization*, 11 vols (National Library, Ireland, 1965–)

Hayes, T., *England's hope against Irish hate* (Lambeth Palace Library, London, 1600)

Hennessey, W. M., ed., *Annals of Lough Ce: a chronicle of Irish affairs, 1014–1590*, 2 vols (London, 1871)

Herbert, W., *Croftus: sive de Hibernia Liber*, eds A. Keaveney and J. Madden (Irish Manuscripts Commission, Dublin, 1992)

Hinton, E. M., *Ireland through Tudor eyes* (Philadelphia, 1935)

Historical Manuscripts Commission, *9th report for Barnstaple, Plymouth and Rochester*, 3 vols (London, 1883–1884)

Historical Manuscripts Commission, *Guide to the reports, I Topographical and II Persons* (London, 1870–1911)

Historical Manuscripts Commission, *Foljambe* (London, 1897)

Historical Manuscripts Commission, *Ormond MSS*, new series, I (London, 1902)

Historical Manuscripts Commission, *Salisbury (Cecil) MSS*: vols iv–xii, xiii (addenda, 1509–1596), xiv (addenda, 1596–1603) and xv–xviii – calendars of the MSS at Hatfield House)

Hogan, E., ed., *Description of Ireland in anno 1598* (Dublin, 1878)

Holinshead, R., *Chronicles of England, Scotland and Ireland*, vol. 6 (London, 1808)

Hollis, D., ed., *Calendar of the Bristol Apprentice Book*, 1532–1542 (Bristol, 1949)

Hughes, J. L. J., ed., *Patentee officers in Ireland* (Irish Manuscripts Commission, Dublin, 1960)

Hughes, P. L. and J. F. Larkin, *Tudor royal proclamations*, 3 vols (Yale, 1964–1969)

Irish Manuscripts Commission, *Bishopric of Derry and the Irish of London, 1602–1705* (Dublin, 1968)

James, T. B. and A. L. Merson, eds, *Third book of remembrance of Southampton* (1514–1602) (Southampton, 1979)

Jennings, B., ed., *Wild geese in Spanish Flanders* (Irish Manuscripts Commission, Dublin, 1964)

Jones Pierce, T., ed., *Calendar of Clenennau letters and papers* (*National Library of Wales Journal* supplement, Cardiff, 1947)

King, D., *The history of the county palatine and city of Chester*, ed. G. Ormerod (London, 1819)

Kinney, A., ed., *Historical documents of the age of Elizabeth* (Connecticut, 1975)

Knyvett, H., *The defence of the realm* (London, 1596)

Lambarde, W., *A perambulation of Kent* (1596) (facsimile edn, London, 1970)

Latimer, J., ed., *Annals of Bristol in the sixteenth century* (Bristol, 1900)

Leland, J., *Itinerary*, ed. Toulmin Smith (London, 1906–1908)

Lewis, E. A., ed., *Welsh port books*, 1550–1603 (Cymmrodorion Records Society, Cardiff, 1927)

Livock, D., ed., *City chamberlain accounts of the late sixteenth and early seventeenth centuries* (Bristol Record Society, xxiv, Bristol, 1966)

Loades, D. M., ed., *The papers of George Wyatt* (Camden Society, London, 1968)

Lodge, E., ed., *Illustrations of British history*, vols I–III (London, 1838)

Lombard, P., *De Regno Hiberniae*, ed. P. F. Moran (Dublin, 1868)

Longfield, A. K., ed., *Fitzwilliam accounts 1560–1565* (Annesley collection) (Irish Manuscripts Commission, Dublin, 1960)

Lynch, J., *Cambrensis Eversus*, ed. M. Kelly, 3 vols (Dublin, 1848–1852)

MacCarthy, D., ed., *Life and letters of Florence McCarthy Mor* (Dublin, 1867)

Maclean, J., ed., *Letters of Sir Robert Cecil to Sir George Carew* (Camden Society, London, 1864)

Maxwell,. C., ed., *Irish history from contemporary sources* (London, 1923)

McGurk, J. J. N., ed., *Calendar of Edward, Lord Wotton's lieutenancy letter book*, in *Archaeolgia Cantiana* (Ashford, 1967)

McNeill, C., ed., *Tanner letters* (Irish Manuscripts Commission, Dublin, 1943)

Monson, W., *Naval tracts*, ed. M. Oppenheim (Navy Record Society, London, 1902–1914)

Morley, H., ed., *Ireland under Elizabeth and James* (London, 1890)

Morley, H., ed., Sir John Davies' 'A Discovery of the True Causes why Ireland was never entirely subdued...', in *Ireland under Elizabeth and James* (London, 1890), 218–221

Morrin, J., ed., *Calendar of patent and close rolls of Chancery in Ireland, Henry VIII – Elizabeth*, 2 vols (Dublin, 1861–1862)

Morris, R. H., *Chester in Plantagenet and Tudor reigns* (Chester, 1893)

Moryson, F., *An itinerary ... and a description of Ireland*, ed. J. McLehose, 4 vols (Glasgow, 1907–1908)

Murdin, W., *A collection of state papers relating to affairs in the reign of Queen Elizabeth from the year 1571–1596* (London, 1759)

Naunton, R., *Fragmenta Regalia*, ed. E. Arber (London, 1895)

Notestein, W., H. Simpson and F. H. Relf, eds, *Commons debates, 1621* (New Haven, 1935)

O'Clery, M., *The life of Red Hugh O'Donnell*, ed. P. Walsh, parts i, ii (Dublin, 1948, 1957)

O'Donovan, J., ed. and trans., *Annals of the kingdom of Ireland by the Four Masters*, 7 vols (Dublin, 1851)

O'Sullivan Beare, P., *Historiae Catholicae Iberniae compendium* (Lisbon, 1621), ed. and trans. in part by M. J. Byrne in *Ireland under Elizabeth* (Dublin, 1903)

Owen, G., *The Taylor's cussion* (a sixteenth century commonplace book of G. Owen on Pembrokeshire) (facsimile edn, London, 1906)

Perrot, J., *Chronicle of Ireland, 1584–1608*, ed. H. Wood (Irish Manuscripts Commission, Dublin, 1933)

Platter, T., *Travels in England in 1599*, trans. and ed. C. Williams (London, 1937)

Prothero, G., *Select statutes and other constitutional documents illustrative of the reigns of Elizabeth and James I* (Oxford, 1913)

Raines, F. R., ed., *The Derby household books* (Chetham Society, xxxi, Manchester, 1853)

Read, C., ed., *William Lambarde and local government* (Ithaca, 1962)

Redington, J,. ed., *Calendar of Treasury papers, 1577–1696* (London, 1868)

Rich, B., *A new description of Ireland* (1610), ed. E. Hogan (Dublin, 1878)

Rich, B., *Looking glass wherein Her Majesty may view Ireland, 1599*, in the *Calendar of the state papers, Ireland*, vol. 205, pp. 45–52, under 1599

Rich, B., *Pathway to military discipline and practise* (London, 1587)

Salter, H. E., ed., *Oxford Council Acts 1583–1626* (Oxford Historical Society, lxxxvii, Oxford, 1928)

Scott Thomson, G., ed., *Calendar of Twysden lieutenancy papers* (Ashford, 1926)

Seyer, R., *Memorials historical and topographical of Bristol*, 2 vols (Bristol, 1821–1823)

Smythe, J., *Instructions, observations and orders mylitarie* (London, 1595)

Smythe, J., *Certain discourses concerninge the formes and effects of divers sorts of weapons* (1590), ed. J. R. Hale (New York, 1964)

Spencer Scott, H., ed., *The journal of Sir Roger Wilbraham* (Camden Society, London, 1902)

Spenser, E., *A view of the present state of Ireland* (1633), ed. W. L. Renwick (Oxford, 1970)

Stafford, T., *Pacata Hibernia* (1633), ed. S. O'Grady, 2 vols (Dublin, 1896)

Stanihurst, R., *A treatise conceringe a plain and perfect description of Ireland* (1577), in R. Hollinshed's *Chronicles of England, Scotland and Ireland* (London, 1808 edn).

Strype, J., *Annals of the Reformation*, 2 vols (Oxford, 1820–1840)

Tait, J., ed., *Lancashire quarter session records* (Chetham Society, lxxvii, Manchester, 1919)

Select bibliography

Tawney R. and E. Power, eds, *Tudor economic documents*, vol. ii (London, 1924)
Tenison, E. M., ed., *Elizabethan England,*, 14 vols (Leamington, 1933–1961)
Treharne, J. M., ed., *The Stradling correspondence* (Camden Society, London, 1840)
Twemlow, J. A., ed., *Liverpool town books* (Liverpool, 1918)
Vanes, J., ed., *Bristol records* (Bristol, 1979)
Wake, J., ed., *Musters, beacons and subsidies in the county of Northamptonshire, 1586–1623* (Northants Record Society, iii, London, 1926)
Williams, S., ed., *Letters written by John Chamberlain during the reign of Queen Elizabeth* (Camden Society, lxxix, London, 1861)
Willis Bund, J. W., ed., *Calendar of quarter sessions records, Worcestershire* (Worcester, 1899–1900)
Wilson, K. P., ed., *Chester customs accounts 1301–1566* (Liverpool, 1969)
Young, S., ed., *Annals of the Barber Surgeons of London* (London, 1890)

Secondary sources (later works)

Published books and articles

Alsop, J. D., 'Government, finance and the community of the exchequer', in *The reign of Elizabeth I*, ed. C. Haigh (London, 1985), 101–124
Andrews, J. H., 'The Irish surveys of Robert Lythe', *Imago Mundi*, xix (1965), 22–31
Andrews, J. H., 'Geography and government in Elizabethan Ireland', *Irish Geographical Studies* (1970), 179–219
Andrews, J. H., 'An early map of Inishowen', *Bulletin of the Friends of the Library, Trinity College*, 73 (1973), 19–25
Andrews, K. R., *Elizabethan privateering* (Cambridge, 1966)
Andrews, K. R., *et al.*, eds, *The westward enterprise; English activities in Ireland, the Atlantic and America, 1480–1650* (Liverpool, 1978)
Appleby, A. B., *Famine in Tudor and Stuart England* (Liverpool, 1978)
Appleby, J. C., 'The fishing ventures of Nicholas Weston of Dublin', *Dublin Historical Record*, 39 (1986), 150–155
Appleby, J. C., *A calendar of material relating to Ireland from the High Court Admiralty examinations 1536–1641* (Dublin, 1992)
Ashton, R., *The crown and the money market 1603–1640* (London, 1960)
Axon, W. E. A., *The annals of Manchester* (Manchester, 1886)
Aydelotte, F., *Elizabethan rogues and vagabonds* (Oxford, 1913)
Bagwell, R., *Ireland under the Tudors*, 3 vols (London, 1885–1890)
Baines, E., *History of Lancashire* (reprint of 1864 edn, Manchester, 1968)
Beck, J., *Tudor Cheshire* (Chester, 1969)
Beckett, J., *Confrontations: studies in Irish history* (London, 1972)
Berry, W., *Pedigrees of families in the County of Kent* (Maidstone, 1830)
Bindoff, S., *Tudor England* (London, 1950)
Blackwood, B. G., *The Lancashire gentry and the Great Rebellion* (Chetham Society, xxv, Manchester, 1978)
Bossy, J., 'The counter reformation and the people of Catholic Ireland, 1596–1641', *Historical Studies*, 8 (1971), 155–169
Boynton, L., 'The Tudor provost marshal', *English Historical Review*, 77 (1962), 437–455
Boynton, L., *The Elizabethan militia* (London, 1967)
Bradshaw, B., 'The Elizabethans and the Irish', *Studies*, 66 (1977), 38–50

Bradshaw, B., 'Sword, word and strategy in the reformation in Ireland', *Historical Journal*, 21 (1978), 475–502

Bradshaw, B., 'Native reaction to the westward enterprise; a case study in Gaelic ideology', in *The westward enterprise*, eds K. R. Andrews, N. P. Canny and P. E. P. Hair (Liverpool, 1978), 65–85

Bradshaw, B., *The Irish constitutional revolution of the sixteenth century* (Cambridge, 1979)

Bradshaw, B., 'The Elizabethans and the Irish; a muddled model', *Studies*, 70 (1981), 233–244

Brady, C., 'Spenser's Irish crisis; humanism and experience in the 1590s', *Past and Present*, 111 (1986), 17–49

Brady, C., *Interpreting Irish history* (Dublin, 1994)

Brady, C., *The chief governors: the rise and fall of reform government in Tudor Ireland, 1536–1588* (Cambridge, 1994)

Brady, C. and R. Gillespie, eds, *Natives and newcomers; essays on the making of Irish colonial society 1534–1641* (Dublin, 1986)

Bridenbaugh, C., *Vexed and troubled Englishmen* (Oxford, 1976)

Buckatzsch, E. J., 'The geographical distribution of wealth in England 1086–1843', *Economic History Review*, 2nd series, 3 (1950), 180–202

Burke's Irish family records (5th edn, London, 1976)

Burne, S. A. H., ed., *Staffordshire sessions records* (Stafford, 1933)

Butler, W. F. T., *Gleanings from Irish history* (Dublin, 1925)

Butterworth, A., *Old Cheshire families* (London, 1932)

Byrne, M. J., *Ireland under Elizabeth* (Dublin, 1903)

Byrne, M. St Clare, *Elizabethan life in town and country* (reprint, London, 1957)

Campbell, M., *The English yeoman under Elizabeth and the early Stuarts* (New Haven, 1942)

Canny, N. P., 'The treaty of Mellifont and the re-organization of Ulster 1603', *Irish Sword*, 9 (1969–1970), 249–262

Canny, N. P., 'Hugh O'Neill and the changing face of Gaelic Ulster', *Studia Hibernica*, 10 (1970), 7–35

Canny, N. P., *The formation of the Old English elite in Ireland* (Dublin, 1975)

Canny, N. P., *The Elizabethan conquest of Ireland: a pattern established, 1565–1576* (Hassocks, 1976)

Canny, N. P., *The upstart earl* (Cambridge, 1982)

Canny, N. P., *From Reformation to Restoration* (Dublin, 1987)

Canny, N. P., *Kingdom and colony: Ireland in the Atlantic world 1560–1800* (Baltimore, 1988)

Challis, C. E., *The Tudor coinage* (Manchester, 1978)

Chamberlain, F., *The sayings of Queen Elizabeth* (London, 1923)

Chambers, A., *Granuaile; the life and times of Grace O'Malley* (Dublin, 1979)

Charles, B. G., *George Owen of Henllys: a biography* (Aberystwyth, 1973)

Clark, P., *English provincial society from the Reformation to the Revolution: religion, politics and society in Kent 1500–1640* (Hassocks, 1977)

Clark, P., ed., *The English commonwealth* (London, 1979)

Clark, P. and P. Slack, eds, *Crisis and order in English towns 1500–1700* (London, 1972)

Clarke, A., *The Old English in Ireland 1625–1642* (London, 1966)

Coburn Walshe, H., 'The rebellion of William Nugent 1581', in *Religion, conflict and co-existence in Ireland*, eds R. V. Comerford et al. (Dublin, 1990), 26–52

Cockle, M. J. D., ed., *Bibliography of English military books 1642 and of contemporary foreign books* (London, 1900)

Corish, P., ed., *The history of Irish Catholicism*, 4 vols (Dublin, 1967)

Cosgrove, A., ed., *A new history of Ireland, vol. ii, medieval Ireland 1169–1534* (Oxford, 1987)

Coward, B., 'Disputed inheritances; some difficulties of the nobility in the late sixteenth and early seventeenth centuries', *Historical Research Bulletin of the Institute of Historical Research*, 44 (1971), 204–214

Crawford, J., *Anglicising the government of Ireland ... 1556–1578* (Dublin, 1993)

Cruickshank, C. G., 'Dead pays in the Elizabethan army', *English Historical Review*, 53 (1938), 93–97

Cruickshank, C. G., *Elizabeth's army* (Oxford, 1970)

Cunningham, B., 'The composition of Connaught in the lordship of Clanrickard and Thomond, 1577–1641', *Irish Historical Studies*, 24 (1984), 1–14

Darby, H. C., ed., *Historical geography of England* (Cambridge, 1963)

Davies, C. S. L., 'Provisions for armies, 1509–1550', *Economic History Review*, 2nd series, 17 (1964), 234–248

Dawtry, J., *The Falstaff sage* (London, 1927)

Dewar, M., *Sir Thomas Smith: a Tudor intellectual in office* (London, 1964)

Dietz, F. C., *English public finance, 1558–1641* (reprint, New York, 1964)

Dodd, A. H., *A history of Carnarvonshire, 1284–1900* (Carnarvon, 1968)

Dolley, M., 'Anglo Irish monetary polices, 1172–1637', *Historical Studies*, 7 (1969), 45–64

Dunlop, R., 'Sixteenth century maps of Ireland', *English Historical Review*, 20 (1905), 309–337

Dunlop, R., 'Sixteenth century schemes for the plantation of Ulster', *Scottish Historical Review*, 22 (1924–1925), 51–60; 115–126; 199–212

Edwards, R. D., *Church and state in Tudor Ireland* (Dublin, 1935)

Edwards, R. D., 'Ireland, Elizabeth I and the counter reformation', in *Elizabethan government and society*, eds S. T. Bindoff, J. Hurstfield and C. H. Williams (London, 1960), 315–339

Edwards, R. D., *Ireland in the age of the Tudors: the destruction of the Hiberno–Norse civilization* (London, 1977)

Edwards, R. D. and M. O'Dowd, *Sources for early modern Irish History, 1534–1641* (Cambridge, 1985)

Ellis, S., 'England in the Tudor state', *Historical Journal*, 26 (1983), 201–212

Ellis, S., *Tudor Ireland: crown, community and the conflict of cultures 1470–1603* (London, 1985)

Ellis, S., *Reform and revival: English government in Ireland, 1470–1534* (Woodbridge, 1986)

Ellis, S., *The pale and the far north; government and society in two Tudor borderlands* (Galway, 1988)

Ellis, S., 'Economic problems of the church; why the reformation failed in Ireland', *Journal of Ecclesiastical History*, 41 (1990), 239–265

Elton, G., *Modern historians on British history 1485–1945* (Cambridge, 1970)

Elton, G., *Studies in Tudor and Stuart politics and government*, 3 vols (Cambridge, 1974–1983)

Elton, G., 'Taxation for war and peace in early Tudor England', in *War and economic development*, ed. J. M. Winter (Cambridge, 1975), 257–292

Emmison, F. G., *Elizabethan life* (Chelmsford, 1973)

Everitt, A., *Change in the provinces: the seventeenth century* (Leicester, 1969)

Falkiner, C. L., *Illustrations of Irish history and topography* (London, 1904)

Falkiner, C. L., *Essays relating to Ireland* (Dublin, 1909)

Falls, C. *Elizabeth's Irish wars* (London, 1950)

Flower, R., *The Irish tradition* (Oxford, 1947)

Ford, A., *The Protestant reformation in Ireland, 1590–1641* (Frankfurt am Main, 1985)

Fortescue, J. W., *The history of the British army*, vol. i (London, 1899)

Foster, F. F., *The politics of stability* (Royal Historical Society, London, 1977)

Freeman Foster, F., *The politics of stability* (Royal Historical Society, London, 1977)

Froude, J. A., *The English in Ireland* (London, 1901)

Gardiner, S. R., *History of England* (London, 1883)

Glasgow, T., Jr, 'The Elizabethan Navy in Ireland, 1558–1603', *Irish Sword*, 7 (1965/1966), 291–307

Gleason, J. H., *The justices of the peace in England, 1558–1604* (Oxford, 1969)

Gribble, J. B., *Memorials of Barnstaple* (Barnstaple, 1830)

Hagan, J., ed., 'Some papers relating to the Nine Years War from the Borghese Collections of the MSS Vat. Archives', *Archivium Hibernicum*, 3 (1914), 241–296

Haigh, C., *Reformation and resistance in Tudor Lancashire* (Cambridge, 1975)

Hale, J. R., 'Sixteenth century explanations of war and violence', *Past and Present*, 2 (1971), 3–26

Hale, J. R., ed., *Renaissance war studies* (London, 1983)

Hall, H., *Society in the Elizabethan age* (London, 1888)

Harland, J., ed., *The Lancashire lieutenancy under the Tudors and Stuarts* (Chetham Society, xlix, Manchester, 1859)

Harrison, W., 'Leland's itinerary', *Transactions of the Lancashire and Cheshire Antiquarian Society*, 28 (1910), 40–58

Hasler, P. W., *The House of Commons, 1558–1603*, 3 vols (London, 1981)

Hasted, E., *History and topographical survey of the county of Kent*, 12 vols (Canterbury, 1797–1801)

Hayes-McCoy, G. A., *Scots mercenary forces in Ireland, 1565–1603* (Dublin, 1937)

Hayes-McCoy, G. A., 'Strategy and tactics in Irish warfare, 1593–1601', *Irish Historical Studies*, 2 (1941), 255

Hayes-McCoy, G. A., 'The Army of Ulster, 1593–1601', *Irish Sword*, 1 (1950), 105–117

Hayes-McCoy, G. A., 'Gaelic society in Ireland in the late sixteenth century', *Historical Studies*, 4 (1963), 45–61

Hayes-McCoy, G. A., *Irish battles* (London, 1969)

Henley, P., *Spenser in Ireland* (Dublin, 1928)

Henry, L. W., 'Contemporary sources for Essex's lieutenancy in Ireland, 1599', *Irish Historical Studies*, 11 (1958–1959), 8–17

Henry, L. W., 'The earl of Essex and Ireland, 1599', *Historical Research Bulletin of the Institute of Historical Research*, 32 (1959), 1–23

Hill, C., *Intellectual origins of the English Revolution* (Oxford, 1965)

Hill, G., *An historical account of the MacDonnells of Antrim* (Belfast, 1973, reprint, Ballycastle, 1976)

Hill, J. W. F., *Tudor and Stuart Lincoln* (Cambridge, 1956)

Holdsworth, W., *A history of English law*, vol. i (London, 1903)

Hoskins, W. G., 'Harvest fluctuations and English economic history 1480–1619', *Agricultural History Review*, 12 (1964), 28–46

Hoskins, W. G., *The age of plunder, 1500–1547* (London, 1976)

Housden, J. A. J., 'Early posts in England', *English Historical Review*, 18 (1903), 714–718

Hughes, C., *Shakespeare's Europe* (London, 1903)

Hurstfield, J., *The Queen's wards: wardship and marriage under Elizabeth I* (London, 1958)

Hurstfield, J., *Freedom, corruption and government in Elizabethan England* (London, 1973)

Jackson, D., *Intermarriage in Ireland 1550–1650* (Montreal, 1970)

Jackson, K., *A Celtic miscellany* (London, 1951)

Jarvis, R. C., 'The head port of Chester and Liverpool, its creek and member', *Transactions of the Historic Society of Lancashire and Cheshire*, 102 (1950), 69–90

Jones, E. G., 'Anglesey and invasion, 1539–1603', *Transactions of the Anglesey Antiquarian Society* (1946), 26–37

Jones, E. S., *The Trevors of Trevalyn and their descendants* (privately printed, 1955)

Jones, F. M., *Mountjoy; the last Elizabethan deputy* (Dublin, 1958)

Jordan, W. K., 'Social institutions in Kent, 1480–1660', *Archaeologia Cantiana*, 75 (1961)

Jordan, W. K., *The charities of rural England 1480–1660* (London, 1961)

Jordan, W. K., *Social institutions of Lancashire, 1480–1660* (Chetham Society 3rd series, vol. ii, Manchester, 1962)

Jorgensen, P., 'Theoretical views of war in Elizabethan England', *Journal of History of Ideas*, 13 (1952), 469–489

Judges, A. V., *The Elizabethan underworld* (London, 1965)

Kearney, H. F., 'The Irish and their history', *History Workshop Journal*, 31 (1991), 149–155

Lambert, G. W., 'Sir Nicholas Malby', *Journal of the Galway Archive Society*, 23 (1948/1949), 1–13

Leatherbarrow, J. S., *Elizabethan recusants in Lancashire* (Camden Society, 2nd series, no. 110, London, 1947)

Lennon, C., 'The great explosion in Dublin 1597', *Dublin Historical Record*, 42 (1988)

Lennon, C., *Sixteenth century Ireland; the incomplete conquest* (Dublin, 1994)

Lennon, C., 'Dublin's great explosion of 1597', *History Ireland*, 3, no. 3 (1995), 29–34

Lewis, E. A., ed., Analysis of the extant port books of N. Wales', *Transactions of the Honourable Society of Cymmrodorion*, 12 (1927)

Lloyd, H. A., 'The Essex inheritance', *Welsh Historical Review*, 7 (1974), 13–39

Lloyd, H. A., 'Corruption and Sir John Trevor', *Transactions of the Honourable Society of Cymmrodorion* (1975), 79–85

Loeber, R., *A biographical dictionary of architects in Ireland, 1600–1720* (Dublin, 1981)

Longfield, A., *Anglo-Irish trade in the sixteenth century* (London, 1929)

Loomie, A. J., *The Spanish Elizabethans* (New York, 1963)

MacCaffrey, W. T., *Exeter, 1540–1640* (Cambridge, Mass., 1958)

MacCaffrey, W. T., *Elizabeth I: war and politics 1588–1603* (Princeton, 1992)

MacCaffrey, W. T. and I. F. W. Beckett, *The Manchester history of the British army* (Manchester, 1991)

MacCarthy-Morrough, M., *The Munster plantation: migration to southern Ireland 1583–1641* (Oxford, 1986)

Machiavelli, N., *Arte della guerra*, ed. and trans. J. Mazzoni and M. Casella (Florence, 1929)

McCaughan, M. and J. C. Appleby, eds, *The Irish Sea: aspects of maritime history* (Belfast, 1989)

McConica, J., *English humanists and Reformation politics* (Oxford, 1965)

McGurk, J. J. N., 'Levies from Kent to the Elizabethan wars, 1589–1603', *Archaeologia Cantiana*, 88 (1973), 57–72

McGurk, J. J. N., 'Lieutenancy and recusancy in Elizabethan Kent', *Recusant History*, 4 (1974), 157–170

McGurk, J. J. N., 'The clergy and the militia, 1580–1610', *History*, 60 (1975), 198–210

McGurk, J. J. N., 'Royal purveyance in the shire of Kent, 1590–1614', *Historical Research Bulletin of the Institute of Historical Research*, 50 (1977), 58–68

McGurk, J. J. N., 'A levy of seamen in the Cinque ports, 1602', *Mariner's Mirror*, 66 (1980), 137–144

McGurk, J. J. N., 'A survey of the demands made on the Welsh shires to supply soldiers for the Irish war 1594–1602', *Transactions of the Honourable Society of Cymmrodorion* (1983), 56–68

McGurk, J. J. N., 'William Camden: civil historian or Gloriana's propagandist', *History Today*, 38 (1988), 47–53

McGurk, J. J. N., 'Rochester and the Irish levy of October 1601', *Mariner's Mirror*, 74 (1988), 57–66

McGurk, J. J. N., 'Casualties and welfare measures for the sick and wounded of the Nine Years War in Ireland 1594–1602', *Journal of the Society for Army Historical Research*, 68 (1990), 22–35; 188–204

McGurk, J. J. N., 'Wild geese: Irish in European armies (sixteenth–eighteenth centuries)', in *Patterns of migration*, vol. i, ed. P. O. Sullivan (Leicester, 1992), 36–62

McGurk, J. J. N., 'Trinity College Dublin, 1592–1992', *History Today*, 42 (1992), 41–47

Melling, E., *Kentish sources: the poor* (Maidstone, 1964)

Moody, T. W., *The Londonderry plantation, 1609–1614* (Belfast, 1937)

Moody, T. W., F. X. Martin and F. J. Byrne, eds, *A new history of Ireland, vol. iii, early modern Ireland* (Oxford, 1976)

Morgan, H., 'Faith and fatherland or Queen and country, an unpublished exchange between O'Neill and the state at the height of the Nine Years War', *Dúiche Néill (Journal of the O'Neill Country Historical Society)*, no. 9 (1984), 9–65

Morgan, H., 'The colonial venture of Sir Thomas Smith', *Historical Journal*, 28 (1985), 261–278

Morgan, H., 'The end of Gaelic Ulster: a thematic interpretation of events between 1534 and 1610', *Irish Historical Studies*, 26 (1988), 8–32

Morgan, H., *Tyrone's rebellion: the outbreak of the nine years war in Tudor Ireland* (Dublin, 1993)

Morrill, J. S., *Cheshire, 1630–1660* (Oxford, 1974)

Muir, R., *History of Liverpool* (London, 1970)

Murphy, D., *Cromwell in Ireland* (Dublin, 1883)

Myers, A., 'Tudor Chester', *Journal of the Chester Archaeological Society*, 63 (1980), 43–57

Neale, J. E., 'Elizabeth and the Netherlands, 1586–89', *English Historical Review*, 45 (1930), 373–396

Neale, J. E., *Elizabeth I and her parliaments, 1584–1601*, 2 vols (London, 1953–1957)

Neale, J. E., *Essays in Elizabethan history* (London, 1959)

Neale, J. E., *The Elizabethan House of Commons* (revised edn, London, 1963)

Nicholls, K. W., *Gaelic and Gaelicised Ireland in the later middle ages* (Dublin, 1972)

Nicholls, K. W., *Land, law and society century Ireland* (Dublin, 1976)

Notestein, W., *The English people on the eve of colonization* (New York, 1954)

Oman, C., *A history of the art of war in the sixteenth century* (London, 1937)

Oppenheim, M., *The maritime history of Devon* (Exeter, 1968)

Outhwaite, R. B., *Inflation in Tudor and early Stuart England* (London, 1969)

Outhwaite, R. B., 'Who bought Crown lands? A pattern of purchases 1589–1603', *Historical Research Bulletin of the Institute of Historical Research*, 44 (1971)

Overall, W. H. and H. C. Overall, eds, *An analytical index to the series of records known as Remembrancia, AD 1579–1664* (London, 1878)

Owen, G. D., *Elizabethan Wales: the social scene* (Cardiff, 1962)

O'Domhnaill, S., 'Warfare in sixteenth century Ireland', *Irish Historical Studies*, 5 (1946), 29–54

O'Dowd, M., 'Gaelic economy and society', in *Natives and Newomers*, eds C. Brady and R. Gillespie (Dublin, 1986), 120–147

O'Fiach, T., 'The O'Neills of the Fews (S. Armagh)', *Seanchas ard Mhacha*, 8 (1973), 1–64

Palmer, W., *The problem of Ireland in Tudor foreign policy 1485–1603* (Woodbridge, 1994)

Parker, G., *The army of Flanders* (Cambridge, 1972)

Parker, G., *Europe in crisis 1598–1648* (Glasgow, 1979)

Parkes, J., *Travel in England in the seventeenth century* (London, 1925)

Pearl, V., *London and the outbreak of the Puritan Revolution* (London, 1964)

Phillips, W. A., ed., *History of the Church of Ireland*, 3 vols (London, 1933–1934)

Picton, J. A., *Memorials of Liverpool* (Liverpool, 1873)

Pine, L. G., ed., *Burke's landed gentry of Ireland* (London, 1958)

Pinkerton, W., 'The "overthrow" of Sir John Chichester at Carrickfergus in 1557', *Ulster Journal of Archaeology*, 5 (1857), 188–209

Quinn, D. B., 'A discourse on Ireland, c. 1599', *Proceedings of the Royal Irish Academy*, 47 (1942), 151–166

Quinn, D. B., 'Agenda for Irish history, 1461–1603', *Irish Historical Studies*, 4 (1945), 258–269

Quinn, D. B., 'Ireland and sixteenth century European expansion', *Historical Studies*, 1 (1958), 20–32

Quinn, D. B., *Ralegh and the British Empire*, 2nd edn (London, 1962)

Quinn, D. B., 'The Munster plantation: problems and opportunities', *Journal of the Cork Historical and Archaeological Society*, 71 (1966), 19–41

Quinn, D. B., *The Elizabethans and the Irish* (Ithaca, 1966)

Quinn, D. B., *England and the discovery of America 1481–1620* (London, 1974)

Quinn, D. B., 'Renaissance influences on English colonization', *Transactions of the Royal Historical Society*, 5th series, 25 (1976), 73–93

Read, C., ed., *William Lambarde and local government* (Ithaca, 1962)

Rich, E. E., 'The population of Elizabethan England', *Economic History Review*, 2nd series, 2 (1950), 247–265

Roebuck, P., 'The making of an Ulster great estate; the Chichesters ... 1599–1648', *Proceedings of the Royal Irish Academy*, 79, section C, no. I (1979)

Rowse, A. L., *Tudor Cornwall* (London, 1969)

Royal Historical Society, *Annual bibliographies of British and Irish history* (London, 1975–1995)

Scammell, G. V., 'Manning the English merchant service in the sixteenth century', *Mariner's Mirror*, 56 (1970), 131–154

Schofield, R., 'Taxation and the limits of the Tudor state', in *Law and government under the Tudor*, eds C. Cross *et al.* (Cambridge, 1988), 227–255

Scott Thomson, S., 'The origin and growth of the office of deputy lieutenancy', *Transactions of the Royal Historical Society*, 4th series, 5 (1922)

Scott Thomson, S., *Lords lieutenants in the sixteenth century* (London, 1923)

Senior, C. M., *A nation of pirates* (Newton Abbot, 1976)

Sharp, B., *In contempt of all authority: rural artizans and riot in the west of England, 1558–1660* (London, 1980)

Sheehan, A. J., 'Official reaction to native land claims in the plantation of Munster', *Irish Historical Studies*, 23 (1983), 297–318

Silke, J. J., 'The Irish appeal to Spain; some light on the genesis of the Nine Years War', *Irish Ecclesiastical Record*, 5th series, 92 (1959), 279–290; 362–371

Silke, J. J., 'Why Aguila landed at Kinsale', *Irish Historical Studies*, 13 (1963), 236–245

Silke, J. J., 'Hugh O'Neill, the Catholic question and the papacy', *Irish Ecclesiastical Record*, 5th series, 104 (1965), 65–79

Silke, J. J., *Kinsale: the Spanish intervention in Ireland* (Liverpool, 1970)

Silke, J. J., 'The Irish Peter Lombard', *Studies*, 64, no. 254 (1975), 143

Slack, P., ed., *Rebellion, popular protest and the social order in early modern England* (Cambridge, 1984)

Smith, A. G. R., *The emergence of a nation state; the commonwealth of England, 1529–1660* (London, 1984)

Smith, J. P., *The genealogists' atlas of Lancashire* (Liverpool, 1930)

Stone, L., 'The anatomy of the Elizabethan aristocracy', *Economic History Review*, 18 (1948), 1–41

Stone, L., *The family, sex and marriage in England, 1500–1800* (London, 1979)

Thirsk, J., ed., *The agrarian history of England and Wales, 1500–1640* (Cambridge, 1967)

Touzeau, J., *The rise and progress of Liverpool, 1557–1835* (Liverpool, 1910)

Vanes, J., *The port of Bristol in the sixteenth century* (Bristol, 1977)

Vanes, J., ed., *Documents illustrating the overseas trade of Bristol in the sixteenth century* (Bristol Record Society, xxxi, Bristol, 1979)

Wark, K. E., *Elizabethan recusancy in Cheshire* (Chetham Society, 3rd series, xxix, Manchester, 1971)

Webb, H., 'English military surgery during the age of Elizabeth', *Bulletin of the History of Medicine*, 15 (1944), 261–275

Webb, H., ed., *Elizabethan military science: the books and the practice* (Madison, 1965)

Wernham, R. B., *The return of the armadas* (Oxford, 1994)

Willan, T. S., *Studies in Elizabethan foreign trade* (Manchester, 1959)

Woodward, D. M., *The trade of Elizabethan Chester* (Hull, 1970)

Wrigley, E. A., ed., *An introduction to English historical demography* (London, 1966)

Wrigley, E. A. and R. S. Schofield, *The population of England, 1541–1871; a reconstruction* (Cambridge, Mass., 1981)

Unpublished theses

Armour, C., 'The trade of Chester and the state of the Dee Navigation 1600–1800', PhD (University of London, 1956)

Ashby, R., 'The organization and administration of the Tudor Ordnance Office', BLitt (University of Oxford, 1972)

Caspari, F., 'The influence of the Renaissance on the English concept of the state', BLitt (University of Oxford, 1936)

Everitt, A., 'Kent and its gentry, 1640–1660', PhD (University of London, 1957)

Hartley, T., 'The office of Sheriff in Kent, c. 1580–1620', PhD (University of London, 1970)

Higgins, G. P., 'County government and society in Cheshire c.1590 to 1640', MA (University of Liverpool, 1973)

Kent, J., 'The social attitudes of members of parliament, 1590–1624', PhD (University of London, 1971)

Long, P. R., 'The wealth of the magisterial class in Lancashire, c.1590–1640', MA (University of Manchester, 1968)

Marriott, P. J., 'Commission of the peace in Cheshire 1536–1603', MA (University of Manchester, 1974)

Treadwell, V., 'Irish financial administrative reform under James I; the customs and state regulation of Irish trade', PhD (Queen's University, Belfast, 1960)

Index

k. = killed in action and refers to captains and commanders only; n. = note number

Lightning Source UK Ltd.
Milton Keynes UK
UKOW06f1520070515

251086UK00001B/38/P